An Introductory Guide to
EC Competition Law and Practice

Australia
The Law Book Company
Brisbane, Sydney, Melbourne, Perth

Canada
Carswell
Ottawa, Toronto, Calgary, Montreal, Vancouver

AGENTS

India
N.M. Tripathi (Private) Ltd
Bombay

Eastern Law House (Private) Ltd
Calcutta

M.P.P. House
Bangalore

Universal Book Traders
Delhi

Aditya Books
Delhi

Israel
Steimatzky's Agency Ltd
Tel Aviv

Pakistan
Pakistan Law House
Karachi, Lahore

An Introductory Guide to EC Competition Law and Practice

Fifth Edition

Valentine Korah, LL.M., Ph.D.

*Professor Emeritus of Competition Law, University College London;
Visiting Professor, Fordham Law School and College of Europe,
Bruges; Barrister*

Foreword to Fourth Edition by Judge René Joliet,
Court of Justice of the European Communities

LONDON
SWEET & MAXWELL
1994

First published by ESC Publishing Ltd, Oxford
as An Introductory Guide to EEC Competition Law and Practice
First Edition 1978
Second Edition 1981
Third Edition 1986
Fourth Edition 1990

Fifth Edition 1994
Published by Sweet & Maxwell Limited of
South Quay Plaza, 183 Marsh Wall, London E14 9FT
Typeset by Create Publishing Services Ltd, Bath
Printed by Information Press, Eynsham, Oxford

A CIP catalogue record for this book is available from
the British Library

ISBN 0 421 53290 4

© Valentine Korah

Foreword to the Fourth Edition

Competition law is a major part of Community law measured, not so much by the proportion of cases involving articles 85 and 86 of the Rome Treaty which are decided by the European Court of Justice in relation to the total volume of litigation before it, as by reason of the economic, financial and intellectual interest of the issues which are at stake and by reason of the considerable attention which decisions receive in legal literature.

It is a field in itself, which requires a very special skill in sorting out and analysing the facts, an understanding of pricing mechanisms, a knowledge of how business actually operates and, last but not least, policy evaluations. It is often argued that cartel agreements can never last very long and that, unless based on statutory measures, single-firm monopolies are almost invariably subject to challenge and will soon be unable to keep their stronghold upon the market. But the practical questions are: how long and how soon. For, meanwhile, consumers and competitors may be badly hurt.

Hence the importance of competition law, which is designed to do away with all artificial barriers erected through collusion or unilateral exclusionary tactics. The need for it will soon be discovered by central and eastern European countries which, after the collapse of their centrally-planned economic systems, are trying to turn to a market economy at the same time as they start enjoying basic political freedoms.

Whether, in the EEC, competition law is really 'about the legal enforcement of competition' or merely 'about who is to decide whether industrialists shall on a particular occasion be free to act non-competitively and in what way they are going to be free not to act competitively'[1] is still a matter open to debate. I shall not discuss it here. Part of the answer will be found in Valentine Korah's book. But what is certain is that, although the EEC Commission is not making many more than ten decisions a year, the case law is now very abundant — especially if one adds the Court's judgments under article 173 or 177 of the Rome Treaty — and has grown enormously in complexity. And case law is not the only thing to look at. Apart from the transport regulations, there are no fewer than eight[2] EEC Commission group exemption regulations which businessmen and their advisers have to take into account before drafting their co-operation, distribution or licensing agreements. It has become a

---

1 Jeremy Lever, *Enterprise Law of the 80s*, eds. Frederick M. Rowe, Francis G. Jacobs and Mark R. Joelson, A.B.A., p. 97.
2 Since this Foreword was written, a ninth has been added on insurance.

risky venture to find one's way through that forest of cases and regulations, for paths are as yet not always clearly marked. Moreover, some institutional changes, such as the creation of the Court of First Instance, are not going to make that task easier. Although whole libraries have been devoted to competition law, a concrete and concise guidebook was needed to provide students and businessmen with a survey of this complex field. This has been the purpose of Valentine Korah in writing what she calls her 'Little Yellow Book.'

No-one is better qualified for that job. Valentine Korah has written extensively and expertly about both the U.K. law of restrictive trade practices and EEC competition law, has wide experience in economics, has taken part in, and even organised, innumerable conferences for practitioners, maintains contacts with civil servants responsible for law enforcement, knows the case law extremely well and never gets tired of reading the decisions prepared by DGIV of the Commission, even the most obscure ones.

Readers will not only find a description of the law in Valentine Korah's book. I am sure that they, and especially EEC civil servants, will greatly benefit from her critical views. I myself am very much inclined to agree with her when she criticises the legalistic and formalistic approach often taken by DGIV officials, and when she stresses that, by not relating specific facts to its legal appraisal, the EEC Commission misses a wonderful opportunity to educate people dealing with competition law — including its own officials. But Valentine Korah is not altogether pessimistic. She regards DGIV officials as more open to outsiders' views than any national administration she knows of (see 14.1). I hope very much that the future will prove her to be right. Meanwhile, I am very pleased to wish the fourth edition of her Little Yellow Book all the attention and success it deserves.

August 1990   Judge René Joliet
                                                 Court of Justice of the
                                                 European Communities

Preface

Businesses, large and small, are increasingly operating in more than one member state of the European Union. Even those whose activities are confined to a single member state or who export to Europe from outside the common market may find that the EC competition rules apply to them, as any substantial restriction of competition within even a single member state may have repercussions on trade between member states. A contract made by foreigners outside the common market is subject to the competition rules if it is implemented and restricts competition within the common market.

Since the beginning of 1994, very similar rules have applied throughout the European Economic Area, which includes Austria and the three Scandinavian states.

Firms may be heavily fined or unable to enforce important provisions in their contracts if they do not take account of the EC competition rules. The maximum fine is 10 per cent. of the undertaking's turnover for the previous year, and in *Pioneer*[1] the Court of Justice of the European Communities held that this relates to the total turnover of the whole group of companies, all products, worldwide. The maximum has never been reached, and is limited by the doctrine of proportionality. If only a small part of the undertaking's activities is affected, the infringement is less grave than if all its activities are. Nevertheless, agreements fixing prices and allocating markets have been subject to very heavy fines — the producers of Polypropylene were together fined nearly 58 million ECUs. On appeal, the Court of First Instance quashed some of the fines and reduced others,[2] but this was on grounds that parts of the infringements had not been established, rather than that the fines were excessive. Fines of 10 and 11 million ECUs were imposed on individual producers, some £792 million in all.

Heavy fines can also be expected for anything that is considered by the Commission to deter trade across national boundaries, or for action of a dominant firm perceived to be taken to deter new entrants to the market from growing.[3] Most large firms are well advised by in-house lawyers or those in private practice, but small firms may not know when to seek advice and may be tempted to save this expense, which is likely to be proportionately higher for them.

---

1   (100–103/80) [1983] E.C.R. 1823.
2   Resulting in total fines 54·5 million ECUs.
3   A non-EC firm was fined 75 million ECUs for abusing a dominant position within the common market in *Tetra Pak II* [1992] 4 C.M.L.R. 551, subject to appeal.

This book was originally written to help businessmen to comply with the EC competition rules, or at least to know when to consult a lawyer. It might also help them to collect their thoughts and the relevant information before seeking advice and thereby reduce the cost of obtaining it. In fact, however, lawyers and law students have also been buying the book. Consequently, in the third edition, I added short sections on price theory which few lawyers in Europe used to learn about at university, although the position is changing. Businessmen who are more familiar with how markets are likely to work can skip these passages. For the convenience of lawyers, multiple citations to the cases mentioned in the text are to be found in the tables.

Throughout, I have tried to explain the rules critically in the light of the objectives they are intended to achieve. It is important to understand the problems of policy, partly because it helps one to argue a case before the Commission or a court and partly because I hope that the book may help to educate those who may later become officials or work at the Court. In the fourth edition, I added a final chapter, critical of the bifurcation of article 85(1) and (3).

I have supported the text with short bibliographies at the end of most chapters, as well as a more general bibliography and a glossary at the end of the work. The tables and appendices are fuller than is usual for a book of this size. Clearly, those practising substantially in the field will need to progress to a larger book appending more legislation, and I cannot recommend too warmly Barry Hawk's loose leaf book, listed in the main bibliography. It is brought up to date every two or three years, and revised material is expected shortly after the fifth edition of this book is published.

My shorter book is intended to be practical. Considerable space is devoted to the remedies for infringing articles 85 and 86. Advice is given on the problems that are not legal in the narrow sense of the term, such as the steps to be taken when faced with the possibility of an inspection from the Commission's Competition Department, DGIV, or the advantages and disadvantages of notifying an agreement to it.

I would have liked to keep the book as short as the first edition, but the Commission's practice of developing new rules for each new type of transaction that it faces rather than using broad economic categories, such as naked and ancillary restrictions and horizontal, vertical or conglomerate transactions, has led to the EC competition rules becoming more and more complex. It seems to me that the time has now come for using footnotes to contain at least one citation to each decision or judgment. Nevertheless, I have not attempted to write a full practitioners' work, but have kept it fairly short.

I always wanted Judge Joliet to write a foreword to one of my books.

Most of the problems now current in competition law are dealt with in his book on the Rule of Reason, published in 1967. He was the first person to criticise the practice of finding any important restriction of conduct anti-competitive even if without protection some kind of investment would not have been forthcoming. I have learned a great deal from the books and articles he wrote while he was teaching at Liège. They are very easy to read, because he takes the trouble to analyse clearly before he starts to write. He also has the gift of the vivid phrase. I would prefer to read his work in French than that of most people in my own tongue.

I was, therefore, delighted when he agreed to write a foreword to the fourth edition, despite the book becoming ready at a time that was personally inconvenient for him. I am most grateful for his encouragement, support and the interesting things that he says.

I am also indebted to Fordham University School of Law. I teach courses there each spring semester on EC competition law and on technology licensing. Fordham has supported me in many ways, provided me with the use of a fast computer and has made available funds for research assistance.

I am also most grateful to my friend and former student, Yvette Verleisdonk, for doing far more than most research assistants. She practised in the area for three years and has updated parts and suggested all sorts of changes.

My former extraordinarily able research assistant, Warwick A. Rothnie transformed the fourth edition of this work. He is now the author of *Parallel Imports*, published by Sweet & Maxwell. We have written three books together and, although he is now a busy practitioner in Australia, he has kindly read through most of this edition too and made many excellent and perceptive comments.

I now refuse to write books unless the publisher agrees to invite Miss Kate Elliott to copy-edit them. She manages to get more information into a table of cases than anyone I know. I prepared it initially, Rothnie added further information for the fourth edition, Ms Verleisdonk checked the new cases in this edition and Miss Elliott checked it all and added information that had never even occurred to us.

I should like to thank all these people and also the publishers, who have encouraged and supported a cantankerous author over the years.

June 1994
                                            Valentine Korah
                              University College London and
                         Fordham University School of Law

Table of Contents

Table of Cases

References in bold type are to discussions in the text.

Hoechst AG and Others *v.* Commission (46/87 & 227/88), 21 September 1989, [1989] E.C.R. 2859, [1991] 1 C.E.C. 280.
5.7.2

Hoffmann-La Roche & Co. AG *v.* Centrafarm Vertriebsgesellschaft Pharmazeutischer Erzeugnisse mbH (102/77), 23 May 1978, [1978] E.C.R. 1139, [1978] 3 C.M.L.R. 217, C.M.R. 8466.
9.4.4.1

Hoffmann-La Roche & Co. AG *v.* Commission (Vitamins) (85/76), 13 February 1979, [1979] E.C.R. 461, [1979] 3 C.M.L.R. 211, C.M.R. 8527.
Comment: L. Zanon (1981) 15 J. World Trade Law 305.
1.2, 4.2.5.1, 4.3.1, 4.3.2.2, 4.3.2.4

Höfner and Elser *v.* Macrotron GmbH (C-41/90), 23 April 1991, [1991] E.C.R. I-1979, [1993] 4 C.M.L.R. 306, [1993] 1 C.E.C. 238.
1.9.7

Hugin—Liptons Cash Registers and Business Equipment Ltd. *v.* Hugin Kassaregister AB (78/68/EEC), 8 December 1977, O.J. 1978, L22/23, [1978] 1 C.M.L.R. D19, C.M.R. 10007.
4.2.4, 4.3.3.4, 10.9

Hugin Kassaregister AB *v.* Commission (22/78), 31 May 1979, [1979] E.C.R. 1869, [1979] 3 C.M.L.R. 345, C.M.R. 8524.
2.3.2, 4.2.4, 4.3.3.4

Hydrotherm Gerätebau GmbH *v.* Compact de Dott. Ing. Mario Andreoli e C. Sas (170/83), 12 July 1984, [1984] E.C.R. 2999, [1985] 3 C.M.L.R. 224, C.M.R. 14112.
2.2.1, 8.3.5, 10.5.4

Iberian Trading (U.K.) Limited—BPB Industries plc *v.* Commission (T-65/89), 1 April 1993, [1993] E.C.R. II-389, [1993] 5 C.M.L.R. 32, [1993] 1 C.E.C. 713.
4.2.3.1

Ideal-Standard's distribution system, O.J. 1985, L20/38, [1988] 4 C.M.L.R. 627, C.M.R. 10662.
8.3.3

Ideal-Standard—IHT Internazionale Heiztechnik GmbH *v.* Ideal-Standard GmbH (C-9/93), 22 June 1994, not yet reported.
9.4.4

IFTRA rules for producers of virgin aluminium (Re) (75/497/EEC), 15 July 1975, O.J. 1975, L228/3, [1975] 2 C.M.L.R. D20, C.M.R. 9769.
7.2.1

IFTRA rules on glass containers—Re European Glass Manufacturers (74/292/EEC), 15 May 1974, O.J. 1974, L160/1, [1974] 2 C.M.L.R. D50, C.M.R. 9658.
7.2.2

IGR Stereo-Television (1981 and 1984), *Eleventh and Fourteenth Reports on Competition Policy* 63 and 76 respectively.
13.2.3

Inno (GB-Inno-BM NV) *v.* ATAB (Vereniging van de Kleinhandelaars in

269/82), 10 December 1985, [1985] E.C.R. 3831, [1987] 3 C.M.L.R. 661, C.M.R. 14265.
7.1.3
Stergios Delimitis—see Delimitis (Stergios).
Sugar cases—Re the European Sugar Cartel: Cooperatiëve Vereniging 'Suiker Unie' UA *v.* Commission (40–48, 50, 54–56, 111 & 113–114/73), 16 December 1975, [1975] E.C.R. 1663, [1976] 1 C.M.L.R. 295, C.M.R. 8334.
2.2.1, 2.2.4.2, **4.2.7**, 4.3.2.2, 8.7

Télémarketing—Centre Belge d'Etudes du Marché-Télémarketing SA (CBEM) *v.* Compagnie Luxembourgeoise de Télédiffusion (311/84), 3 October 1985, [1985] E.C.R. 3261, [1986] 2 C.M.L.R. 558, C.M.R. 14246.
4.3.2.5, 4.3.3.4
Tepea BV *v.* Commission (28/77), 20 June 1978, [1978] E.C.R. 1391, [1978] 3 C.M.L.R. 392, C.M.R. 8467.
2.3.2
Tetra Pak (88/501/EEC), 26 July 1988, O.J. 1988, L272/27, [1990] 4 C.M.L.R. 47, C.M.R. 11015.
4.3.2.6, 13.2.3, **14.2.6**
Tetra Pak Rausing SA *v.* Commission (T-51/89), 10 July 1990, [1990] E.C.R. II-309, [1991] 4 C.M.L.R. 334, [1990] 2 C.E.C. 409.
1.2, 4.3.1, 4.3.2.6, 8.3, **8.3.6, 8.6**
Tetra Pak II—Elopak Italia Srl *v.* Tetra Pak (92/163/EEC), 24 July 1991, O.J. 1991, L72/1, [1992] 4 C.M.L.R. 551, [1992] 1 C.E.C. 2145.
Pref., 1.8, 4.3.2.4, 4.3.2.5, 4.3.3.3, 5.10, **7.5**
Tetra Pak II—Tetra Pak Rausing SA *v.* Commission (No. 2) (T-83/91), not yet reported.
7.5, 8.3
Thetford Corporation *v.* Fiamma SpA (35/87), 30 June 1988, [1988] E.C.R. 3585, [1988] 3 C.M.L.R. 549, C.M.R. 14497.
4.3.3.1, **9.4.2**, 14.3.1
Thomson/Pilkington (M51), O.J. 1991, C279/19, [1991] 4 C.M.L.R. 897.
12.2.4
Transocean Marine Paint—Re the Transocean Marine Paint Association (No. 1) (67/454/EEC), 27 June 1967, J.O. 163/10, [1967] C.M.L.R. D9.
7.6.1
Transocean Marine Paint Association *v.* Commission (17/74), 23 October 1974, [1974] E.C.R. 1063, [1974] 2 C.M.L.R. 459, C.M.R. 8241.
5.8.1
TWD Textilwerke Deggendorf *v.* Bundesrepublik Deutschland (C-188/92), 9 March 1994, not yet reported.
6.3.4

UIP—Re the Application of United International Pictures BV (89/467/EEC), 12 July 1989, O.J. 1989, L226/25, [1990] 4 C.M.L.R. 749, [1989] 2 C.E.C. 2019.
7.2.3, 13.2.4.2
United Brands Company (Re) (76/353/EEC), 17 December 1975, O.J. 1976, L95/1, [1976] 1 C.M.L.R. D28, C.M.R. 9800.
4.2.1, 4.2.5.1, 4.3.3, 5.7.1

II ENGLISH CASES

III GERMAN CASES

IV U.S. CASES

Continental TV Inc. *v.* GTE Sylvania Inc., 433 U.S. 36 (1977), 694 F.2d 1132, 53
   L. Ed. 2d 568 (1982).
      7.1.3
Eastman Kodak, 112 S.Ct. 2072 (1992).
      4.2.4
Monsanto *v.* Spray-Rite, 465 U.S. 752 (1984).
      2.2.2.1
Rothery Storage & Van Co. *v.* Atlas Van Lines, Inc., 792 F.2d 210, 226,
   (D.C.Cir. 1986).
      7.1.3
Topco Association Inc. *v.* U.S., 405 U.S. 596, 131 L.Ed.2d 515, 92 S.Ct. 1126
   (1972).
      7.1.3
U.S. *v.* Addyston Pipe & Steel Co., 85 Fed. 271 (6th Cir., 1898).
      7.1.1, 7.1.2
U.S. *v.* Penn-Olin Chem. Co., 378 U.S. 158, 12 L.Ed.2d 775, 84 S.Ct. 1710
   (1964).
      13.2.1

V OTHER CASES

SACEM, Cons. Conc. (France), Avis 93-A-05, 20 April 1993.
      4.3.3.1
Queensland Wire (Australia), 1989 ATPR 40–925.
      4.3.2.5

Table of Legislation

Subordinate Legislation
The O.J. citations of notices, regulations and directives adopted after the Special Edition are given in this table.

---

1   A convenient collection of the authentic texts of the regulations and notices has been published by the Commission: Competition law in the European Communities (Situation at 31 December 1989), 1990, ISBN 92–826–1307–0, Catalogue number CB-42–90–001-EN-C.

National Legislation

1 Introduction

1.1 The common market

Many economic advantages were expected to flow from the establishment of the common market. Goods and services could be produced in the areas most suited to each and sold where they were wanted. In a larger geographic market there might be greater opportunities for specialisation. In many industries firms might be able to grow to a size at which they enjoyed economies of scale and scope in production and distribution, while leaving room for other producers to compete with them.

The European Economic Community (EEC) was formed by the six original member states in 1958 under the EEC treaty, which I shall usually call 'the treaty.' The various objectives of the EEC were set out in article 2 of the treaty. These included an accelerated raising of living standards and a continuous and balanced expansion of economic activity to be achieved through the establishment of a common market. The treaty of Maastricht, which came into force on 1 November 1993, supplemented the earlier treaties and created a European Union when it added a common foreign policy, as well as co-operation in the environmental and social areas and the aim of achieving a monetary union between the member states. The treaty of Maastricht changed the name of the EEC to the European Community (EC).

All economic resources should be free to move throughout the common market, unimpeded by national boundaries. Consequently, the treaty provides for the free movement of goods, services, workers and capital and the right to establish a business in other member states. It would, however, be of little use to abolish government restrictions such as customs barriers and quotas between member states if these could be replaced by cartels, under which traders in different member states agree reciprocally to keep out of each other's home market. Agreements restricting competition are, therefore, controlled by the competition rules in the treaty. Herr von der Gröben, the first Member of the Commission responsible for competition policy, and others believe that these rules also have a longer term function — to encourage the expansion of efficient firms and sectors of the economy at the expense of those less good at supplying what people want to pay for. There is concern, however, that the rules may be being applied so as to protect smaller firms at the expense of larger, irrespective of efficiency.[1]

---

1   See 1.3.2.2 and 1.3.2.5 below.

1.2 The competition rules

The main competition rules governing undertakings in the public and private sectors are set out in articles 85 and 86 of the EC treaty (reproduced in Appendix I: they were not amended by the treaty of Maastricht). The first forbids, as incompatible with the common market, collusion that may affect trade between member states and has the object or effect of restricting competition within the common market. The second forbids the abusive exploitation of a dominant position. Article 85 controls agreements between undertakings and article 86 the conduct, unilateral or otherwise, of firms that are subject only to remote competitive pressures.

Conduct may infringe both articles. In *Vitamins*,[2] the Court confirmed the Commission's decision that Hoffmann-La Roche had infringed article 86 by granting discounts to large buyers who had bought or who agreed to buy a large proportion of their requirements from it, making it difficult for its smaller suppliers to compete. Such a contract might also be forbidden by article 85. In *Tetrapak*,[3] the Court of First Instance upheld a decision condemning under article 86 the acquisition by a dominant firm of a potential competitor that had an exclusive licence to the main alternative technology.

1.2.1 *Article 85 — collusion that restricts competition*

Article 85(1) prohibits collusion between undertakings which may affect trade between member states and has the object or effect of restricting competition within the common market. It provides that:

'(1) The following shall be prohibited as incompatible with the common market: all agreements between undertakings, decisions by associations of undertakings and concerted practices which may affect trade between member states and which have as their object or effect the prevention, restriction or distortion of competition within the common market, and in particular those which ...'

There follows a list of examples of conduct assumed to be anti-competitive, without any distinction being drawn between agreements between competitors and those between firms operating at different levels of trade or between restrictions that are necessary to make some legitimate transaction viable and those that are not.[4]

Article 85(2) provides that agreements that infringe the article are void

2 *Hoffmann-La Roche & Co. AG* v. *Commission (Vitamins)* (85/76) [1979] E.C.R. 461. See 4.3.2.2 below.
3 (T-51/89) [1990] E.C.R. II-309.
4 See 7.1 below.

and, although the Court ruled that the nullity applies only to the clauses having the prohibited object or effect, national courts will not be able to order parties to fulfil their contracts if the provisions in question infringe article 85(1). This can have far reaching consequences. When enforcing an exclusive agreement one may be met by a Euro-defence that, in its legal and economic context, parts of the agreement infringe article 85(1) and are void.

Article 85(3) provides for exemptions from the prohibition. These can be granted only by the Commission, the executive body of the EC and not by courts asked to enforce an agreement.

In *Pronuptia*,[5] for instance, it was argued in the German Supreme Court that a franchise agreement for three cities in the Federal Republic was contrary to article 85(1) and void and that, consequently, the franchisor could not recover the agreed royalty payments. Meeting this defence requires an analysis of the market, which may be expensive and difficult for both counsel and judges. It increases the cost of litigation and makes it more difficult to obtain advice on whether contracts can be enforced.

1.2.2 *Article 86 — the abuse of a dominant position*

Article 86 prohibits the abusive exploitation of a dominant position:

> 'Any abuse by one or more undertakings of a dominant position within the common market or in a substantial part of it shall be prohibited as incompatible with the common market in so far as it may affect trade between member states. Such abuse may, in particular, consist in: . . .'

The examples relate to exploitation, to conduct that oppresses buyers and sellers dealing with a dominant firm: charging too much, paying too little, restricting production or markets, discriminating against some firms and so making it difficult for them to compete downstream, and refusing to supply the monopolised product without some other product the buyer would prefer to obtain elsewhere. Indeed, 'abuse' is a poor translation of the term 'abusive exploitation' used in the authentic texts of the treaty in most languages. It was thought that the article forbids the exploitation of market power to harm customers and suppliers: that is, that it provides for regulation of prices charged by powerful firms. This is not practicable in view of the tiny resources the Community devotes to enforcing the competition rules. More importantly, it would be inconsistent with the liberal spirit in which the Community was created.

In *Continental Can* v. *Commission*,[6] the Court held that the

---

5   (161/84) [1986] E.C.R. 353.
6   (6/72) [1973] E.C.R. 215.

acquisition by a dominant firm of a potential competitor might infringe article 86, although the shareholders in the target company had not been harmed; nor was it alleged that they had been forced to sell their shares because Continental Can enjoyed a dominant position. As buyers may be harmed indirectly by the reduction of competition, the Court construed the words 'abusive exploitation of a dominant position' to include conduct that affects the structure of the market by absorbing a potential competitor, and not only conduct that exploits the lack of competition.

It is difficult to advise firms on the application of article 86, as it has been held that even firms that have little power over prices may be dominant, and it is not clear what conduct is forbidden. The Community Courts have had difficulty distinguishing conduct that excludes others through efficiency, by giving better value for money, from methods of exclusion not based on the merits. They have used a formula suggesting that competition on the basis of performance is lawful, but it is not clear what is included in this category (4.3.1 below). Consequently, conduct that would not infringe the US law may infringe that of the EC.

1.2.3 *The interpretation of the competition rules and the integration of the common market*

Both articles 85 and 86 and the regulations that implement them must be read in the light of the objectives of the treaty. Article 2, as amended at Maastricht, provides that

> 'The Community shall have as its task, by establishing a common market *and an economic and monetary union and by implementing the common policies or activities referred to in articles 3 and 3a,* [and progressively approximating the economic policies of member states,] to promote throughout the Community a harmonious development of economic activities, a continuous and balanced expansion, *sustainable and non-inflationary growth respecting the environment, a high degree of convergence of economic performance, a high level of employment and of social protection,* [an increase in stability, an accelerated] *the* raising of the standard of living [and closer relations between the States belonging to it] and *economic and social cohesion and solidarity among member states.'*[7]

One might think that the common market is the mechanism by which the expansion, stability and so forth are to be achieved, but market integration has been elevated in competition cases to an aim in itself,[8]

---

7   I have italicised the words added by the treaty of Maastricht and placed those it deleted in square brackets.
8   See *Consten & Grundig* v. *Commission*, (56 & 58/64) [1966] E.C.R. 299, 2.3.1 and 2.4 below.

and is pursued in a mechanical way, even when this leads to reduced competition and may delay the integration of the market.[9]

Article 3, as amended at Maastricht, provides that,

> 'For the purposes set out in article 2, the activities of the Community shall include, as provided in this treaty and in accordance with the timetable set out therein:
> (a) the elimination, as between member states, of customs duties and of quantitative restrictions on the import and export of goods, and of all other measures having equivalent effect;
>
> ...
>
> (g) the institution of a system ensuring that competition in the internal market is not distorted; ...'

The Court of Justice of the European Communities (hereafter usually called 'the Court' or 'the Community Court') has held more than once that both articles 85 and 86 should be construed in the light of these provisions, even when there is a fairly clear literal interpretation to the contrary. In *Continental Can*, for instance, the Court interpreted article 86 not only as a provision under which the conduct of firms already dominant which harmed consumers directly could be regulated but also as one forbidding the weakening of any remaining potential competition by a firm already dominant, as this might harm consumers in the longer term.[10]

1.2.4 *The treaty covers all sectors of the economy*

The competition rules apply to services as well as goods and to licences of incorporeal property such as patents, but there are some special sectors. Most coal and steel products are subject to the treaty of Paris which established the European Coal and Steel Community (ECSC) and not to the EC treaty. The ECSC treaty contains somewhat similar competition rules in articles 65 and 66, but the Commission has greater power to intervene over these two products and the competition rules cannot be enforced in the courts of member states until the Commission has found an infringement.[11] Coal and steel precedents must therefore be applied to the EC only with caution. They will be ignored in this book, as will the provisions of the Euratom treaty which relates to nuclear energy, another sector to which, by virtue of article 232(2) (EC), the EC treaty does not apply to the extent that there are special rules for Euratom.

9 See, for instance, 1.3.2.5 and 2.4 below.
10 See also 1.2.2 above and 4.3.2 below.
11 *H.J. Banks & Co.* v. *British Coal Corporation* (C–128/92), not yet reported. See 6.1 below.

Regulations have made special provision modifying the competition rules as regards agriculture (regulation 26/62). Moreover, for products such as corn, skimmed milk powder and butter, elaborate protection has been created through intervention authorities which are required to buy any intervention products offered to them at the prices fixed by the current applicable regulations. For some products — mainly those grown in Northern Europe — this floor is supported by Community levies on imports from outside the common market. For other agricultural products, such as olive oil, there is far less protection. But there is little temptation for private firms to agree on common prices or quotas for some of the products subject to the common agricultural policy. Even when there is no such protection, national common rules for the agricultural products listed in annex 2 to the treaty are treated more favourably than in most industries.[12] Nevertheless, in principle, agriculture is also subject to the competition rules. In *Frubo* v. *Commission*,[13] for example, the Court upheld the Commission's decision that some of the rules of membership of associations of importers and wholesalers taking part in a fruit auction infringed article 85.

⚹ Shortly after the main implementing regulation for the competition rules, regulation 17, was adopted by the Council, transport was excluded from its application by regulation 141/62. Other implementing regulations dealing with the application of the competition rules to transport by land and inland waterway were adopted by regulation 1017/68. This became effective in the mid-1980s as the Commission took its first decision on the *EATE levy*,[14] condemning an agreement between transport brokers to charge an extra 10 per cent. on exports to be used to promote transport by river boat.

The Council and Commission have, more recently, adopted implementing regulations for air and sea transport. Regulation 3975/87,[15] which applies articles 85 and 86 to air transport, covers only flights between Community airports. In *Ahmed Saeed*,[16] the Court held that, in the absence of implementing legislation, agreements relating to flights between the Community and third countries are only subject to the competition rules through articles 88 and 89 of the treaty. Consequently, such agreements enjoy provisional validity until they are condemned or exempted by the national authorities or the Commission. Article 86,

12   *French New Potatoes* [1988] 4 C.M.L.R. 790.
13   (71/74) [1975] E.C.R. 563.
14   [1988] 4 C.M.L.R. 677, confirmed on appeal, (272/85) *ANTIB* v. *Commission* [1987] E.C.R. 2201.
15   O.J. 1987, L374/1, amended by regs. 1284/91, O.J. 1991, L122/2, and 2410/92, O.J. 1992, L240/18.
16   (66/86) [1990] 4 C.M.L.R. 102.

however, is directly applicable to all flights. The procedural provisions of regulation 3975/87 are largely parallel those of regulation 17/62. Regulation 3976/87[17] empowers the Commission to issue group exemptions in the air transport sector. Pursuant to this power, Regulation 1617/93 exempts joint planning and co-ordination of capacity on intra-Community flights, consultation on tariffs and schedules and agreements on the allocation of slots. Regulation 83/91[18] exempts agreements relating to computer reservation systems. The implementing regulation for maritime transport is 4056/86. It is not intended to deal with any of the special sectors in this book.

1.3 The economics of market power

Resources in the world are limited, but demand for them is not. In socialist economies or wartime, resources have been allocated by officials and rationing. The free market solution is to ration through the market. On the supply side, firms good at producing things that people want will flourish and have more to spend than those less good at it. This has the advantage that the market encourages firms to produce efficiently what people want to buy. Even if one firm is so successful that it expands and produces most of a particular product, its profits may be noticed or guessed by other firms, which are encouraged to produce something similar. So the successful firm is not likely to go on enjoying market power for long unless, for some reason, other firms cannot enter the market freely and those already in the market are unable to expand.

Competition also works on the demand side of the market. If the cost of fish increases, some people who used to eat fish may eat more meat or eggs. A monopolist will not be profitable unless there are both barriers to entry on the supply side of the market and no adequate substitutes for the product supplied on the demand side. In the short term, many firms appear to have market power: they can raise their prices without losing much trade. Economists, however, frequently assume a period of time long enough to build new production facilities. Consequently, they tend to perceive most markets as competitive.

Most economists welcome the 'invisible hand' of competition to allocate scarce resources in accordance with consumer choice, to avoid waste in acquiring market power and to stimulate efficiency. The Community lacks the governmental resources to regulate many markets, so it is particularly important that resources be allocated by the market.

17 O.J. 1987, L374/9, amended O.J. 1990, L217/15 and by reg. 2411/92.
18 As amended by reg. 3618/92.

1.3.1   *Welfare economics — efficiency*

An unduly high price for products that people continue to buy is not necessarily bad: who is to say that sellers do not welcome high prices as much as buyers dislike them? Most monopolists are large firms, most of the capital of which is owned by institutions such as life assurance and pension funds. A pensioner may enjoy the extra income yielded by the monopoly profit as much as the monopolist's customers dislike the extra charge. These issues relate to how wealth should be distributed in the Community. They are of political and philosophical concern, better resolved through the tax and welfare systems.

Since Adam Smith, however, it has been clear that if prices are raised above cost, some people who would buy the product if it were available at cost (including a normal profit on the resources committed) will not be prepared to pay the higher price and will spend their money on something else. A firm exercising market power to raise prices above cost will have to produce less than it would otherwise have done. Consumers will be worse off: the loss in their welfare is the demand for the monopolised product foregone less what it would have cost, when the money is spent on other things consumers value less in terms of the resources used to produce them. No one benefits from this loss, so it is sometimes called 'the deadweight loss.'

Richard Posner goes further and alleges that a more important cause for concern over high prices is the waste of resources spent on acquiring and maintaining market power.[19] Competitors have to organise and enforce an agreement to keep prices up, or persuade politicians to regulate the industry and keep others out, and so forth. These resources could be better spent on producing more goods and services for consumption.

A third objection to market power is that it reduces the incentive to increase efficiency. In a competitive market, firms that do not efficiently produce what buyers want to pay for may go out of business. This helps to ensure that only the more efficient survive and there is pressure on firms to prune their costs or provide better bargains in other ways.

If efficiency be the only goal of competition policy there will be little need for officials to intervene. In the absence of government regulation, few industries are protected by significant barriers to entry that will protect the incumbent firms from competition by equally efficient firms.

---

19 *Antitrust Law: An Economic Perspective* (1976), ed. University of Chicago, Chap. 1.

1.3.2 *Other reasons for controlling market power*

Efficiency is not the only objective of the EC competition rules.

1.3.2.1 *Market integration* — Competition in the common market is also intended to further market integration, an overriding aim considered by some to be more important than efficiency. Articles 85 and 86 are intended to support the rules for free movement by preventing firms from replacing protection enjoyed for over a century as a result of state action by agreements to keep out of each other's markets. Hence, anything like an export ban is likely to be condemned under the competition rules.

1.3.2.2 *Small and medium-sized firms* — Integration brings with it the risk that small and medium-sized firms, formerly protected by customs duties and quotas, may find it difficult to compete successfully with larger firms operating from other member states. To mitigate this risk, the Commission has encouraged collaboration between them, especially where they carry on business in different member states.

The Commission has also shown concern for foreclosure of firms that would like to enter a market, whether or not their possible entry would benefit consumers.

Another populist view is that small is beautiful and workers are entitled to be their own bosses. Many difficulties face a small business trying to enter a market or to expand, such as the lack of capital, managerial expertise and so forth. If the concern of the law be to protect small and medium-sized firms, market power will be perceived as far more pervasive than if the sole concern is with efficiency, and this may account for the Commission's view that any exclusive rights are highly suspect.

1.3.2.3 *Fair competition* — Some Europeans desire competition also to help to achieve fairness within the economy. 'Fair competition' is listed as desirable in the preamble to the EC treaty. The meaning of the term is not clear. Should small firms be helped to compete against supermarkets, even if they are less efficient in producing what consumers want to buy and have to charge more? Where one firm has invested in promotion for the benefit of a brand as a whole, is it fair to let other firms take advantage of this investment for free?

1.3.2.4 *Political freedom* — Another strand of thought, enshrined in the German constitution and also reflected in the preamble to the EC treaty, is that every citizen should have a chance to enter a market as part of his political freedom. He may fail and go under, but he should have a chance to try.

The notion of competition at Community level has also been influenced by the different policies in member states, particularly in Germany and France. Although it has largely been based on liberal ideas of free markets, competition policy has not been oblivious of social and human demands.

1.3.2.5 *Conflict of goals* — How far competition law is capable of furthering all these goals without a considerable loss in efficiency is controversial. Small firms that are efficient need no special treatment. Help required for those that are not reduces efficiency to the extent that it consumes resources and encourages the growth of firms that are less efficient.

The ability to trade across national frontiers has increased competition within the EC, but when member states have different laws, for instance those relating to patents or maximum prices, it may not be possible to sell at all in some member states and still less to sell at the same price throughout the common market. Many of these different measures have been harmonised under the 1992 programme for market integration, but some differences in laws remain. Nevertheless, export bans and price discrimination have been prohibited without any analysis of the reasons for imposing them.

For example, at a time when, contrary to Community law, France prohibited the advertising of whisky but not of alcohol distilled from fruit which was produced in France and several member states taxed whisky more heavily than the locally produced liquor, the British firm, Distillers, charged some £5 a case more for whisky that was to be exported from the UK. It claimed that this was necessary because on the Continent, owing to high and discriminatory taxes, demand had to be increased through the promotional efforts of its exclusive dealers. These would not be able to afford to keep three months' stock and perform other promotional activities if at popular times, such as Christmas, local supermarkets which did not bear these expenses were able to import large quantities and undercut them. Yet in the United Kingdom, because demand was very elastic to price differences, Distillers would lose sales to other brands if it were to charge the extra £5.

The Commission did not meet this argument but adopted a decision condemning the extra charge for exports.[20] Distillers, therefore, divided its brands, ceasing to supply 'red label' in the United Kingdom and

20   *Distillers* [1978] 1 C.M.L.R. 400.

raising the prices of two other brands. These brands continued to be promoted on the Continent but ceased to be bought in the UK, whereas distributors on the Continent ceased to invest in promoting the others, which could be bought cheaply by parallel importers from the United Kingdom. I have been told that Distillers' sales of the three brands which could not be bought cheaply in the UK increased on the Continent more than those of its other brands.

Demand in the United Kingdom was more responsive to price; that on the Continent to promotion. There was no way in which the same brands could be sold at the same prices in the two markets. This was recognised by Advocate General Warner when the case was appealed, but for procedural reasons the Court did not consider the issue.[21]

In this case, the Commission's simple view that an extra charge for the whisky exported to other member states divided the common market must actually have delayed its integration. When the illegal discrimination on the Continent against whisky ended, Distillers had different brands known in the two areas. The Commission objected to the symptom of differential prices before the cause, the illegal discrimination in taxes, was removed. Moreover, it is more difficult to introduce a foreign product than to continue to sell that to which the local population is accustomed. The Commission failed to analyse the transaction *ex ante*, from the time when Distillers was trying to persuade its distributors to spend money promoting its brands, but looked only *ex post*, to competition at the time of the decision from the firms that wanted to take a free ride on that promotion and undercut the distributors without having to make the same investments.[22] It did not consider whether, without the investment induced by the territorial protection, parallel importers would have wanted to stock Distillers' products.

1.3.3 *Barriers to entry and substitutes may define the relevant market*

Where there are many suppliers to whom buyers can turn, a firm that offers bad bargains will soon lose business. Consequently, competition both acts as a spur to efficiency and determines price levels. Market power — power over price and other components of bargains — assumes, therefore, on the supply side that there are entry barriers preventing new firms from entering a profitable market as prices rise and

---

21 *Distillers* v. *Commission* (30/78) [1980] E.C.R. 2229.
22 In 1983, the Commission did announce its intention of exempting Distillers' conditions of sale in so far as they permitted an additional charge for 'Red Label' to Continental dealers, [1983] 3 C.M.L.R. 173. Although the exemption was never adopted, Distillers did charge the differential, and was delighted to find that UK buyers still bought the brand. The notice and its subsequent conduct related to one brand only, so the other brands remained split.

that few firms have, or can, overcome them. It also presupposes, on the demand side, that there are no substitutes to which buyers can turn. If the price of pears rises, some fruit eaters will turn to grapes or apples and some growers of other fruit may start planting pear trees.

Even if they collaborate, existing pear growers are unlikely to have much market power unless there is government regulation excluding new fruit growers, limiting the number of fruit trees that may be planted or providing a minimum price at which the government will buy up surplus pears. Competition from substitutes often operates more rapidly than the entry of new firms into the market or the expansion of existing firms — it takes time to build a plant or for a fruit tree to become sufficiently mature to bear much fruit, but each mechanism controls market power for most products.

Substitutes on both sides of the market, the ease with which suppliers can enter or expand and that with which consumers can turn to other products are considered in the United States to define the market relevant to assessing whether a firm or firms enjoy market power. It is not irrelevant to the definition of the relevant market under EC law, but the concept is less clear (4.2.3–4.2.3.5 below).

1.3.3.1 *Substitutes on the demand side* — In *United Brands*,[23] the Court confirmed the Commission's view that bananas were in a separate market from apples and oranges, partly because the very young or old and infirm could not manage other fruit, although there was no way of discriminating against these people. In fact, they were protected from high prices by the loss of sales to healthy people, who ate far more bananas than did the toothless, that would result if the price of bananas were raised.

1.3.3.2 *Barriers to entry* — In *Michelin*[24] the Court excluded the possibility of other firms entering the market to supply heavy tyres because it takes too long to build a factory. Most economists, in Europe as well as in the United States, state that competition works only in the long term, which is defined to mean the time needed to build the necessary facilities.

If the only goal of competition policy is efficiency, there are few entry barriers that matter. Entry of equally efficient firms is obstructed only by something that is more difficult for the new entrant than for the old. The fact that I have a factory and you do not is no entry barrier, because I had to sink resources into mine, and you are no worse off having to pay for yours.

On this basis, many economists, especially those associated with the

23   (27/76) [1978] E.C.R. 207.
24   (322/81) [1983] E.C.R. 3461.

University of Chicago, assert that there are only two kinds of entry barriers that exclude equally efficient firms: a minimum efficient scale of operation that is large in relation to the market and government regulation of all kinds. The more traditional view is that an established firm may adopt practices, such as a discount structure, that make it hard for smaller firms to compete successfully. Much of the current debate is concerned with problems of information, including reputation. Where the product is difficult for clients to assess, they may tend to go to the firm with the established reputation. The Commission and Court have considered that the need to invest in technology, a well developed marketing system and other benefits for which the incumbent had to provide resources may increase market power, but they would not keep out equally efficient firms. EC law is, however, concerned to protect not only efficient firms, but also competitors who may want to enter the market whether or not the possibility of entry may help consumers.

If a single plant can reprocess all the spent nuclear fuel in Europe substantially more cheaply than could smaller plants, it would be unprofitable for a second firm to establish a smaller plant.[25] Consequently, the first firm to enter the market on an efficient scale may have considerable power over price. It can charge at a level that merely covers its costs, including a return on capital and compensation for unusual risks, or it could make a higher charge up to the point where it pays someone to enter the market on a smaller scale. There are few products for which the minimum efficient scale of operation does not permit several plants in the common market, after allowance has been made for the higher costs of delivery from a single plant, customers' desire to have more than one source and so on. Moreover, scale economies at the level of the firm, such as spreading investment in r & d over a large turnover, may be outweighed by problems of running a large organisation.

Large capital requirements, in themselves, are not now treated as important barriers to entry by Chicago economists and some others.[26] If a market is profitable, there are enough large firms that can raise the finance to enter it. An existing supplier will not be able to maintain high prices for long. If, however, one is concerned, as some are in Europe, with the welfare of small firms which can raise capital only at greater cost than a larger incumbent, the need for capital may constitute a barrier to entry.

25   The facts in *KEWA* [1976] 2 C.M.L.R. D15.
26   Oliver Williamson, *Markets and Hierarchies, Analysis and antitrust implications: a study in the economics of internal organization*, New York, Free Press (1975), 11–113 and 'Delimiting Antitrust', 76 Georgetown L.J. 271.
Some economists and others believe that if significant investment is required it may be many years before anyone undertakes it. Moreover, only very large firms or joint ventures will be potential entrants.

On the other hand, even if one is concerned only with efficiency for the benefit of consumers, quite small amounts of capital may be a barrier to entry to small markets. Once there is a baker in a remote village, it may not pay another to install a large oven, or transport the bread from a distance, even if a loaf is a penny or two dearer than in the neighbouring town. It is not the amount of capital that is relevant, but whether there is likely to be sufficient demand for the product to yield a normal return once the new entrant has invested his capital.

There is not much that can be done about local market power, apart from improving the infrastructure of roads, canals, the postal service, telecommunications and so forth. Sometimes it is eroded by new entry at a point between the existing suppliers. Sometimes the possibility of hit and run entry may constrain the incumbent, when capital can easily be withdrawn from the market. Unfortunately, the new entrant often has sunk costs that cannot be withdrawn without significant loss.

A prevalent entry barrier is government regulation. If town planning authorities will allow only one fish and chip shop or launderette in an area, few local inhabitants will go to the trouble and expense of going further for a cheaper source of supply. Even so, the fish fryer or organiser of the launderette may not make undue profits — it is the owner of the land who can earn a monopoly rent by charging more for occupying licensed premises. A pub in the United Kingdom that loses its licence to sell alcohol on the premises without a meal suffers a dramatic loss of capital value. The prospect of monopoly profits may be capitalised. If the barrier to entry is removed by deregulation, the incumbent may suffer a reduction in the value of his premises.

Patents, copyrights and other intellectual property rights confer an exclusive right by law, so are an example of government regulation, though they may be justified as pro-competitive. Perceived *ex post*, after the investment in innovation has been made, important intellectual property rights may well constitute entry barriers. The exclusive right of the holder keeps other firms out. Perceived *ex ante*, when an undertaking is deciding whether to invest in innovation, however, the expectation of such rights may increase competition. The hope of monopoly profits resulting from an exclusive right creates an incentive to invest. If exclusive rights were not obtainable, some sorts of innovation that can be easily copied might not take place at all.

Pharmaceutical firms spend a substantial part of their turnover on research and development and on the trials drugs must undergo before they can legally be released to the public. Yet it is easy to copy a drug once its therapeutic effects are known. Little research and development would be financed for products that can be reverse engineered if anyone could undercut the inventor by copying the invention without incurring the costs of research and development. Such people are often called 'free riders.' They take a 'free ride' on the investment of the innovator.

Whether an exclusive right for 20 years, provided the invention is novel and not obvious, is the protection that yields the best amount of investment in research and development cannot be known, but almost everyone now recognises that patent protection is required if the common market is to compete in developing, disseminating and using advanced technology. 'Free riders' create major difficulties for firms investing in many contexts. In the short term they increase competition and reduce prices, but in the longer term the possibility of 'free riders' may discourage the very investment that creates the competition. When parallel importers were enabled to take advantage of the promotion paid for by Distillers' dealers on the Continent, the dealers ceased to promote and the brands became less attractive even to parallel importers.

This has not always been the prevailing view of economists. In the 1950s economists and lawyers associated with Harvard were concerned by many factors that would not now be treated in the United States as serious entry barriers. As a reaction to Nazi domination, West German economists and politicians just after the second world war were so concerned about entry barriers that patents, copyright and other intellectual property rights were distrusted. Many countries still reduce the value of patents by providing for compulsory licensing. This distrust of exclusive rights may account for the Community policy of reducing the benefits of holders of such rights (Chapters 9 and 10 below).

If one of the goals of competition policy is to enable small firms to enter markets, then entry barriers are pervasive. Many markets can be supplied only after considerable capital investments are made or technology developed. These are not barriers to the entry of an equally efficient firm unless the firm already in the market acquired these assets more cheaply, which is rarely the case after allowance has been made for general inflation. The Community Court has treated many costs as if they were entry barriers, such as a good distribution system, a technological lead or capital requirements. It should be realised that a firm protected only by such resources is not in a position to hold its customers or suppliers to ransom except in the short term. To control the conduct of firms with such fragile protection may discourage large European firms from making investments to enable them to compete aggressively.

1.4 EC institutions

1.4.1 *The Council*

The legislative body of the EC is still the Council of Ministers, not the European Parliament, which used to be little more than a debating chamber, although it now has a power of co-determination on many matters.

The principal regulations implementing the competition rules have been made by the Council, which consists of ministers of member states. Until the Single European Act came into effect in 1987, major regulations used to be made only if no state opposed them. The procedure for adopting such regulations was therefore not unlike the haggling that frequently precedes the conclusion of international treaties.

Since 1987, harmonising legislation under article 100A of the EC treaty has been adopted by the Council by qualified majority. The Council may adopt such legislation in co-operation with the Parliament.[27] This has increased the influence of the Parliament.

A new co-determination procedure has been introduced in Article 189b for harmonisation under article 100A. Proposed legislation is adopted in two phases. Parliament has a legislative veto. If Parliament rejects a proposed measure, and repeats its rejection on the second reading, the measure cannot pass. The Council cannot overrule Parliament even by voting unanimously. Parliament often proposes amendments. If the Council disagrees with the proposal, it is considered by a Conciliation Committee composed of members of the Council and Parliament. A possible compromise proposed by the Committee must be adopted by qualified majority in the Council and simple majority in Parliament. If one of them fails to act within the prescribed period, the measure lapses.

Nevertheless, legislation is still adopted on a proposal of the Commission to the Council and is not initiated by the European Parliament. In the field of competition, some measures may be adopted under article 87 and are therefore not subject to the co-operation or co-decision procedure, although they may be adopted by qualified majority in the Council. Legislation proposed under article 235 to fill a gap in the treaty still requires unanimity and the proposed regulation giving the Commission power to control mergers was blocked politically for a decade and a half until a regulation controlling concentrations between very large firms was adopted at the end of 1989 (Chapter 12 below).

The Council's greater willingness to legislate on the Commission's proposals, however, seems to be affecting legislation in the competition field. It has recently adopted implementing regulations for air and maritime transport.

---

27   Now arts. 100A and 189c of the EC treaty as amended at Maastricht.

1.4.2 *The Commission — the executive of the Communities*

The Commission is the executive arm of the EC. In practice each member state according to its size appoints one or two members to the Commission. Each member of the Commission is responsible for one or more policy areas. These political heads of the Commission must take their formal decisions on competition policy collegiately. They are served by a small secretariat, divided into Directorates General — DGs — each responsible for one policy area. Currently Mr. Van Miert is responsible *inter alia* for competition. DGIV assists him on competition matters.

There are fewer officials working for the Commission in all departments than are employed by any one of the major departments of the UK civil service. There is not the manpower for much regulation, which is one reason for reliance upon market forces. Some attempt is made to appoint officials from each member state proportionately to the size of its population. The tradition of the Service is far more open than that of the British civil service. Members and their officials consult far more on proposed legislation and are willing to speak to those interested. Traditionally, however, there has been less horizontal consultation between different departments than in the British civil service. Originally, officials reported to their boss and he to his until matters were sorted out by the Members of the Commission. There is a growing tendency, now, for matters to be sorted out informally between officials from different Directorates General.

1.4.3 *The Community Courts*

Originally there was a single Community Court, but in 1989 the Court of First Instance, called the Tribunal in some member states, started to operate in competition and staff cases. Its jurisdiction was significantly increased in 1993 and 1994. It now includes state aids, dumping and many other matters, save for actions brought by or against member states. The original court is still called the Court of Justice of the European Communities and I will call it 'the Court' or 'the Community Court.'

Both courts consist of judges appointed collectively by the member states, but in practice each nominates one judge and the others accept him, with a thirteenth judge coming from one of the larger member states. Advocates General in the Community Court are mostly appointed by the four larger member states, but the other member states appoint two Advocates General in turn.

Because the Court started by being both the supreme constitutional court and the ultimate court of appeal, while many of its decisions were also at first instance, the Advocates General performed a useful function. They may operate a little like a judge at first instance, reading and hearing the arguments and giving an unbiased opinion. Nevertheless, the analogy should not be pressed too far: there is normally no further hearing and after the opinion is delivered the Court continues to give judgment automatically.

The office of Advocate General works well when individuals attempt to analyse the problems rationally. It works less helpfully when an individual Advocate General tries to find out which way the Court will go, and leans that way. I regret that some assess their success by how often they are followed by the Court.

The Court does not publish dissenting or individual judgments, only a single collegiate judgment. Naturally, independent judges of high standing, caring about the development of Community law, do not always perceive issues in identical fashion. They have to agree on the words of their judgment, if not its meaning. This tends to lead to obscurity. Sometimes, inconsistent statements are left in, or at least statements with a very different emphasis. Sometimes, a wide principle is followed by a narrower proposition, sufficient to deal with the facts before the Court. Sometimes, key paragraphs are left obscure, again probably in an attempt to achieve a consensus. Recently, the Court has tended to answer only as much as it need, rather than use the questions put to it to develop broad principles of law, as it did in the early days.

The Court's backlog has been growing by almost 50 cases a year, and it now takes at least two years to obtain a preliminary ruling (1.5.2.1 and glossary).

The new Court of First Instance established under the Single European Act now hears appeals from the Commission in competition cases and, since 1993, in many other matters. The Court of First Instance has taken some of the pressure off the Community Court and, although some of its decisions have been appealed, the appeal must be confined to points of law, so the files to be examined by the Community Court should be far less massive. It is not yet clear where the line should be drawn between facts and law. The law in different member states varies. The Court treats inferences from the primary facts as law, so has little jurisdiction.

The procedure before both Courts is mostly written, a feature made necessary by the linguistic difficulties caused by multiple official languages, now nine.[28] There is a short oral hearing, but each party is

---

28   In theory, also Irish. The EC treaty was translated into Gaelic, but the Irish do not normally insist on its use.

restricted usually to an hour or less to meet new points or go over the salient features of its case.

1.5 Enforcement of the competition rules

There are two main ways in which the competition rules are enforced. The Commission has been empowered by regulation 17 to find whether conduct infringes article 85 or 86 and to grant individual exemptions. There is now some discussion of the possibility of the Commission delegating its powers in relation to article 85(1) to national competition authorities in cases involving primarily a single member state. The prohibitions in articles 85 and 86 also give rise to actions in tort in national courts. Moreover article 85(2) renders agreements that infringe that article void. The prohibition of article 86 may also cause a transaction to become void on the ground that it is illegal.

1.5.1 *Enforcement by the Commission*

The competition rules are largely enforced by the Commission. Not only has it been empowered by the Council to enact some subordinate legislation granting group exemptions from the prohibition of article 85(1) and providing forms for notifying agreements of which individual exemption is required, but article 9 of regulation 17/62 also gives it the exclusive right to grant individual exemptions.[29] Moreover, it has powers to obtain information from firms and to order undertakings to terminate an infringement of article 85 or 86 and to impose fines. Its powers and procedures are described in Chapter 5 below. The Commission operates formally through the decisions of its members which must be adopted collegiately. When it acts informally by administrative letter, the parties to an agreement are not bound.

1.5.1.1 *The role of the Court under articles 173 and 175* — By virtue of article 173 of the treaty, the parties to whom a decision is addressed and others to whom it is of direct and individual concern have the right to appeal to the Community Court. Such an appeal now lies to the Court of First Instance. It is not a rehearing of the merits, but the court is required to consider whether the Commission has violated the treaty in substance or procedurally. Seldom did the Community Court go far in investigating the facts found by the Commission, but in several cases involving horizontal cartels the Court of First Instance has gone very far in re-examining the evidence on which the Commission's decision was based.

29   See 5.6 below.

_..uer article 175, the Commission may also be sued in the Court of First Instance for failing to take action required by the treaty, but few such actions have succeeded under the competition rules, largely because many of the Commission's powers are discretionary.

1.5.2 Enforcement by national courts

The competition rules, like many others in the treaty, were incorporated into the law of the six original member states on the establishment of the common market, although the first implementing regulation was adopted only in 1962. The rules became part of the law of the first three new member states (the United Kingdom, Denmark and the Republic of Ireland) by reason of their accession to the Community at the beginning of 1973. They applied to Greece on its accession at the end of 1980 and to Spain and Portugal from 1986. Similar rules now apply throughout the EEA.

Agreements that infringe the competition rules are prohibited and the highest courts in several large member states have held that damages lie for infringing articles 85 and 86. Indeed, it is now virtually certain that Community law requires national courts to give an adequate remedy to those injured by breach of the treaty.[30]

Moreover, provisions in contracts that infringe article 85 are void *pro tanto* and national courts should not enforce them.[31] As mentioned at the end of 1.2.1 above, this gives rise to considerable difficulty, as it may be necessary to analyse the market in order to assess the effect of an agreement or the conduct of a dominant firm on competition and, frequently, it may not be simple to tell whether an agreement infringes article 85 or may be enforced. Sometimes national courts will have to adjourn to enable the Commission to decide whether to exempt the agreement. The problems will be analysed shortly in Chapter 6 below.

1.5.2.1 Preliminary rulings under article 177 — It is important that courts in the various member states should apply Community law uniformly. Consequently, article 177 of the treaty requires ultimate courts of appeal and permits lower courts and tribunals, but not arbitrators, to ask the Community Court for a preliminary ruling as to the construction of the treaty, or the validity or construction of subordinate legislation. Should the defendant to an action for breach of contract, for instance, plead that the agreement is void under article 85(2), the civil or commercial court may request the Community Court for a ruling on the

---

30   *Cf. Francovich* v. *Italy* (C–6 & 9/90) [1991] E.C.R. I–5357 and *Factortame* (221/89) [1990] E.C.R. I–2433.
31   *Marty* v. *Lauder* (37/79) [1980] E.C.R. 2481.

interpretation of Community law or the validity of subordinate legislation.

Judgments given on this ground are, by and large, less helpful than those given on an appeal from a decision of the Commission. The Court is supposed to give an abstract ruling rather than apply it to the facts, although, on occasion, it has applied the law. It frequently reformulates the questions asked of it so as to be as helpful as possible. For this purpose, it is customary for the referring court to forward the whole file to the Community Court. If it does not do so, it is difficult for the Court to reformulate the questions.

Since the 1960s, with political stalemate on many matters in the Council, the Court has often taken on the role of furthering the integration of the common market. Many of its judgments, such as *Continental Can*,[32] have changed what most people thought to be the law, and it is misleading to study Community legislation without becoming familiar with the Court's work. Even though legislation can now more easily be adopted by the Council, the Court continues to develop the law.

1.5.3 *Possible enforcement by national competition authorities*

The Commission suffers from inadequate resources to cope with all its files and is considering whether it could delegate its powers over some of them to national competition authorities. At the moment there is little incentive for national authorities to perform the Commission's tasks under articles 85 and 86. They are more likely to invoke national law.

National authorities have no power to grant exemptions under article 85(3), and if they follow the Commission's practice under article 85(1) they will have to forbid many agreements that increase competition. Moreover, when the Bundeskartellamt was about to forbid one joint venture, the Commission, which had approved a state aid for it, trumped the national authority by granting an exemption under article 85(3).[33]

1.5.4 *The co-existence of national competition rules*

National legislation that controls restrictions of competition was for three decades hardly affected by Community law, save to the extent that national law takes into account the ease of trade between member states. Undertakings are required to comply with both systems because the competition rules have direct effect on the law of member states. In

---

32 Cited at 1.2.2 above.
33 *Ford/Volkswagen*, O.J. 1993, L20/14. See H.-Peter von Stoephasius in Piet Jan Slot and Alison McDonnell (eds.), *Procedure and Enforcement in EC and U.S. Competition Law — Proceedings of the Leiden Europa Instituut Seminar on User-friendly Competition Law*, p.33.

Wilhelm v. *Bundeskartellamt*[34] the Community Court confirmed that national authorities may proceed against an alleged infringement under national law. The Bundeskartellamt was entitled to investigate and punish the four members of an alleged cartel operating in the Federal Republic, even after the Commission began to investigate the same industry throughout the Community. Nevertheless, the Court qualified its ruling:

> '4. ... However, if the ultimate general aim of the treaty is to be respected, this parallel application of the national system can only be allowed in so far as it does not prejudice the uniform application throughout the Common Market of the Community rules on cartels and of the full effect of the measures adopted in implementation of those rules. ...
>
> '5. ... The treaty ... also permits the Community authorities to carry out certain positive, though indirect action with a view to promoting a harmonious development of economic activities within the whole Community.'

The exact scope of these paragraphs is not clear, but they seem to indicate that national authorities should not forbid the implementation of agreements that have been exempted under Community law, at least where the exemption was of an individual agreement on grounds of the benefits to be obtained from collaboration. Whether a group exemption preempts the application of national law is controversial. Some officials responsible for enforcing national competition laws fear that the Commission granted some group exemptions for anti-competitive activities in order only to dispose of its backlog of cases and on account of its wish to be able to keep control over them.

In the last few years, many member states have adopted national rules corresponding to articles 85 and 86 and the merger regulation. Lawyers may have to visit several countries to clear an important merger or joint venture, if it is not subject to the merger regulation.

1.6 Extraterritorial competence

The Commission has long assumed that any agreement having a prohibited effect in the common market is caught, even if the agreement be made outside the common market by foreigners who carry on no activities within the common market. In *Wood Pulp,*[35] the Court adopted the traditional territorial theory of international law. It held that if a contract made by non-nationals outside the common market is implemented within it, the Commission is competent. It is not clear whether a foreigner can be fined for making an agreement to keep out of

---

34   (14/68) [1969] E.C.R. 1.
35   (89, 104, 114, 116, 117 and 125–129/85) [1988] E.C.R. 5193.

the common market. Would the agreement be 'implemented' by a failure to trade within the Community?

There are provisions similar to articles 85 and 86 in free trade agreements — the treaties entered into between the Communities and various other countries, which used to be in force with the members of EFTA. The Court in *Wood Pulp* added, in relation to the Finnish firms involved, that articles 85 and 86 are the methods whereby the Community gives effect to its obligations under the Free Trade Agreements to prohibit agreements that restrict trade between the Community and the other Party. The EC competition rules can, therefore, be applied despite the existence of the Free Trade Agreements.

1.7 The European Economic Area (EEA)

In January 1994, the EEA treaty entered into force and replaced the Free Trade Agreements for most of the members of EFTA. Austria, Finland, Iceland, Liechtenstein,[36] Norway and Sweden joined the member states of the common market in closer relations than in a free trade area. Switzerland put the proposal to a referendum which was negative and had to withdraw. The EEA treaty has provisions corresponding to those of the EC treaty, but the institutional provisions are rather different. The EFTA countries have accepted the case law and practice of the Communities and the treaty will largely be enforced through the Commission of the European Communities, but in specific cases by the EFTA Surveillance Authority (ESA), the administrative body of the EEA. The decisions of the ESA are subject to appeal to the EFTA Court in Geneva, but those of the Commission relating to the EEA are subject to appeal to the Court of First Instance in Luxembourg.

Articles 53 and 54 of the EEA treaty[37] correspond to Articles 85 and 86 of the EC treaty and article 57 enables the EC Commission to control mergers that may create or strengthen a dominant position as a result of which competition is impeded within the European Economic Area.

The provisions of the EEA treaty are directly effective in Austria, which is a monist state — the provisions of international Conventions enjoy the force of law. The other countries, which are dualist, have expressly incorporated the provisions of the EEA into national law.

Annex XIV to the EEA treaty incorporates the various regulations adopted by the Communities in relation to competition and protocol 28 incorporates the doctrine of exhaustion of intellectual property rights[38] developed in the EC in relation to the whole EEA.

36 Liechtenstein is not yet a member, but is likely to ratify soon.
37 Set out at the end of Appendix 1 below.
38 Set out in App. 1 below and described in Chap. 9 below.

It is too early to write on the experience under the EEA treaty. In theory, it should be interpreted and applied in the same way as that of the EC. Officials of the ESA have been working with DGIV in order to gain experience of its practice and there are provisions for the Commission and ESA to communicate with each other. They will send each other copies of notifications and so forth. The ESA has been able to hire some very able lawyers who have studied EC law seriously. The usefulness of the EEA treaty will, however, be greatly reduced if Austria, Finland, Norway and Sweden join the Community shortly, as contemplated.

1.8 The importance of the competition rules

It is very important to consider the EC and EEA competition rules when planning a firm's production and marketing policy. The Commission and EFTA Surveillance Authority have power to impose on undertakings that have deliberately or negligently infringed the competition rules fines of up to 10 per cent. of their turnover for the previous year (5.10 below). Ignorance of the law is no excuse if the firms ought to have known that their conduct was anti-competitive. In *Pioneer*,[39] the Court confirmed that the 10 per cent. limit may be based on the turnover of the entire group of companies, worldwide and for all products. On the other hand, when the infringement has affected only a small part of a large firm's activities, the fine may be reduced in accordance with the doctrine of proportionality: the remedy should not exceed the harm. The balance between these factors is unclear. Fines for what the Commission conceives as clear offences, such as price fixing cartels or the imposition of export bans that are not ancillary to any pro-competitive transaction (7.1.2 below) have been increasing and fines exceeding 10 million ECUs (over £7 million) have been imposed on some individual firms for price fixing cartels, especially when the market of some member states is reserved to the local producer. Tetra Pak was fined 75 million ECUs for abusing a dominant position in various ways.[40] Many large commercial and industrial firms employ their own lawyers and are well advised on EC competition matters, but some smaller firms have been fined substantial sums and also need advice.

The other main sanction is that provisions which restrict competition within the common market contained in contracts which affect trade between member states are automatically void by virtue of article 85(2). Consequently, a manufacturer suing its exclusive dealer in the English High Court for actively selling outside his territory may be met with the

39   (100–103/80) [1983] E.C.R. 1823.
40   *Tetra Pak II* [1992] 4 C.M.L.R. 551, subject to appeal. The way the value of the ECU is determined is explained in the glossary.

defence that an export restraint is contrary to article 85(1) of the treaty and does not merit exemption. If the brand the dealer is appointed to sell has a significant impact on the market, parts of the agreement may be void — a total ban on exports almost certainly would be. Some territorial protection is exempted under various regulations applying to exclusive dealing agreements and technology licences, but export restrictions that go further than the exemption may also prevent the group exemption from applying to clauses whereby the dealer agrees not to handle competing products and the manufacturer agrees not to sell directly to any other dealer within the dealer's territory, in which case those clauses may also be void.

In *Ford*,[41] when the brand owner refused to supply right hand drive vehicles freely on the Continent, the exclusive dealing provisions that could be exempted by regulation 67/67 might have become void, although it might not have paid Ford to rely on this nullity at the cost of sacrificing its continuing relationship with its dealers. Investments based on the assumption that such provisions are enforceable may prove unfruitful and even lead to insolvency.

When drafting a contract one should consider whether one is likely to want to enforce it, in which case the agreement must be drafted so as not to infringe the competition rules. On the other hand, if it is the other party who is to make the initial investment and who is most likely to wish to sue, some firms may take less trouble to exclude an illegal provision. They may be able to use such a clause to renegotiate the contract later. This is, however, conduct not lightly to be undertaken since agreements that infringe article 85 are prohibited and may give rise to an action in tort by third parties. Moreover, unless the agreement is notified to the Commission, it may attract the imposition of fines. When negotiating, one should guard against the danger of making it difficult to enforce the agreement in national courts.

It is not sufficient to ensure that the contract itself is legal, and then by a nod or a wink make it clear that one will not compete with a friend. Concerted practices are illegal as well as contracts, and the contract itself may be tainted if it is the means whereby an illegal concerted practice is to be implemented.[42]

Common market law affects agreements even if they are confined to firms in a single member state. *Brasserie de Haecht* v. *Wilkin (1)*[43] related to the tie of a single café to a small Belgian brewery, but the Court ruled that if most Belgian cafés were tied to one brewery or another for a

---

41   *Ford* v. *Commission* (228 & 229/82) [1984] E.C.R. 1129.
42   See 2.2.4–2.2.4.2 below.
43   (23/67) [1967] E.C.R. 407. See also *Stergios Delimitis* v. *Henninger Bräu* (C-234/89) [1991] E.C.R. I-935.

long time, it might be difficult for other firms to enter the Belgian market. In *Belasco*,[44] the Court and Advocate General Mischo observed that it is difficult to maintain high prices within one country unless action is taken to exclude imports. This is what may affect trade between member states.

The EC competition rules are of wide application and enforced by important sanctions. It may be costly to remain ignorant of them.

1.9 State measures to protect firms from competition

Although later chapters of this book are confined to analysing articles 85 and 86, which apply only to undertakings, it may well be that the worst distortions to competition are caused by state intervention. Without state protection, cartels seldom survive for long. State subsidies are illegal under articles 92–94 of the treaty in so far as they may affect trade between member states, although there are some exceptions and more discretionary exemptions. Taxation that discriminates in favour of locally produced products is controlled under article 95 and some distortions of trade between member states caused by the buying practices of state monopolies can be controlled under article 37.

These provisions are often not conceived as being part of the competition rules, and the control of discriminatory taxation is not dealt with by the Competition Department of the Commission in Brussels, DGIV, but by DGIII, which is responsible for the internal market.

More generally, article 3(g)[45] provides for

'the institution of a system ensuring that competition in the common market is not distorted.'

It is hardly surprising that the Community should have wished to control anti-competitive state measures. Articles 85 and 86 are not addressed to member states directly, but to undertakings. Even in a fully federal system, however, a supreme court must not act too strongly when expanding federal law at the expense of state rights. The member states transferred very little of their sovereignty to the European Communities. The Community Courts have no physical powers and must rely on the courts of member states to apply their rulings. If such courts are outraged, the application of Community law is prejudiced and the Community Court has trodden warily when considering state action that facilitates anti-competitive agreements or makes them unnecessary.

Article 5(2) requires member states to refrain from any measure which could jeopardize the attainment of the objectives of the treaty. From this

---

44   *Belasco* v. *Commission* (246/86) [1989] E.C.R. 2117.
45   Article 3(f) until the provisions were renumbered by the treaty of Maastricht.

very general provision, the Court has ruled in a series of cases that effect should not be given by national courts to measures which encourage, require or reinforce the effects of an agreement that infringes article 85(1).[46]

1.9.1   *Government encouragement or persuasion is no defence to article 85*

It is clear that non-binding action such as mere persuasion or encouragement by a government to enter into an anti-competitive agreement is no defence — hardly even mitigation — under the competition rules.

For instance, in *BNIC* v. *Clair*,[47] the Court stated that the recommendation by a private trade association of minimum prices for cognac and the *eaux de vie* from which it is distilled infringed article 85, although the association was set up by ministerial order. The minister also appointed the members of the board and sent a nominee to its meetings. The Court added that the recommendation was not excused by a subsequent ministerial order that made the prices binding on non-members.

The minister initiated and supervised the cartel and ensured its success by making it illegal for outsiders to undercut it. In the United States that might have sufficed for the cartel to be treated as the exercise of governmental power not subject to the antitrust laws.

1.9.2   *State measures reinforcing the effects of anti-competitive agreements*

In *BNIC* v. *Aubert*,[48] the Court ruled that the ministerial order extending the effect of the same anti-competitive agreement to bind all traders in *eaux de vie* was itself subject to articles 3(f), 5(2) and 85 in combination. It could not be relied upon as a basis for prosecuting a trader who exceeded maximum quotas fixed by the agreement. The national law itself was ruled to be subject to Community law, which takes priority.

Similarly, in *Belgian Travel Agents*[49] the Court ruled that the Belgian state should not prosecute a travel agent for sharing its commission with a customer when this was prohibited by a royal decree that gave legal effect to the rules of professional conduct that forbade such price competition, even though the original agreement had expired — it had become unnecessary once the national law of 1966 took its place. This judgment was less controversial in that the government had not encouraged

---

46   1.9.2 below.
47   (123/83) [1985] E.C.R. 391.
48   (136/86) [1987] E.C.R. 4789.
49   *Vlaamse Reisbureaus* (311/85) [1987] E.C.R. 3801.

and supervised the restrictive agreement as the minister had done in *BNIC* — it merely reinforced the agreement that had been freely made.

1.9.3 *State measures that delegate the fixing of prices to citizens*

In *Leclerc* v. *Au Blé Vert*,[50] Leclerc operated a supermarket chain with a reputation for price cutting. The French Lang Act, however, required publishers or importers of books to fix minimum retail prices for the books they published or imported, and it was made a criminal offence for retail sales to be made at a discount of more than 5 per cent. Provision was made for competitors and various kinds of trade associations to seek an injunction or damages, as well as for criminal prosecutions to be brought.

Leclerc sold various titles below the permitted level and at the suit of several competing booksellers was ordered to comply with the law. The Court of Appeal at Poitiers, however, asked the Community Court for a preliminary ruling whether the French law infringed the EC rules of competition in the light of articles 3(f) and 5(2).

Leclerc argued that the law was not simply price control by the state, since the prices could be fixed freely by publishers and importers. In effect, Leclerc argued that the Lang Act set up a resale price maintenance system which it would be illegal for the undertakings to arrange. The Commission, however, asked the Court to distinguish state measures from agreements between undertakings, since article 85 applies only to the conduct of undertakings.

The Court referred at paragraph 15 to a principle it had established in somewhat obscure terms in 1977 and which underlies its later judgments:

> 'Whilst it is true that the rules on competition are concerned with the conduct of undertakings and not with national legislation, member states are none the less obliged under the second paragraph of Article 5 of the treaty not to detract, by means of national legislation, from the full and uniform application of Community law or from the effectiveness of its implementing measures; nor may they introduce or maintain in force measures, even of a legislative nature, which may render ineffective the competition rules applicable to undertakings (*cf.* judgment in *Wilhelm* v. *Bundeskartellamt*,[51] and judgment in *Inno* v. *ATAB* at paragraph 31.[52])'

The Court observed that the French law did not compel the conclusion of agreements, but only unilateral conduct. It then went on to consider whether the Lang Act deprived the competition rules of their effectiveness by making collusion unnecessary. It mentioned that the French

50   (229/83) [1985] E.C.R. 32.
51   See 1.5.4 above.
52   (13/77) [1977] E.C.R. 2115.

measure protected book prices on cultural grounds, that the resale prices of books are maintained in many member states and that the Commission had, so far, attacked only one system of resale price maintenance for Dutch language books embracing two member states, and not a national system.

The Court concluded at paragraph 20 that, as Community law then stood, article 5, combined with articles 3(f) and 85, was not sufficiently well defined to prevent member states from enacting legislation such as that in issue.

1.9.4 Anti-competitive state measures making agreements between undertakings unnecessary

Judge Joliet has since argued[53] that the Court did object in principle to national measures, such as the Lang Act, for depriving article 85 of its effect. A private firm should not be able to dictate the terms on which other firms deal. Nevertheless, he says that the Court declined to strike down the Act as unconstitutional on grounds of legal certainty.

The argument, based on the failure of the Commission to challenge the resale price maintenance of books, may well mask a compromise. It was not accepted in relation to package tours in *Belgian Travel Agents*.[54] Nevertheless, more member states permit an exception to prohibitions of resale price maintenance for books than for travel agents. In all these cases, the government had enabled existing traders to fix the prices at which others were allowed to trade.

In *Cullet* v. *Leclerc*[55] however, where the French government itself had fixed minimum prices for petrol, there was no question of delegating its discretion to firms that might want protection from outsiders, and the Court held that article 85 was not deprived of its effectiveness. In the absence of inter-brand competition, however, the law was even more anti-competitive than the Lang Act.

In *Van Eycke*,[56] the Court went out of its way to rule that article 5(2) forbids governments to delegate to associations of private banks decisions as to rates of interest. It seems that the government did not delegate its powers, so the legislation was presumably valid. Some commentators consider that this was a strong *dictum*, in as much as interest rates were closely allied to monetary policy which, before Maastricht, was reserved to member states by title 2 of the treaty. What the

53 Cited bibliography, 1.11 below.
54 Cited at 1.9.2 above.
55 (231/83) [1985] E.C.R. 305.
56 (267/86) [1988] E.C.R. 4769.

Court objected to, however, was the delegation of the government's discretion to a particular group of undertakings that might operate in its own interest.

At a speech at the University of Liège in November 1993,[57] Luc Gyselen argued that the Court's alternative rulings in *Van Eycke* were incompatible: first it said that for a measure to infringe article 5(2) there must also be an agreement between undertakings. Secondly, it suggested that the delegation of discretion would infringe article 5(2), presumably in the absence of any such agreement.

Where, as in the case of books, the products are heterogeneous, the government cannot possibly set a mandatory price, so must delegate the price fixing to individual producers. The Court ruled in *Leclerc*[58] that this may infringe article 5(2). Where, like petrol, the products are homogeneous, however, the government may impose controls. The Court has not addressed this argument. It has not articulated the reasons for distinguishing measures where the right to fix the prices is delegated to businessmen. It seems unlikely that governments would fix the price at a more desirable level than would individual suppliers.

Without articulating its reasons, the Court held in 1993 that national measures that make it unnecessary for undertakings to agree, such as a national legislative prohibition on an agent sharing his commission with his customer, do not infringe article 5(2), even though a horizontal agreement between the agents would certainly restrict competition and might well affect trade between member states.[59] Such legislation may well be more anti-competitive than that which has been condemned under article 5(2), but in 1993 the Court seems to have been unwilling to cut back state power.

1.9.5   *State measures are subject to the rules for free movement*

Some government intervention to protect local traders may infringe article 30, which prohibits quantitative restrictions on imports, including measures that bear more heavily on imports than on domestic production. Such action can be restrained by the Commission operating under article 169 and, since it has direct effects, article 30 can be used by citizens as a defence to prosecution under the offending law.

In *Au Blé Vert*,[60] the Court found that the provisions relating to books imported from other member states did infringe the rules for the free

57   To be published in an expanded form *op. cit.*, to be published in the E.L.R. checklist, bibliography at 1.11 below
58   Cited at 1.9.3 above.
59   *Meng* (C–2/91), *Ohra* (C–245/91) and *Reiff* (C–185/91), judgments of 17 November 1993.
60   Cited at 1.9.3 above.

movement of goods, which are addressed to member states. The French law required the importer, not the publisher, to fix the resale prices. So a dealer could prevent its competitors from undercutting it and thereby reduce demand for imported books. The law did not apply to imported books the same régime as for those published in France. The law was later amended and became valid.[61]

1.9.6 Conclusion on article 5(2)

There is considerable regulation in Europe that might interfere with 'undistorted competition,' but the Court has been cautious in invoking article 5(2). It has not accepted that government persuasion is a defence to an agreement that infringes article 85. It has condemned as contrary to a combination of articles 3(f), 5(2) and 85 government measures that require, favour or reinforce agreements that infringe article 85. It has gone further and condemned national measures that delegate to a private firm or trade association the fixing of terms on which outsiders may trade.

It has, however, drawn back from ruling that a government measure might be invalid when there had never been any agreement restricting competition in the common market. Further action against anti-competitive regulation must probably be left to measures of harmonisation under articles 100 and 100A[62] of the treaty, and to article 90, which empowers the Commission to take action against state monopolies (1.9.7 below).

1.9.7 Special and exclusive rights (article 90)

Until 1992, DGIV devoted considerable resources to enforcing article 90, set out in Appendix 1 below. The provision restrains state measures protecting public undertakings and undertakings to which the state has granted special or exclusive rights contrary to the rules of the treaty, expressly mentioning the competition rules. Paragraph (2) provides a derogation for revenue producing monopolies or undertakings entrusted with services of general economic interest. The third paragraph enables the Commission to enforce the provisions of article 90 by directives and decisions. In effect, it can legislate on state measures conferring exclusive rights without going through the Council by invoking article 90(3) together with some other provision in the treaty.

Until 1992, DGIV devoted considerable resources to enforcing article

---

61   *Libraries de Normandie* v. *L'Aigle Distribution, Centre Leclerc* (254/87) [1988] ECR 4457.
62   As revised at Maastricht. It is subject to the new co-determination procedure under art. 189(b) and legislation can be passed by a qualified majority.

90 and the Court has construed it very broadly. The exception in paragraph 2 has been narrowly construed, and in *Italy* v. *Commission*,[63] the Court upheld a decision that British Telecom had infringed article 86 before it was privatised. It was an undertaking carrying on commercial operations, although it was owned by the government. It enjoyed exclusive rights and the terms on which it forwarded telex messages from Europe did not obstruct the performance of the task of providing a universal telephone service assigned to it.

There was some doubt about what public bodies amount to 'undertakings.' The German state labour exchange was held to constitute an undertaking in *Höfner and Elser* v. *Macroton*,[64] because it carried on an economic activity finding jobs, although it made no charges for its service and could not make profits. In *Poucet*,[65] however, it was held that the office for dispensing national insurance and health payments in France was not an undertaking for various reasons: it enjoyed no discretion and the social security system was based on the principle of solidarity, so that those with bad health were subsidised by the more fortunate.

In *Merci* v. *Gabrielli*,[66] the exclusive right to unload and transship cargoes was entrusted under Italian legislation to a co-operative of workers in the port of Genoa. When a cargo of steel arrived, the workers in the co-operatives were on strike, but the ship was not permitted to use its own tackle to unload. The cargo owner sued in Italy and the Community Court was asked to make preliminary rulings under article 177.

The co-operatives were ruled to be undertakings (paragraph 9). The port was considered a substantial part of the common market within the meaning of article 86 because of the large amount of trade from other member states that passed through it (paragraph 15). The statutory exclusive right led to the co-operatives enjoying a dominant position (paragraph 14). The Court also ruled that Italy infringed article 90 if the mere exercise of the exclusive right by the co-operative infringed article 86, or if the exclusive right were capable of creating a situation in which the undertaking was caused to commit an abuse, by one of four acts (paragraph 19):

—requiring payment for services that were not requested;
—charging disproportionate prices;

63   (41/83) [1985] E.C.R. 873.
64   (C–41/90) [1991] E.C.R. I–1979, paras. 20–23.
65   *Poucet and ors.* v. *Assurances Générales de France & ors*, (C–159 & 160/91) 17 February 1993, shortly reported at C.M.R. 96, 832.
66   *Merci Convenzionali Porto di Genova* v. *Siderurgica Gabrielli* (C–179/90) [1991] E.C.R. I–5889.

—refusing to use modern technology; or

—price discrimination.

The Court added that even in the context of article 90, article 86 was directly effective and created rights for individuals, which national civil courts were required to protect (paragraph 23). The cargo owner may be able to sue the government for infringing article 90, although it may be harder to quantify the damage than it was in *Francovich*,[67] and also the co-operatives for infringing article 86.

In *Corbeau*,[68] a former postman was prosecuted for infringing the Belgian postal monopoly by carrying on a business of collecting mail within the city of Liège and promising to deliver it by next morning for a charge of one Belgian franc less than the cost of a stamp. He was skimming the cream — delivering the letters that took little effort and not those to distant or remote parts of the country. The Community Court ruled that although the obligation of universal service imposed on the post office did come within the derogation of article 90(2), to refuse permission to others to compete by providing a superior service on any terms was contrary to article 90 in combination with 86.

It is not clear what the petty criminal court in Liège should do. Should it work out how great a profit the post office needs on each letter within a substantial town in order to subsidise delivery at a distance or to areas where few people live? Such a task is difficult for a regulatory Commission and virtually impossible without one. If it does not do this, would the postal service have to decide the matter itself, subject to review by the Commission which could make a decision under article 90(3)?

Recently, while member states were having difficulty ratifying the treaty of Maastricht, the Commission hesitated to use its powers under article 90(3) to legislate by directive or make individual decisions against member states, although it did adopt two directives[69] earlier on terminal equipment for telephones and on value added services. Nevertheless, the Community Court has been asked to interpret article 90 by national courts and it may well be that complainants harmed by the failure of some liberalisation initiatives may take the matter before the Court through suit in a national court followed by a reference under article 177.

Community law under article 90 has developed rapidly at the expense of state regulation. Significant progress has been made on telecommunications. At some point, the Court may relent and give greater recognition to state rights.

67   Cited at 1.5.2 above.
68   (C–320/91) judgment of 19 May 1993, not yet reported.
69   Dir. on Terminal Equipment, Dir. 88/301, O.J. 1988, L131/73. The Community Court upheld the Dir. in *France* v. *Commission* (202/88) [1991] E.C.R. I–1223. See also the Services Dir. Dir. 90/388, O.J. 1990, L192/10.

1.9.8 State aids

Possibly the most important way for states to distort trade is by the grant of aid. Politicians are subject to strong temptation to be seen to decrease unemployment in a marginal constituency by subsidising failing firms, even if the inefficiency leads in the longer run to greater unemployment through the loss of work to international competitors once the aid is reduced. Aids are controlled by DGIV under articles 92–94 of the treaty. Article 92(1) provides that:

'... any aid granted by a member state or through state resources in any form whatsoever which distorts or threatens to distort competition by favouring certain undertakings or the production of certain goods shall, in so far as it affects trade between member states, be incompatible with the common market. ...'

The concept of an aid from state resources is very broad and covers not only grants, loans at a low rate of interest and deferment of tax liabilities, but also schemes of aid financed by compulsory contributions by all traders including those who do not benefit and, in general, any gratuitous advantage.

The worst sufferers from state aids may be firms in the same industry locally that have to meet subsidised competition, profitable firms in the same country that have to pay taxes higher than they might otherwise be in order to provide the state resources and the workers that these would otherwise employ. These effects, however, are not on trade between member states so are not restrained by article 92. The Commission can control aids only in so far as firms in another member state suffer too.

Since the Commission has a discretion to authorise aids, article 92 is not directly applicable until the Commission makes an individual decision refusing to authorise an aid. All new state aids are illegal, however, unless notified by the government to the Commission and approved by it, and this provision does have direct effect. The Commission may, and normally does, require the state to recover at least part of the aid illegally paid after it has been spent.

State aids increased as the unemployment statistics deteriorated in the early 1980s. The Commission has taken more decisions condemning them and the Community Court has confirmed its powers, but condemned some decisions of the Commission for failing adequately to state the reasons on which they were based. The Commission's later decisions have set out its reasons better and it has been clarifying its practice on the control of aids. Appeals from decisions on state aids that are not brought by member states now go before the Court of First Instance, which may well require the Commission's practice to be more open.

Interesting remedies may have become available in this area. Previously, if a firm's competitor obtained a state aid, the natural reaction was to seek one too. Now the firm may complain to the Commission, and it is strongly arguable that a firm that suffers can recover damages from the state.[70] This field is also developing. The Member of the Commission responsible for competition policy has been spending more time on government measures than on the activities of firms in the private sector. Unfortunately, the problems are politically charged and it has not always been possible to deal with them as a matter of routine. The Commission's work on state aids is described annually in its reports on Competition Policy.

1.10 The plan for the book

In this book it is intended first to analyse the substantive law enacted by articles 85 and 86, then the main implementing regulation 17/62. This will place the reader in a position to understand the case law on the extent to which agreements and other conduct that infringe the competition rules may be void.

In Chapters 7 to 13 various kinds of agreements and concentrations will be considered, mainly under article 85, but occasionally article 86 is relevant to agreements. I shall start in Chapter 7 to analyse conduct that almost certainly infringes the article and should be abrogated forthwith; then, from Chapter 8, permissible kinds of agreement, such as bilateral exclusive dealing, technology licences and other forms of collaboration such as specialisation agreements and joint ventures. Chapter 13 will analyse the law relating to mergers and Chapter 14 will contain more general comments.

While this book is intended to be introductory, the basic controversial problems are addressed. It is hoped that sufficient citations of authority have been made, mainly in the bibliographies, for readers to refer easily on particular points to more detailed analysis. Some of the larger practitioners' books are described in the main bibliography at the end. Shorter, more specialised works are listed at the ends of most chapters. The table of cases at the beginning of the book gives multiple citations, as different readers may have access to different series of reports, and the

---

70   The Court's language in *Francovich* v. *Italy*, cited at 1.5.2 above, was far broader than necessary to deal with a dir. which the Italian government failed to implement. The Court made it clear that national courts must provide an effective remedy for infringements of Community law. See 6.1 below.

In *Francovich*, it was easy to quantify the damages. It would be far harder to show what damage had been suffered from a competitor receiving a state aid. An injunction might be the sensible remedy, but a national court should also grant damages for injury already suffered.

glossary may be helpful when the meaning of technical terms is not precisely known.

1.11 Bibliography

Theofanis Christoforou and *David B. Rockwell*, 'European Economic Community Law: The Territorial Scope of Application of EEC Antitrust law — the Wood Pulp Judgment' (1989) 30 Harvard Int'l. L.J. 195.

Luc Gyselen, 'State Action and the Effectiveness of the EEC treaty's Competition Provisions' (1989) 26 C.M.L.Rev. 33.

——, 'Anticompetitive state Measures under the EC Treaty: Towards a Substantive Legality standard,' to be published in E.L.R. checklist 1994.

Trevor C. Hartley, The Foundations of European Community Law, 2nd. ed., 1988, Clarendon Law Series, Oxford.

Allan B. Hoffman, 'Anti-competitive State Legislation condemned under Articles 5, 85 and 86 of the E.E.C. treaty: How far should the Court go' [1990] E.C.L.R. 11.

René Joliet, 'National Anti-competitive Legislation and Community Law,' in Barry Hawk (ed.) [1988] *Fordham Corporate Law Institute*, Chap. 16.

Kurt Markert, 'Some Legal and Administrative Problems of the Co-Existence of Community and National Competition Law in the EEC' (1974) 11 C.M.L.Rev. 92.

F. M. Scherer and *Ross, op. cit.*, main bibliography.

Kurt Stockmann, in Barry Hawk (ed.) [1987] *Fordham Corporate Law Institute*, Chap. 12, part III, p.265, from p.278.

2 Analysis of Article 85(1)

2.1 Introduction

Article 85(1) prohibits collusion that restricts competition and threatens the unity of the common market. The kinds of cartels that were made before the second world war, whereby all the producers in an industry fixed minimum prices and divided markets by quota or otherwise are clearly forbidden. Economic theory predicts that they are likely to lead to prices being raised and less being bought than when competition determines the price of goods and services (1.3 and 1.3.1 above and 2.2.4.1 below). Other agreements may restrict competition between one of the parties and other persons, as in the case of protection given to dealers who perform pre-sales services which may also increase competition between different brands or result in other benefits to the economy. Even if agreements are caught by article 85(1), they may be exempted by the Commission under article 85(3). In practice, however, the Commission has not got the resources to grant many individual exemptions and granted only 16 in the four years from 1990 to 1993.[1]

To infringe article 85(1), three conditions must be satisfied. There must be:

(1) some form of collusion between undertakings,
(2) which may affect trade between member states, and
(3) which has the object or effect of restricting competition within the common market.

Each of these three elements must be examined in some detail in this chapter. In Chapter 3 it is intended to describe shortly article 85(3), which provides for exemptions from the prohibition of article 85(1), and article 85(2), which provides that agreements infringing the article as a whole shall be void. It is, however, difficult to understand the problems created for firms by automatic nullity until the procedures for notification and exemption have been explained in Chapter 5, so nullity and other sanctions will not be considered until Chapter 6.

2.2 Collusion between undertakings

Article 85(1) prohibits as incompatible with the common market

'all agreements between undertakings, decisions by associations of undertakings and concerted practices ...'

1 See 6.4.1.2 below.

The various elements in this part of the definition must be considered separately.

2.2.1 *Undertakings*

'Undertaking' is a broad concept, which seems to have the same meaning in articles 85, 86 and 90.[2] It covers any collection of resources to carry out economic activities. It embraces a company, partnership, sole trader or an association, whether or not dealing with its members. A trust company authorised to police a cartel was held by the Commission to be an undertaking.[3]

The liberal professions were once thought to be sufficiently outside commerce not to be undertakings, but this became more doubtful when an inventor was held to be an undertaking when exploiting his inventions.[4] World class opera singers were treated as undertakings by the Commission in *RAI/Unitel*.[5] A lawyer has been held in *Reyners*[6] to be sufficiently commercial to benefit from the freedom of establishment, so why should he not be subject to the competition rules? Employees acting as such are almost certainly not undertakings — they act for their employer.

A group of companies is treated as a single undertaking. In *Hydrotherm* v. *Andreoli*[7] the Community Court held that a man, the company and the partnership that he controlled were but one undertaking. Commission regulations and notices which apply only to undertakings below a certain size, whether made before or after that judgment, contain provisions for aggregating the turnover of all the companies within the group, and each has a definition of 'group.' The definitions adopted earlier included affiliated companies that were only one quarter owned, but the more recent ones have referred to a link of 50 per cent. In *Gosmél Martel-DMP*,[8] the Commission decided that a 50/50 joint venture did not constitute a single undertaking because it was subject to control by more than one parent.

Most of the Court cases have been concerned with the imputation of a subsidiary's conduct to the parent, and in *Commercial Solvents*[9] the conduct of a 51 per cent. subsidiary was attributed to its parent when the

2   See 1.9.7 above for some cases under art. 90.
3   *Italian Cast Glass* [1982] 2 C.M.L.R. 61. See also 1.9.7 above for the wide concept of 'undertaking' in recent judgments.
4   *Reuter/BASF* [1976] 2 C.M.L.R. D44.
5   [1978] 3 C.M.L.R. 306.
6   (2/74) [1974] E.C.R. 631.
7   (170/83) [1984] E.C.R. 2999.
8   [1992] 5 C.M.L.R. 586.
9   (6 & 7/73) [1974] E.C.R. 223.

subsidiary had followed the policy decided by the parent. A fine was imposed jointly and severally on the Italian subsidiary and its US parent. Where, however, a subsidiary disobeyed instructions when discouraging exports, the parent had done nothing wrong and the Court confirmed in *BMW Belgium* v. *Commission*[10] that it was the subsidiary that should be fined.

A parent company may be liable for the conduct of a subsidiary which was acquired later,[11] at least where it continued to pursue the same policy after acquisition. In *Johnson & Johnson*,[12] the Commission imposed fines jointly and severally on a parent, its subsidiaries and a sub-subsidiary, without alleging any infringement by the parent or intermediate companies, nor invoking any theory that the group should be considered a single entity.

The other question is whether an agreement between a parent and/or its subsidiaries can infringe article 85. In *Centrafarm* v. *Sterling*,[13] Advocate General Trabucchi suggested that, although the allocation of tasks between dependent subsidiaries may not infringe article 85(1), it is unlawful to limit the freedom of action of third parties. These two views are hard to reconcile: if a firm allocates the task of serving the French market to its French subsidiary, it will probably restrain its German subsidiary from trading there. This prevents third parties from buying in France from the German subsidiary. The Court accepted the first view and ruled that a parent may allocate tasks within the corporate group without making an agreement between undertakings to which article 85(1) applies. It did not qualify this by reference to the freedom of third parties and must be taken to have rejected the view of the Advocate General to the extent that it is not compatible.

Where the subsidiary of a state-owned company is privatised and no longer subject to control by its former parent, agreements between them may become subject to article 85[14] and, where a subsidiary is sold by a company in the private sector, a geographic restriction of competition between it and another member of the former group of companies may infringe article 85(1).[15]

A federation of public authorities for water supply was fined as an undertaking for helping to exclude parallel imports of washing machines

10 (32 & 36–82/78) [1979] E.C.R. 2435.
11 *Sugar*, (40–48, 50, 54–56, 111, 113 & 114/73) [1975] E.C.R. 1663, paras. 76–88.
12 [1981] 2 C.M.L.R. 287.
13 (15/74) [1974] E.C.R. 1147.
14 *Austin Rover Group/Unipart* [1988] 4 C.M.L.R. 513.
15 *Quantel International-Continuum/Quantel SA* [1993] 5 C.M.L.R. 497.

into Belgium,[16] but in *Bodson* v *Pompes Funèbres des Régions Libérées,*[17] the Court ruled that concessions granted by communes acting as public authorities were not agreements between 'undertakings.' The local authorities were not carrying on an economic but an administrative activity. The Court also stressed that *Centrafarm* v. *Sterling* applies only where the parent dictates the market strategy of the subsidiary.

'Decisions of associations of undertakings' are considered at 2.2.3 below. Their recommendations may also be treated as agreements between their members, and fines have been imposed on individual members. Members of a trade association are not treated as a single undertaking.

2.2.2 *Agreements*

The concept of agreement clearly includes a contract, but is broader. In *ACF Chemiefarma NV* v. *Commission,*[18] a contract fixing prices and quotas for supplying quinine to much of the world expressly excluded the common market, but the parties entered into a written 'gentlemen's agreement,' enforceable by arbitration, to extend its application to the common market. This and the implementing oral and written arrangements were held to amount to 'agreements' within the meaning of article 85(1), even after they were put into mothballs by the parties, since they intended the prices fixed previously to continue in the common market. The Commission added that, even if this suspension ended the legally binding character of the agreement, it would remain a 'concerted practice.'

In *BP Kemi,*[19] an agreement that had never been signed was held by the Commission to be part of an 'agreement' since it had been implemented by the parties. The Commission also held that two separate contracts, one signed and the other implemented, each dependent on the other, formed part of the same agreement. It is thought, but not established, that when a later contract is dependent on the first but the first is made without any assurance that the second will be made, they form separate agreements: that an option and its exercise, for instance, are not parts of the same agreement. The exact scope of the term 'agreement' is seldom important because the category of 'concerted practices' catches less formal agreements once they have been implemented. The Commission easily infers an agreement or concerted practice from conduct and might do so from the exercise of an option.

16   *Anseau* [1982] 2 C.M.L.R. 193.
17   (30/87) [1988] E.C.R. 2479, para. 18.
18   (41/69) [1970] E.C.R. 661.
19   [1979] 3 C.M.L.R. 684.

In *Polypropylene*,[20] the Court of First Instance approved the Commission's finding of a single infringement consisting of an agreement and a concerted practice where it would have been artificial to split a single course of conduct to affect prices collusively into separate agreements and concerted practices.

2.2.2.1 *Unilateral conduct in the context of a long term contract* — The Court has been extending the concept of collusion. In *AEG Telefunken* v. *Commission*,[21] it condemned AEG's practice of refusing to supply distributors operating on low margins, even when they were qualified to offer the services required for consumer electronic goods before and after sale. It was argued that even if AEG had adopted such a practice, it would be unilateral conduct on its part. The Court held that:

> '38 ... On the contrary, it forms part of the contractual relations between the undertaking and resellers. Indeed, in the case of the admission of a distributor, approval is based on the acceptance, tacit or express, by the contracting parties of the policy pursued by AEG which requires *inter alia* the exclusion from the network of all distributors who are qualified for admission but are not prepared to adhere to that policy.'

It may be argued that the Court considered that each dealer was allowed to supply only approved dealers, in which case a refusal to approve a qualified dealer results in a contractual provision that other dealers should not supply a particular outlet. The law on what is often called 'selective distribution' is considered at 8.3.3 below.

The Commission and Court have long treated conditions of sale as forming part of the long term contract on which sales are regularly made to a dealer. In *Sandoz*,[22] the prices of pharmaceutical products were controlled in Italy, so Sandoz had an interest in deterring parallel exports to countries where prices were not controlled. Its invoices bore the words 'export prohibited.' The Court held that this was not a unilateral act outside article 85(1) on two grounds: the invoices contained other important terms, so were not merely accounting documents and the Court held that they

> 'formed part of the general framework of commercial relationships which the firm undertook with its customers.' [paragraph 10, my translation from the French]

The Court went on to suggest that when Sandoz first appointed a distributor and the latter received these invoices after every order, the

---

20   *E.g., Hercules* v. *Commission*, (T–7/89) [1991] E.C.R. II–1711.
21   (107/82) [1983] E.C.R. 3151. Contrast the US Supreme Court in *Monsanto* v. *Spray-Rite*, 465 U.S. 752 (1984).
22   (277/87) reported only in summary [1990] E.C.R. I–47.

distributor tacitly accepted Sandoz' normal method of distribution by settling its accounts on the basis of the invoices, whether or not the distributor actually abided by another term. The distributors were not condemned for infringing article 85 in this decision. The Court's use of the concept of 'tacit acceptance' may explain the term 'tacit' in *AEG*. The Court seems not be treating the parties as if they had made an agreement when they had not, but rather to be inferring agreement from conduct, which is less worrying.

2.2.2.2 *Unsatisfactory evidence on which collusion is sometimes found—* There is also concern that the Commission may sometimes find an agreement or concerted practice on somewhat unsatisfactory evidence. Fortunately, the Court of First Instance has been taking great pains to ensure that the Commission takes more care to prepare its cartel decisions properly. The Commission, however, lacks sufficient resources and not all the case handlers know what is required to establish a cartel.

The Commission's decisions in *Italian Flat Glass*[23] were quashed in part and the fines reduced or quashed[24] when the Court of First Instance, of its own motion, read several hundred handwritten notes in Italian. It found that, when transcribed by the Commission as part of its evidence, a significant part of one document that favoured the parties had been excised[25] and that not all the conduct alleged had been established. In *Polypropylene*[26], too, the evidence against some of the fringe participants was held to be inadequate.[27]

2.2.3. *Decisions by associations of undertakings*

In *Vereeniging van Cementhandelaren* v. *Commission*,[28] the Court held that this phrase includes recommendations by a trade association to its members, even if they are not binding. Such recommendations have also been treated by the Court as agreements between the members who implemented them at general meetings, for instance in *Belasco*,[29] where the Court confirmed the Commission's decision fining the members and not just the association. Sometimes all the members of a trade

23   [1992] E.C.R. II–1403.
24   (T–68,77 & 78/89) [1992] E.C.R. II–1403.
25   It will not be possible for the over-stretched legal service to check that case handlers do not do this in future. The competition department will have to put its own house in order.
26   (T–7/89) [1991] E.C.R. II–1711; (T–1/89) [1991] E.C.R. II–869; (T–2/89) [1991] E.C.R. II–1087; (T–3/89) [1991] E.C.R. II–1179; (T–4/89) [1991] E.C.R. II–1523; (T–6/89) [1991] E.C.R. II–1623; (T–8/89) [1991] E.C.R. II–1833.
27   See 2.2.4.2 below.
28   (8/72) [1972] E.C.R. 977.
29   (246/86) [1989] E.C.R. 2117.

association are themselves trade associations, but in *BNIC* v. *Clair*,[30] the Court treated recommendations of the federal association as coming within the phrase. Although the association had been established on ministerial instigation and was supervised by the minister's delegate, its conduct was condemned under article 85 in combination with article 5(2). The minister had reinforced the effect of the private agreement and jeopardised the objectives of the Community (1.9.2 above). In *FRUBO*,[31] two trade associations made an agreement which was not enforceable except by each association requiring its members to comply. Nevertheless the Court upheld a finding that there was an agreement between undertakings.

Some trade associations organise exclusive trade fairs for their members and, in a series of cases, the Commission has required that the conditions of participation be altered so as to enable members to exhibit elsewhere for a period between the international fairs.

2.2.4 *Concerted practices*

2.2.4.1 *Economic considerations* — Classic cartels between competitors fixing prices or allocating production or sales have long been thought anti-competitive and contrary to the public interest because, if they are successful, prices are likely to be higher than they would be under free competition (1.3.1 above). Consequently, some people who would have bought at the competitive price, and would have liked to pay at least as much as the costs of production and distribution including a normal return on capital, will be forced to spend their money on other things which they want less. Scarce resources are misallocated. Moreover, cartels tend to be inefficient. Even ill-equipped firms must be accommodated within the cartel to reduce price cutting.

Such cartels seldom work effectively unless the number of participants is very small, or they are backed by state intervention, since it pays each participant to cheat and expand its production by selling at less than the agreed price to a few large customers who can be relied upon to keep quiet. Once this is suspected, the others may cut prices even further and cartels tend to break down.[32] Even OPEC (the Organisation of Petroleum Exporting Countries) could not keep the prices for oil much above the level they might have reached without the cartel for very long, although, owing largely to the self restraint of its largest producer, it did manage to raise prices in its early years and to cause a world wide recession.

---

30 (123/83) [1985] E.C.R. 391, and 1.9.1 above.
31 (71/74) [1975] E.C.R. 563.
32 But not always: see Baker, *op.cit.*, bibliography, 2.5 below.

In industries with only a very few producers, whether worldwide or in a small local market protected by the cost of freight and other entry barriers, suppliers may be able to raise prices above the competitive level without making any price fixing agreement. If firm A sells at above its long term marginal costs, including a return on the capital employed, firm B may find that it pays it to sell at the same price when there is spare capacity in the industry. Unless B expects to be able to force A out of the market or thinks that overall demand would expand enough, it will not increase its share of the market at A's expense if it undercuts A, since A would have to reduce its prices to B's level or lose as much of its market as B could supply. Each will have some market power, if the other does not act competitively.

The same argument would apply to some extent even if there were four or five suppliers in the market. If there were dozens, it would be difficult to find out what secret discounts competing firms were giving. Owing to the lack of transparency, the oligopolistic interdependence would probably break down. If the industry were very concentrated, each firm taking its own independent decisions over a period of time would realise that these would affect its competitors' decisions. If it were to reduce prices, the others would be forced to do so too unless there were a shortage of capacity.

If one company were to announce a price rise, its competitors would know that that company would not be able to maintain the rise unless most of them were to follow it. So the others would be under pressure to respond rapidly to such an announcement. Even if there were no collusion, the firms might act as if there were.

The question arises whether parallel conduct that is not collusive, such as that described above, but which has much the same effect as a price fixing agreement infringes article 85(1). Is market behaviour, adopted in the knowledge and hope that competitors will follow it, a concerted practice if, in fact, competitors do follow? Enabling competitors to learn of a price rise plus the hope that they would follow or maintain it might amount to an intention to collude.

The difficulty for an enforcement agency is that there is no point in prohibiting such behaviour. As costs rise in times of inflation, one firm after another would have to leave the industry if it could not raise prices without the risk of substantial fines. At the very least, they would not build new capacity as old plant became obsolete or worn out.

The sensible remedy to prevent conscious parallelism is to ensure that nothing is done to prevent other firms entering the industry so that the number of suppliers becomes too great for cheating to be controlled. One problem with this policy in the common market is that many entry barriers are created by national or local licensing requirements and other action by member states which there is little power to control under the EC treaty, although some progress has been made under article 90.[33] Where there are substantial entry barriers, it would be sensible to control mergers which lead to more concentrated markets. The Commission's power to do this has been limited.[34] There has, therefore, been pressure on the Commission to extend the concept of 'concerted practices' in order to control parallel behaviour under article 85. The unfortunate result has been that in concentrated markets it may be difficult to raise prices without incurring a risk of being fined.

2.2.4.2 *Legal precedents* — In *Dyestuffs*,[35] the Community Court observed that article 85 distinguishes concerted practices from agreements and decisions in order to bring within the competition rules

> '64 ... a form of co-ordination between undertakings which, without having reached the stage where an agreement properly so-called has been concluded, knowingly substitutes practical co-operation between them for the risks of competition.'

This passage may have been intended to distinguish the German practice at that time, according to which only a binding written agreement infringed the earlier sections of the law. In both *Dyestuffs* and the *Sugar Cartel*,[36] the Court said that for the few firms in a concentrated market to take account of each other's market behaviour does not amount to a concerted practice. In *Dyestuffs*, for instance, it said:

> '118. Although every producer is free to change his prices, taking into account in so doing the present or foreseeable conduct of his competitors, nevertheless it is contrary to the rules on competition contained in the treaty for a producer to co-operate with his competitors, in any way whatsoever, in order to determine a co-ordinated course of action relating to a price increase and to ensure its success by prior elimination of all uncertainty as to each other's conduct regarding the essential elements of that action, such as the amount, subject-matter, date and place of the increases.'

This passage raised concern that the Court's phrase, 'co-ordinated course of action,' might be broader than collusion. Acting in a way that makes it easier for suppliers or buyers not to compete, for instance by giving considerable notice of price increases in a trade journal, might amount to a concerted practice if competitors follow the rise. There are other facilitating devices that make it easier for suppliers not to compete in concentrated markets, such as promising many customers that they

33 See 1.9.7 above.
34 4.3.2.1, 4.4 and Chap. 12 below.
35 (48, 49, 51–57/69) [1972] E.C.R. 619.
36 Cited at 2.2.1 above.

will receive any discounts given to anyone else. This makes it less attractive to give secret discounts to other buyers, the only kind of price competition likely in a concentrated market.

It is not clear that the Court understood the way that prices may be fixed without collusion in concentrated markets. At paragraph 66, it said:

'Although parallel behaviour may not by itself be identified with a concerted practice, it may however amount to strong evidence of such a practice if it leads to conditions of competition which do not correspond to the normal conditions of the market, having regard to the nature of the products, the size and number of the undertakings and the volume of the said market.'

It went on to refer to stabilising prices at a level different from that to which competition would have led. This is unknowable. In the absence of collusion, prices might be at the competitive level, or the level that maximises the profits of a monopolist in the short term, or anywhere in between. A firm can set the prices anywhere it wants within that range and, unless some of the others charge less, it can profitably maintain them at that level. If the market be oligopolistic, over time it is likely that market power will lead to higher prices even in the absence of collusion. The one cheering feature of the judgment is that at paragraph 68 the Court did refer to the factual evidence on which the Commission had found the concertation.

In the *Dyestuffs* case,[37] the Commission had found that the price increases on three occasions were 'concerted,' partly because the producers had met and partly because of various other items of circumstantial evidence of collusion. On the first occasion, six out of the ten firms which were fined and which supplied about 85 per cent. of the dyestuffs in the common market had sent notices of increases to their subsidiaries in Italy by telex on the same evening (ICI used the telephone, Francolor did not sell much outside France and ACNA had no need to communicate since it was already in Italy). They had used much the same wording to give similar detailed instructions, for example to refuse to backdate invoices.

The Court seems to have placed less weight on these circumstances, but did point out that the three increases showed progressive co-ordination, which consisted mainly of the leader announcing his intended price rise for a particular country further in advance. The final increase was announced by Geigy at a meeting of the producers three months in advance. This gave time for the largest supplier in France to announce in public a rather larger increase there, as prices had previously been frozen by the government and so had not been increased when those in other

37   Cited at n. 35 above.

countries had been. The others had time to follow this and each announced the larger increase for France before the smaller increase originally intended was implemented. The price increases on all the Community markets (except Italy, where the Italian producer had refrained from following the increase announced by the others on the second and third occasions) came into effect on the same day.

From this judgment and that in *Sugar*, there was concern that merely announcing one's price increases to customers or in the trade press would amount to a concerted practice if competitors made similar price increases.

In the *Polypropylene* cases, the question to be answered by the Court of First Instance was not whether parallel conduct on the market was the result of collusion. The Commission had found ample documentary evidence that 15 petrochemical companies had worked out a complex scheme of arrangements with the purpose of setting and implementing target prices and quotas. There was clear evidence of collusion, but there were hardly any effects on the market. As one expert stated, the initiative had 'no more than a placebo effect on nervous branch managers.'[38] The Court of First Instance held that the existence of an intent to concert is sufficient to establish a concerted practice, even if there are no actual effects.[39]

In *Rhône-Poulenc*, the Court of First Instance also confirmed that:

'126. Those schemes were part of a series of efforts made by the undertakings in question in pursuit of a single economic aim, namely to distort the normal movement of prices on the market in polypropylene. It would thus be artificial to split up such continuous conduct, characterized by a single purpose, by treating it as consisting of a number of separate infringements. The fact is that the applicant took part — over a period of years — in an integrated set of schemes constituting a single infringement, which progressively manifested itself in both unlawful agreements and unlawful concerted practices ...'

It added that 'the Commission was also entitled to characterize that single infringement as "an agreement and a concerted practice," since the infringement involved at one and the same time factual elements to be characterized as "agreements" and factual elements to be characterized as "concerted practices".'

Recently, in its judgment in *Wood Pulp*,[40] the Court significantly limited the concept of 'concerted practices.' The pulp producers

---

38   As cited by Judge Vesterdorf, acting as Advocate General, [1991] E.C.R. II–869.
39   *Shell* v. *Commission*, (T–11/89) [1992] E.C.R. II–757, 881, para. 299. *Rhône-Poulenc* v. *Commission*, (T–1/89), [1991] E.C.R. II–867, 1073, paras. 120–124.
40   (C–89, 104, 114, 116, 117 and 125–129/85) [1993] 4 C.M.L.R. 407.

announced maximum prices quarterly in advance to their customers. The Court said:

'64. In this case, the communications arise from the price announcements made to users. They constitute in themselves market behaviour which does not lessen each undertaking's uncertainty as to the future attitude of its competitors. At the same time when each undertaking engages in such behaviour, it cannot be sure of the future conduct of others.

65. Accordingly, the system of quarterly price announcements on the pulp market is not to be regarded as constituting in itself an infringement of Article 85(1) EEC.'

While the Court has said that consciously parallel behaviour by itself does not amount to a concerted practice, concerting has easily been inferred by the Commission as in the *PVC* and *LdPE* decisions (especially that against Shell),[41] if the parties have been in communication with each other. It is still not entirely clear whether the announcement of price changes well in advance to customers or in a trade journal constitutes the necessary element of co-ordination. Advance warning does make it easier for other producers to decide how far to follow the announced rise, and for the original leader to resile wholly or partly if its lead is not fully followed.

On the other hand, there may be sensible commercial reasons for announcing price rises in advance. Customers may make fixed price contracts and want notice of a change in their costs; a temporary glut may be cleared; in markets where there are few suppliers, price competition may take the form of tough negotiations for individual discounts and time may be required for these to take place.

In *SACEM*,[42] the various national copyright collection societies in the EC had entered into reciprocal licences, so the rights of their copyright holders to royalties in other member states were enforced by the local collection society. Although each society remained entitled to license public performances of music in other member states, none of them was willing to license the operators of discothèques in France. The discothèque operators used little other than Anglo-American music and would have liked licences confined to such music at the lower royalty payable to the collecting societies outside France. They argued that the refusal of each society to grant licences of their rights in France was a concerted practice. SACEM replied that it would be onerous for each of the copyright societies to grant such licences abroad, as they would have to negotiate them and check what was being played. Since there was

41   (T–11/89) [1992] E.C.R. II–757, from p.793.
42   *Lucazeau* v. *SACEM* (110/88) and *SACEM* v. *Debelle* and *SACEM* v. *Soumagnac* (241 & 242/88), para. 18 and *Ministère Publique* v. *Tournier* (395/87), para. 24, [1989] E.C.R. 2565.

another explanation of parallel conduct, the Court held that it was not collusive.

At paragraph 24 the Court referred to *Dyestuffs* and said that:

> 'Nevertheless, such a concertation should not be presumed when the parallel behaviour can be explained by reasons other than the existence of concertation. Such may be the case when the copyright collection societies in other member states would have to organise an individual system of management and an individual monitoring system in another country, if they were to allow direct access to their repertoire.' [my translation from the French transcript]

I hope that recognition that price cuts are likely to be copied by competitors would be treated as a sufficient reason to explain identical lists of prices.

2.2.4.3 *Horizontal agreements to exchange information* — Since it is illegal to agree with competitors about prices, firms have adopted practices that tend to make strong competition less likely. Agreements between competitors to exchange detailed information about price changes or output may well be treated as having the object or effect of restricting competition.[43] If competitors will immediately know of orders obtained by discounts, there may be no incentive to make the cut. Usually there are clear agreements to exchange information, but the actual exchange without prior agreement was treated in *COBELPA*[44] as a concerted practice.

2.3 'Which may affect trade between member states'

The condition that trade between member states be affected is easily satisfied. Even an agreement confined to activities in a single member state may infringe article 85(1). The concept of trade is very broad, and covers all economic activities relating to goods or services, even the right of a trader in one member state to set up business in another.[45]

2.3.1 *Market integration*

The condition that trade between member states may be affected has been construed in the light of the need to establish and maintain a single market — export boosters are as divisive as import deterrents. In its first judgment on appeal from the Commission, *Consten and Grundig* v. *Commission*,[46] the Court said:

---

43   7.2.2 below.
44   [1977] 2 C.M.L.R. D28.
45   See 2.3.2 below.
46   (56 & 58/64) [1966] E.C.R. 299, at 341.

'The concept of an agreement "which may affect trade between member states" is intended to define, in the law governing cartels, the boundary between the areas respectively covered by Community law and national law.'

In itself, this does not help us much to draw the line. Moreover, in *Wilhelm* v. *Bundeskartellamt*,[47] the Court ruled that some agreements may be subject to both national and Community law. The condition about trade between member states limits the scope of Community law. It limits that of national law only to the extent that Community law takes precedence. The next paragraph of *Grundig* was more helpful in deciding where Community law ceases to apply:

'[W]hat is particularly important is whether the agreement is capable of constituting a threat, either direct or indirect, actual or potential, to freedom of trade between member states in a manner which might harm the attainment of the objectives of a single market between states. Thus the fact that an agreement encourages an increase, even a large one, in the volume of trade between states is not sufficient to exclude the possibility that the agreement may "affect" such trade in the above-mentioned manner.'

Grundig had agreed with Consten that Consten should be its exclusive dealer in France. It agreed to supply no one else in France, and Consten agreed not to handle competing brands, to promote Grundig products, to arrange for an after-sales service, to buy in minimum quantities, order regularly in advance and make sales forecasts.

Incurring these costs would be worth while for Consten only if it could reap where it had sown. The investment was risky, in that the costs were 'sunk': the effort would be wasted unless it could be recovered through the sale of Grundig products at a time when an import licence was required to import them.

To encourage Consten's commitment to this expenditure, Grundig tried to confer absolute territorial protection on Consten, by isolating the French market. Its distributors in other member states and dealers in Germany were forbidden to export, as was Consten. Moreover, all Grundig machines of that period bore the mark Gint (Grundig International) as well as the Grundig mark. Consten was allowed to register Gint as a trade mark under French law, and so was able to sue for trade mark infringement anyone importing commercially or selling without its consent a machine bearing that mark.

When a third party, UNEF, started to buy Grundig apparatus in Germany and sell it in France at lower prices than Consten's dealers charged, Consten sued it for trade mark infringement, and also for the French tort of unfair competition, on the ground that UNEF knew that

47   (14/68) [1969] E.C.R. 1. See 1.5.4 above. See also *Société La Technique Minière* v. *Maschinenbau Ulm* (56/65) [1966] E.C.R. 235, at 247.

sales by the German dealers were in breach of their contracts with Grundig and would undermine Consten's exclusive distributorship. Not only did the Court uphold the Commission's decision that the agreement infringed article 85, it upheld its order that neither party should make it difficult for dealers and other buyers to obtain Grundig apparatus elsewhere. Of this limitation to the market sharing function of trade marks, patents etc. far more will be said in Chapter 9.

To return to the concept of affecting trade between member states, the Court added that:

> '[T]he contract between Grundig and Consten, on the one hand by preventing undertakings other than Consten from importing Grundig products into France, and on the other hand by prohibiting Consten from re-exporting those products to other countries of the common market, indisputably affects trade between member states.'

The insulation of the French market from the lower-priced German one clearly affected trade between the countries, but the second passage I have quoted from the Court's judgment is far broader. The Court deliberately refrained from considering linguistic points in the four Community languages as to whether the 'effect' must be harmful, but returned to the basic principle of the free movement of goods, the treatment of the whole Community as a single market.

In fact, sales of Grundig's products in France increased substantially between 1957 when the contract was made and the Commission's decision in 1964, but the Court stated that this did not prevent there being an effect on trade between member states. One might think that the increase was due to other matters, such as the expansion and final abrogation of quotas and reduction of customs duties under the transitional provisions of the treaty.

Sometimes, as in *Grundig*, the Court has referred to the deflection of trade and at others to the competitive structure of the market when considering whether trade between member states has been affected. Both concepts have been related to the integration of the market. In *Commercial Solvents*,[48] a case involving article 86 which is subject to the same condition about affecting trade between member states, the Court stated that any abuse of a dominant position leading to the elimination of a competitor downstream in Italy was prohibited, although the Court went on to refer to the possibility of Zoja, the competitor, exporting to Germany and France. It may be that different members of the Court were using different tests.

In *Groupement des Fabricants de Papiers Peints de Belgique* v.

---

48   Cited at 2.2.1 above. See also the quotation at 2.3.4 below.

Commission, Advocate General Trabucchi suggested a third meaning for the condition as the common market matures[49]:

> 'Moreover, as has been brought out in legal writings, ... in a unified multi-
> national market, within which there are no longer any national frontiers
> impeding the movement of goods, the ... criterion ["may affect trade between
> member states"] must assume a significance to match the new situation which
> has come into being; it must be interpreted in such a way as to bring within the
> prohibitions of article 85 agreements in restraint of competition which affect
> the attainment of the objectives for which the common market was estab-
> lished. In this sense, the criterion relating to the effect of the restriction of
> competition on trade between member states serves to define that restriction
> itself by requiring that, in order to come within the purview of Community
> law, it must be of importance within the ambit of the Community system in
> respect of the objectives pursued.'

As Professor Paul Ulmer has written, even unimportant cartels in a small member state are likely to have effects outside the country; quite major restrictions in a large member state may not. The effects on cross-frontier trade may be the first problems faced by a new common market, but as it becomes mature, the criterion should become the importance of the restriction of competition.

In *Groupement des Papiers Peints*, the Court did not take up the idea invoked by its Advocate General, but it was resuscitated by Jonathan Faull[50] when he worked in the *cabinet* of the member of the Commission responsible for competition. Furthermore, in *Consten and Grundig*, the Court started by stating that the function of the condition was to define the relative spheres of national and Community law. If so, Advocate General Trabucchi's view has much to commend it.

There is no need to prove an actual effect on trade between states; a potential effect is enough. The goods immediately subject to an agreement may not move between member states, but if there is or may be trade between member states in the products of which they form part, the condition is fulfilled. In *BNIC* v. *Clair*,[51] an agreement relating to *eaux de vie* was held to infringe article 85, although little was exported, since the cognac made from them was.

2.3.2 *Condition often fulfilled even if agreement is confined to a single member state*

An agreement confined to activities in a single member state may infringe article 85(1). In *Vereeniging van Cementhandelaren* v.

---

49   (73/74) [1975] E.C.R. 1491, at 1522–1523.
50   'The Enforcement of Competition Policy in the European Community: a mature system' [1991] *Fordham Corporate Law Institute* 139.
51   (123/83) [1985] E.C.R. 391.

Commission,[52] a Dutch trade association, of which most Dutch cement dealers were members, recommended the prices at which its members should sell in the Netherlands. It was argued that, as this did not apply to exports, it did not 'affect trade between member states,' but the Community Court answered:

'29. An agreement extending over the whole of the territory of a member state by its very nature has the effect of reinforcing the compartmentalization of markets on a national basis, thereby holding up the economic interpenetration which the treaty is designed to bring about and protecting domestic production.
30. In particular, the provisions of the agreement which are mutually binding on the members of the applicant association and the prohibition by the association on all sales to resellers who are not authorized by it make it more difficult for producers or sellers from other member states to be active in or penetrate the Netherlands market.'

In the light of the facts of the case, this was a particularly strong statement. What seems to have kept imports out of the Netherlands, at least until very shortly before the Commission's decision, was an agreement, the subject of separate proceedings,[53] between the cement producers in neighbouring states under which they agreed how much each might export to the Netherlands. The more the Cement Dealers' Trade Association restrained price cutting in the Netherlands by established dealers, the more others would be encouraged to import cement and undercut them. The agreement may have increased imports, but that, presumably, is irrelevant. The Court is concerned that the common market should be treated as a unit, and price fixing throughout the Netherlands affects the pattern of trade by creating a distortion along the Dutch border.

The judgment is explained in *Belasco* v. *Commission*,[54] where Advocate General Mischo and the Court observed that cartels confined to a single member state have to take measures to oppose imports, and that is why national agreements may normally be prohibited.

Where there are direct restrictions on imports or exports between member states, the conditions of application for the prohibition are usually satisfied. Nevertheless in *Hugin* v. *Commission*,[55] despite the presence of an export ban, the Court quashed a decision that article 86 was infringed by refusing to supply Liptons, a small firm that operated only within a radius of 30 miles of London. The judgment makes sense, however, if the condition about trade between member states is meant to

52 Cited at 2.2.3 above.
53 *Cimenteries* (8–11/66) [1967] E.C.R. 75.
54 See 2.2.3 above.
55 (22/78) [1979] E.C.R. 1869.

distinguish important agreements, subject to Community competence, from minor ones to be dealt with only by national authorities.[56] No such argument was articulated in the judgment.

In other cases where only one member state is directly affected it used to be impossible to foretell the outcome. Sometimes the Court asked the Commission to spell out the mechanism restraining imports or exports; yet in other cases, such as *FRUBO*,[57] and most of the recent cases, it observed that currents of trade are appreciably affected and confirmed an infringement even if no mechanism restraining trade across frontiers was indicated.

The concept of 'appreciable' effect (2.4.1 below) increased the unpredictability. Sometimes, as in *Tepea*,[58] the Court would quash the Commission's condemnation, observing that there were no appreciable effects on trade between member states. Yet in *Société de Vente de Ciments et Bétons* v. *Kerpen & Kerpen*,[59] the Court ruled that a restriction accepted by a buyer in one part of the Federal Republic of Germany on selling in another part of it might infringe article 85, and that the effect on inter-state trade was perceptible, because the contract related to 10 per cent. of the cement exported from France to the Federal Republic of Germany. It is thought that this may be a dangerous precedent. Where an insignificant part of the demand in state A is satisfied by imports from state B, it is thought that effects on inter-state trade are not necessarily significant, whatever the restriction.

2.3.3 *The condition has recently been further narrowed*

In the last decade, several propositions have been established by the Court which have further reduced the importance of the condition that trade between member states must be affected. In *Windsurfing* v. *Commission*,[60] the Court stated that, although it is only the particular provisions that restrict competition that are void, if the agreement as a whole affects trade between member states, article 85 may be infringed even if the restrictions of competition do not affect such trade.

In *Pronuptia*,[61] the Court included in the concept of effect on trade between member states the possibility of a firm becoming established in another member state. Trade is not confined to the movement of the goods or services, but extends also to the right of establishment and the free movement of the suppliers.

56 See 2.3.1 above.
57 Cited at 2.2.3 above, at para. 38.
58 (28/77) [1978] E.C.R. 1391.
59 (319/82) [1983] E.C.R. 4173.
60 (193/83) [1986] E.C.R. 611.
61 (161/84) [1986] E.C.R. 353.

In *Fire Insurance*,[62] the Court observed that foreign insurance companies were allowed to operate in the Federal Republic of Germany only if they set up a branch there. This, however, did not prevent an arrangement limited to the insurance of fire risks in the Federal Republic being found to affect trade between member states. The minimum premium recommended by the trade association must have affected the financial relationship between the foreign head office and its German branch and made it harder for foreign firms to enter by competing on premiums.

2.3.4 *The comparable provision in article 86 is similarly construed*

The construction of the term 'may affect trade between member states' in article 86 has been similar. In *Commercial Solvents* v. *Commission*,[63] the Community Court, referring expressly to article 85 as well, said that the condition should be applied in the light of articles 2 and 3(f)[64] of the treaty. The abuse of a dominant position alleged in that case consisted of refusing to supply raw materials to a small pharmaceutical firm which competed downstream. It was argued that this did not affect trade between member states, since 90 per cent. of the final product was exported to non-member countries and most of the rest was sold in Italy, where the complainant manufactured it. The Court responded:

> '33. The Community authorities must therefore consider all the consequences of the conduct complained of for the competitive structure in the common market without distinguishing between production intended for sale within the market and that intended for export. When an undertaking in a dominant position within the common market abuses its position in such a way that a competitor in the common market is likely to be eliminated, it does not matter whether the conduct relates to the latter's exports or its trade within the common market, once it has been established that this elimination will have repercussions on the competitive structure within the common market.'

This all-embracing statement, which almost read the condition about inter-state trade out of the competition rules, was followed by the observation that the victim of the abuse had in fact been exporting part of its production to France and the Federal Republic of Germany. These paragraphs may represent a compromise, some members of the Court wanting to establish the broad principle, while others were prepared to go no further than was required by the facts of the case.

---

62   *Verband der Sachversicherer* v. *Commission* (45/85) [1987] E.C.R. 405, at para. 49.
63   See 2.2.1 above.
64   Now art. 3(g) as amended at Maastricht.

2.3.5 Under the EEA

Articles 53 and 54 of the EEA treaty forbid the same sorts of conduct as articles 85 and 86 of the EC Treaty when 'they may affect trade between the Contracting Parties.' Article 2(c) EEA provides that the term 'Contracting Parties' sometimes refers to the EC and sometimes to its member states. This is not very helpful. It is thought that for the EEA to apply there must be at least one non-EC member state affected. When only EC member states are affected, however, their conduct will remain subject to the EC competition rules.

2.4 'Have as their object or effect the prevention, restriction or distortion of competition within the common market'

Although this phrase is followed by a list of examples, the list is not exhaustive. In *Consten and Grundig* v. *Commission*[65] it was not only the market-sharing effects of the absolute territorial protection that had the object of restricting competition and so fell within the prohibition but, probably, also the exclusivity provisions whereby Consten agreed not to handle competing apparatus and Grundig to supply no one in France other than Consten, although these do not figure in the list given in article 85(1). In Chapter 8, however, it will be seen that such restrictions are frequently exempted. Moreover, the Court quashed the Commission's decision in part for failing to give reasons for condemning the exclusivity.

To be caught, arrangements must have 'as their object or effect' the prohibited effects on competition. The Court held in *Consten and Grundig* that there is no need to examine the effects of an agreement if its object is to restrict competition. Consten and Grundig asked the Court to quash the Commission's decision for not having made an analysis of the market for the kinds of equipment affected by the agreement; the Commission had not stated even that Grundig was an important brand name. The Court stated that the brand was important, but perceived the issue *ex post* from 1964 when the Commission adopted a decision and not *ex ante* when the agreement was made and Consten had to establish the name in France.[66]

In 1957, when Consten undertook to incur costs promoting the product, before the common market had removed quotas, it incurred significant risks. It might not be able to obtain import licences for many or even for any items of equipment. Even if Consten managed to obtain a quota, the expenditure would have to be spread over a limited number of

65   Discussed at 2.3.1 above.
66   See 8.5.1 below.

sales and would be wasted unless Consten were able to sell the Grundig product. The costs were sunk. Consequently, it would need unusually high profits if it was to be successful.

A high margin would attract imports from Germany, where there were no quotas and average costs and risk would be less. Such traders would take a free ride on Consten's investment in making the product acceptable. Unless Consten could be protected sufficiently from these parallel imports, it might well have found the risk unacceptable.

If Grundig could not have found someone to promote its product in the early days, Grundig products might have been less attractive for the parallel importers. The Commission never investigated how much protection was necessary to induce the optimal amount of investment in promotion. Nor was the question raised whether Grundig, which backed its judgement as to the amount of protection needed with its expectation of profit, was better able to judge than officials in the Commission.

The Court said that the Commission had found that the object of this agreement was to restrict competition between Consten and any other dealers. It had properly taken into account not just the agreement in issue but the whole network of Grundig distribution agreements, which clearly attempted to insulate the national markets from competition from other distributors of the same brand.

Frequently, the Commission says merely that certain kinds of conduct are restrained and asserts that this has the object of restricting competition even if, without the restriction, no one could sensibly have entered the market. Normally, it states that an exclusive territory given to a dealer or licensee restricts the supplier or licensor from appointing another dealer or licensee and has the object of restricting competition contrary to article 85(1). Nevertheless, it states when granting an exemption under article 85(3) that, without an exclusive territory, no one could have been found to develop the market or tool up. If this is so, competition must have been increased, so this practice seems to me to be contradictory.

There is no general possibility of exemption from the prohibition in the US Sherman Act, so the judges were able to limit the prohibition to agreements that were unlikely to have significant pro-competitive benefits. The possibility of exemption in the EC has caused difficulty. It has encouraged Commission and Court to interpret the prohibition widely. Some say that if the increase in inter-brand competition caused by the entry of Grundig into the French market were to take the exclusive agreement outside article 85(1), there would be no function for article

85(3). It would probably have to be used only when consumers benefit from non-competitive advantages, such as a cleaner environment.

To see whether an agreement has 'the effect' of restricting competition, however, a market analysis is required. In *La Technique Minière* v. *Maschinenbau Ulm*[67] the Court stated that if an agreement, considered in its economic and legal context, does not have the object of restricting competition:

> 'the consequences of the agreement should then be considered and for it to be caught by the prohibition it is then necessary to find that those factors are present which show that competition has in fact been prevented or restricted or distorted to an appreciable extent.
>
> The competition in question must be understood within the actual context in which it would occur in the absence of the agreement in dispute. In particular, it may be doubted whether there is an interference with competition if the said agreement seems really necessary for the penetration of a new area by an undertaking.'

The Court continued that, to decide whether an exclusive dealing agreement is:

> 'prohibited by reason of its object or of its effect, it is appropriate to take into account in particular the nature and quantity, limited or otherwise, of the products covered by the agreement, the position and importance of the grantor and the concessionaire on the market for the products concerned, the isolated nature of the disputed agreement or, alternatively, its position in a series of agreements, the severity of the clauses intended to protect the exclusive dealership or, alternatively, the opportunities allowed for their commercial competitors in the same products by way of parallel re-exportation and importation.'

This judgment in which, under article 177 of the EC treaty, the Court interpreted Community law for a national court to apply uses two concepts possibly to exclude the application of the prohibition of article 85(1). The first is that the competition excluded was not possible — the firm could not have penetrated the other member state without co-operation from a local exclusive dealer who would need protection to induce investment. The second concept is that only if the agreement substantially foreclosed other dealers would it infringe article 85(1).

That second concept was reaffirmed in 1991 in *Stergios Delimitis* v. *Henninger Bräu*[68] in relation to the converse situation where a tenant agreed to acquire all the beer for his bar from his landlord. The Court required a national court to make a full analysis of the market to see whether so many outlets were tied to one or other of the brewers for so long that insufficient free outlets remained or came on the market to take

---

67 Cited at 2.3.1 above, pp.249–250.
68 (C–234/89) [1991] E.C.R. I–935.

the supply of another brewer of a viable size for distribution entering the market or expanding.

The Court continues to insist also on the first concept: that clauses that make a transaction viable do not infringe article 85(1). In *Nungesser*,[69] it held that an open exclusive licence under plant breeders' rights did not in itself infringe article 85(1) because it was needed to induce the investment of both parties and, in *Coditel (2)*,[70] that exclusive licences of performing rights did not do so, even though in the circumstances, they conferred absolute territorial protection.

In *Pronuptia*,[71] the Court ruled that many ancillary restrictions on conduct do not infringe article 85(1) where they are necessary to make the franchising system work, since franchising, in itself, is not contrary to article 85(1). Nevertheless, the Court ruled that the effect of two clauses in combination — an exclusive territory, coupled with an obligation to sell only from the franchised outlet — may confer absolute territorial protection, and infringes article 85(1) once the network is widespread.

Even so, the clauses should be exempted if necessary to induce the franchisee to make the necessary investments. The Advocate General invoked the first and advised the Court that competition policy is concerned only with the horizontal effects of vertical agreements: that in the absence of substantial market power or restrictions on cross border trade, franchise agreements do not infringe article 85(1).

These cases are all examples of ancillary restrictions required to make a pro-competitive transaction viable which are explained further at 7.1.2 below. There are, however, a few judgments, such as *Windsurfing*,[72] where the Court has treated any important restrictions on conduct as having the object or effect of restricting competition.

There is also a growing series of articles in the law reviews advocating a more flexible approach to article 85(1), on the policy ground that the Commission has the exclusive power to exempt agreements from article 85(1) and that it lacks sufficient resources to make many exempting decisions. Agreements that infringe article 85(1) are void unless they are actually exempted.

It is generally thought that a national court should not enforce restrictive provisions in contracts that infringe article 85(1), but should adjourn until the Commission decides whether to grant an individual exemption.[73] Moreover, exemption may be made subject to conditions,

69   (258/78) [1982] E.C.R. 2015, and 10.3 below.
70   (262/81) [1982] E.C.R. 3361, and 10.3 below.
71   (161/84) [1986] E.C.R. 353 and 8.5.1 below.
72   Cited at 2.3.3 above.
73   See 6.2 onwards, below.

while a clearance cannot. It is, therefore, very important to European business that ancillary clauses be outside the prohibition and not merely merit exemption. Unless a national civil court can enforce restrictive clauses that are reasonably ancillary to pro-competitive kinds of collaboration, the lack of legal certainty may prevent industry in the common market from keeping up in international markets.

Despite the clear rulings by the Court, the Commission has rarely taken into account under article 85(1) whether, without the protection from competition agreed, the basic activity would have been commercially attractive. Often it has found that an agreement is caught by the prohibition of article 85(1) and granted an exemption on the ground that, without an exclusive territory, no dealer or licensee could have been found. Although if this were the case, one would have thought that the agreement should have been cleared rather than exempted.

The Commission's recent decisions on joint ventures, technology licences and franchising have found that many important clauses do not infringe article 85(1), although it has exempted, and not cleared, exclusive territories.

For competition to be restricted, it is not necessary that any obligation should be accepted. In *Kali und Salz/Kali Chemie* v. *Commission*,[74] the Court treated an option to require Kali und Salz to buy any potash not required by Kali Chemie itself as if Kali Chemie were bound to sell it to Kali und Salz, since Kali Chemie had no distribution network for the product and its declining sources of supply would not warrant the expense of establishing one. It was, therefore clear that it would exercise its option and the option restricted competition contrary to article 85(1).

2.4.1 *'Appreciable' effects*

The Court has confirmed an implied condition that the restriction of competition and the possible effect on trade between member states should be noticeable. In *Völk* v. *Vervaecke*,[75] Völk made less than 1 per cent. of the washing machines produced in Germany, and the Court ruled that even absolute territorial protection granted to its exclusive distributor for Belgium and Luxembourg would not infringe article 85(1) if it did not restrict competition and noticeably affect inter-state trade.

The Commission has tried to reduce the uncertainty surrounding this *de minimis* rule by issuing a notice on Minor Agreements in 1970. This was reissued in amended forms in 1977 and 1986. In the Commission's view, agreements between undertakings engaged in the production or supply of goods are not caught if:

74   (19 & 20/74) [1975] E.C.R. 499.
75   (5/69) [1969] E.C.R. 295.

'— the goods or services which are the subject of the agreement (hereinafter referred to as 'the contract products') together with the participating undertakings' other goods or services which are considered by users to be equivalent in view of their characteristics, price and intended use, do not represent more than 5 per cent. of the total market for such goods or services (hereinafter referred to as 'products') in the area of the common market affected by the agreement and
— the aggregate annual turnover of the participating undertakings does not exceed 200 million ECU.'[76]

This is followed by standard provisions which combine half-owned companies together with the participants in making these calculations. So large corporate groups are excluded.

The relevant geographic market is said in paragraph 14 usually to be the whole of the common market, although it may be a smaller area where the goods cannot be moved cheaply, either because of the high cost of freight in relation to the value of the products, or because there are barriers to trade across national frontiers resulting from state intervention. As the latter are reduced in accordance with the rules for the free movement of goods, the relevant market will more often be the whole of the common market. This sensible view of the Commission is important as it probably relates to all competition proceedings, not merely to those that qualify under the notice as having insignificant effects. A limited market analysis may be necessary to decide what substitutes count on the demand — but not on the supply — side of the market.

Another new feature of the latest version of the notice is point 16, which states that it does not apply:

'where in a relevant market competition is restricted by the cumulative effects of parallel networks of similar agreements established by several manufacturers or dealers.'

This may deprive the notice of most of its value. Small firms are most likely to be concerned in distribution or franchising agreements, and likely to be part of a network, competing with other networks. If, however, the Commission construes the words 'competition is restricted' realistically, the notice may continue to be useful. Agreements in which large commercial firms participate do not come within its terms.

The Court has referred to the notice only once, when it considered it in mitigation of a fine. Advocates General,[77] observe from time to time that the notice does not bind the Community Court: *Völk* v. *Vervaecke* had laid down a *de minimis* rule. The notice's greatest importance derives from the Commission's practice in following it when vetting agreements notified to it.

76 O.J. 1986, C231/2, point 7.
77 E.g., Mr. Warner in *Miller Schallplatten* v. *Commission* (19/77) [1978] E.C.R. 131.

2.5 Bibliography

Jonathan B. Baker, 'Recent Developments in Economics that Challenge Chicago School Views' (1989) 58 Antitrust L.J. 645.

Theofanis Christoforou and *David B. Rockwell*, 'European Economic Community Law: The Territorial Scope of Application of EEC Antitrust law — the Wood Pulp Judgment' (1989) 30 Harvard Int'l. L.J. 195.

John Daltrop and *John Ferry*, 'The relationship between articles 85 & 86: *Tetra Pak*' [1991] E.I.P.R. 31.

Jonathan Faull, 'Effect on Trade between member states and Community — Member State Jurisdiction' [1989] *Fordham Corporate Law Institute* 485.

Ian Forrester and *Christopher Norall*, 'The Laïcization of Community Law: self-help and the rule of reason: how competition law is and could be applied' (1984) 21 C.M.L.Rev. 11.

Luc Gyselen, 'Vertical Restraints in the Distribution Process: strength and weakness of the Free Rider Rationale under EEC Competition Law' (1984) 21 C.M.L.Rev. 648.

René Joliet, 'La Notion de Pratique Concertée et l'Arrêt *I.C.I.* Dans une Perspective Comparative' [1974] c.d.e. 251.

——, *The Rule of Reason in Antitrust Law* (see main Bibliography).

——, 'Trademark Licensing Agreements under the EEC Law of Competition' (1984) 5 Northwestern J. of Int'l. L. & Bus. 755, from 773.

Stephen Kon, 'Article 85, para. 3: A Case for Application by National Courts' (1982) 19 C.M.L.Rev. 541.

3 Exemptions and Nullity

3.1 Introduction

This chapter deals briefly with the second and third paragraphs of article 85. The treaty expressly provides that agreements which infringe article 85 are prohibited and void. The main implementing regulation[1] provides for the Commission to impose fines and daily penalties. It is also becoming clear that Community law provides for private actions for damages by those harmed by such agreements (6.1 below).

Not all agreements that perceptibly restrict competition and may affect inter-state trade are prohibited. Some forms of collaboration restrictive of competition may have beneficial effects and are capable of exemption by the Commission under article 85(3). Exercising powers granted by the Council, the Commission has granted seven group exemptions of general application and specific ones in the sectors of vehicles, maritime and air transport and insurance. It also grants a few individual exemptions in most years, ten in 1988 — more than ever before or since — although more often it merely closes the file and sends a 'comfort letter' (6.3.4 below).

3.2 Article 85(3)

The prohibition in article 85(1) may be declared inapplicable to any agreements or category of agreements provided that they have certain characteristics; they must contribute to the improvement of the production or distribution of goods, or promote technical or economic progress. The first two criteria do not often apply to services, but the last two frequently do so. Moreover, a fair share of the benefits must be passed on to consumers; the agreement must not impose restrictions that are not indispensable for achieving these benefits or afford the parties the possibility of eliminating competition in respect of a substantial part of the products in question.

The earlier decisions relied largely on improving the production and distribution of goods, but for the last two and a half decades increased attention has been paid to the promotion of economic and technical progress as the Commission has exempted technology licences.

In deciding whether a share of the benefits which go to consumers is fair, the Commission has not quantified the benefit. Exclusive distribution agreements have been exempted on the ground that consumers benefit from the additional choice made possible through the existence

1 Chap. 5 below.

of a local firm charged with the promotion of goods often from another member state that otherwise might not easily penetrate the market. 'Consumers' is rather a misleading translation of the French '*utilisateurs.*' In most of the authentic texts (other than English), the word means ultimate buyers, whether for private or business use. The 'consumers' of a bus, for instance, were held to be bus companies and tour operators, not commuters or tourists.[2]

3.3 Group exemptions

Until 1965, the Commission probably had power to grant exemption only to individual agreements. By regulation 19/65, however, the Council empowered it to make regulations exempting classes of exclusive distribution and exclusive purchasing agreements and of agreements licensing intellectual property rights. The Commission's exercise of these and of powers granted subsequently will be analysed in Chapters 8, 10, 11 and 13 below.

These regulations have the advantage that those who can clearly bring their agreements within the terms of such a regulation are able to rely on the agreements not being void under article 85(2).

There are, however, disadvantages in having to bring a transaction within a block exemption. The first is that the Commission is required to specify the provisions that may and may not be inserted. The black lists of clauses and conditions that prevent the application of the regulation are wide and not always easy to apply. So it is not always certain whether an agreement is exempt at the time when the firms may have to make investment decisions. Block exemptions should be certain in their application.

The second disadvantage is that the parties may distort agreements that would make the common market more competitive and may contribute to the integration of the economies of member states in order to fall within the terms of a group exemption. This may reduce efficiency and at times may even make the agreement more restrictive.

A third disadvantage is that some of these exemptions, for instance that for automobile distribution (1985), attempt to make the agreement fair for dealers, by inserting clauses protecting their interests. This seems misguided. As the Advocate General said in *Pronuptia*,[3] competition policy is not directly concerned with fair bargains. Moreover, the fairness of a bargain does not depend on specific terms, but on the bargain as a whole. A dealer may prefer to buy at a lower price than be given specific forms of protection prescribed in general terms.

2   *ACEC/Berliet* [1968] C.M.L.R. D35.
3   (161/84) [1986] E.C.R. 353.

Nevertheless, when an agreement can be framed to benefit from one of these group exemptions, the risk of illegality and nullity is avoided and the task of the parties' advisers is made far easier. There is no need to analyse the market to ascertain whether article 85(1) is infringed, either when negotiating the agreement or when enforcing it.

In three of the group exemptions granted since 1984, the Commission has introduced a new procedure, loosely referred to as 'the opposition procedure.' Provided that there are no blacklisted restrictions, an agreement may be exempt under the regulation even if there is some restriction of competition not specifically exempted, provided that the agreement is notified to the Commission which does not oppose the exemption within six months or withdraws its opposition at any time. In theory, this enables more agreements to be exempted simply under the group exemption, while giving the Commission a chance to check that they are not anti-competitive (10.5.4 below). In practice, however, the black lists are so extensive that the procedure has been little used.

Apart from this short description, there is little point in analysing the provisions of article 85(3) in the abstract. It is more useful to discuss the particular kinds of contracts and clauses that have been exempted in practice. As will be seen in Chapter 5, only the Commission has power to grant exemptions, and if it decides to grant an exemption, it recites that the various conditions are fulfilled. If it does not wish to do so, it recites that at least one is not. It must, however, take care to give adequate reasons for so doing, or the decision may be quashed as in *Kali und Salz/Kali Chemie*.[4]

3.4 Nullity

It is important to distinguish between agreements that are not caught by article 85(1) and those that are caught but merit exemption, as until exemption is granted, whether individually or through a group exemption, the provisions in the agreement restrictive of competition cannot be enforced in national courts (6.2 below).

Article 85(2) provides that 'any agreements or decisions prohibited by this Article shall be automatically void.' Nevertheless, it is not the whole of an agreement that is rendered void by article 85(2), but only those provisions that restrict competition. In *La Technique Minière* v. *Maschinenbau Ulm*,[5] and *Société de Vente de Ciments et Bétons* v. *Kerpen & Kerpen*,[6] the Court ruled that only those provisions that infringe article

4   (19 & 20/74) [1975] E.C.R. 499.
5   (56/65) [1966] E.C.R. 235.
6   (319/82) [1983] E.C.R. 4173.

85 are void. In *Consten and Grundig*,[7] the Court quashed the decision for not specifying how much of the agreement was contrary to article 85. Whether the rest of the agreement can be severed and enforced is a question for the national court asked to enforce the contract (6.3.4 below).

Moreover, article 85(2) applies only if the agreement infringes article 85 as a whole, that is, if the agreement is not exempted under article 85(3). Where the agreement is capable of exemption but has not been exempted, this creates a difficulty for a civil court asked to enforce a contract, as only the Commission can grant an exemption. It is, however, difficult to explain the developments in the case law about nullity until the first implementing regulation, no. 17/62, has been briefly analysed, so this will be postponed until Chapter 6.

---

7   (56 & 58/64) [1966] E.C.R. 299, 2.3.1 and 2.4 above.

4 Abuse of a Dominant Position

4.1 Objections to economic strength

As explained at 1.3–1.3.3.2 above, the most important objection to market power expressed by classical economists is that a firm insufficiently constrained by competitive pressures may be able to operate inefficiently for long periods or earn high profits through charging prices higher than would be possible in more competitive conditions. The higher prices would reduce demand and lead to too little of the monopolised product being made and to resources being used to make things less wanted by consumers.

The emphasis of modern economics is even more general, but is still focused on the wide discretion enjoyed by firms with market power to pursue a variety of goals and choose a range of productive means, unconstrained within wide limits by market pressures. In most markets, many firms may enjoy some discretion over their production and marketing strategies, but this is not the general independence that enables high prices or inefficiency to be maintained over long periods and without risk.

Chicago economists and the enforcement authorities in the US during the Reagan era were concerned only with protecting those dealing with a dominant firm from exploitation. To further this objective, it is necessary to control only firms which are protected from competition by equally efficient firms. Consequently the only entry barriers relevant are those that would keep out equally efficient firms. It is widely agreed that entry barriers include government licensing and, in some circumstances, a minimum scale of operation that is large in relation to the market (1.3.3–1.3.3.2 above). It is less clear that lack of access to capital or lack of reputation would keep out equally efficient firms.

In the EC, however, there is concern also that large firms may make it hard for smaller firms to compete, even if the latter are less efficient (1.3.2.2 above). The preamble to the treaty refers to many factors other than efficiency, such as social policy, fair competition, peace and liberty. To protect small firms that are less efficient, it may be necessary to control the conduct of firms that have no power over price. To serve these objectives, which may detract from efficiency, entry barriers may be perceived as pervasive, including all the investments to be made by the new entrant, even if the incumbent had to make similar investments.

Article 86 provides:

'Any abuse by one or more undertakings of a dominant position within the common market or in a substantial part of it shall be prohibited as incompatible with the common market in so far as it may affect trade between Member States. Such abuse may, in particular, consist in:

(a) directly or indirectly imposing unfair purchase or selling prices or other unfair trading conditions;

(b) limiting production, markets or technical development to the prejudice of consumers;

(c) applying dissimilar conditions to equivalent transactions with other trading parties, thereby placing them at a competitive disadvantage;

(d) making the conclusion of contracts subject to acceptance by the other parties of supplementary obligations which, by their nature or according to commercial usage, have no connection with the subject of such contracts.'

The treaty was influenced by theories of workable competition current in the 1930s to 1950s and based on the paradigm of the structure of the market, which affects the conduct of firms, which affects their performance. Later it was seen that each of these elements affects the other two. Article 86 is not expressed to prohibit uncompetitive structures or conduct that leads to them: the existence or acquisition of market power. It is expressed to restrain conduct by a dominant firm that harms those with whom it deals. It will be seen (4.3.2–4.3.2.6), however, that the Community Court has interpreted the notion of abuse widely to include some kinds of conduct by a firm already dominant that extend or consolidate its market power by restricting the remaining competition, even minimally. Hence, conduct that adversely affects the structure of the market may be forbidden by article 86.

4.2 Dominant position

4.2.1 What is a dominant position?

Given the fluidity of the indications of dominance, it is not easy, especially for jurists, to determine how dominant a firm may be, and both the Commission and Court have failed to make clearly and cogently reasoned decisions.

In its decision in *Continental Can*,[1] the Commission defined the concept of a dominant position in much the same terms as would an economist:

'3. Undertakings are in a dominant position when they have the power to behave independently, which puts them in a position to act without taking into account their competitors, purchasers or suppliers. That is the position when, because of their share of the market, or of their share of the market combined with the availability of technical knowledge, raw materials or capital, they have the power to determine prices or to control production or

1   [1972] C.M.L.R. D11.

distribution for a significant part of the products in question. This power does not necessarily have to derive from an absolute domination permitting the undertakings which hold it to eliminate all will on the part of their economic partners, but it is enough that they be strong enough as a whole to ensure to those undertakings an overall independence of behaviour, even if there are differences in intensity in their influence on the different partial markets.'

The Commission focused on the discretionary power of the monopolist to set its prices and make other market decisions without being tightly constrained by competitive pressures. It referred to the need for capital and technology, although such barriers to entry could be surmounted in the long run by many firms if monopoly profits would thereby be earned. On appeal,[2] Advocate General Roemer approved of the Commission's definition and the Court more or less accepted it by implication.

Later, it became clear that dominance in the EC differs from the economists' concept of power over price: it is a legal concept developed by Commission and Court. In *United Brands*, the Commission[3] found and the Court[4] confirmed that United Brands was dominant in a market where it was unsuccessfully fighting a price war with its chief competitor and had made losses in four out of the last five years.

4.2.2 *How to assess whether a position is dominant*

In *Continental Can*, the Court insisted on the Commission analysing a firm's market power in two steps: first, it should define the relevant market and then it should assess the firm's dominance therein.

Unfortunately markets do not always have clear limits: there may be substitutes that are not perfect, in which case selecting a narrow definition will overstate the market power of a firm supplying a large proportion of the defined product. If it raises prices above the competitive level, it will lose many sales. A wide definition, however, will indicate a smaller market share which understates it. Competition from close substitutes may constrain the firm's conduct closely and in the short term, while that from more remote substitutes only in the longer term when customers have time to adapt to the new product. Both, however, may be expected to affect its conduct.

4.2.3 *Relevant market*

4.2.3.1 *Relevant product market — substitutes on both the demand and supply side of the market* — The Court has repeatedly required the

2   (6/72) [1973] E.C.R. 215, paras. 33–36, and p.257, *per* Roemer A.G.
3   [1976] 1 C.M.L.R. D28.
4   (27/76) [1978] E.C.R. 207.

Commission to define the relevant market and give reasons for its definition. In *Continental Can* v. *Commission*,[5] the Court quashed the Commission's finding that Continental Can was dominant over the supply of cans used for meat and fish products and for metal closures other than crown corks. The Commission had to some extent considered substitutes on the demand side of the market, the possibility of meat and fish suppliers using plastic and glass containers: but it had not considered substitutes on the supply side, how easily the makers of cylindrical cans could start making the more complex shapes used for meat and fish. If it were easy to switch production in this way, Continental Can would have had little discretion: if it were to raise prices significantly above costs (including a normal return on capital), it would pay one of the other can makers to enter a profitable market by making cans for meat and fish. Continental Can would foresee the likelihood of such entry, so would be unlikely to initiate the price rise which would not pay except in the very short term. Hence, it would be constrained by potential competition even in the short term.

The Court, however, did not consider the possibility of a completely new entrant obtaining a technology licence from, say, American Can, but only of the maker of cylindrical cans making the irregular shaped ones used for meat and fish; or of a canner starting to make its own cans.

Although, like the Court in *Continental Can*, many economists consider that substitutes on both the supply and demand side of the market define it, some decisions in the EC adopted in the late 1970s and 1980s, seeming to rely on the German practice and precedents, used a test based on demand substitution to define the market. Ease of entry and the availability of substitutes were considered only when dominance within that market was assessed. Consequently, there has been a tendency for the Commission, sometimes supported by the Court,[6] to approach the definition of the market by asking:

(1) what firm is being accused;
(2) what products sold by it are involved in the complaint;
(3) who buys them; and
(4) what else could be used by those customers with minimal adaptation to their business?

Where the firm is alleged to have buying rather than selling power the converse questions are relevant.

This is a different test from that given in *Continental Can*. The Commission looks to substitutes mainly on the demand side and only in

5 Cited at 4.2.1 above.
6 *E.g.*, in *Michelin* [1982] 1 C.M.L.R. 643; on appeal, (322/81) [1983] E.C.R. 3461, and 4.2.3.2–4.2.8 below.

the short term. It may result in a very narrow market being relevant where customers are dependent on a supplier but the latter has little power to charge excessive prices because new suppliers can easily enter once they have built or adapted a factory.

Where there are competitive pressures from outside the market as defined, the test may not be very helpful to an assessment of power over price, but the difficult questions are postponed until a second stage and if there are such pressures the firm accused can bring them to the attention of the Commission to show that it is not dominant even within the narrow market. In *British Plasterboard*,[7] the Commission considered the availability of substitutes not when defining markets, but at the later stage when assessing market power. It does not matter at which stage the assessment takes place, as long as it is not neglected.

The Commission's practice accords with the methods of analysis used in assessing dominance under German cartel law. Nevertheless, there seems to be little point in defining a market at all if products that are excluded from the definition become relevant later. The Court in its most recent judgments has been referring to substitutes on both sides of the market.[8]

In some cases, the criteria for defining the market have been based on the nature of the complaint. As there is no complainant, however, control of mergers under the new regulation has been based on the structure of the market. Consequently, rather broader markets have often been the starting point for the analysis of mergers under the regulation (12.2.3 below). It is hoped that the expertise of the merger task force will spread to other parts of DGIV and influence the analysis under article 86.

Markets have been even more narrowly defined also from the demand side. In *United Brands*,[9] the Court upheld the Commission's choice of bananas as the relevant market:

'22. For the banana to be regarded as forming a market which is sufficiently differentiated from the other fruit markets it must be possible for it to be singled out by such special factors distinguishing it from other fruits that it is only to a limited extent interchangeable with them and is only exposed to their competition in a way that is hardly perceptible.'

It confirmed, however, that oranges were not interchangeable with bananas and apples only to a limited extent, despite evidence of the easing of banana prices and a reduction in the quantities sold during the

---

7 [1990] 4 C.M.L.R. 464, para. 108, where the Commission said that the possible substitution of wet plaster could be taken into account when considering whether a dominant position exists. Confirmed on appeal (T-65/89) [1993] 5 C.M.L.R 32.
8 See, *e.g.*, *Hilti* v. *Commission* (T-30/89) [1992] 4 C.M.L.R. 16.
9 Cited at 4.2.1 above.

seasons for summer fruit and oranges, perhaps because of a finding in a report by the Food and Agriculture Organisation in 1975 that 'the price of oranges in all cases had no significant impact on banana consumption.'

In its decision, the Commission was concerned about the need of the young, the old and the infirm who may have difficulty eating other fruit. The interests of the toothless, however, are sufficiently protected by the inability of the dominant firm to discriminate against them. It would lose so much market share from the rest of the population that it would not be worth raising prices to exploit the weak.

Few economists would define a market so narrowly. Indeed, when considering under article 95 of the EC treaty whether a tax imposed on bananas by Italy protected Italian soft fruit, the Court held that 'bananas must be regarded as being in partial in competition with such fruit.'[10] In view of the influence of the decisions under the merger regulation which are beginning to influence other parts of DGIV,[11] however, it is doubted whether the Commission would select quite such a narrow market these days.

4.2.3.2 *Relevant geographic market* — It is the abuse of the dominant position only within the common market that could be challenged. For some products, economists might say that the relevant market is worldwide, as the sole producer of a substance in the common market would have no monopolistic discretion were the market liable to be swamped by imports. In *Wood Pulp*,[12] the Court confirmed that the relevant market under article 85 was global. In *Filtrona*,[13] a complainant appealed against the dismissal of its complaint by the Commission which argued that cigarette filters could be sold worldwide and that, consequently, the only buyer in Spain did not enjoy a dominant position over their acquisition.

In *Michelin*,[14] however, the Commission fined the Dutch subsidiary of a French company for abusing its dominant position over the supply of tyres for heavy vehicles in the Netherlands at the dealer level without enquiring whether the dealers' customers could easily have bought Michelin tyres outside that country. If they could have done so,

10   *Commission* v. *Italy* (184/85) [1987] E.C.R. 2013, para. 12.
11   See also 4.2.3.4 below.
12   (89, 104, 114, 116–117 and 125–129/85) [1988] E.C.R. 5193.
13   (220/89) O.J. 1989, C211/9. The case was dismissed on procedural grounds and the Court never considered the substantive issue. See also *Bayer/Gist* [1976] 1 C.M.L.R. D98, where the Commission looked to world markets (excluding countries then behind the iron curtain for which no statistics were available); and *KEWA* [1976] 2 C.M.L.R. D15, where it looked to the whole of Europe.
14   Cited at 4.2.3.1.

Michelin's Dutch subsidiary, Michelin NV, could not have earned a monopoly profit from dealers without driving them out of business to its own disadvantage.

The Court[15] confirmed the Commission's selection of the Netherlands as the relevant market on the ground that the decision was addressed to the Dutch subsidiary, whose activities were concentrated in the Netherlands; its main competitors also carried on activities there through local subsidiaries; the alleged abuse related to discounts given to dealers there and dealers there obtained their supplies only from suppliers operating there. So the Court held that the Commission was right to take the view that the competition facing Michelin NV was mainly on the Dutch market and that was the 'level at which the objective conditions of competition are alike for traders.' It did add, however, that this did not exclude the position of the Michelin group and its competitors as a whole and a much wider market being relevant to the existence of a dominant position on the relevant product market.

It may well have been that the Michelin group was equally dominant in the areas outside the Netherlands, but this was not established. It may also be objected that it is for the Commission to establish the existence of a dominant position, and I regret that no analysis was made of competitive forces from outside the Netherlands either when defining the relevant market or when finding that Michelin was dominant within it. Earlier, in *Continental Can*,[16] Advocate General Roemer pointed out that metal closures for glass containers came to Germany from as far away as Poole in the UK and this indicated that the relevant market for closures was far wider than North West Germany.

Where a narrow market is taken as relevant, however, the firm alleged to be dominant should take the initiative to defend itself and prove that competitive pressures from outside the market defined as relevant are so strong that it is futile to concentrate only on it. As in the case of product markets, it does not greatly matter whether this is done at the stage of defining the relevant market, or when the dominant position is being assessed, as long as it is done.

In its notice on minor agreements,[17] the Commmission states its view that:

> '13. The relevant geographical market is the area within the Community in which the agreement produces its effects. This area will be the whole common market where the contract products are regularly bought and sold in all Member States. Where the contract products cannot be bought or sold in a

15 Cited at 4.2.3.1 above, at paras. 23–28.
16 Cited at 4.2.1 above.
17 O.J. 1986, C231/2.

part of the common market, or are bought and sold only in limited quantities or at irregular intervals in such a part, that part should be disregarded.

14. The relevant geographic market will be narrower than the whole common market in particular where:
— the nature and characteristics of the contract product, *e.g.*, high transport costs in relation to the value of the product, restrict its mobility: or
— movement of the contract product within the common market is hindered by barriers to entry to national markets resulting from state intervention, such as . . .'

Although the notice purports to deal only with the concept of appreciability, the Commission seems to be using the same criteria for defining the relevant market under article 86.

Both Court and Commission have, however, selected narrow markets where they fear that a firm controls an essential facility. The port of Genoa, for instance, was considered a substantial part of the common market in view of its importance to trade into and out of Italy.[18] The Commission has been accepting even narrower markets.

4.2.3.3 *Time scale* — In *Michelin*,[19] the Court accepted that the Commission should assess the cross elasticities of supply and demand, but it assessed the alleged barriers to entry on a shorter time scale than would be used by economists, in Europe as well as America. They say that competition operates in the long term, defined as the time needed to build new plant.

In *Michelin*, however, the Court observed that it takes time to build a factory or for customers to assess the quality of a new brand of heavy tyres. So the creation of new capacity could be ignored. Yet Michelin could not have exploited its position for long or at all if Goodyear could profitably have built a factory in the Netherlands. The need to discourage it from doing so would constrain Michelin's conduct meanwhile.

On the shorter time scale, which is used in many decisions of the Commission and judgments of the Court, entry barriers are pervasive. They include the need to invest in plant, an established reputation, a good commercial network, access to technology and many other assets of existing firms which do not give them power to maintain high prices for any length of time without risk, or even the certainty, of losing market share. Those familiar with the US decisions of the last two decades will be amazed by some of the EC ones and *vice versa*.

18 *Merci Convenzionali Porto di Genova* v. *Siderurgica Gabrielli* (C–179/90) [1991] E.C.R. I–5889.
19 Cited at 4.2.3.1 above.

4.2.3.4 *Wider markets suggested by the Court* — Recently the Court has been less willing to confirm a finding of dominance. In *Ahmed Saeed*,[20] it suggested that charter, rail or road transport might be substitutes for scheduled flights for a particular route. In *Alsatel* v. *Novasam*,[21] the Court suggested that the whole of France might be the relevant geographic market since the licences granted by regional authorities to provide the telephonic installations were valid for the whole country and not merely for a particular region. The Court also rejected the Commission's narrow definition of the market as that for the hire of telecommunications equipment. Consumers had the option of buying the equipment from other suppliers and the Court ruled that this was also relevant. Nevertheless, in a press release[22] over a year later, the Commission treated cola drinks in Italy as the relevant market.

4.2.3.5 *The fallacy of defining markets to assess market power* — One of the drawbacks of assessing market power by reference to substitutes on the demand and supply side is that a firm with power over price is likely to have raised it above the competitive level to the point where, if it raised it a little further, it would lose substantial sales. Consequently, even a firm with considerable market power and charging far more than it would have been able to do had the market been more competitive will usually face competition from substitutes at the prices it is actually charging. If the market power is already being exploited, the firm will probably be subject to competitive pressures. There is no simple solution to this problem as, in the absence of close competitors, it is not possible to tell what the competitive price would be. Neither the Commission nor the Court has addressed this problem.

Another problem is that it is difficult to assess the extent to which higher prices of product A would cause customers to buy other products or new firms to enter the market for A, especially the latter. Unless there is excess capacity in the market for the substitutes, which I shall call B, the price of B would rise as suppliers of B switched to make A. How many buyers of B would switch as its price rose? The series of questions about substitutes may be endless.

4.2.4 *Customer dependence*

In 1977, an extension to the concept of dominant position was made by the Commission in two decisions that were subject to appeal. In

20   (66/86) [1989] E.C.R. 803, at para. 39.
21   (247/86) [1988] E.C.R. 5987.
22   IP(90)7.

ABG,[23] it decided that during a period of acute shortage, when a maximum price for petrol had been imposed by the Dutch government at a level that did not permit suppliers to cover the cost of replacing it:

'76. ... their customers can become completely dependent on them for the supply of scarce products. Thus while the situation continues, the suppliers are placed in a dominant position in respect of their normal customers.'

Advocate General Warner recommended that this should not be accepted by the Court:

'In a temporary emergency of the kind here in question, a trader cannot distribute his scarce supplies regardless of the attitude of his customers. He must have it in mind that, once the emergency is over, they will have memories of the way in which they were treated by him during the period of scarcity. Contractual customers will expect the favourable treatment to which their contracts entitle them, both as a matter of law and as a matter of commercial honour ...'

He considered that the case was about the allocation of supplies, not about pricing, so did not consider whether a supplier can have market power when he is not allowed to sell at a price that would enable him to cover his replacement costs. The Court did not consider whether BP enjoyed a dominant position.

In *Hugin/Liptons*,[24] the Commission found that Hugin, which supplied 12 per cent. of the cash registers in the common market, did not enjoy a dominant position in respect of cash registers. The spare parts for these, however, were mostly not interchangeable with those of other cash registers. Hugin cash registers could therefore not be maintained, repaired or rebuilt without Hugin parts and Hugin was found to enjoy a dominant position over such spares throughout the world and, consequently, in the common market. Hugin therefore:

'has a dominant position for the maintenance and repair of Hugin cash registers in relation to companies which need a supply of Hugin spare parts. It follows, therefore, that Hugin AB and Hugin U.K. hold a dominant position for these products and services in that substantial part of the Common Market consisting of England, Scotland and Wales. Such dominant position extends to the business, such as Liptons carried on, of reconditioning and repairing used Hugin cash registers which also depends upon a supply of Hugin spare parts.'

---

23   [1977] 2 C.M.L.R. D1; quashed on appeal: *BP* v. *Commission* (77/77) [1978] E.C.R. 1513, at p.1538.
24   [1978] 1 C.M.L.R. D19, at para. 62.

In *Hugin* v. *Commission*,[25] the Court confirmed that Hugin enjoyed a dominant position in relation to such owners. Subsequently, however, it refrained from citing *Hugin* in *Volvo* v. *Veng*[26] and it may be that there is no longer a consensus in the Court that a firm is dominant over supplies of spares for its own products. Nevertheless, *Hugin* does not go very much further than the Court's earlier judgment in *General Motors Continental*,[27] confirming that the only firm allowed by Belgian law to provide an inspection and certification service was dominant over the supply of that service. In both cases the dominance started only when the product had been acquired. When choosing which brand to buy, the lack of competition at the next stage might be taken into account by the cautious buyer, but once the object had been acquired there was only one firm to which the customer could turn.

In the United States, the Supreme Court in *Eastman Kodak*,[28] held that a firm might have sufficient market power over spare parts for the equipment it produced for a refusal to supply parts to independent maintainers to amount to monopolisation contrary to article 2 of the Sherman Act. There was some evidence that some customers for imaging equipment did not calculate the cost of maintaining it over its useful life when first buying it. The Supreme Court, therefore, referred the case back for further findings of fact.

The Commission remains concerned that intellectual property rights over spare parts may enable the holder to prevent third parties from supplying repair and maintenance services. It has prepared both a regulation and a directive to ensure that design laws provide that after three years compulsory licences will be granted when fitting an extension or replacement part which will necessarily infringe.[29]

In *British Leyland*,[30] the Court confirmed a finding that British Leyland had infringed article 86 when it refused to make available type approval documents that would have facilitated the import of certain models from the Continent. Only British Leyland was in a position to make them available.

The notion of customer dependence may well derive from the German

---

25   (22/78) [1979] E.C.R. 1869. See paras. 7–10, although the Commission decision was quashed on the ground that Liptons operated only within a radius of 30 miles from London, so the abuse did not affect trade between member states.
26   (238/87) [1988] E.C.R. 6211 and 10.9 below. Nor did it or the A.G. cite *Hugin* in *Renault* (53/87) [1988] E.C.R. 6039, although it was cited by the parties.
27   (26/75) [1975] E.C.R. 1367.
28   112 S.Ct. 2072 (1992).
29   Proposal for a directive on Community Design (94/C29/02), COM(93)342 *final* — COD 463, submitted by the Commission, on 3 December 1993. A reg. is also proposed. See also Magill, discussed at 10.9 below.
30   (226/84) [1986] E.C.R. 3263.

concept of sub-groups against whom a supplier can discriminate and over which he is dominant. *Hugin* is almost identical in facts and reasoning to an earlier decision of the German Supreme Court in *Registrierkassen*.[31]

4.2.5   *Assessment of dominant position*

In all its judgments since *United Brands*, the Court has defined a dominant position as

> 'a position of economic strength enjoyed by an undertaking which enables it to prevent effective competition being maintained on the relevant market by giving it the power to behave to an appreciable extent independently of its competitors, customers and ultimately of consumers.'[32]

The last two lines sound like the economists' concept of power over price. A monopolist, unconstrained by competitive pressures, enjoys a discretion in his pricing and other market decisions. The application of competition policy to the conduct of such a firm may protect those with whom it deals.

The concept of economic strength which enables an undertaking to prevent effective competition, however, may encompass a different idea: that of being able to exclude other firms, efficient or otherwise — the power to foreclose. Control by a competition authority over such strategic behaviour may help a firm's competitors. If the firms that might be excluded are as efficient as the dominant firm, control by the Commission may increase consumer welfare, but if they are less efficient than the dominant firm, control may lead to worse bargains for consumers.

4.2.5.1   *Barriers to entry and market share* — The Court has not expanded in its judgments on its definition of a dominant position, but has concentrated on developing a list of relevant factors: the Commission and Court commonly look to barriers to entry as well as to market shares although, as described at 4.2.3.3 above, it has treated as entry barriers short term factors that would not be so treated by economists. Frequently, the Commission has pointed to the size of investment needed, although this would not exclude other large firms from a profitable market unless the minimum size of an efficient plant were very large in relation to the market or its expected expansion. Only in that case would a potential new entrant be deterred by the expectation that its investment in a new plant would lead to excess capacity and unprofitable prices.

In *United Brands*,[33] the Commission found that United Brands did

---

31   WuW (BGH) 1238 (1972).
32   Cited at 4.2.1 above, para. 65.
33   Cited at 4.2.1 above.

enjoy a dominant position over the supply of bananas in six member states, although the barriers to entry listed by the Commission do not appear to have been high and, before the Court, United Brands stated that it had made losses for four out of the last five years.

It sold some 45 per cent. of the bananas in Benelux, the Federal Republic of Germany, Denmark and Ireland, more than twice as many as its nearest rival. It had been active in plant research and developed a more prolific and disease-resistant variety of bananas. It owned plantations in different parts of the tropics, which gave it an advantage in regularity of supply when natural disasters hit a particular part of the growing area.

On the other hand, competitors could also buy or establish plantations in diverse areas and some planters had surplus bananas for sale. United Brands itself bought half the bananas it sold on the relevant market. United Brands owned enough refrigerated vessels to ship over half the bananas it sent to Europe through the ports of Rotterdam and Bremerhaven; but there is a charter market for such ships and ownership can be a disadvantage when freight rates slump. It had also arranged for very careful quality control and extensive promotion of the bananas it had packed in the tropics bearing the Chiquita mark. Chiquita bananas were found by the Commission to fetch some 30–40 per cent. more than unbranded ones, and by the Court 7 per cent. more than rival brands.

The Court pointed out that United Brands supplied between 41 and 45 per cent. of the market it had defined as relevant: several times as much as that supplied by the next largest banana company. From the cumulative advantage of all these factors the Commission found, and the Court confirmed, that United Brands was dominant, without finding any one of the advantages vital, or considering the possibility of new entrants coming in at one level only, buying bananas and chartering ships, etc. or of existing suppliers expanding the scale of their business.

Nevertheless, it seems that United Brands had no power over price. On an accounting basis, at least, it had made losses in four out of the previous five years, and was fighting a price war in Denmark.

In *Hoffmann-La Roche* (*Vitamins*),[34] the Court again stressed the importance of market shares:

'41. Furthermore although the importance of the market shares may vary from one market to another the view may legitimately be taken that very large shares are in themselves, and save in exceptional circumstances, evidence of the existence of a dominant position.

An undertaking which has a very large market share and holds it for some time, by means of the volume of production and the scale of the supply which

34 (85/76) [1979] E.C.R. 461.

it stands for — without those having much smaller market shares being able to meet rapidly the demand from those who would like to break away from the undertaking which has the largest market share — is by virtue of that share in a position of strength which makes it an unavoidable trading partner and which, already because of this secures for it, at the very least during relatively long periods, that freedom of action which is the special feature of a dominant position.'

Later in its judgment, the Court confirmed a finding of dominance solely on the basis of market percentages in the eighties, although it held that further indications were necessary to establish dominance over other vitamins where the market shares were in the forties and fifties. By stressing market shares that endure and barriers to expansion, it is hoped that the Court was presupposing barriers to entry, without which market power cannot exist.

In *AKZO*,[35] the Court considered that a stable market share of 50 per cent. or more raised a presumption of dominance, although it added that the Commission was right to consider other factors. It is thought that, in the absence of any entry barriers, even very high market shares do not indicate a dominant position.

There is now rather less concern that in a competitive market — and there was considerable evidence of competition in the sale of bananas — a firm with a large market share that is considerably larger than its competitors' may be found to enjoy a dominant position, especially if competition is possible only from large firms or from those operating on a different basis from the existing suppliers.

4.2.5.2 *Conduct* — The Commission also stressed United Brands' behaviour, from which dominance in some part of the area might have been inferred: geographical price discrimination, from which it seems that monopoly profits may have been earned in some countries; and the restriction on the sale of green bananas, which the Commission interpreted as an export restriction intended to insulate the high price areas. This would have made commercial sense only if the firm expected to have some market power, so it was sensible to treat it as an indication of such. Since it is usually so difficult to tell whether a firm is earning monopoly profits, however, it is hoped that the level of prices or charges will seldom be used as an indication of a dominant position.

4.2.6 *Collective dominance*

Article 86 refers to an abuse 'by one or more undertakings' of a dominant position. The Commission has been trying to establish

35   (62/86) [1991] E.C.R. I–3359, paras. 58–62.

collective dominance when two or more firms act under a cartel agreement. In its decision in *Italian Flat Glass*,[36] the Commission condemned under article 85 agreements between three firms allocating quotas and fixing prices and also condemned the same firms for abusing a collective dominant position because they presented themselves on the market as a single entity.

On appeal, the Court of First Instance[37] accepted that collective dominance might exist when, for instance, two independent undertakings shared a technological lead enabling them to behave to an appreciable extent independently of their competitors. It denied, however, that the Commission could 'recycle the facts' from which it had established an agreement contrary to article 85(1) to establish a dominant position. It also observed that, before finding a dominant position, the Commission would have had to define the relevant market and establish a lack of imports from outside the geographical area accepted.

The Commission has continued to allege joint dominance enjoyed, for instance, by the members of a shipping conference,[38] and under the merger regulation.[39] It wants to establish its competence over mergers that make a market more concentrated, and which may reduce price competition without leading to a single undertaking being dominant.

4.2.7 *'Substantial part of the common market'*

Article 86 prohibits an abuse of a dominant position within a substantial part of the common market. It is not entirely clear how large an area, or what proportion of the supply amounts to 'a substantial part of the common market.' In *Sugar*,[40] the Court stated that

> '371. . . . the pattern and volume of the production and consumption of the said product as well as the habits and economic opportunities of vendors and purchasers must be considered.'

So, precedents relating to different products will not be of much assistance. In his opinion in *BP* v. *Commission*,[41] Advocate General Warner treated the qualification as a *de minimis* rule. He concluded that the fact that BP's customers in the Netherlands took less than 0·5 per cent. of the motor spirit supplied in the common market did not prevent them from amounting to a substantial part of the common market. He seemed to assume that the limitation need not be purely geographical, provided

---

36   [1990] 4 C.M.L.R. 535.
37   *Italian Flat Glass* (T–68,77 and 78/89) [1992] E.C.R. II–1403, at para. 358.
38   *E.g.*, *French-West African Shipowners' Committees* [1993] 5 C.M.L.R. 446, para.
69.   *Nestlé/Perrier*, M100 [1993] 4 C.M.L.R. M17, and 12.2.3 below.
40   (40–48, 50, 54–56, 111, 113 & 114/73) [1975] E.C.R. 1663.
41   Cited at 4.2.4 above, at p.1537.

that there is some other factor dividing customers. Yet, in *Pigs and Bacon Commission* v. *McCarren*,[42] he said that a particular current of trade, such as the export of Irish bacon to Great Britain, did not constitute a 'part of' the common market.

4.2.8 *Conclusion on dominant position*

On the basis of the precedents, it is not easy to advise a client what the relevant market may be. The Commission has considerable discretion in selecting it. It is arguable that this does not matter, since the key question is the extent of the competitive pressures on the firm. Provided that pressures from outside the market selected as relevant are taken into account, few firms need be found dominant that do not have power over price. In *Italian Flat Glass*,[43] the Court insisted on the Commission establishing that Italy was the relevant market despite a considerable quantity of imports.

A greater cause for concern is the short time scale over which the Court and Commission have considered barriers to entry. If, as the Court stated in *Michelin*,[44] it takes too long to build a new plant for new entry to be relevant, firms that have substantial market shares but are subjected to intense competitive pressures may be held to be dominant and substantially constrained by article 86 in their market behaviour. Even in *Continental Can*, the Court looked only to firms that could start making the relevant kinds of cans with only a slight adaptation of their business. The Commission and, perhaps, the Court are concerned about the effects of market power during the period before the harsh treatment of customers or suppliers induces entry.

Under the merger regulation, however, the Commission is looking concretely to see which firms might enter were the merged firms to increase prices. In *Alcatel/Telettra*,[45] although the combined market share of the two firms for transmission equipment in Spain was 81 per cent. and for microwave equipment 83 per cent., the Commission concluded that the market was contestable. It observed that Telefonica, the only customer in Spain, had a policy of buying from more than one source and had said that it would be prepared to buy abroad, and the Commission indicated specific firms that might well compete. Consequently, it decided that the merger was not likely to create a dominant position as a result of which effective competition would be significantly

---

42   (177/78) [1979] E.C.R. 2161, at p.2216.
43   Cited at 4.2.6 above.
44   Cited at 4.2.3.1 above.
45   M18 [1991] 4 C.M.L.R. 778, at paras. 37–49.

impeded. This is in marked contrast to most of the Commission's decisions under article 86.

The Director General of Competition at the Commission is taking steps to help the greater economic content of the merger decisions to spread to other directorates. Officials who have worked for the merger task force are joining the policy directorate of DGIV.

4.3 'Abusive exploitation'

4.3.1 Introduction to 'abusive exploitation'

Article 86 is not expressed to prohibit the existence or acquisition of a dominant position, but only its abusive exploitation. The authentic English text of the treaty uses the single word 'abuse,' but most of the other languages use the double concept of 'abusive exploitation,' which might be thought to forbid harsh treatment of those with whom the dominant firm deals. Since the Court's judgment in *Continental Can*,[46] however, it has become clear that conduct by a dominant firm that reduces such competition as remains in the market is also treated as abusive.

In *Vitamins*,[47] the Court said that abuse is an objective concept. In the judgments given since *United Brands*[48] and concerned with attempts by a firm found to be dominant to increase market share, such as *Michelin*,[49] the Court has added that:

> '70. Article 86 covers practices which are likely to affect the structure of a market where, as a direct result of the presence of the undertaking in question, competition has already been weakened and which, through re-course to methods different from those governing normal competition in products or services based on traders' performance,[50] have the effect of hindering the maintenance or development of the level of competition still existing on the market.'

The sentence quoted is difficult to understand. Yet, unless some meaning can be extracted, we are left only with a list of practices that have already been held to be abusive or otherwise, and no means of advising what further practices may be considered abusive.

John Kallaugher[51] traces the sentence quoted back through the idea

46   Cited at 4.2.1 above.
47   Cited at 4.2.5.1 above.
48   Cited at 4.2.3.1, above.
49   Cited at 4.2.3.1 above. The following quotation is from *Michelin*, because of poor translations into English of the earlier judgments.
50   This is a poor translation of the German authentic text which speaks of 'competition on the basis of performance.' In *AKZO* (62/86) [1991] E.C.R. I–3359, para. 70, the Court used the term 'competition on the merits.'
51   *Op. cit.*, bibliography, 4.5 below.

of undistorted competition referred to in article 3(f),[52] to theories of workable competition current from the 1930s to the 1950s, according to which the structure of the market affects conduct which in turn affects performance. It has since been recognised that in fact each of these may affect the other two.

Kallaugher analyses the passage quoted to establish that the concept of abuse is objective as opposed to subjective — it does not depend on the ill will of the dominant firm. The conduct must be likely to influence the structure of the market through recourse to methods different from those that condition normal competition on the basis of performance.

The concept of competition based on performance is familiar in German law. In the law of unfair competition it is used to describe the kind of conduct that is expressly permitted, even if it harms competitors. It has also been applied under section 22 of the German Competition Act as a criterion for assessing the abuse of a dominant position. The classic forms of competition on the basis of performance include price competition (if not predatory); improvement in quality, including r & d; or in services to customers; even advertising. However much such competition may exclude competitors it is lawful.

Competition on the basis of performance is not identical with the US concept of economic efficiency; nor does it include such 'normal' conduct as mergers and acquisitions, exclusive dealing agreements or loyalty discounts, which are not necessarily illegal under US law.

Kallaugher rejects the relevance of proportionality, which has been advocated by some authors, as the main criterion for abuse.[53] However much competition on the basis of performance excludes others, it is permitted. Where refusals to sell are justified by the buyer's failure to look after a product, proportionality may have a role to play,[54] but the role is subsidiary.

Many of the cases since *United Brands* have been concerned with steps taken by monopolists to increase their market share. The unfair abuses considered from 4.3.3 are less likely to affect the structure of the market unfavourably, and in these cases[55] the Court has not used the kind of

---

52   Now art. 3(g) by virtue of the treaty of Maastricht.
53   Some of these are cited and followed in the A.G.'s opinion in *Tetrapak* (T–51/89), [1990] E.C.R. II–309, from para. 69. The Court of First Instance did not consider it.
54   *United Brands*, cited at 4.2.1 above and considered at 4.3.3.4 below.
55   *E.g.*, in *Ahmed Saeed*, 4.2.3.4 above, at paras. 42–46, the Court refers to unfair prices, which may be excessively high or excessively low. In *Bodson* v. *Pompes Funèbres* (30/87) [1988] E.C.R. 2479, paras. 30–35, and *Lucazeau* v. *SACEM* (110/88) [1989] E.C.R. 2521, paras. 21 *et seq.*, the Court considered only *indicia* as to whether prices were excessive. It did not give a basic definition of 'abuse' in these cases heard under art. 177.

definition of abuse that I have quoted from *Michelin*. High prices may attract new entry to the market and improve its structure. The requirement that structure be affected may apply only to exclusionary practices.

4.3.2 *Reduction of competition prohibited by article 86*

The Court in *Continental Can* v. *Commission*[56] construed article 86 as prohibiting conduct that substantially reduces competition. Continental Can held 85 per cent. of the shares in Schmalbach, a company found to enjoy a dominant position in part of the Federal Republic of Germany over the supply of tins for meat and fish products and of metal closures for glass containers other than crown corks. It caused another of its subsidiaries to make a bid for all the shares of Thomassen, a company that made a large proportion of all such tins and nearly half the metal closures in the Netherlands. The Commission condemned this as eliminating potential competition in respect of these products.

The Community Court quashed the decision on its facts, since the Commission had not established its findings that the makers of other kinds of can could not easily start making fish and meat cans, nor had it given reasons for excluding crown corks from the market in metal closures. Nevertheless, in the light of the basic articles of the Treaty — 2 and 3(f)[57] — it concluded that, in principle, conduct that substantially reduces competition is prohibited by article 86.

> '26. ... the provision is not only aimed at practices which may cause damage to consumers directly, but also at those which are detrimental to them through their impact on an effective competition structure, such as is mentioned in Article 3(f) of the Treaty. Abuse may therefore occur if an undertaking in a dominant position strengthens such position in such a way that the degree of dominance reached substantially fetters competition, i.e. that only undertakings remain in the market whose behaviour depends on the dominant one.'

Although the Commission's decision was quashed on the facts, the Court clearly interpreted article 86 to prohibit anti-competitive conduct by a firm that already enjoys a dominant position in the common market. In this case, the merger reduced the number of existing competitors, but the Court's reasoning has been applied to other practices thought to bar the entry or expansion of other firms such as loyalty rebates given by a dominant firm (4.3.2.2 below).

4.3.2.1 *Control of mergers* — Although in *Continental Can*[58] the

56 Cited at 4.2.1 above.
57 Now art. 3(g) as revised at Maastricht.
58 Cited at 4.2.1 above.

Commission clearly obtained power to control acquisitions by firms already dominant, when these substantially reduce competition, it has not since exercised that power in any formal decisions. At the end of 1989, the Council finally adopted a regulation conferring power on the Commission relating to very large mergers and concentrative joint ventures between large firms. The way that mergers may be dealt with thereunder will be considered in Chapter 12 below.

4.3.2.2 *Systematic discrimination* — In several cases, the Court has confirmed the condemnation of discount systems which it considered made competition by smaller competitors more difficult. These have been considered discriminatory and, when *ad hoc*, unfair or, when systematic, anti-competitive. At this point, only the second objection will be considered. Unfair discrimination is considered at 4.3.3.3 below.

Systematic discrimination may foreclose smaller firms and make it harder for them to compete on the merits. A buyer entitled to an extra 1 per cent. discount on all its purchases if it buys, say, 70 per cent. of its requirements from the dominant firm will require a very much lower price before it buys more than 30 per cent. from other firms. It will lose the 1 per cent. not merely on the extra amount bought elsewhere, but also on the amount that is actually bought from the dominant firm.

Where a buyer is dependent on the dominant firm for a substantial part of the range of products it needs or some of its customers favour the dominant firm's brands, it will have to buy a significant amount from the dominant firm. Loyalty discounts will lead to other suppliers being foreclosed not only from those parts of the demand which can be supplied only by the dominant firm, but from all but 30 per cent. of the market.

Progressive rebates, such as an extra 1 per cent. on total purchases during the year for every 100 tons bought, may have a similar foreclosing effect. The dominant firm's customer is unlikely to buy elsewhere until he is sure that he will attain the maximum discount possible.

Discounts that reflect the savings to the dominant firm of delivering a container or barge full, on the other hand, may be justified. They encourage customers to organise their business so as to enable the supplier to adopt low cost methods of delivery. Other kinds of cost savings, however, are less easy to quantify and, consequently, to justify.

The concern about foreclosing others reflects the desire in the EC to protect the interests of traders wanting to enter a market. After the Community Court had condemned conduct that substantially reduced potential competition in *Continental Can*,[59] the Court confirmed the

59   Cited at 4.2.1 above.

condemnation of requirements that customers should buy only from a dominant firm, and loyalty discounts promised to those buying most of their requirements from it in *Sugar*.[60] This was confirmed in *Hoffmann-La Roche (Vitamins)*[61] on two grounds. First, requirements obligations and loyalty discounts foreclose competition and, secondly, they come within the examples of abuse listed in article 86. They may make it harder for smaller makers of vitamins, who cannot supply a large percentage of a large customer's requirements, to compete and their effect is

> '90. ... to apply dissimilar conditions to equivalent transactions with other trading parties in that two purchasers pay a different price for the same quantity of the same product depending on whether they obtain their supplies exclusively from the undertaking in a dominant position or have several sources of supply.'

This seems to be a reference to article 86(c):

> 'applying dissimilar conditions to equivalent transactions with other trading parties, thereby placing them at a competitive disadvantage;'

although it might be argued that where one buyer agrees to take a percentage of its requirements from the dominant firm, he is not party to a transaction equivalent to that with a buyer who buys the same quantity without such a commitment. Moreover, Roche's customers used the vitamins for different purposes and it was not shown that they were competing down stream. These qualifications in paragraph (c) may have been read out of the treaty.

At paragraph 111 the Court also pointed out that loyalty discounts granted across the board on the proportion of all vitamins bought also had a tying effect contrary to article 86(d): a customer who needed some vitamins that Roche produced, but other firms did not, would have to buy part of its requirements from Roche and would have an incentive to buy its other requirements from Roche in order to earn the higher discount.

It is not easy to distinguish competing on the merits from artificially making business more difficult for competitors. Nor is it always possible to distinguish price-cutting, which is allowed, from exclusionary rebates, which are prohibited. In *Vitamins*, the Court distinguished quantity discounts that it considered were legal from loyalty rebates that were not. A quantity discount is based on the volume of products bought from the same firm, and a loyalty discount on the proportion of

60   Cited at 4.2.7 above.
61   Cited at 4.2.5.1 above.

requirements bought from it. Yet quantity discounts may also foreclose small firms who cannot supply large quantities. The Court also referred to article 86(c) and (d) and it may be that conduct listed in article 86 should be assumed not to be competition on the merits.

In *Michelin*,[62] the Court confirmed the Commission's condemnation of incentive rebates given to dealers who had met their targets and had sold more than they had in a previous year. Such rebates are frequently given in order to encourage dealers to try harder. It may be easy to maintain last year's turnover but difficult to expand it. The rebates were based on the quantities sold, yet a fine was imposed, despite the statement in *Vitamins* that quantity discounts are permissible. Perhaps both Commission and Court were swayed by the practice of Michelin of not writing down in advance the target levels of each dealer, as uncertainty might result in the dealer continuing to press sales of Michelin tyres even after he thought he had probably achieved his target.

In *Continental Can*,[63] the Court stated that conduct leading to a substantial reduction of competition might infringe article 86. In *Hoffmann-La Roche*, however, the amount of foreclosure for some vitamins was small. It granted loyalty rebates to only 22 of its largest customers and for some vitamins I am told that less than 2 per cent. of the market was foreclosed — possibly insufficient for the agreement to infringe article 85(1). At paragraph 123, however, the Court ruled that:

> 'since the course of conduct under consideration is that of an undertaking occupying a dominant position on a market where for this reason the structure of competition has already been weakened, within the field of application of Article 86 any further weakening of the structure of competition may constitute an abuse of a dominant position.'

Consequently, even a small reduction of competition may infringe article 86.

The EC notion of hindering competitors seems to have been strongly influenced by the distinction developed in Germany between competition on the basis of performance, such as charging lower prices or supplying better products, which is permissible for a dominant firm even if its competitors are harmed, and other forms of competition that are permissible only for firms that are not dominant (4.3.1 above). The courts in Germany have held that loyalty rebates are not included in the notion of competition based on performance, and condemn them under national cartel law as the use of economic strength to manipulate the market unless they are *de minimis*.

The Commission's treatment of rebates given to dealers who achieve a

---

62   Cited at 4.2.3.1 above.
63   Cited at 4.2.1 above.

target may follow the German practice. In *Fertigfutter (Pet Foods)*,[64] the Berlin Court of Appeal found an annual rebate system abusive, but suggested that a system with shorter reference periods would be legal. The Federal Cartel Office subsequently accepted (under protest) a rebate system based on quarterly reference periods by the same firm. This solution would enable a dealer to qualify in the first quarter, keeping in stock such products as it could not sell, and then to buy from other firms during the second quarter, when he had disposed of his stocks. That would not be so effective in encouraging a distributor to improve its performance, but would make sales easier for competing firms.

According to a press release,[65] the Commission accepted target rebates granted by Coca Cola in Italy when they were based on a three month period, although it objected to target rebates based on a reference period of a whole year.

4.3.2.3 *Refusals to supply* — These too may be thought of both as unfair and as reducing competition. The two objections have not been clearly distinguished by the Court and are considered together at 4.3.3.4 below.

4.3.2.4 *Predatory pricing* — There is a large literature on predatory pricing in the US. The courts there have mostly accepted the Areeda/Turner test of predation,[66] which is based on a criterion of efficiency: sales below average variable cost are usually predatory, but provided the dominant firm can cover its variable costs, it is not inefficient for it to sell additional units.

On this basis of a very low level of costs, there cannot be much predatory pricing unless entry barriers are very high. The dominant firm would lose on each sale it makes and to drive out a competitor it would have to supply the increased quantities demanded at a low price. This would hardly pay if the new entrant were to try again to enter the market after a period of price cutting, or the person who bought its plant from the liquidator could do so. Only a firm more concerned with turnover or market share than with profits would think it worth while.

Others have been concerned that lowering prices where it might most hurt actual or potential competitors may be prevalent and effective. In *Concrete Roofing Tiles*,[67] the UK Monopolies and Mergers Commission accepted that the dominant firm, Redland, did not sell below average variable cost. Indeed, even its most heavily discounted prices were not

64 WuW (OLG) 2463 (1980).
65 Press Release IP(90)7, 9 January 1990.
66 *Op. cit.*, bibliography, 4.5 below.
67 1981 H.C. 120.

clearly below the full costs of using the plant at a high level of capacity utilisation. Yet the Monopolies Commission concluded that

'the established suppliers are able to contain new entrants' market penetration and accompanying price competition at relatively low cost to themselves by means of selective discounting. We regard Redland's behaviour as an indication of how deep selective discounting may be used by established firms as a means of preserving their dominant position. Such behaviour which operates as a barrier to entry may in the circumstances of this industry be expected to operate against the public interest.'[68]

The criterion used to define predation in that report was selective price cutting with an intent to exclude just where a new competitor entered the market. The reliance on intention has the disadvantage that most competitors would like their rivals to disappear. Sophisticated firms are usually well advised not to send threats or produce memoranda for inspectors to find alleging an intent to exclude. The less sophisticated may be caught.

Other criteria are based on average cost. Sales below average total costs, including overheads, are common. When there is excess capacity any sensible firm would sell a bit more even if the additional sales make only a small contribution towards overheads. Such sales make commercial sense even with no intention or likelihood of excluding a rival and then raising prices again.

Many American courts have followed the Areeda/Turner test and treated sales below average variable costs as predatory, on the basis that such sales make no commercial sense without the hope and probability of eliminating a competitor and raising prices later.

Unfortunately, this is not always true. Firms frequently do not cover even their variable costs when first introducing a product to the market. Products are not always worth what they cost when they have become technically obsolescent or unfashionable, or when the original acquisition was commercially mistaken. It should not be wrongful to sell these at less than their variable cost as determined historically.

There is danger that if price predation is treated as abusive, price competition will be chilled. There is no satisfactory definition of predation, of distinguishing competition on the merits from excluding others by illegitimate means, and there is significant room for judges and officials to get the answer wrong.

In *AKZO*,[69] the Commission condemned predatory pricing largely on the basis of internal memoranda and threats by AKZO to deter a smaller

---

68   *Report of the Monopolies and Mergers Commission on the Supply of Concrete Roofing Tiles* (1981–1982) H.C. 12, para. 10.57.
69   O.J. 1985, L374/1, appeal cited at 4.2.5.1.

firm, ECS, from supplying the market for making plastics. It imposed a
fine of 10 million ECUs.

AKZO produces organic peroxides for use in the plastics industry and
also makes compounds of benzoyl peroxide, one of the organic peroxides, for use as a whitening agent for flour. ECS, a small company
operating in the UK, also makes a nearly full assortment of flour
additives in the UK.

When ECS began to sell organic peroxides to the makers of plastics in
1979, AKZO made direct threats against ECS in meetings with the aim
of making ECS withdraw from the plastics sector. Thereafter, AKZO
systematically offered and supplied flour additives to ECS's clients at
abnormally low prices while maintaining its prices to other customers.

On appeal,[70] after repeating the definition of abuse given in *Vitamins*
the Court said:

> '70. It follows that Article 86 prohibits a dominant undertaking from
> eliminating a competitor and thereby strengthening its position by using
> methods other than those which come within the scope of competition on the
> basis of quality. From that point of view, however, not all competition by
> means of price can be regarded as legitimate.
>
> 71. Prices below average variable costs (that is to say, those which vary
> depending on the quantities produced) *by means of which a dominant under-
> taking seeks to eliminate a competitor* must be regarded as abusive. A domin-
> ant undertaking has *no interest in applying such prices except that of
> eliminating competitors so as to enable it subsequently to raise its prices* by
> taking advantage of its monopolistic position, since each sale generates a loss,
> namely the total amount of the fixed costs (that is to say, those which remain
> constant regardless of the quantities produced) and, at least, part of the
> variable costs relating to the unit produced. [my emphasis]
>
> 72. Moreover, prices below average total costs, that is to say fixed costs
> plus variable costs, but above average variable costs, must be regarded as
> abusive if they are determined as part of a plan for eliminating a competitor.
> Such prices can drive from the market undertakings which are perhaps as
> efficient as the dominant undertaking but which, because of their small
> financial resources, are incapable of withstanding the competition waged
> against them.
>
> 73. These are the criteria that must be applied to the present case.'

These rules of thumb are exceedingly worrying. A stricter test is applied
in the context of a plan to drive out a competitor, yet competition on the
merits drives out competitors. A rule based on intent leads to lawyers
preventing sophisticated clients from making threats or leaving memoranda about intent for Commission inspectors to find. Perhaps the

---

70   Cited at 4.2.5.1, above.

AKZO rule is a little narrower than one based just on intent; it is only when a *plan* is discovered that the stricter test applies.

In cyclical industries it is normal to sell below average total costs during the down turn of the business cycle, and recoup during the upturn. Can one impose fines on the ground that the former prices are predatory and the latter excessive?

Frequently it is not possible to determine average variable costs. Moreover, if judged on a historical basis, the sale of products that are either technically obsolescent or out of fashion might be predatory. That problem did not arise as AKZO continued to make organic peroxides, but I would argue that one should take into account the words I have italicised in paragraph 72: sales below average variable cost could have no object other than that of driving out a competitor and recouping later. Low promotional prices make commercial sense without the hope or probability of charging excessive prices later.

Another way of treating the disposal of obsolescent products so as to avoid the danger of predatory pricing would be to take into account the opportunity cost rather than historical cost. If the value of a product is less than was paid for it, the cost of the opportunity to sell would be well below the historical cost of acquisition.

Unfortunately, the Commission followed the statement that prices below average variable costs are predatory in *Tetra Pak II*,[71] without taking into account the reasons for the rule. First it condemned Tetra Pak for refusing to supply the aseptic equipment over which it enjoyed a dominant position to dairies and suppliers of fruit juice without also supplying the cartons, in the supply of which there was more competition. It went on (at paragraph 157) to object to the sale in the UK of non-aseptic machinery at prices below variable cost, without taking into account the profits from the tied cartons. It also condemned the sale of machinery in Italy as being below average variable cost when the purchase was made from a fellow subsidiary, but we are not told the cost to that subsidiary. Only if the sales price and other associated income falls below the variable cost to the corporate group should the Commission infer an intent and likelihood of later charging excessive prices.

4.3.2.5 *Tying* — The last example of an abuse listed in article 86 is tying. If a dominant firm refuses to supply goods or services over which it has a dominant position to those wishing to use them to provide a further service, it may be able to exclude firms from the second market. In the US, fear of this has decreased substantially as it will rarely pay a monopolist to tie for this reason. He is free to charge the monopoly

71 [1992] 4 C.M.L.R. 551, para. 149.

profit for the item over which he has market power and, to the extent that he charges more than a competitive price for the tied product, he will be able to obtain that much less for the monopolised product. Ties may well, therefore, have other objectives that may increase efficiency.

One of the most frequent reasons for tying is to meter the use of some input. A royalty for the use of a machine, technology or marketing know-how is accepted as legitimate, but it is not always possible to prevent the licensee from cheating and not disclosing all the use made of the input. Sometimes, therefore the supplier requires the licensee to buy only from him some consumable as a means of measuring use. This argument does not seem to have been put in *Vaessen/Moris*[72] and has not been accepted in the block exemptions.

Another reason for tying is to ensure that a dealer stocks a full line of products and not merely those for which demand is greatest. This is treated in the group exemption for exclusive distribution as an obligation which does not prevent the application of the regulation.

Some monopolists have their charges regulated and may have to take any monopoly profits available in the tied market. For them, tying may extend market power to an unregulated activity. Whether this is desirable depends on whether the regulation itself is desirable.

In Europe, there is considerable concern over tying and other refusals to supply. Profit maximisation may not be such a strong motivating force in Europe, where governments constantly try to persuade private firms to reduce national unemployment and dominant positions may be supported by exclusive rights given by law, sometimes protected even from the market for corporate control — from being acquired by other firms — so their managers do not need to maximise profits to stay in business.

Moreover, efficiency is not the only objective of Community competition law: freedom for other traders to enter and prove themselves in a market is also protected in the interests of the trader. There is, therefore, greater concern about tying in Europe.

In *Hilti*,[73] the Commission condemned unilateral tying under article 86 for the first time. The Court of First Instance confirmed the decision, but Hilti conceded that if it was in a dominant position tying was illegal, so it was not necessary for the Court to decide the issue. On appeal to the Community Court, the matter was not in issue.

Shortly after the decision in *Hilti* was adopted, the Court gave a preliminary ruling in *Télémarketing*.[74] The Compagnie Luxemburgeoise

---

72 [1979] 1 C.M.L.R. 511.
73 [1989] 4 C.M.L.R. 677, on appeal (T–30/89) [1991] E.C.R. II–1439.
74 (311/84) [1985] E.C.R. 3261, at para. 27.

de Télédiffusion (CLT) stopped accepting spot advertisements that indicated a telephone number to be used by the public to obtain further information, unless the number given for Belgium was that of its own subsidiary. The Court ruled that:

> '... an abuse within the meaning of Article 86 is committed where, without any objective necessity, an undertaking holding a dominant position in a particular market reserves to itself or to an undertaking belonging to the same group an ancillary activity which might be carried out by another undertaking as part of its activities on a neighbouring but separate market, with the possibility of eliminating all competition from such undertaking.'

CLT's alleged conduct can be analysed as a tie. The Court relied on its judgment in *Commercial Solvents*[75] where it had held that an unjustified refusal by a dominant firm to supply raw materials to a former competitor downstream in order to reserve for itself the market for a final product may infringe article 86. Similarly, a refusal by a firm dominant over the transmission of advertisements to Belgium to transmit telemarketing spots unless its own answering service were used may be an abuse of a dominant position, in the absence of a technical or commercial justification. The Court did not indicate whether it was guided by the desire to make the market for telemarketing in Belgium more competitive, or to enable a firm to stay in the market when it had not been shown to be less efficient than CLT's subsidiary.

In *Tetra Pak II*,[76] the Commission imposed a fine of 75 million ECUs, the highest ever on a single firm, for various items of conduct by a very dominant firm, including tying. Tetra Pak invented a machine with which one could aseptically make and fill a carton with milk or fruit juice, so that the resulting product would have a shelf life of six months. The Commission found that Tetra Pak was dominant over the machines and cartons for use with them. Tetra Pak also made machines for filling cartons non-aseptically, which permitted a shorter shelf life, and may have been less dominant over this machinery.

Tetra Pak required the customers to whom it supplied machines to use only Tetra Pak cartons and to obtain them from the Tetra Pak subsidiary within the member state where the customer was operating. Sometimes the obligation was limited to the cartons needed for a specific machine, sometimes it was quite general (paragraphs 116–121).

---

75   (6 & 7/73) [1974] E.C.R. 223, 4.3.3.4 below. Compare the judgment of the Australian High Court in *Queensland Wire* [1989] ATPR 40–925, where a refusal to sell a semi-manufactured product, Y-Bars, was condemned on the ground that the conduct made commercial sense only because it would exclude a competitor from the market down stream.
76   Cited at 4.3.2.4 above.

4.3.2.6 *Other exclusionary conduct* — The list of practices is not closed. In *Boosey & Hawkes*,[77] the Commission found that when its distributor started to make its own brass band instruments, Boosey & Hawkes abruptly ceased supply, started vexatious litigation and other harassing tactics while the distributor's production arrangements were still vulnerable. The Commission adopted a decision under article 86 imposing interim measures requiring supplies to be provided.

In *Napier Brown/British Sugar*,[78] the Commission imposed a fine of 3 million ECUs on British Sugar for refusing to supply a former customer who wanted to enter a downstream market, and for imposing a price squeeze.

In *Tetra Pak*,[79] the Commission condemned a dominant firm for acquiring a company that enjoyed an exclusive licence for rival technology that was being developed and having the licence assigned to it.

4.3.3 *Unfair competition also prohibited by article 86*

As explained at 4.3.1 above, article 86 forbids the abusive exploitation of a dominant position. A dominant firm may not charge too much or do other things that harm those with whom it deals, even though overcharging might operate as a signal to attract other firms into the market and so increase competition. The Commission and Court have been concerned as much with fair competition as with free competition.

4.3.3.1 *Unfair prices* — Although anti-competitive conduct adopted by dominant firms is now illegal, the Commission has not avoided the difficulties of deciding when prices and other terms are fair. In several decisions, it has attempted to protect those dealing with dominant firms directly, by reference to the practices listed in article 86.

In *General Motors Continental*,[80] the Court confirmed, in principle, that it is an abuse to charge prices that are excessive in relation to the 'economic value' of a service. In that case, it was not necessary to decide on what criteria prices should be held to be excessive, since the firm had already reduced them very substantially before the Commission intervened. On this ground, and because of other mitigating circumstances, the Court ruled that GMC's dominant position had not been abused.

In *United Brands*,[81] the Commission found that United Brands' prices for bananas in Germany, Denmark and Benelux were excessive on three

77   [1988] 4 C.M.L.R. 67, Boosey & Hawkes submitted, so no final decision on the merits was required.
78   [1990] 4 C.M.L.R. 196.
79   [1990] 4 C.M.L.R. 47, confirmed on appeal, cited at 4.3.1 above.
80   Cited at 4.2.4 above.
81   Cited at 4.2.1 above.

grounds: first, they exceeded prices in Ireland, on which it considered that profits were being earned; secondly, they were 20–40 per cent. higher than the prices of unbranded bananas, and only about half of this differential could be justified by differences in quality and advertising costs; and thirdly, prices for Chiquita bananas were higher than for other brands. On appeal, the Court confirmed that[82]:

> '248. The imposition by an undertaking in a dominant position directly or indirectly of unfair purchase or selling prices is an abuse to which exception can be taken under article 86 of the Treaty.
> 249. It is advisable therefore to ascertain whether the dominant undertaking has made use of the opportunities arising out of its dominant position in such a way as to reap trading benefits which it would not have reaped if there had been normal and sufficiently effective competition.'

This is reminiscent of the approach adopted by the Bundeskartellamt of comparing the prices of the dominant firm in Germany with those in more competitive markets. It has, however, been accepted by the Federal Supreme Court with reserve because of its unreliability. That court has insisted on a considerable additional margin being allowed to the dominant firm.[83]

Recently, in cases where the Court was giving a preliminary ruling and did not have to decide itself whether charges were unfair, it has suggested comparisons with charges made in other markets. In *Lucazeau* v. *SACEM*,[84] the operators of French discothèques complained that SACEM, the French copyright collecting society, was charging more for licences of performing rights than were the similar collecting societies in other member states. The discothèques wanted licences mainly for English language works, but were not permitted to take a licence confined to these at a lower royalty. SACEM replied that different methods of calculation were used in different member states and that the results were not comparable. The Court concluded that:

> '25. When an undertaking holding a dominant position imposes scales of fees for its services which are appreciably higher than those charged in other member states, and where a comparison of the fee levels has been made on a consistent basis, this difference must be regarded as indicative of an abuse of a dominant position. In such a case it is for the undertaking in question to justify the difference by reference to objective dissimilarities between the situation in the member state concerned and the situation prevailing in all the other member states.'

82   (27/76) [1978] E.C.R. 207.
83   *Vitamin B12*, WuW/E (BGH) 1435 (1976) and *Hoffmann-La Roche*, WuW/E (BGH) 1445 (1976).
84   (110/88) [1989] E.C.R. 2521. See also *Bodson* v. *Pompes Funèbres*, cited at 4.3.1 above, at para. 31.

The Court's statement is welcome in that it does admit of justifications. The limit to the usefulness of such a test is that the basis of
comparison is rarely uniform. Quite apart from different methods of
calculation, conditions are frequently so different in different parts of
Europe that foreign experience is of limited value. In one country labour
costs may be higher, but fuel costs lower and so forth. Nevertheless, the
dominant firm is required to analyse and establish reasons for price
differences where the basis of comparison is homogeneous.

In *United Brands*,[85] the Community Court quashed the Commission's
decision that UBC's prices were excessive because the Commission
should at least have asked United Brands about its costs. It also
suggested, without specifying them, that there might be other ways of
objectively determining whether prices were too high.

It seems from paragraph 251 of *United Brands* that if prices do not
exceed costs, including, presumably, a reasonable profit on the capital
used, they cannot be excessive, but in *Lucazeau* v. *SACEM*, the Court
added that if the dominant firm's costs were higher than those of firms
providing the same service elsewhere, prices might be excessive, even if
profits were not. If prices do exceed reasonable costs, it may be necessary
to consider whether they are fair, presumably by comparing prices
elsewhere.

In *United Brands,* the Court added that the 7 per cent. premium
enjoyed by Chiquita bananas over rival brands did not necessarily show
that the price of Chiquita bananas was excessive. It is uncertain whether
a larger premium might have done so. The comparison with unbranded
bananas was not considered by the Court.

Although the Court is prepared to consider justifications, its acceptance that excessive prices may infringe article 86 is disturbing. How is
the economic value of a product to be determined, if not through the
market? A firm may be condemned and fined for having charged a price
which the Commission later decides exceeds the economic value of the
product. The cost plus approach ignores the function of pricing as a
signal encouraging new entrants. If prices and profits are high, new firms
may be attracted into the market over, at least, modest entry barriers.

Many people think that only if natural barriers to entry — those not
imposed by state measures — are very high, should this 'invisible hand'
of competition be sacrificed to price regulation. Because of the impre-
ciseness of the legal criteria, price regulation *ex post facto* — the condemnation of excessive prices in the past — is even more worrying than
regulation for the future. Moreover, price regulation is a far cry from the
liberal inspiration of the treaty, and made more serious where, as in

85   Cited at 4.2.1 above.

United Brands, the Court treated as dominant a firm subject to substantial competition and with no power over price.

The Commission has been loath to decide whether prices are excessive and has left the question of SACEM's pricing policy to the French Courts. It has been condemned by the French competition authority, the Conseil de la Concurrence.[86]

Nevertheless, it is hard to criticise the Court for condemning excessive prices given the wording of article 86(a). Since *United Brands*, the Commission has not been condemning excessive prices. The cases have come to the Court under article 177 from national courts.

The Court has not been consistent when dealing with intellectual property rights. It emphasised in *Volvo* v. *Veng*[87] that the 'very subject matter of' an intellectual property right is the power to exclude others and that there is no duty to grant licences, even in return for a reasonable royalty. Yet immediately afterwards, in that case and in *Renault*,[88] it suggested that charging too much for the product protected by the right or a refusal to sell it might amount to an abuse. If the intellectual property right is justified on the ground that it fosters creative activity,[89] its very function is to enable holders to charge whatever the market will bear. The Court did not have to decide how much monopoly profit is justified by the intellectual property right, but left the impossible task to the national court under article 177. In *Renault*, paragraph 17, it did cite its earlier judgment in *Parke Davis*[90] for the proposition that the holder 'may lawfully call for a return on the amounts which he has invested in order to perfect the protected design.' At the end of each of his opinions on the second question, Advocate General Mischo stated that:

> '"the inventor" is entitled to recover not only his production costs in the strict sense and a reasonable profit margin but also his research and development expenditure.'

He then added in *Renault* that the national court should have to decide the extent to which this had already been recovered from the sale of new cars.

Personally, I regret this 'cost plus' approach. The function of intellectual property rights is to enable the person financing innovation to obtain the prices that the market will bear. If this is accepted in relation to article 36, it should also be accepted under the competition rules. The market should decide on the value of the innovation. If the price a

---

86   *Avis* No. 93–A–05 of 20 April 1993.
87   Cited at 4.2.4 above.
88   Cited at 4.2.4 above, para. 15.
89   *Thetford* v. *Fiamma* (35/87) [1988] E.C.R. 3585, para. 19.
90   (24/67) [1968] E.C.R. 55.

dominant firm may charge be limited to cost plus a reasonable return, the incentive to risky innovation may be drastically reduced.

Even if one accepts, as I do not, that excessive prices for products protected by intellectual property rights are illegal, problems remain. Neither the Court nor the Advocate General expressly stated that the cost would have to include the amounts spent on abortive research and development. Alternatively, they might have stated that the amount spent on successful development should be multiplied by a factor allowing for the risk of its not being profitable. The second criterion would be impossible to apply in a predictable manner.

Some parts of a vehicle need replacement more often than others. It may not be possible to obtain much return on the design of parts that rarely wear out, yet the vehicle would not be saleable without them. Its original price must include a sum for the total cost of designing those parts and making the various components compatible. If only the cost of designing front wing panels, or other parts that need frequent replacement, is used as the basis for ascertaining a reasonable price for those replacement parts, the manufacturer of the whole vehicle may fail to make an adequate return.

It is not possible to reconcile what the Court said about the function of intellectual property rights entitling the holder to refuse a licence with its view that excessive prices might be abusive. Although the view about excessive pricing appears in the Court's ruling, it did not form part of the questions asked by the referring court, so may not have been sufficiently argued. (See also 10.9 below.)

The judgments in *Volvo* and *Renault* are difficult to reconcile with the judgment of the Court of First Instance in *Magill*.[91]

4.3.3.2 *Other unfair terms* — In *BRT* v. *SABAM*,[92] the Court condemned restrictions imposed on the authors, composers and publishers who were members of a performing rights society in so far as these were not justified by the need for the society to strengthen its power when negotiating with national radio and television stations, etc. over copyright licences.

Unfair buying terms for services are also prohibited by article 86. In *Eurofima*,[93] a case that did not proceed to a formal decision, the Commission persuaded an important buyer of railway stock to stop inviting tenders for development contracts on terms that unlimited patent licences be granted to it without further remuneration.

91   (T–69, 70 & 76/89) [1991] E.C.R. II–485.
92   (127/73) [1974] E.C.R. 51 and 313.
93   [1973] C.M.L.R. D217.

4.3.3.3 *Ad hoc discriminatory pricing* — In *United Brands*,[94] the Court confirmed the condemnation of the kind of *ad hoc* price discrimination that enables a firm held to be dominant to maximise its profits by charging what each market will bear. This is an example of the unfair or exploitative practices which article 86 was originally intended to control. In *United Brands*, a supplier charged different prices for identical boxes of bananas delivered free on rail at the port, according to the member state to which the boxes were going. The Court stated that:

'217. The price in any given week is calculated so as to reflect as much as possible the anticipated yellow market price in the following week for each national market.'

It was simple to prove discrimination in this market since boxes of identical branded bananas were delivered free on rail at the two ports of Rotterdam and Bremerhaven, to which the freight was virtually identical. Local VAT charges and freight from the ports were paid by United Brands' customers. Prices were set when the bananas were already at sea in answer to offers from the distributor/ripeners. At that time the supply for the following week was fixed by the quantity of bananas at sea and it might have been argued that price discrimination encouraged United Brands to give priority to those areas where bananas were most strongly wanted. To this the Court objected:

'229. The interplay of supply and demand should, owing to its nature, only be applied at each stage where it is really manifest.

230. The mechanisms of the market are adversely affected if the price is calculated by leaving out one stage of the market and taking into account the law of supply and demand as between the vendor and the ultimate consumer and not as between vendor (UBC) and the purchaser (the ripener distributors). ...

232. These discriminatory prices, which varied according to the circumstances of the Member States, were just so many obstacles to the free movement of goods and their effect was intensified by the clause forbidding the resale of bananas while still green and by reducing the deliveries of the quantities ordered.'

UBC claimed that the weekly variations in price were due to various factors that were hard to predict when a decision was taken in the tropics as to the number of bananas to be shipped, such as weather, differing availability of other fruit, holidays, strikes, government measures and currency fluctuations. One might think that these factors, leading to a temporary local shortage in some weeks, would lead to short term monopoly rents to be taken by either United Brands, its distributor/ripeners or the retailers. In other weeks, there might be a surplus of

94   Cited at 4.2.1 above.

which United Brands would have difficulty in disposing and prices would not cover average costs.

The Court's view that it should not be United Brands that took the risk of these fluctuations has several disadvantages. First, since distributors were prohibited from selling the bananas while they were still green and were capable of distant travel, the distributors in places where the prices were low were not entitled to sell to distributors for places where they were higher. The distributors did not compete with each other. The Court, however, condemned the clause on the ground that it operated as an export deterrent.

Secondly, even when this restriction was amended after it had been found to infringe article 86 to entitle the distributors to sell to other approve banana ripeners, it is not clear that once the bananas had arrived in the European ports the distributors had sufficient knowledge of the market as a whole to ensure that the bananas would go to places where the demand was strongest. It may be that they would have developed resources to monitor the various markets in the longer term.

More important is the incentive that the Court gave to United Brands to do its own distribution and ripening.

Without discussing these considerations, the Court spoke of adverse effects on the mechanism of the market, but did not spell out what these were. It ignored the function of prices in signalling to suppliers the markets in which their services are most valued.

It is hoped that the prohibition of discriminatory pricing to maximise profits will be confined to geographical discrimination backed by territorial protection, which shows up the lack of unity of the common market.[95] In the United States, the Robinson Patman Act, which prohibits price discrimination generally, has been very seriously and cogently attacked in the literature, by both White House task forces and in 1977 by the Department of Justice, for interfering with price competition.

Many markets, especially for components, are served by few suppliers, and in such markets overt price competition is unlikely, even in the absence of collusion. Each firm knows that it will not gain market share by charging less than its competitors since overt price cuts will be matched immediately, so it will not increase its market share. In such markets, the only sort of price competition likely is in secret discounts to important buyers who bargain toughly. It is hoped that this will not be discouraged by fears of article 86.

4.3.3.4 *Refusal to supply* — There is considerable case law on refusals to

95　See, e.g., *Tetra Pak II* [1992] 4 C.M.L.R. 551, at paras. 154–155 and 160.

supply. In *Commercial Solvents* v. *Commission*,[96] the Court upheld the Commission's decision that Commercial Solvents, the only producer in the world on an industrial scale of raw materials from which the drug ethambutol could be made, enjoyed a dominant position in the common market. The Court confirmed that it was abusive to refuse to supply the raw material to Zoja, one of three makers of ethambutol in the common market. The basis of the decision is not entirely clear. Zoja had asked to be released from its contract to buy the raw materials, but when it became impossible to buy them elsewhere, Zoja complained to the Commission that it could no longer obtain them from Commercial Solvents or its subsidiary. The Commission ordered that minimum quantities be supplied, but it is not clear whether it was protecting the interest of Zoja in carrying on a profitable trade, which it had developed, or whether it was protecting the interests of those who paid for the drug.

Advocate General Warner treated the refusal to supply as an extreme example of discrimination contrary to article 86(1)(d) — there was no price at which Zoja could obtain supplies of the drug. Nevertheless, he suggested that there might be a justification for not supplying a product over which a firm is dominant. He suggested that it might be lawful never to supply a new product, but to manufacture the derivative product oneself from the beginning. Certainly, such a possible justification would increase the incentive to invest in the original innovation.

There were pro-competitive reasons for objecting to the elimination of Zoja as an independent maker of ethambutol. Commercial Solvents was the only maker of the raw materials in the world and barriers to entry, consisting of know-how, seem to have been high. Zoja was one of only three makers of the derivative in the common market and had partially overcome the barriers to entry created by patents. Its demand for supplies of the raw material would make it easier for a new entrant at the level of the raw materials to use its capacity profitably, but this argument was not urged.

The Court confirmed the Commmission's decision but did not distinguish between free and fair competition, although one of the judges, Pescatore, has stated in public that the Court had to come to the help of a small producer, Zoja. The precedent has been extended to cases where dominance was less marked, even transitory, and the customer far less important.

In *ABG*,[97] BP had refused to supply petrol to a Dutch co-operative that had ceased to be a regular customer some months before a shortage of crude oil developed in 1973 when OPEC first raised prices and

---

96   Cited at 4.3.2.5 above.
97   Cited at 4.2.4 above.

boycotted the Netherlands. The Commission alleged that in a period of crisis, buyers could obtain petrol only from their former suppliers. Such a supplier, therefore, enjoyed a dominant position over its former customers (4.2.4 above). It reasoned that BP should have supplied all its customers with the same proportion of the amounts it had supplied in an earlier period, which, it suggested, might be 12 months. Mr. Warner, the Advocate General, however, said on appeal[98]:

> 'In my opinion such a rule, which manifestly is not expressed in article 86, could be held to be implicit in the terms of that article only if it were equitable, practical and generally accepted. It appears to me that it would be none of these things.'

It would be unfair to contractual and regular customers. It would be impractical in that suppliers would not know when the duty to supply arose as it is seldom possible to tell how long a crisis will last. Moreover, no such rule is generally accepted — the Rijksbureau, the Dutch government body set up to help those with insufficient supplies of petrol, used different formulae at different times when it was supporting ABG.

The Court quashed the decision, holding on cumulative grounds that the reduction of supplies to ABG was not an abuse. Its judgment is so specific that it is unlikely to be a precedent in future, so Mr. Warner's opinion is important.

In *Hugin/Liptons*,[99] the Commission condemned Hugin, which it found to be in a dominant position over the spare parts for the cash registers it made, for ceasing to supply its former exclusive distributor for the United Kingdom with the spares it needed to repair and maintain the large number of Hugin cash registers it had bought for renting out. To British lawyers and businessmen, the decision came as a surprise. Liptons could have protected itself by entering into a long term contract for the supply of spares before investing in machines. The Commission provided it with a windfall gain. Belgian exclusive dealers, however, are protected against termination of their contracts, so such protection must seem natural in some member states.

The refusal to supply might be seen as anti-competitive in that it restricted Lipton's ability to rent out Hugin registers. Hugin, however, was not dominant in the supply of registers and we are not told there was any scarcity of registers to hire.

The precedent was ignored in *Renault*,[100] and *Volvo* v. *Veng*,[101] where the spare parts were protected by intellectual property rights, on the

98   At 1539 (E.C.R.).
99   Cited at 4.2.4 above. See that section generally.
100 Cited at 4.2.4 above.
101 Cited at 4.2.4 above.

ground that the exclusive right is part of the very subject matter of the right (4.3.3.1 above). Nevertheless, the Court ruled that it might be abusive neither to give independent repairers a licence, nor to supply them with parts on reasonable terms. Perceived *ex ante*, the exclusive rights encourage investment by making it possible to charge high prices. So it is difficult to reconcile the requirement to supply or license with the Court's statement about the specific subject matter of the right. It was, however, relied on by the Court of First Instance in *Magill* (10.9 below).

In *Hugin*, despite an export ban accepted by another dealer, which prevented Liptons from obtaining supplies indirectly, the Court quashed the decision on the ground that the refusal to supply a firm that operates only locally does not affect trade between member states. It did not consider whether the refusal to supply was abusive.

In *United Brands*,[102] the Court confirmed the Commission's condemnation of the reduction in supplies to Olesen, one of United Brands' distributors in Denmark. United Brands' ripener/distributors were allowed to handle competing goods and in 1969, Olesen had become the only Danish distributor for a rival brand 'Dole' supplied by the Standard Fruit Company. Four years later, Olesen had taken part in an advertising campaign for Dole bananas, and United Brands argued that Olesen was selling fewer and fewer Chiquita bananas, while deliberately pushing Dole bananas. United Brands then reduced its supplies to Olesen. The Court's attitude to this reduction in supplies to a customer, far less important than was Zoja in *Commercial Solvents*, by a firm with no power over price was strong:

> '182. ... it is advisable to assert positively from the outset that an undertaking in a dominant position for the purpose of marketing a product — which cashes in on the reputation of a brand name known and valued by consumers — cannot stop supplying a long standing customer who abides by regular commercial practice, if the orders placed by this customer are in no way out of the ordinary.'

The Court went on to consider whether United Brands' conduct was justified and held that a dominant firm can take only reasonable steps to ensure that its produce is properly sold. If Olesen was spoiling the bananas, presumably United Brands should have complained to Olesen and kept records of its complaints before cutting off supplies, instead of doing nothing for four years.

The Court considered also that United Brands' conduct had interfered seriously with the independence of small and medium sized firms. It would discourage independent conduct by other ripener/distributors, and this may explain its concern. It had earlier observed that the

102   Cited at 4.2.1 above.

restriction on selling green bananas prevented Olesen from obtaining Chiquita bananas from other ripener/distributors.

In *Télémarketing*,[103] the Court treated as a refusal to supply what might be called a tie.

4.3.4 Refusals to deal based on grounds of nationality

Refusals to supply have been condemned not only when they were thought unfair or restrictive of competition, but also when based on grounds of nationality. In *GVL*,[104] the Court confirmed that it was abusive for the only collecting society in Germany for a particular kind of copyright to be prepared to collect royalties for artists established outside the Federal Republic only if they were of German nationality. Article 7 prohibits discrimination on grounds of nationality and article 86 has been used to implement it.

4.4 Conclusion

Cases decided under article 86 in the last two and a half decades have given rise to concern. From the Court's judgment in *United Brands*,[105] it seems that firms meeting substantial competition may be treated as dominant if they have over 45 per cent. of the market and are considerably larger than their competitors. Many firms with no power over price may find themselves in a dominant position under this test. Dominance seems to be decided as a matter of status, independently of the particular abuse being alleged, although when the abuse is structural, as in the case of mergers, the precedents may develop wider concepts of a relevant market. Indeed, in the last decade the Court has been suggesting that markets may be wider than seemed likely earlier. In the past, small markets have been investigated for dominance, for example Hugin spare parts, and the certification of Opel cars bought abroad by residents as being fit to be driven on Belgian roads.[106]

Once dominant, a firm may not discriminate, at least geographically. It may, and probably should, charge more for supplying in small quantities or at a distance, when freight charges, etc., are borne by the supplier, but it seems not to be permitted to earn substantially higher profits in one member state than in others. Nevertheless, I hope that dominant firms may still be allowed to give secret discounts to important customers to secure an order. Were they not, the competitive process would be considerably impaired.

103   Cited at 4.3.2.5 above.
104   (7/82) [1983] E.C.R. 483.
105   Cited at 4.2.1 above.
106   *General Motors Continental*, cited at 4.2.4 above.

Mainstream economists, such as J. Bain, working in the 1950s, were concerned that entry barriers were pervasive, and feared systematic price discrimination, such as loyalty discounts, might inhibit entry. The UK Monopolies and Mergers Commission articulated this theory cogently in its *Report on the Supply of Metal Containers*.[107] Given the European interest in protecting competitors and its associated fear of entry barriers that would keep out even less efficient firms, it is not surprising that loyalty discounts have been attacked under article 86. It is, however, difficult to advise an important firm how to compete effectively without incurring the risk of being fined.

The prohibition on overcharging by firms with only slight market power is also worrying. Article 86(a) forbids unfair prices, but does not set up any machinery for determining fair prices. It is difficult to reconcile price regulation with competition in the same market. High profits are the signal attracting new firms into a market. The problems are particularly acute where there are intellectual property rights encouraging innovation by enabling the holder to charge more.

Inability to terminate dealers is also worrying from the point of view of providing an efficient service to customers. Many goods and services need careful handling or services at the point of sale. These may be ensured only if the manufacturer or brand owner can discipline his dealers, ultimately by dismissal. Firms subsequently found to be dominant appear to be in danger of being fined if they have carried out such discipline, unless they can justify each particular action to the Commission. The consequences of a complaint by a dealer refused supplies are very serious unless the dominant firm keeps careful records of complaints it has made to the dealer about its competence.

My fear is that the competition rules are not being used to enable efficient firms to expand at the expense of the less efficient, but to protect smaller and medium sized firms at the expense of efficient or larger firms. I am concerned that the interests of consumers, and the economy as a whole, in the encouragement of efficiency by firms of any size is being subordinated to the interests of smaller traders.

The Competition Department of the Commission was staffed for many years largely by jurists to whom justice between two parties may seem important, especially in the light of some of the Continental laws protecting existing traders, and whose education has not encouraged them to think at the margin, to look to the effects of a ruling on the operation of the economy as a whole, nor to ensure that incentives to efficient performance are provided. The attitudes of many officials and of the Court, however, are becoming far more flexible.

107   1970 H.C.P 6.

4.5 Bibliography

Gregory B. Adams, 'Antitrust Constraints on Single Firm Refusals to deal by Monopolists in the European Economic Community and the United States' (1985) 20 Texas Intl. Law Jnl. 1.

Areeda and *Turner*, 'Predatory Pricing and Related Practices under Section 2 of the Sherman Act', 88 Harv. L.Rev. 697 (1975).

Charles Baden Fuller, 'Article 86 EEC: Economic Analysis of the Existence of a Dominant Position' [1979] 4 E.L.R. 423.

William Bishop, 'Price Discrimination under Article 86; Political Economy in the European Court' (1981) 44 M.L.R. 282.

——, Essay on predatory pricing in a forthcoming volume to be published in my honour, eds. Peter Alexiadis and John Kallaugher, Sweet and Maxwell.

Frank H. Easterbrook, 'Monopolization: Past, Present Future,' 61 Antitrust Law Journal 99.

Eleanor Fox, 'Abuse of a Dominant Position under the Treaty of Rome — a Comparison with U.S. Law,' in Barry Hawk (ed.) [1983] *Fordham Corporate Law Institute*, also reply by *V. Korah*, 367 and 423.

Luc Gyselen, 'Abuse of Monopoly Power Within the Meaning of Article 86 of the EEC Treaty: Recent Developments' [1989] *Fordham Corporate Law Institute* 597.

René Joliet, *Monopolization* — cited in general Bibliography.

——, 'Le controle des Monopoles dans la CEE' [1976] 4949 Journal des Tribunaux 217.

John Kallaugher, notes for a conference organised by ESC in London on 27 March 1990.

Thomas E. Kauper, 'Whither Article 86? Observations on Excessive Prices and Refusals to Deal' [1989] *Fordham Corporate Law Institute* 651.

Valentine Korah, 'Interpretation and Application of Article 86 of the Treaty of Rome: Abuse of Dominant Position within the Common Market' (1978) 53 *Notre Dame Lawyer* 768.

——, 'The Control of Mergers under Article 86 of the Rome Treaty: Continental Can' (1973) 26 C.L.P. 82.

——, 'Concept of a Dominant Position within the Meaning of Article 86' (1980) 17 C.M.L.Rev. 395.

——, Case note on *Michelin* (1982) 7 E.L.R. 130.

——, 'The paucity of Economic analysis in the EEC decisions on competition — Tetra Pak II,' *Current Legal Problems* 148.

Richard Rapp, 'Predatory pricing and entry deterring strategies: the economics of *AKZO*' [1986] E.C.L.R. 233.

John Temple Lang, 'Some Aspects of Abuse of Dominant Positions in European Community Antitrust Law' (1979) 3 *Fordham International Law Forum* 1.

——, 'Monopolisation and the definition of "abuse" of a dominant position under Article 86 EEC treaty' (1979) 16 C.M.L.Rev. 345.

Jacques A. Van Damme, (ed.), 1977 Bruges Week, *Regulating the Behaviour of Monopolies and Dominant Undertakings in Community Law*.

Lucio Zanon, 'Price Discrimination and Hoffmann-la Roche' [1981] 15 J.W.T.L.
305.
——, 'Price Discrimination under Article 86 of the EEC Treaty: A Comment on
the *UBC* Case' (1982) 31 I.C.L.Q. 36.

5 Enforcement under Regulation 17

5.1 Introduction

If the competition rules are to be effective in helping to integrate the common market and improve efficiency and market access, they must be enforced. The sanction of nullity under article 85(2) of the treaty may be applied by national courts or through the advice given by lawyers and requires no action at Community level. Nullity is, however insufficient to control horizontal agreements, those between producers or dealers of similar products at the same trading levels. Their interests are likely to remain congruent and they might well implement anti-competitive agreements even if they are not enforceable in the courts.

Civil judges, who are usually generalists rather than experts in competition law and policy, are likely to find the problems difficult. So, the sanction of nullity of contract has grave drawbacks. The application of article 86 is particularly difficult for non-specialist courts and has been enforced under the first implementing regulation of the Community.

Until 1962, there was a little enforcement of the competition rules by the competent authorities in the Federal Republic of Germany, but in that year the Council adopted the first implementing regulation, no. 17 (set out in Appendix II). This empowered the Commission to enforce the competition rules in various ways and it was hoped that it would lead to their uniform interpretation and application, despite the very different attitudes towards competition and various kinds of distortion of it adopted by national laws.

At that time there was, for instance, no competition law in Italy, Belgium or Luxembourg, while the attitude in the Federal Republic of Germany towards vertical agreements between a single manufacturer and each of its dealers was more favourable than that towards horizontal agreements between those competing with each other, and exemptions were discretionary. The French practice, however, was stricter towards vertical agreements than towards horizontal, because, when most European countries had introduced rationing to cope with the shortages after the second world war, it was concerned that all dealers should be able to obtain supplies fairly. If the conditions under French law for exemption applied, exemption was automatic.

Regulation 17 resolved these differences by providing for a single Community authority with exclusive power to grant exemptions. The conditions for exemption in article 85(3) are so vague that the Commission has considerable discretion in appreciation, whether or not exemptions are theoretically automatic when the conditions of article 85(3) apply.

The provisions under the EEA treaty are similar. By virtue of article 56, where the agreements affect trade only between the EFTA states, the EFTA Surveillance Authority (ESA) is the relevant authority. Where trade between EC member states is affected, the Commission is the competent authority. In other cases, where trade between an EFTA and an EC member state is affected, the ESA has competence if one third of the turnover of the undertakings concerned is in the EFTA area. It seems that many EFTA firms have more than two-thirds of their turnover in the EC, so much of the work will be done by the Commission.

In order to ensure uniform standards, the two authorities are required by article 58 to co-operate with each other. It will be interesting to see whether the ESA follows the practice of the Commission in finding that most exclusive agreements infringe article 53, or whether it is more willing to follow the judgments of the Court.

5.2 Basic provision (article 1)

The regulation confirms that conduct prohibited by articles 85 and 86 is illegal, even if there has been no prior decision to that effect. Community law is harsh for those who reasonably thought that their conduct was not illegal. While the legality of many agreements under article 85 is now fairly clear, that of others depends on an analysis of the market or of the need for ancillary restrictions, and it is almost always hard to give clear advice in relation to article 86.

5.3 Negative clearance (article 2)

The Commission may certify that, on the basis of the facts in its possession, there are no grounds under article 85(1) or article 86 for action on its part in respect of an agreement, decision or practice. A negative clearance is not an exemption (5.6 below), but a statement of the Commission's opinion, which probably does not bind either national courts or the Community Court, because the terms of the decision are so limited. Where full disclosure has been made, however, negative clearance should be taken into account by national courts when deciding whether an agreement is invalid under article 85(2).[1]

---

1 See 6.3.4 below for the case law on comfort letters. A decision, binding on the parties to whom it is addressed, can hardly have less effect.

5.4 Termination of infringement (article 3)

The Commission may order the parties to terminate an infringement. This is the main way in which the competition rules can be enforced. With no provision for treble damages, actions for tort in national courts have not developed as in the United States. The procedure leading up to a decision under article 3 will be described shortly at 5.8–5.8.3 below. The Commission is required to define the conduct that is to be terminated, so that the parties may know what is forbidden by the decision.[2] A decision under article 3 is important to the parties, who are therefore protected by the requirement that they be heard. Appeals from such a decision lie to the Court of First Instance, with a further appeal, limited to points of law, to the Community Court.

Sometimes the Commission acts under article 3 on its own initiative, sometimes on the basis of the notification of an agreement to it by the parties thereto (5.5 below), but frequently it acts on a complaint. Although the procedure is inquisitorial, when there is a complainant which continues to take an active part in the proceedings, it may become almost adversarial. A complainant, as well as the parties, has a right to be heard before the Commission makes a decision. A complainant, however, is not entitled to a formal decision: provided that the Commission considers the complaint carefully and gives a good reason for not pursuing it, it may reject the complaint without taking a decision under article 3.[3]

The Community Court held in *Camera Care*[4] that the Commission may also grant interim relief to a complainant when there is immediate danger of serious and irreparable harm. Such decisions have been rare and cannot be adopted rapidly. The Commission has substantial discretion whether to take such measures, and it is difficult to force it to do so. Nevertheless, in *La Cinq*,[5] the Court of First Instance quashed the Commission's decision not to grant interim measures on the ground that it is not necessary to establish an infringement with certainty: *prima facie* evidence is enough. Moreover it objected to the Commission's finding that there was no danger of serious and irreparable harm.

Interlocutory relief is obtainable far faster in the English High Court (6.1 below). The complainant there is liable for the defendant's costs and risks having to compensate him if he eventually loses on the merits. The Commission may also require an undertaking to that effect as a

---

2   Warner A.G. in *Commercial Solvents* (6 & 7/73) [1974] E.C.R. 223, at 271–273.
3   *Automec II* (T–24/90) [1992] 5 C.M.L.R. 431, described at 6.1 below.
4   (792/79R) [1980] E.C.R. 119. See *La Cinq* (T–44/90) [1992] 4 C.M.L.R. 449.
5   (T–44/90) [1992] E.C.R. II–1.

condition of granting relief. In some other member states it takes longer
to get injunctions and in some no interim relief is possible.

5.5 Notification (articles 4 and 5)

A system of notification has been established under articles 4 and 5 of
regulation 17. Article 4 applies to 'new agreements': those made after the
regulation came into force on 6 February 1962 — and article 5 to 'old
agreements': those made before. A new group of 'old agreements' was
added by the accessions of the new member states in 1973, 1981 and 1986
and others will probably be added if Austria, Finland, Norway and
Sweden join the European Union (see 1.7 above). 'Accession agreements' is a technical term comprising agreements which became subject
to article 85 only because of the accession of new member states. These
include agreements that restrict competition between undertakings trading in the new member states, or possibly between those in one of them
and a firm in one of the existing member states. The latter may well,
however, already have infringed article 85(1).

Both articles provide that an agreement must be notified if the parties
wish it to be exempt. There is no duty to notify, but the possibility of
exemption or comfort letter is one incentive and freedom from fines
under article 15(5) is another.[6] Exemption is not possible for the period
before notification. There are, however, certain agreements listed in
article 4(2), as amended, that may be exempted retrospectively to a date
before notification. These are agreements that in 1962 were thought to
do least harm to competition and the integration of the common market,
and a few others that have been added subsequently. They represent an
attempt by the Commission and Council to limit the number of notifications of innocuous agreements with which the Commission does not
have sufficient staff to deal.

5.5.1 Reorganisation of DGIV, the Competition Department

Notifications are being dealt with faster than formerly. In 1984, the
Competition Department[7] was reorganised so that Directorates B, C
and D, which are responsible for handling individual agreements, each
specialise in a particular industry. Consequently, when a case handler
first reads a notification he should already be familiar with the industry.

To prevent one industry being treated differently from another without good reason, a co-ordination division was established in Directorate
A, which is also responsible for new policies and legislation. Originally,

6 See 5.10 below.
7 See glossary.

one official was responsible for technology licences, others for horizontal agreements and so forth. Now they seem to be less specialised.

Each case handler is now responsible for conducting his own inspections. The integration of the roles of detective and decider has been much criticised on the ground that a detective may find it difficult fairly to assess the evidence. To some extent the greater willingness of the Court of First Instance to quash decisions on the ground that the Commission's procedures have been unfair has lessened the need to return to the old procedure where the roles were separate. Nevertheless a firm may have to suffer the cost and trauma of a complete investigation including an adverse decision, before it can appeal.

The reorganisation of DGIV has helped to speed up the Commission's procedures considerably and led to its policy being applied more efficiently. Nevertheless, the Commission manages to adopt 20 formal decisions or fewer in most years.[8] By the end of 1992 the average period for scrutinising notifications of co-operative joint ventures was over two years.

At the end of 1992, the Commission decided further to speed up its vetting of notifications, starting with structural co-operative joint ventures.[9] Within two months of receiving all the information, the Commission has promised to inform the parties in writing whether their agreement gives rise to doubts concerning its compatibility with the competition rules. If not, they will receive a comfort letter. If an actual decision is required, the process will take longer. This is apart from delays caused by the need for translations for publication in the *Official Journal*.

5.5.2 *Forms for notification (regulation 27)*

Regulation 27/62, as amended,[10] prescribes form A/B to be used when notifying an agreement. An identical form must be used for notifications under the EEA treaty. A far more complicated form CO is required for notifying mergers (Chapter 12 below). Form A/B is being redrafted along the lines of form CO to require considerably more information at least for structural joint ventures so that the Commission can deal with them far faster, but it may apply to notifications of all sorts of agreements. Thirteen copies have been required under regulation 17 since the

---

8   In 1992, 20, Commission's *22nd Annual Report*, p. 83; in 1991, 13, Commission's *22nd Annual Report*, p.60.
9   Those where substantial investment is required. Commission's *22nd Annual Report*, for 1992, points 122–124.
10   By reg. 2526/85. The same form is appended to the EEA treaty.

accession of Spain and Portugal at the beginning of 1986, one for the Commission and one for each member state. Since 1994, a fourteenth copy has been required for the EFTA Surveillance Authority. Fewer copies of supporting material need be sent but, if they are not duplicated, they will probably not be seen by the competent authorities in member states, which advise the Commission. In *Distillers*,[11] the Community Court held that the use of form A/B is compulsory. In *Dutch Book Association* v. *Eldi Records*,[12] however, it held:

> '11. ... that an agreement may be regarded as properly notified in its entirety and may therefore benefit from the effects of an agreement which has been notified, where its entire text has been attached to the notification form, even though only some of the clauses of the agreement are quoted on the form, provided that the description given there constitutes a fair and accurate record of the provisions which at the time were considered most important.'

Parties are asked for information about the market, their competitors and any entry barriers. They should make a reasonable attempt to answer carefully and truthfully all the questions on the form and in the annex attached to the regulation. For the notification to be effective, the information furnished must be complete and in accordance with the facts. It is easier to ensure that the information is complete now that form A/B requires more detailed information under Regulation 2526/85.[13]

Although form A/B provides for applications for negative clearance as well as for exemption, an application for negative clearance does not qualify as a request for exemption. Nor does it prevent the imposition of fines.[14] Consequently, most applications for negative clearance are accompanied by a request in the alternative for exemption. This can be done at the same time and on the same form. One has also to make out a case that, if the Commission thinks the agreement is caught by article 85(1), it merits exemption.

A complaint need not be made on any particular form, although form C has been prepared for this purpose by the Commission. If one wants the Commission to commence proceedings, however, it is sensible to use it, as it saves the Commission from having to take one internal administrative step.

In any sort of notification, it is sensible to separate the confidential parts from the rest and even to prepare a non-confidential version of the

---

11   (30/78) [1980] E.C.R. 2229.
12   (106/79) [1980] E.C.R. 1137.
13   The new form being prepared will request even more information.
14   *John Deere* [1985] 2 C.M.L.R. 554.

confidential part, so that the expurgated version can be shown to any other parties interested.

5.5.3 *Whether to notify*

This important question will be postponed until 6.4, since the decision affects the enforceability of contracts.

5.6 Exemption (articles 6–9) and comfort letters

The Commission was given exclusive competence to grant individual exemptions by article 9(1) of regulation 17. By virtue of article 6(1), a decision exercising this power should state a date from which the exemption should take effect. Except for agreements excused from notification, no exemption may be given under article 6(1) for a period before the agreement was notified nor, according to Commission practice, will it be given unless the agreement qualifies therefor as it stands.

Sometimes the Commission brings pressure on the parties to amend their agreement so as to eliminate or alter provisions that the Commission considers are unduly restrictive or not necessary to obtain the benefits that result from the agreement. Once this is done, an exemption may be given from the date of the amendments.

As mentioned at 3.2 above, the Commission has also adopted regulations granting exemptions to classes of agreement, but they are not made under regulation 17. An opposition procedure has been established under some of the group exemptions.[15] These provide that an undertaking may notify its agreement and, if the Commission does not oppose the exemption within six months or withdraws its opposition at any time, the agreement will be exempt under the group exemption. If the Commission opposes the exemption of an agreement notified under the opposition procedure,[16] regulation 17 applies to the agreement. By not opposing or at any time withdrawing its opposition to the exemption, however, the Commission can ensure that an exemption is granted by a group exemption without having to take all the procedural steps required for an individual one.

Far more often than granting an individual exemption, the Commission sends a 'comfort letter,' informing the parties that there is no reason for it to take further action and that it is closing the file. There are three grounds for so doing. First, the Commission may state that from the facts it has, the agreement does not appear to infringe article 85(1) or,

15 The procedure started with the group exemption for patent licensing agreements and continues to operate under the group exemption for r & d, considered at 13.5 below.
16 See 10.5.4. below.

secondly, that it falls within a group exemption. Either kind of letter is helpful, since a national court should take it into account when asked to enforce a contract.[17] A letter stating that the agreement merits exemption may be a Trojan horse, as it implies that the agreement falls within the prohibition of article 85(1) and national courts have no power to grant the exemption (6.3.4 below).

Sometimes, too, the Commission sends 'discomfort letters' before closing the file. This would make it dangerous not to abrogate the provisions to which the Commission objects.

Attention must be given by businessmen and their advisers to the question whether provisions unlikely to be accepted by the Commission should be abrogated before notification, or whether they should be included in the hope that the Commission may not immediately consider the agreement. The restrictions on competition or parallel imports may be useful meanwhile.

A business considering adopting this course must be aware of the drawbacks involved. It will not be possible to enforce in national courts clauses that are clearly contrary to article 85(1). Some black clauses may prevent the application of a group exemption. The time gained is no longer measured in years, but in months.

A further disadvantage of including black clauses is that they may encourage the Commission to give priority to the agreement and the case handler may start his investigation with the attitude of a crusader, believing that the parties are trying to restrict competition. It may be difficult to persuade him to change his mind once he has taken a preliminary view.

Many firms take the view that, unless the agreement has only insignificant effects on competition, there is much to be said for excluding the sort of clause that is habitually condemned: price fixing, market sharing, especially the insulation of national markets, where these clauses are not necessary ancillary parts of a pro-competitive transaction, collective boycotts and reciprocal exclusive dealing (Chapter 7 below). Such clauses are likely to attract immediate enforcement proceedings. It is often not clear whether other clauses are anti-competitive and these may be left in, to be the subject of negotiation with the Commission, unless the need to enforce the contract expeditiously is vital.

As soon as the Commission opens proceedings, it will be vital to negotiate about the removal of any anti-competitive provisions if an exemption of others is desired.

In the case of 'old agreements,' however, the decision whether to

17   *Guérlain* (253/78 & 1–3/79) [1980] E.C.R. 2327.

abrogate any anti-competitive clauses is less important. Under article 7, the 'dirty past' may be swept under the carpet. Once agreements are amended so as not to infringe article 85(1) or to merit exemption, the Commission has power to validate them retrospectively, even if they included anti-competitive provisions. Where, however, one of the parties does not consent to the notification, article 7 cannot be invoked against it. This may be important to protect those who have relied on the invalidity of some of the provisions. Where standard forms are used, and the wording remains identical with those being used at the relevant date, the agreement will be treated as old.[18] This may be important, since standard forms which may not have changed over the years are often used for terms of sale or distribution agreements. Even if the terms have changed, but the restrictions have not, the agreements would qualify as 'old'. In *Dutch Book Association* v. *Eldi*,[19] the Community Court held that the notification of the complete text of an old agreement appended to form B in due time conferred provisional validity on all the provisions within its original scope, even though attention was not drawn to clauses that did not appear restrictive in 1963. Since notification, some classes of books had ceased to come within the terms of the restrictions, but the Court stated that this would not prevent the agreements from being old if the original class books were brought in again.

By virtue of article 8, exemption may be granted subject to conditions and obligations and must be limited in time. Some exemptions have been renewed, although the conditions for the exemption may be stricter if the firms have grown meanwhile. Exemptions may also be withdrawn by the Commission when there is a change in the circumstances basic to the grant of the exemption, or where, for example, the decision was based on incorrect or incomplete information.

5.7 Obtaining information (articles 11–14)

The Commission may find much of the information it requires in its files of notifications and, as the new form A/B came into use in 1985, more market information has been included, but more is sometimes required. Frequently, the Commission starts proceedings on the basis of a complaint made under article 3, in which case the complainant may provide a considerable amount of information both about the market and the conduct of the firm suspected of an infringement. The Commission may receive replies to informal enquiries, complaints from those harmed by a practice or from Members of the European Parliament, or

18   *Rochas* v. *Bitsch* (1/70) [1970] E.C.R. 515.
19   Cited at 5.5.2 above.

may read the information in the press. It also has two ways in which it may obtain information under regulation 17.

5.7.1 Requests for information (article 11)

'11(1). ... [T]he Commission may obtain all necessary information from the Governments and competent authorities of the Member States and from undertakings and associations of undertakings.'

There is probably no duty to comply with a request for information, but if the information be supplied, it must be prepared carefully, as small penalties may be imposed under articles 15(1) and 16 for supplying false information deliberately or negligently. Moreover, it may be difficult to convince officials later that it was inaccurate. If no information is supplied or not as much as is requested, however, the Commission may take a decision under article 11(5), in which case, if the information requested is not supplied within the time allowed, the Commission may impose a small fine under article 15(1)(b) or daily penalties under article 16. This procedure would involve two decisions, one under article 11(5) requiring the information to be furnished and another under article 15 or 16 imposing the fine or penalty.

Officials may experience considerable difficulty in obtaining a decision from the members of the Commission. Very few lawyers choose to be obstructive and leave the official to get a decision if he can, although this has the advantage that the Commission is required to specify more precisely what information is required. Most think, however, that it is more important not to antagonise the person handling the case from day to day and who will have considerable influence over the final decision.

The Commission does not know how firms keep their files, and it may ask questions which it would be time-consuming to answer. Often a prompt telephone call to Brussels analysing the difficulties will result in the case handler agreeing to accept information more readily obtainable that will serve his purpose. Sometimes, he may ask for the information that can easily be provided to be sent within the deadline but give a longer period to answer other questions. The deadlines for answering questions are short, seldom more than four to six weeks. Priority should be given to answering requests for information and the task of supervision should be given to someone intelligent. He may have to delegate a good deal of his normal work to devote time and thought to this. Preliminary estimates should not be lightly given as, if they are later retracted, the Commission may believe the first statement as it did in *United Brands*.[20] False information can easily be given through

---

20   [1976] 1 C.M.L.R. D28, para. 100; the retraction is made clear by the Court on appeal at (27/76) [1978] E.C.R. 207, para. 243.

carelessness. One firm, asked for its share of the market in the whole EC and in each member state, produced figures for its share of sales from America in each area, as those were the figures readily available. These far larger market shares made its conduct appear much more serious. Fortunately, the error was spotted and corrected before the information was sent. It is vital to ask of whoever answers the questions supplementary questions about the sources from which information was obtained.

The Commission's power is to obtain all 'necessary information.' The Commission has wide discretion to decide whether particular information is necessary.[21] It is difficult to establish that information required is not necessary. If some utterly irrelevant information is requested, one may refuse to provide it, giving reasons. The Commission might accept these, but if not, might compel the information by a decision under article 11(5), as it did in *RAI/UNITEL*.[22] An appeal under article 173 can be taken to the Court of First Instance against this, but would be advisable only in an extreme case. The information would have to be utterly irrelevant not to be necessary. In *Acciaieria di Brescia* v. *High Authority*[23] the Court held under the ECSC Treaty that the High Authority was entitled to demand accounts of engineering as well as coal and steel production in order to see that the dividing line between the EC and ECSC treaties had been properly drawn. It also suggested that officials might use information found to guide their further enquiries.

There is no power to take a decision against governments and competent authorities, and it is far from clear whether the Office of Fair Trading (OFT), which is a competent competition authority in the United Kingdom, is required to give information requested of it. There are two classes of agreements that may infringe article 85(1) that are not entered on the public register of restrictive trading agreements in the United Kingdom: there is a special secret section for particulars of registrable agreements that it is contrary to the public interest to disclose; and particulars of export agreements are required to be notified to the OFT but are not registrable. Confidentiality 'of information with respect to any particular business' is protected under United Kingdom law, unless there is a directly applicable Community obligation to disclose it to the Commission. There is no case law on the subject, despite similar problems under the law of some of the original member states. It may well be that the Commission would not press the OFT for information which it has power to obtain for itself.

21   *AM&S v. Commission* (155/79) [1982] E.C.R. 1575.
22   [1978] 3 C.M.L.R. 306.
23   (31/59) [1960] E.C.R. 71.

5.7.2 Inspections (article 14)

Usually the Commission starts an investigation by requesting information, but it also has the power to inspect an undertaking, enter its
premises, examine books and other business records and ask for oral
explanations on the spot. The procedures under articles 11 and 14 are
independent and the Commission may request additional documents
after it has carried out an inspection of the premises.[24]

There is a two-step procedure[25] as under article 11, but no need to
make a request under paragraph 1 before making a decision to inspect
the premises under paragraph 3.[26]

Under paragraph (1), an inspector may come with a simple mandate,
but there is no duty to admit him. Where inspectors arrive unexpectedly
they will probably be armed with a decision made under paragraph (3)
and, if this is not complied with, the Commission has power to impose a
fine under article 15(1)(c) or daily penalties under article 16(1)(d) in
much the same way as for non-compliance with a request for information made by decision.

There is, however, no direct power under Community law actually to
enter premises. Therefore, article 14(6) requires member states to assist,
and in the United Kingdom the Crown has obtained an injunction from
the Commercial Court to assist an inspection, in terms similar to an
Anton Piller order obtainable to discover breaches of copyright law.[27] A
similar procedure in Germany was confirmed by the Court in *Hoechst* v.
Commission.[28]

It may not be sensible to refuse entry to Commission inspectors. The
Commission might not unreasonably infer that the undertaking has
something to hide and might make adverse findings of fact on the basis
of such information as it may have. Indeed, inspectors are usually
admitted when only a mandate is produced, although when mandates
are drawn very widely, asking for sight of documents which may enable
the Commission to ascertain whether an infringement of article 85 or 86
has been committed in relation to a specified product, there is something
to be said for refusing admission until a decision, which is subject to
appeal, is produced. Routinely, it takes the Commission two weeks to
prepare a decision but, once, where the member of the Commission

24 *Orkem v. Commission* (374/87) [1989] E.C.R. 3343, at para. 14; *Solvay* v. *Commission* (27/88) [1989] E.C.R. 3355, at para. 14.
25 The two step procedure was considered by the Court in *Hoechst* (46/87 & 227/88)
[1989] E.C.R. 2859.
26 *National Panasonic* v. *Commission* (136/79) [1980] E.C.R. 2033.
27 See annex to the First House of Lords' report cited in the bibliography to this
chap. at 5.12 below.
28 Cited in n. 25 above.

responsible for competition was available to sign it, a decision was taken the same day.

Once a firm agrees to submit to such an investigation, it cannot bring it to an end unilaterally and it is not enough to deny knowledge in answer to broadly phrased questions and leave the inspectors to search the files, or to provide to help the inspectors someone who has recently joined the firm and is ignorant of its past conduct.[29] The Commission claims that under its inquisitorial procedure, the firm being investigated is required to assist it effectively.[30] No list of documents, however, has to be provided as in English proceedings for discovery.

In *Orkem v. Commission*, the Court held that the right against self-incrimination has no bearing on investigations in the field of competition law. Consequently, the Commission may compel an undertaking to provide information concerning facts known to it, even if the information may be used to establish anti-competitive conduct. It would, however, be contrary to the rights of the defence for the Commission to compel an undertaking to answer questions which might constitute an admission of an infringement which it is for the Commission to establish. The distinction between the two propositions is not always clear.

It is important to arrange in advance for an appropriate committee to meet the inspectors from the Commission. This should include a lawyer and good shorthand secretaries to take a record of what is asked for, provided or refused, and the reasons given for any refusal. The Commission does not normally make its record available to the parties. The lawyer will, doubtless, inspect the mandate, though it is unlikely to be insufficient, and he may wish to advise his client not to provide certain documents, for instance on the ground that they are privileged or irrelevant.

The Commission may then make a decision requiring the document to be produced, as it did in *AM&S*.[31] Such a decision enables the undertaking to appeal against it to the Community Court, and this is the procedure to settle a dispute as to whether the Commission is entitled to a particular document.

In *AM&S*, the Court held that a firm being investigated enjoys what in England is called 'legal professional privilege,' and in France, '*le secret professionnel*.' It need not produce correspondence with a lawyer, registered at the bar[32] of a member state and not employed by his client, in

29　*Fabbrica Pisana* and *Fabbrica Lastre di Vetro Pietro Sciarra* [1980] 2 C.M.L.R. 354 and 362.
30　The Court in *Orkem* v. *Commission*, cited above, at para. 27, held that the undertaking must 'co-operate actively.'
31　Cited at 5.7.1 above.
32　This term includes solicitors.

order to obtain or give legal advice. At one time, it was hoped that the Commission would not demand to see advice given by in-house lawyers, but in *John Deere*[33] it relied on such advice to show that the firm knew it was infringing article 85, and deserved a heavier fine.

More frequently, a lawyer may object to oral questions on the spot, as these deprive individuals of the time to think or check that is allowed by a request for information. It may be that the right to compel an oral explanation if the inspection is by decision is confined to questions arising out of the documents.[34] The Commission considers that it is entitled to demand to see an individual who is, for instance, shown by the documents to have attended a meeting with competitors. The point has sometimes been contested but never decided. The firm's committee should include someone of sufficient seniority to authorise the disclosure of the information.

It is usual for a firm to make its photocopier available to the inspectors and to take a second copy of each document for itself, so that it knows some of the evidence the Commission has and can later send explanations of documents that might look suspicious if read out of context. Occasionally, the Commission offers to pay for the photostats and will do so if pressed. The alternative may be to have the inspectors for days taking longhand notes or they may leave before the firm has established points in its favour.

It is dangerous to refuse documents on the grounds that they have been destroyed, unless a good reason can be given for their destruction. In *German Machine Blacksmiths*[35] documents were refused on the ground that the directors had ordered their destruction, and the Commission issued a decision under article 14(3) requiring the firm to submit to an investigation, at its Düsseldorf offices, into various classes of documents including those relating to its joint office in Zürich, outside the Community. If the firm fails to produce the documents, the Commission may require it, by decision made under article 16(1)(d), to pay penalties of up to 1,000 ECUs (defined in the glossary) *per* day indefinitely. If it does produce them, it will have difficulty in persuading the Commission of its honesty in view of its earlier statement that they had been destroyed.

The destruction of records on an *ad hoc* basis is very dangerous, though many firms legitimately arrange for systematic destruction of old documents that the national law does not require to be kept in order to save storage space. Even the failure to take minutes of a meeting between

33   Cited at 5.5.2 above.
34   Warner A.G. in *National Panasonic*, cited above, at p. 2066.
35   [1978] 1 C.M.L.R. D63.

a supplier's dealers to discuss cross-frontier trading was treated by the Commission as evidence of a concerted practice in *Pioneer*.[36]

Officials making an inspection habitually bring with them a memorandum setting out the rights of the firm being inspected, *inter alia*, to bring in its lawyer, although the inspection will not be long delayed to enable a lawyer to come.[37]

It is important to realise that the procedure is inquisitorial and not adversarial. One must try to find out what the Commission officials suspect as clearly as possible. If it is wrong, do not merely deny the suspicions but produce evidence to demonstrate the correct facts. The Commission suggests that the firm being investigated should take the initiative and use the inspection to bring out points in the firm's favour and not merely respond passively to questions asked.

This may, however, encourage loose talk which is noted down and may later appear in the Commission's case against the firm. It may be sensible to arrange a meeting of managers concerned with the matter being investigated shortly after an inspection in case there are points that can be forwarded to Brussels which were overlooked in the strained atmosphere of the inspection. Any misconceptions should be corrected before they have time to colour the case handler's approach to the situation.

The investigatory powers of the Commission may be delegated to competent authorities in member states such as the OFT, but this is rarely done in practice. An official from the OFT, however, normally attends inspections in the UK to give the Commission any assistance it may require.

5.7.3 *Sector enquiries (article 12)*

The Commission has power to make enquiries into a whole sector of the economy, such as brewing in Belgium or the supply of margarine to the Continent. The provisions of articles 11 and 14 apply also to such enquiries. Few have been made.

5.8 Procedure (article 19 and regulation 99)

Article 19 provides that the parties shall be given an opportunity of presenting their views before the Commission makes a decision on the merits, that is, one which clears, prohibits or exempts an agreement, or imposes fines. This right is further protected by the hearing regulation,

36   [1980] 1 C.M.L.R. 457.
37   The memoranda for inspection both by simple mandate and those made by virtue of a decision are appended to the *13th Annual Report.*

no. 99/63. The parties to the agreement and others showing a sufficient interest, such as complainants, have the right to make their views known in writing and may also request an oral hearing.

5.8.1 Statement of objections

The Court held in *Transocean Marine Paint (2)*[38] that, if the parties are to be able to present their views effectively, they must be told the case against them and the substance of any conditions which may be attached to the exemption with some particularity. The Commission's practice is to prepare a document, known as the statement of objections, to which the parties are invited to reply within a time limit which varies, but is normally two months, perhaps three months in a complex cartel case. Extra time is allowed over major holiday periods. The 'hearing' is usually fixed for about two months after the end of this period, and since a room and interpreters have to be hired well in advance, it is very difficult to persuade the Commission to delay the hearing, although an extra few weeks may be given for the written reply. The Commission may accept further evidence after the formal hearing while drawing up a draft decision.

5.8.2 Access to the file

In practice the Commission has done more to help the parties than is required by the Court. It is now customary to append to the statement of objections a list of the documents that the Commission has on its file. With the exception of those that are confidential or prepared by officials for the purpose of the case, the parties are entitled to inspect these before completing the answer to the statement of objections. If there are under 50 pages, the Commission will usually send photocopies on request.[39] The documents disclosed include those favourable to the defence. Although the Community Courts have never stated that the Commission is required to provide them, Advocate General Warner considered in *Distillers*[40] that it is and, in *Italian Flat Glass*,[41] the Court of First Instance objected when a passage favourable to one of the firms was deleted from a document that was used. Doctor Ehlermann, the Director General in charge of the competition department, informed the House of Lords Select Committee that safeguards had been introduced

38   (17/74) [1974] E.C.R. 1063.
39   In its *23rd Annual Report*, para. 201, the Commission states that in future it will send copies of all the documents necessary to the defence.
40   Cited at 5.5.2 above, at pp. 2294–2298.
41   (T–68, 77 & 78/89) [1992] E.C.R. II–1403 and see also *Hercules* v. *Commission*, (T–7/89) [1991] E.C.R. II–1711.

to prevent a repetition. He also accepted a duty to give access to documents that are manifestly exculpatory.[42]

Giving access to a large file is very time consuming, since thousands of documents may have to be checked to exclude confidential information. The practice of officials, who were brought up under different legal systems, as to how much disclosure should be given tends to vary. In *Cimenteries*,[43] firms alleged to be members of a large cartel objected that they had been shown only the documents to be used against each of them, and could not assess their position as a whole. The Court of First Instance dismissed the appeal as premature before the Commission had adopted a decision condemning them. This is unfortunate, as the parties may have to go to the trouble and expense of defending themselves, not knowing whether the decision will be quashed at a later stage.

Dr. Ehlermann, the Director General of the Commission's competition department, has said[44] that having to give access to all the documents on the file, subject to confidentiality, is too onerous, especially in cases involving many parties. He wants to provide access only to those documents on which the Commission's case is based and to those that may exonerate the particular party. He proposes to issue new guidelines to this effect.

5.8.3 The hearing

There is little time after receiving the statement of objections to prepare for the hearing, especially when the managers who know what happened are abroad on business. Any surveys that may be necessary to prove a vital point likely to be in issue should probably be put in hand before the Commission's case is received.

In 1982, the Commission appointed a Hearing Officer, now Dr. Johannes.[45] Although employed by the competition department, his independence is guaranteed by his right directly to contact the Member of the Commission responsible for competition policy. Although he is

---

42 Minutes of Evidence to *op. cit.* in bibliography, 5.12 below, from question 419, at p. 106.
43 (T–10–12 & 14/92R) [1992] 4 C.M.L.R. 243.
44 'Development in Community Competition Law Procedures,' address to Association Européenne des Avocats, Brussels, 25 January 1994. In this speech he explained his reactions to the various recommendations of the House of Lords Committee listed in the bibliography at 5.12 below. See also the Commission's *23rd Annual Report*, para. 207, not yet published.
45 Mr. Gilchrist sits for mergers and acts as a second hearing officer for cases under arts. 85 and 86.

responsible for the hearing, he will come to the case new at that point and will have to familiarise himself with the file. He may arrange a meeting with the parties before the formal hearing if there are points on which their views are particularly desired. His task is to ensure that the case of the firm whose conduct is being investigated is understood and taken into account.

His functions begin, however, with the hearing. The recent report of the House of Lords Select Committee suggests that he might be given further functions, such as dealing with objections about access to the file. The Commission intends to extend his mandate during 1994 to permit this.

The hearing often lasts only one day and, as the afternoon may be left for questions from the representatives of member states, there may be only a morning for the parties to take the initiative. Where there are many parties or the issues are complex two to five days is not uncommon. In large cartel cases the hearing may last three weeks. The hearing usually starts with the case handler stating the facts and issues as seen by the Commission. Even the remaining time may not all be available to the parties to the agreement. If there is a complainant he also has a right to be heard, and to hear such of the evidence as is not confidential. Consequently, the parties must divide their address into the parts with no confidential evidence, and those from which the complainant may be excluded.

An Advisory Committee consisting of representatives of the member states must be consulted before a decision is made on the merits, but its opinion is not made public, and its procedure remains a mystery to outsiders.

5.9   Confidentiality (article 20)

Information obtained by requests or inspections may be used only for the purpose of the relevant request (article 20(1)). There is no express restriction on the use of information obtained from notifications, except under the opposition procedure, or from informal chats with officials. Officials of the Commission and of the member states are not, however, allowed to disclose confidential information obtained under any of the provisions of the regulation (article 20(2)).

After the revised form A/B came into operation from 1985, officials placed confidential information in a separate annex, so that the Commission knows what to withhold from a complainant. It is sensible to draft a less precise answer in the non-confidential part of the form for the Commission to show third parties. Even if a document marked confidential' is shown to a complainant, an adverse decision may not be quashed. In *FEDETAB*,[46] the Court did not decide whether the information disclosed to a complainant was covered by '*le secret professionel*,' but refused to quash the adverse decision on the merits on the ground that the improper disclosure had not affected the result.

In *AKZO*,[47] however, the Court objected when the Commission gave a copy of a document that may have been secret to the complainant, without giving AKZO an opportunity to object to its decision to hand the document over, and ordered the Commission to recover the document. This prevented the complainant from using it as evidence in national proceedings.

If the Commission requires the production of highly sensitive information, such as a document containing valuable know-how, try to persuade the Commission that it is not necessary for its purposes, even if a version that may be shown to the complainant is also supplied. When notifying agreements it should be remembered that under article 10(1) copies are sent by the Commission to national competition authorities which in the UK include the Office of Fair Trading and the Department of Enterprise (DTI). Despite this, there is also a requirement under the Registration of Restrictive Agreements (EEC Documents) Regulations 1973, S.I. 1973, No. 450, that the Office be notified of certain steps taken under Community law, including notification of agreements to which the Restrictive Trade Practice Acts apply.

5.10 Fines and penalties (articles 15 and 16)

Article 15(2) provides for fines of up to 1 million ECUs, or 10 per cent. of the turnover for the previous year, for intentional or negligent infringement of article 85 or 86. The amount of fines has increased over time and in 1992, the Swedish firm Tetra Pak was fined 75 million ECUs — three times the previous record for a single firm.

In *Pioneer*[48] the Court confirmed that the Commission was entitled to change its policy and impose a fine far heavier than previously imposed without giving any warning prior to the conduct to be punished. The Court confirmed that the basis for the 10 per cent. was the entire turnover on all products of the group of companies worldwide, but that where the infringement concerned only one item of business, among others, that should reduce the proportionate fine. Often the Commission imposes a fine based on the turnover of the group in the product to which the illegal conduct related, but it has a wide discretion as to what to take

46   (209–215 & 218/78) [1980] E.C.R. 3125.
47   (53/85) [1986] E.C.R. 1965.
48   See 5.7.2 above.

as its base. Turnover is habitually excised from the public decisions, and it is not easy to read into them what weight was given to the various factors stated to be relevant. This gives the Commission considerable discretion.

Fines may also be imposed on a trade association, and in *Groupement des Cartes Bancaires & Europay International* v. *Commission*,[49] the Court of First Instance stated that the turnover of all the members could be aggregated when assessing the fine. If this were not the case, firms contemplating a cartel could avoid the possibility of fines exceeding a million ECUs by operating through a trade association which had little turnover. The association in question had pursued the policy of its members and under its constitution the members were responsible for its conduct. On grounds of preventing law avoidance, it may well be that members would be held responsible irrespective of the constitution of the association. As the Court pointed out, the 10 per cent. test is intended to reflect the economic power of the firms responsible. The Court of First Instance also approved of the Commission having taken into account the amount of profits the members had made from the infringement and some mitigating circumstances.

In *National Panasonic*,[50] the Commission reduced the fine substantially because the firm introduced an effective compliance system shortly after its attempts to control exports were investigated by the Commission.

As mentioned above, fines do not run for the period when an agreement was notified (or before, if it was an 'old agreement' duly notified). By virtue of article 15(6), this concession may be removed by the Commission informing the undertakings concerned that after a preliminary examination it is of the opinion that the agreement infringes article 85(1) and that an exemption is not justified. Since this changes the legal position of the parties, the Court has held that it amounts to what is technically called 'a decision.'[51] This is important as, by virtue of article 190 of the treaty, the Commission is required to give reasons for taking a decision and, by virtue of article 173, the undertaking to which it is addressed has the right to appeal against it to the Court of First Instance, if the reasons be inadequate or the treaty be infringed in some other way. From time to time the Commission states that it intends to make greater use of article 15(6), but so far it has found that such proceedings are almost as troublesome as making a final decision under article 3, and few simplified decisions have been made.

---

49   *Helsinki* agreement (T–39 & 49/92), judgment of 23 February 1994, not yet reported.
50   [1983] 1 C.M.L.R. 497.
51   *Cimenteries* (8–11/66) [1967] E.C.R. 75.

5.11 Miscellaneous

Decisions on the merits, that is, to clear, forbid, exempt or impose conditions on an exemption, are required to be published (article 21). They appear in all the official languages in the *Official Journal* of the Communities, 'Legislation' (L) series. An intention to give a favourable or unfavourable decision is published in the 'Information' (C) series of the *Official Journal* (article 19(3)). Under the new procedure for dealing with structural joint ventures within two months, the Commission publishes a very few facts in the O.J. as soon as possible in order to encourage third parties to submit evidence, without indicating whether its decision will be favourable. Decisions to impose fines or daily penalties are not required to be published, but if they are, they appear in the Legislation series.

A period of prescription has been provided, so that the Commission cannot impose fines more than five years after the termination of conduct infringing article 85 or 86, or more than three years after procedural irregularities, by virtue of the Limitation of Actions (Transport and Competition) Regulation 2988/74 of the Council.

5.12 Bibliography

Theofanis Christoforou, 'Protection of Legal Privilege in EEC Competition Law: the Imperfections of a case,' (1985–1986) 9 Fordham Int'l L. J. 1.

Barry Hawk (ed.) [1993] *Fordham Corporate Law Institute*; many papers consider the problems and limitations of enforcement by national courts and national authorities.

House of Lords, Select Committee on the European Communities, *Competition Practice*, 23 February 1982 (91),

——, Select Committee on the European Communities, *Enforcement of Community Competition Rules*, 7 December 1993, HL paper 7. (These are significant critical reports and the minutes of evidence by officials and practitioners are of exceptionally high quality. The first report resulted in several reforms to DGIV's procedure and the second may well do so.)

Dr. Johannes, contribution to a collection of essays to be published in my honour in 1995, Peter Alexiadis and John Kallaugher (eds.), Sweet and Maxwell.

Julian M. Joshua, 'The Element of Surprise' (1983) 8 E.L.R. 3.

——, 'Proof in Contested EEC Competition Cases: A Comparison with the Rules of Evidence in Common Law' (1987) 12 E.L.R. 315.

——, 'Information in EEC Competition Law Procedures' (1986) 11 E.L.R. 409.

C.S. Kerse, *EEC Antitrust Procedure* (1994) 3rd. ed., European Law Centre at Sweet & Maxwell (London).

Valentine Korah, 'Collaborative joint ventures for research and development where markets are concentrated: the competition rules of the common market and the invalidity of contract,' 15, part II, Fordham Int'l L.J. 248.

Helmut W. Kreis, 'EEC Commission Investigation Procedures in Competition Cases' (1984) *International Lawyer* 19.

Michael J. Reynolds, 'Practical Aspects of Notifying Agreements and the New Form A/B,' Barry Hawk (ed.) [1985] *Fordham Corporate Law Institute* 705.

Piet Jan Slot and *Alison McDonnell* (eds.), *Procedure and Enforcement in EC and US Competition Law, Proceedings of the Leiden Europa Instituut seminar on User-Friendly Competition Law*, Sweet & Maxwell, 1993.

Ivo van Bael, 'The Antitrust Settlement Practice of the EEC Commission,' in Barry Hawk (ed.) [1985] *Fordham Corporate Law Institute* 759.

6 Civil Law Sanctions

6.1 Injunctions and actions for damages

The only sanctions expressly provided by Community law for conduct prohibited by article 85 or 86 are the fines the Commission may impose under regulation 17[1] and, by virtue of article 85(2), the nullity of those provisions in a contract that restricts competition contrary to article 85. The Commission may make a final or interim decision requiring a citizen to cease infringing, but has no power to award damages.

Since the conduct is prohibited by a provision of Community law which is directly applicable in member states,[2] it is virtually certain that infringements give rise to an action for damages in national courts. In *BMW Cars*,[3] the Bundesgerichtshof, the Supreme Civil Court of the Federal Republic of Germany, held that the Community prohibition coupled with the national code on civil procedure provides for damages, although some German lawyers interpret the judgment as deciding only that the fact that the conduct took place outside the Federal Republic did not preclude jurisdiction.

The judgment of the House of Lords, the ultimate English appellate court, in *Garden Cottage Foods* v. *Milk Marketing Board*[4] is strong persuasive authority that damages lie for an infringement of article 86, but the issue was avoided by the majority judgment and Lord Wilberforce considered the question too important to be considered as a side wind to a case on interlocutory injunctions.

In several earlier applications made *ex parte*, an interlocutory injunction had been awarded by the English High Court for a short period, but usually the matter was settled before judgment was given on the basis of argument *inter partes*. In *Cutsforth* v. *Mansfield Inns Ltd.*,[5] however, Sir Neil Lawson in the Commercial Court granted an interlocutory injunction and delivered judgment after two days' hearing *inter partes*. He held that there was a serious issue whether an agreement between a brewer and its tied pubs infringed article 85(1), and thought that it was fairly clear that it was not exempted by regulation 1984/83. The balance of convenience was in favour of an interlocutory injunction, as otherwise a supplier of amusement machines with whom the publicans were not

---

1 5.10 above.
2 *BRT* v. *SABAM* (127/73) [1974] E.C.R. 51 and 313, *Ahmed Saeed* (66/86) [1989] E.C.R. 803, para. 33.
3 (Case KZR 21/78) (BGH) [1980] ECC 213.
4 [1984] A.C. 130, [1983] 3 C.M.L.R. 43.
5 [1986] 1 C.M.L.R. 1.

allowed to deal would lose half its business at very short notice. The judgment did not refer to the *Garden Cottage* case, but there the House of Lords did not hold that damages were in fact the appropriate remedy, only that it should not interfere with the discretion of the trial judge. The *Cutsforth* case was settled before further proceedings ensued.

Since the last edition of this book, the Community Court has continued to hold that national courts must provide adequate remedies for breach of Community law. *Francovich* v. *Italy*[6] related to the vertical effects of a directive that was insufficiently precise in certain respects to have direct effect and could, therefore, not be invoked directly by the plaintiff in a national court. In ruling that the Italian state was liable in damages for not implementing the directive in time, the Court went further than Advocate General Mischo and used language far wider than necessary to decide the case:

> '32. Furthermore, it has been consistently held that the national courts whose task it is to apply the provisions of Community law in cases within their jurisdiction must ensure that those rules take full effect and protect the rights which they confer on individuals (see in particular the judgments in ... *Simmenthal,* and *Factortame,* para. 19).
>
> 33. The full effectiveness of Community rules would be impaired and the protection of the rights which they grant would be weakened if individuals were unable to obtain redress[7] when their rights are infringed by breach of Community law for which a member-State can be held responsible.'

The Court accepted that a government must be liable in damages if the citizen's rights are to be sufficiently protected: although, unlike Advocate General Darmon, it did not define the circumstances in which the state would be so liable. Italy's failure to implement in *Francovich* was particularly flagrant.

Challenges to the validity of administrative action in England must now normally be made by a special procedure in the High Court known as the application for judicial review.[8] This must be done promptly and in any event within three months, although the House of Lords has held that no time limit applies where the applicant challenges the validity of a statute on the ground that it is incompatible with Community law.[9] The court has power under English law to grant interim injunctive relief. At the final hearing it may make an order quashing the decision (*certiorari*),

6   (C–6 & 9/90) [1991] E.C.R. I–5357, judgment of 19 November 1991.
7   'Redress' is broader than 'compensation', which was used in the preliminary translation by the Court, and must include injunctive relief.
8   Supreme Court Act 1981, s. 31 and Rules of the Supreme Court, O. 53. See generally H. W. R. Wade, *Administrative Law* (6th. ed.), chaps. 16–21.
9   See *R.* v. *Secretary of State for Employment, ex p. Equal Opportunities Commission* [1994] 1 All E.R. 910 (H.L.).

grant mandatory and prohibitory injunctions or make a declaration, although the court has discretion to withhold any of these remedies even if the applicant has made out a case. This discretion probably does not apply where Community rights are affected, but the matter has not yet been tested. Until 1993 it was thought that the courts had no jurisdiction to grant injunctions against a minister of the Crown on an application for judicial review, but the House of Lords granted an interlocutory injunction where rights under Community law were involved.[10]

Generally, the fact that a government body has made an invalid administrative decision *in itself* gives no right of action for damages in English law. It follows from *Francovich*, however, that an action for damages may now lie against the government for its breaches of Community law without the need for the plaintiff to show any other cause of action; but no such case has yet come before the English courts.[11]

Where it is necessary to sue a private person for infringing the competition rules, it is thought that the same rule applies, although Luc Gyselen[12] doubts this, on the ground that it is the horizontal effect of a directly effective provision that is in issue rather than the vertical effect of a directive. The language in *Francovich* was very wide indeed. In *H. J. Banks & Co. Ltd.* v. *British Coal Corporation*,[13] Advocate General van Gerven wrote a cogent opinion concluding that damages lay for infringement of the competition rules of the European Coal and Steel treaty as a matter of Community law and not merely as a matter of national law. There was no previous authority to establish even that articles 65 and 66 of that treaty had direct effect. Nevertheless, on the basis of very general principles which apply even more strongly to the EC treaty, he considered that damages lie under Community law.

The Court differed,[14] and concluded that the competition provisions in the ECSC treaty did not have direct effect and that infringements could be sued upon only if the Commission had already made an adverse finding. It observed that article 65(4) provides that:

'The High Authority[15] shall have sole jurisdiction, subject to the right to bring actions before the Court, to rule whether any such agreement or decision is compatible with this article.'

10 *Factortame Ltd. and Others* v. *Secretary of State for Transport (No. 2)* (Case C–213/89) [1991] 1 A.C. 603 (ECJ) and *Factortame Ltd.* v. *Secretary of State for Transport (No. 3)* [1992] 3 W.L.R. 288 (H.L.).
11 I am indebted to my colleague at University College London, Andrew LeSeur, for help on English administrative law.
12 *Op. cit.*, bibliography, 6.6 below.
13 (C–128/92), not yet reported.
14 Judgment of 13 April 1994, not yet reported.
15 Now the Commission.

The ECSC treaty leaves more control with the Commission than does the EC treaty. The Court did not address the issue under the EC treaty, which contains no such provision. Moreover, there is abundant case law to establish that articles 85 and 86 do have direct effect. I still think that damages lie under Community law for breach of articles 85 and 86. Since he was not reversed on this point, Mr. Van Gerven's opinion retains some authority.

It is for national law to establish such procedural rules as what court has jurisdiction, but the remedy must be efficacious, and no worse than that available for infringement of national law.

Since the Commission has insufficient staff to deal with all infringements of Community competition law, it wants more enforcement to be done by national courts. There are, however, many difficulties in the way of a plaintiff that deter such actions. Damages clearly lie under the law of the UK for giving effect to an agreement that should have been notified to the Director General of Fair Trading under the restrictive trade practices legislation but has not been. Nevertheless, no successful action has yet been reported. The Post Office accepted £9 million in settlement of its claim against firms that admitted to agreeing to keep up the prices of the cables they sold to it, and there may well be other instances where money was paid to prevent a claim being pursued.

The same difficulties arise where the action is brought under article 85. The plaintiff would have to establish illegal collusion, but it cannot use the Commission's powers to obtain information under regulation 17, nor can it obtain information on discovery under English law, as there is privilege against disclosing information that might render a person liable to penalties, such as those the Commission can impose under regulation 17.[16] Sometimes some of the evidence may be outside the jurisdiction of the national court being asked to grant relief. Often the evidence may be in several member states and, even with the Brussels Convention, there may not be a defendant in a country with jurisdiction. The plaintiff must also quantify the damages it has suffered, but if it has not been able to enter the market because of the illegal conduct that may well be difficult. Consequently, victims of anti-competitive behaviour often prefer to complain to the Commission.

Moreover, few civil judges have the education or experience to deal effectively with problems of competition law. They tend to be generalists. The same may be true of the Bar, although many younger lawyers are now well educated in that respect. One major drawback is that only the Commission can grant exemptions under article 85(3) and if national

16   *R.T.Z.* v. *Westinghouse Electric Corporation* [1978] 1 C.M.L.R. 100 (H.L.), and 5.10 above.

courts follow the Commission's practice, they may hold that many agreements that actually increase competition by enabling firms to appropriate the benefit of the costs they have sunk are void and illegal. The alternative would be to adjourn while the Commission decides whether to grant an exemption.[17]

On the other hand, a plaintiff has more control of proceedings than a complainant and may negotiate with the defendant and bring them to an end. Moreover, in *Automec II*,[18] the Court of First Instance confirmed that the Commission is not obliged to pursue every complaint to a formal decision. It may choose its priorities and investigate only those files that raise a 'Community interest,' provided that it examines carefully the factual and legal aspects of which it is notified by the complainant and clearly sets out sound[19] reasons for deciding to take no action. In that case the Commission had observed that proceedings were already pending before a Milanese court, which would have power to grant damages. Complainants may now have either to suffer or litigate in national courts.

6.2 Enforcement by national competition authorities

The Commission has also been considering the possibility of delegating its powers under regulation 17 to the competent authorities in member states. Some of them, however, do not have power under national law to enforce the EC rules, although Germany has taken such powers recently.[20] Moreover, they have little incentive to enforce the EC competition rules rather than their national ones: once the national authority has decided to condemn an agreement its prohibition may be trumped by an exemption from the Commission.[21] In addition, a national authority cannot grant an exemption under article 85(3).

17 See 6.3.4 below.

18 (T–24/90) [1992] E.C.R. II–2223.

19 See *B.E.U.C. & National Consumer Council* v. *Commission* (T–37/92), judgment of 18 May 1994, where the Court of First Instance did not consider the reasons given as sufficient.

20 H.-Peter von Stoephasius, in Slot and McDonnell, *op. cit.*, bibliography, 6.6 below, p.32.

In answer to the question at para. 446 of the minutes of evidence attached to the recent report of the House of Lords Select Committee, cited in the bibliography to this chap., Dr. Ehlermann stated that only the UK, Ireland, Denmark and the Netherlands do not have power to apply the Community competition rules.

21 See *Ford/Volkswagen*, O.J. 1993, L20/14, where the Commission had approved a state aid to finance a plant for the joint venture to make multi-purpose vehicles. The Bundeskartellamt was about to prohibit the joint venture when the Commission granted an exemption. See Stoephasius, *op.cit.*, Slot and McDonnell (eds.), bibliography at 6.6 below.

Some of the problems of both national courts and competition authorities might be overcome if, following the lead of the Court, article 85(1) were construed more narrowly under something like a truncated rule of reason.[22] Few exemptions would be needed if pro-competitive agreements were not found to infringe article 85(1).

Now that most member states have enacted legislation similar to articles 85 and 86, national authorities are more likely to invoke national than EC law and will then be able to apply a provision similar to article 85(3).

6.3 Nullity (article 85(2))

Contracts that infringe article 85 as a whole are nullified by article 85(2). Some agreements prohibited by article 85(1) have no legal effects to nullify, but nullity is important for vertical contracts. As early as 1966, the Court held in *La Technique Minière* v. *Maschinenbau Ulm*[23] that it is only those provisions that have the object or effect of restricting competition that are void and that it is for national law to decide whether enough remains for the rest of the contract to be enforceable. It repeated this view as recently as 1991, in *Stergios Delimitis* v. *Henninger Bräu*.[24] Consequently, even if the amount at issue is trifling, a national court may have to make complex market analysis before enforcing a contract.[25]

In *Stergios Delimitis* v. *Henninger Bräu* itself, the Court said that an exclusive purchasing obligation accepted by the tenant of a single beer house provided benefits to both parties and did not have the object of restricting competition. In deciding whether it had that effect, it would be relevant to enquire whether so many bars were tied for so long that it would be difficult for another brewer to find enough outlets to enter the market. The national court should also consider possibilities of a new entrant opening new cafés or buying a chain of them. Even if there were significant foreclosure, it would be only the ties that made a significant contribution to it that would be illegal. The cost of such an enquiry may be large in relation to the small loan in issue, and most lawyers and courts in the UK and other member states are not used to dealing with economic evidence or issues. It should, however, suffice to prove that a new firm could enter the market in any one of these ways to establish conformity with article 85.

22   2.4 above.
23   (56/65) [1966] E.C.R. 235.
24   (C–234/89) [1991] E.C.R. I–935.
25   2.4 above.

6.3.1 *The early case law*

Until the first decisions of the Commission were published in 1964, uncertainty as to the interpretation and application of article 85(1) was complete. In *De Geus* v. *Bosch*,[26] Bosch had appointed an exclusive dealer by an agreement similar to that between *Consten and Grundig*[27] and, before regulation 17 came into force, Bosch and its dealer sued under the Dutch law of unfair competition to restrain a parallel importer. Concerned by the uncertainty then prevailing, the Community Court relied on the principle of legal certainty which it derived from the general principles of law in member states and ruled that agreements made before regulation 17 came into force and duly notified should be treated as provisionally valid until the Commission had come to a decision. In subsequent cases in 1969 and 1970 it went further and ruled that such agreements should be given their full effect meanwhile. This provisional validity might be justified also on the ground that article 7 of the regulation provides for retrospective validation if the agreement is later altered so as not to infringe article 85(1) or to merit exemption.

6.3.2 *The second Brasserie de Haecht case*

Provisional validity was difficult to reconcile with article 85(2) of the treaty; its extent was not clear — the position if the Commission later condemned an agreement which a national court had enforced was never decided, and the Commission was so short of staff that it wanted to rely on the sanction of nullity which did not require intervention by it.

By 1973 when the Community Court gave a preliminary ruling in *Brasserie de Haecht* v. *Wilkin (2)*,[28] the application of article 85 was far clearer than it had been at the time of the *Bosch* ruling in 1962. The Community Court confirmed the provisional validity of old agreements — those made before regulation 17 came into force or before the accession of the relevant member state, but adopted the opposite view for new agreements. It ruled that notification of new agreements does not have suspensive effect. The national court should judge:

> 'whether there is cause to suspend proceedings in order to allow the parties to obtain the Commission's standpoint, unless it establishes either that the agreement does not have any perceptible effect on competition or trade between Member States or that there is no doubt that the agreement is incompatible with article 85.'

26   (13/61) [1962] E.C.R. 45.
27   (56 & 58/64) [1966] E.C.R. 299; 2.3.1 and 2.4 above.
28   (48/72) [1973] E.C.R. 77.

In *Delimitis* the Court said that the national judge *must* adjourn if he considers that the agreement might be exempted.

6.3.3   Old agreements after the second Brasserie de Haecht case

In *De Bloos* v. *Bouyer*,[29] the Court confirmed that until the Commission refuses to grant an exemption, national courts asked to enforce an old agreement duly notified or exempted from notification:

> 'must give such an agreement the legal effects attributed thereto under the law applicable to the contract, and those effects cannot be called in question by any objection which may be raised concerning its compatibility with Article 85(1).'

The Court laid more stress on the general principle of legal certainty than on article 7 of the regulation, which does not apply unless an agreement is in fact duly notified. So even when the agreement is unlikely to be modified to comply with article 85 because the parties are at loggerheads and the defendant wishes to get out of the agreement, provisional validity may apply. Indeed, the Advocate General referred to 'absolute validity.' The position after the Commission has condemned an agreement remains uncertain, but it is thought that unless the validity for the period before the decision remains, the position of the parties would be intolerable. A national court if asked would have to enforce the contract, yet it might later be condemned with retroactive effect by the Commission. Parties might be encouraged to engage in unnecessary litigation merely to crystallise the provisional validity of the contract.

In *Lancôme*,[30] however, the Court further reduced the scope of provisional validity. The Commission had sent a 'comfort letter' stating that in its view an old agreement did not infringe article 85(1) owing to the firm's small market share in each member state and that it was closing its file. The Court ruled that this brought the provisional validity to an end, as it was now unlikely that the Commission would validate the agreement retrospectively under article 7 of the regulation. It added that a national court might take into account the Commission's view that the agreement escaped the prohibition of article 85(1), but ruled that it was not bound by it. It is anomalous that when one modifies an agreement to satisfy the Commission, one may no longer be able to enforce it automatically. It may be, however, that other kinds of comfort letter do not bring the provisional validity to an end: for instance, one stating that the agreement merits exemption; but that the Commission is not giving the

29   (59/77) [1977] E.C.R. 2359.
30   (99/79) [1980] E.C.R. 2511.

agreement any priority. After such a letter it might well proceed to an exemption should the validity of the contract be raised in a national court.[31]

6.3.4 New agreements, comfort letters and short form exemptions

The lack of provisional validity for new agreements has created serious problems, as the Commission makes few decisions granting an individual exemption under article 85(3),[32] but more often sends a comfort letter informing the parties that it sees no reason to intervene and has closed the file (5.6 above). Most agreements that have been notified are being dealt with in this way, and it is unlikely that they will ever be exempted, unless they come within the terms of a group exemption.

In *Guérlain*,[33] the Court ruled that a national court may take into account any view expressed by the Commission in a comfort letter, although it is not binding as either a negative clearance or an exemption. The ruling probably created no great difficulties for the parties in that case, since the letter implied that the vertical selective dealing agreement made by a firm supplying a small proportion of the perfumes and toilet preparations in the common market had no significant effect on competition or trade between member states once the dealers were permitted to sell to authorised outlets outside their area.

Other comfort letters such as that in *Europages*,[34] however, do not make it clear whether the Commission considers that the provisions are not caught by article 85(1), or that they merit an exemption. The distinction is not important to it, but it is vital for a national court, since article 9 of regulation 17 provides that only the Commission may grant an exemption. Unless national courts are fairly robust in treating cases dealt with by comfort letters as being outside article 85(1), there is great danger that many agreements that increase competition, for instance by providing for joint research and development of a new product, but that contain ancillary restraints enabling each party to obtain part of the benefits of the competitive possibilities so created, may not be enforceable. Doubts about the validity of such restraints may inhibit the investment necessary to important collaborative ventures.

The Commission developed another sort of comfort letter in *Rovin*,[35]

31   See the end of 6.3.4 below.
32   See 6.4.1.2 below.
33   (253/78 and 1–3/79) [1980] E.C.R. 2327.
34   [1984] 1 C.M.L.R. 38 and 97.
35   [1984] 1 C.M.L.R. 128 and 87.

stating that in its view an agreement merits exemption and that it is closing its file. Sometimes the intention to send such a letter is published in the *Official Journal* so that third parties may comment but this is unusual because of the trouble of preparing multiple translations. The Commission seems to think that publication would help a national court to enforce the agreement, and in *Lancôme*[36] the Court did stress that the letter could not be treated as a decision of exemption since such decisions require publicity in the *Official Journal*. It is thought, however, that there were other reasons preventing the letter from being a formal decision. The reasoning was probably not sufficient and the letter does not seem to have been approved by the members of the Commission acting collegiately but only by the secretariat.

The kind of letter stating that the agreement merits exemption is particularly unfortunate as it may imply that the agreement is caught by the prohibition of article 85(1), and a national court has no power to exempt. It is just arguable that for a national court to enforce an agreement in such circumstances would not amount to granting an exemption. The problem can be avoided if the court ignores some of the Commission's precedents and follows the Court's rulings on ancillary restrictions. It could then find that the agreement does not infringe article 85(1) and enforce it.

Commission officials have tried to overcome the problems of invalidity by introducing a short form for exemption where the issues are straightforward. In *BP/Kellogg*,[37] the statement of facts published in the *Official Journal* under article 19(3) of regulation 17 and already translated into all the official languages formed part of the decision. A very short legal appraisal was added when the final decision was published. Care is needed to ensure that the appraisal takes into account the economic context of the agreement or it may be quashed on appeal.[38] This, however, is unlikely unless a complainant appeals within the two months permitted by article 173 of the Treaty. The parties are not likely to have fallen out so soon. If a national court were to refer the matter to the Community Court years later under article 177, the Community Court might state that the period of limitation had expired and refuse to consider the matter.[39]

In *Delimitis*, the Court confirmed its earlier case law. When the provision to be enforced clearly infringes article 85(1) and is unlikely to be exempted, the national court cannot enforce it. On the other hand, if

36   See 6.3.3 above.
37   [1986] 2 C.M.L.R. 619.
38   *Groupement des Fabricants de Papiers Peints* (73/74) [1975] E.C.R. 1491.
39   *TWD Textilwerke Deggendorf* v. *Bundesrepublik Deutschland* (C–188/92), judgment of 9 March 1994, not yet reported.

it does not infringe article 85(1), the national court should not refuse to enforce it on grounds of competition law.

More difficult problems arise when the agreement may come within the prohibition of article 85(1), but may still be exempted for the period in issue. The national court may suspend proceedings while the Commission decides whether to grant an exemption. In *Delimitis*, the Community Court added (paragraph 52) that the national court may grant interlocutory relief meanwhile. It added that:

> '53. ... it is also open to a national court, *within the limits of the applicable national procedural rules and subject to article 214 EEC*, to seek information from the Commission on the state of any procedure which the Commission may have set in motion and as to the likelihood of its giving an official ruling on the agreement in issue pursuant to regulation 17. Under the same conditions, the national court may contact the Commission where the concrete application of article 85(1) or of article 86 raises particular difficulties, in order to obtain the economic and legal information which that institution can supply to it. Under article 5 EEC, the Commission is bound by a duty of sincere co-operation with the judicial authorities of the member state, who are responsible for ensuring that community law is applied and respected in the national legal system' (author's emphasis).

The first statement, encouraging the national court to enquire whether the Commission is likely to grant a formal exemption is not controversial, but the second idea, asking the Commission for legal and economic advice, is. In England such advice might well be inadmissible as hearsay.[40] There is also a question of how reliable such information would be.

It seems clear that a national court could grant an interlocutory or permanent injunction to enforce a provision that does not infringe article 85(1), even if there are other provisions in the contract which may, provided that the provisions that are valid are capable of being severed from the rest. The English Court of Appeal in *Chemidus Wavin* v. *TERI*[41] enforced the royalty provision in a patent licence, although there were other clauses that might have infringed article 85. The criterion adopted by the Court was:

> 'whether, after the excisions required by the article of the treaty have been made from the contract, the contract could be said to fail for lack of consideration or on any other ground, or whether the contract would be so changed in its character as not to be the sort of contract that the parties' intended to enter into at all.'

There are no special rules of court dealing with this problem in

40   See Jeremy Lever, *op. cit.*, bibliography, 6.6 below.
41   [1978] 3 C.M.L.R. 514.

England, although cases may have to be adjourned for far longer than
has previously been experienced.

To sum up, a national court should refuse to enforce a provision in a
new agreement if it is caught by article 85(1) and cannot be exempted for
the relevant period, either because it has not been notified and is not
excused from notification under article 4(2) of regulation 17, or it is
pretty clear that it is not the kind of agreement the Commission is likely
to exempt. Where the Commission has stated that the agreement merits
exemption but has closed its file, probably the right course is for the
court to adjourn in the hope that the Commission will then reopen its file
and complete the exemption process. Since the grant of an exemption is
within the exclusive remit of the Commission, it appears from *Automec
II*[42] that the Commission is obliged to proceed to a formal decision if the
parties press. Just before he retired as the member of the Commission
responsible for competition law, Sir Leon Brittan stated that the Commission would abide by the views stated in its comfort letters unless it
had been told lies or circumstances had changed.[43]

This has significantly reduced the problem of nullity. If the Commission sends a comfort letter stating that the agreement merits exemption and one later needs to enforce the contract, one can write asking the
Commission to proceed to a formal decision. If it does not do so
promptly, one can formally request it to do so under article 175 of the
treaty. Unless circumstances have changed, Sir Leon Brittan has promised that it will not change its mind, even if the defendant lobbies. Two
drawbacks remain. Where the transaction is very successful, the parties
may obtain far higher market shares than previously and this might be
treated as a change of circumstances, enabling the Commission to take a
different view in its final decision. Secondly, the need to require a
decision would make litigation slower and more hazardous, and so
reduce the chances of the plaintiff obtaining a favourable settlement.

6.3.5 *Accession agreements*

It has not yet been decided whether accession agreements (5.5 above)
should be treated as old or new agreements for the purposes of enjoying
validity before the Commission makes up its mind. Article 7 of regulation 17 applies to them if they were notified in time, but by the date of
the first accessions group exemptions already operated in two fields and

42   (T–24/90) [1992] E.C.R. II–2223, at para. 7.5.
43   'The future of EEC Competition Policy,' speech at the Centre of European Policy
Studies, Brussels, 7 December 1992. An excerpt is reproduced in Slot and McDonnell,
op.cit., bibliography, 6.6 below, at p.120.

uncertainty about the Commission's attitude to many types of agreement had been considerably reduced. Nevertheless the Commission stated its view that accession agreements do enjoy provisional validity in its *Third Report on Competition Policy*,[44] and the English High Court so held in *Esso Petroleum* v. *Kingswood Motors*.[45]

The Community Court held in *Nouvelles Frontières*,[46] at a time when there was no implementing regulation for air transport, that provisional validity did apply to agreements in that sector. It seems, then, that it is the lack of an implementing regulation rather than the uncertainty in the early days that is the important consideration.

This was confirmed in *Ahmed Saeed*,[47] where the Court relied only on the possibility of subsequent retrospective validation. By ignoring the problem of legal certainty, the Court was able to avoid granting provisional validity to an agreement that might infringe article 86.

6.4 Whether to notify

Whether to notify an agreement is an important strategic decision, to be taken by management. Legal advisers should merely analyse the advantages and disadvantages. There is no duty to notify, only not to infringe.

6.4.1 *Advantages of notifying*

6.4.1.1 *Immunity from fines* — Where there are deterrents to trade between member states or a horizontal cartel, fixing prices and allocating quotas, immunity from fines is not likely to last long. Moreover, where the infringement is clear, it is possible that notification might be considered to be an abuse of the notification procedure and, under the law of several member states, an abuse of law cannot be relied upon. The Community Court might adopt this principle of law and hold that the Commission is entitled to impose fines, despite notification.

When the agreement has been tailored to include only minimal restrictions that are necessary to make a pro-competitive transaction viable, fines are not likely in any event, so this advantage is rarely very great.

6.4.1.2 *Individual exemption* — An individual exemption might be granted, but there have seldom been more than about three a year, although ten were granted in 1988. There was a total of 16 in the four

44 At p. 19.
45 [1974] 1 Q.B. 142.
46 *Ministère Public* v. *Asjes* (209–213/84) [1986] E.C.R. 1425.
47 Cited at 6.1 above.

years 1990–93. An individual exempting decision is very unlikely for the particular contract one is negotiating. In theory, notification under the opposition procedure provided for by the new group exemptions (3.3 above) might result in more exemptions, especially where the restrictions of competition not listed in the regulations are not very great, or the market shares of the firms small. In practice, however, the number has been disappointingly small. There is no provisional validity for notified, new agreements. So, apart from the opposition procedure, notification will seldom help the parties to enforce their contract.

6.4.1.3 *A comfort letter is not an exemption* — Where a comfort letter states that the agreement does not infringe article 85 as in *Guérlain*[48] or comes within a group exemption as in *De Bloos* v. *Bouyer*,[49] this may be taken into account by a national court asked to enforce the contract, so may facilitate enforcement of the contract. Where, as in *Rovin*,[50] however, it states that the agreement merits exemption, it used to be dangerous. A national court may infer that the agreement falls within the prohibition of article 85(1), and the national court has no power to exempt. All it can do is adjourn to enable the Commission to proceed to the grant of a formal exemption.

Since *Automec II*,[51] however, the Commission has probably been under a duty to proceed to a formal decision if the parties proceed under article 175 of the Treaty. Since the member of the Commission responsible for competition policy has stated that the Commission will normally abide by the views expressed in a comfort letter (6.3.4 above), there is now more reason to notify than there was formerly.

6.4.1.4 *Reputation* — Notification may help to develop a reputation for being Communautaire, and enable one to get a favourable view of the agreement to DGIV before a complainant persuades it to the contrary.

6.4.1.5 *Evidence that infringement was intentional* — If an agreement is not notified, management may reconsider the possibility from time to time and rehearse the reasons for thinking the agreement may infringe article 85(1). These documents may later turn up on an inspection unless written by an outside lawyer enjoying legal professional privilege and may indicate to the Commission that the firm knew its agreement was unlawful and result in higher fines.

48   Cited at 6.3.4 above.
49   Cited at 6.3.3 above.
50   Cited at 6.3.4 above.
51   Cited at 6.3.4 above.

6.4.2 *Disadvantages of notifying*

6.4.2.1 *Trouble* — Completing form A/B is burdensome. It cannot be done in ten minutes. Annexes will have to be prepared analysing the market and stating why the agreement does not infringe article 85(1) or why it merits exemption. Soon, a more complex form will be in use, although the Commission intends to take power to waive some of the information in suitable cases. Preparation of notifications usually means collaboration between a manager responsible for the future development of the firm and specialised lawyers and, if waiver is required for some of the information, with DGIV. It is difficult and time-consuming work.

6.4.2.2 *Skeletons* — The Commission may start to ask questions and find skeletons in the cupboard.

6.4.2.3 *National law* — Notifications are sent to the member states, so check that any notifications required by national law have been completed.

6.4.2.4 *Opportunity to renegotiate* — The major disincentive to notification is that one does not know when the Commission will start seriously analysing the notification. In the past one could wait for many years, but with more group exemptions and the reorganisation,[52] DGIV has substantially reduced its backlog. When it does finally consider the agreement, the Commission may require some amendment to be made if it is to grant an exemption, or send a comfort letter, or it may attach conditions and obligations to an exemption. If the bargaining power of the parties has shifted by then, for instance when a patent licensee has invested in tooling up and developing a market, the other party may refuse to amend the agreement without renegotiating the terms, such as the royalties payable.[53] It is this possibility for opportunist behaviour that has discouraged many people from notifying. They clean up the agreement, so that the restrictions are minimal and establish a file showing the need for them; then hope that, when enforcing the agreement in a national court or defending themselves from a complaint to the Commission, they will be able to establish that the agreement does not infringe article 85(1).

---

52 See 5.5.1 above.
53 See the sad story of *ARD*, described at 14.2.6 below.

6.5 Undertakings given to the Commission

In another attempt to speed up its procedures and conserve its resources, the Commission has been accepting undertakings from firms against which it has been proceeding. The case under article 86 against IBM was settled in 1984 by the Commission[54] merely suspending its proceedings indefinitely in return for IBM modifying the practices subject to the complaint. The settlement is expressed not to be enforceable, but there are considerable commercial pressures on IBM to comply and political pressures on the Commission not to recommence complex proceedings. The Commission has completed several annual reviews and states that IBM has complied with its undertakings. In *Hilti*[55] the firm gave an undertaking to abrogate commercial practices that tied the sale of nails to the supply of a powered tool for inserting them rapidly, a market over which the Commission thinks Hilti may be dominant. Should the undertaking be broken, the Commission might proceed to interim measures. In fact, it finalised its decision in 1988. In *Wood Pulp*[56] some of the parties gave a formal undertaking which was incorporated in the decision ordering the termination of a cartel, a factor which led the Commission to impose greatly reduced fines on those firms. On appeal,[57] the Court treated the undertakings as if they were part of the Commission's order and annulled them only in so far as the Court did not confirm the Commission's finding of an infringement. The Commission is accepting undertakings or persuading the parties to alter their agreements in order to speed up its administration and deal with more cases.

6.6 Bibliography

Sir Leon Brittan, cited in Piet Jan Slot and Alison McDonnell (eds.), *Procedure and Enforcement in EC and US Competition Law, Proceedings of the Leiden Europa Instituut seminar on User-Friendly Competition Law*, Sweet & Maxwell, 1993, pp. 115–122.

Jonathan Faull and *Joseph Weiler*, 'Conflicts of Resolution in European Competition Law' [1978] 3 E.L.Rev. 116.

Ian Forrester and *Christopher Norall*, 'The Laïcization of Community Law — Self-Help and the Rule of Reason: How Competition Law is and could be applied' [1983] *Fordham Corporate Law Institute*, chap. 8, from p.305.

Walter van Gerven, 'The Genesis of EEA Law and the Principles of Primacy and Direct Effect' (1992–93) 16 *Fordham Int'l L.J.* 955.

Jeffrey Goh, 'Enforcing EC Competition Law in Member States' [1993] E.C.L.R. 114.

54 Commission's *24th Annual Report*, point 77.
55 [1989] 4 C.M.L.R. 677.
56 [1985] 3 C.M.L.R. 474.
57 [1993] 4 C.M.L.R. 407, at paras. 178–185.

Luc Gyselen, 'Le Juge national face aux règles de concurrence communautaires applicables aux entreprises,' *Journal des tribunaux, Droit européen*, 23 October 1993 (no.2), pp. 25–33.

Barry Hawk (ed.), [1993] *Fordham Corporate Law Institute*, to be published by Transnational Law in 1994; many papers consider the problems and limitations of enforcement by national courts and national authorities.

Mark Hoskins, '*Garden Cottage* Revisited: The Availability of Damages in the National Courts for Breaches of the EEC Competition Rules' [1992] E.C.L.R. 257.

House of Lords, 8th Report of the Select Committee on the European Communities, *Competition Practice*, 23 February 1982 (H.L. 91), now out of print.

——, Select Committee on the European Communities, *Enforcement of Community Competition Rules*, 7 December 1993, HL paper 7. (These are significant critical reports and the minutes of evidence by officials and practitioners are of exceptionally high quality. The first report resulted in several reforms to DGIV's procedure and the second may well do so.)

C. S. Kerse, *op. cit.* main bibliography, at chap. 10.

Valentine Korah, 'The Rise and Fall of Provisional Validity — the Need for a Rule of Reason in EEC Antitrust' (1981) 3 N.W.J. Int'l. L. & Bus. 320.

——, 'Comfort Letters — Reflections on the Perfume Cases' [1981] 6 E.L.R. 14.

——, 'The Judgment in *Delimitis*: A Milestone towards a Realistic Assessment of the Effects of an Agreement — or a Damp Squib?' [1992] 5 E.I.P.R. 167.

Paul Lasok, 'Assessing the Economic Consequences of Restrictive Agreements: a Comment on the *Delimitis* case' [1991] 5 E.C.L.R. 194.

Jeremy Lever, 'U.K. Economic Regulation: Use and Abuse of the Law' [1992] 2 E.C.L.R. 55.

Enric Picanol, 'Remedies in National Law for Breach of Articles 85 and 86 of the EEC Treaty: A Review,' 1983/2 L.I.E.I. 1.

Alan J. Riley, 'More radicalism, Please: The Notice on Co-operation between National Courts and the Commission in applying Articles 85 and 86 of the EEC Treaty' [1993] 3 E.C.L.R. 91.

Mario Siragusa, 'The System of Notification: Summary of the Relevant rules' [1986] *Fordham Corporate Law Institute*, chap. 11, from p.246.

Piet Jan Slot and *Alison McDonnell* (eds.), *Procedure and Enforcement in EC and US Competition Law, Proceedings of the Leiden Europa Instituut seminar on User-Friendly Competition Law*, Sweet & Maxwell, 1993.

Michel Waelbroeck, 'Que reste-t-il de la validité provisoire des ententes' [1974] c.d.e. 169.

Richard Whish, 'The Enforcement of E.C. Competition Law in the Domestic Courts of Member States' [1994] 2 E.C.L.R. 60, Baron de Lancey lecture.

7 Classes of Agreement Clearly Prohibited

7.1 Distinctions between naked and ancillary restrictions of competition and between horizontal and vertical agreements

The Sherman Act 1890 in the US prohibits all agreements, combinations and conspiracies in restraint of trade. This prohibition is as broad as that in article 85(1), and might have been construed to render all commercial transactions illegal: if traders satisfy their needs for supply or demand with particular traders, fewer opportunities remain available to others. To avoid such a preposterous result, the judges early read into the Act a qualification, foreshadowed by the common law doctrine of restraint of trade, that only unreasonable restraints are illegal.

7.1.1 *Naked restraints illegal per se*

Even so, the US courts did not permit parties to justify price fixing cartels or collective boycotts by competitors on the ground that the prices fixed were reasonable, or that a collective boycott was agreed for justifiable purposes, such as restraining infringement of copyright for which the civil remedies were considered to be too weak. In his famous judgment in *US* v. *Addyston Pipe and Steel*,[1] Judge (later President) Taft distinguished a naked cartel between competitors to keep up the price of steel, which was illegal however reasonable the prices set, from restraints ancillary to a wider lawful purpose. In the absence of a competitive market, there is no way of knowing what level prices would have reached but for the cartel. Even if prices were reasonable yesterday, it does not follow that they are today. Judge Taft refused to 'set sail on a sea of doubt' and permit the justification of a cartel on the ground that the prices fixed were reasonable. The issue was not one that courts could resolve.

In this condemnation of naked cartels that are not clothed in any pro-competitive transaction that they make viable, the Commission and Court have followed the American case law, although on different reasoning. The Commission and Court tend, rather, to look to the examples of agreements listed in article 85(1). Nevertheless, price fixing agreements between competitors and collective boycotts have attracted heavy fines and rarely been exempted. The economic objections to market power are explained at 1.3–1.3.2.5 above and to cartels at 2.2.4–2.2.4.3 above.

1 85 Fed. 271 (6th Cir., 1898), affirmed by Supreme Court on other grounds.

7.1.2 *Ancillary restraints may be justified*

As an illustration of the kind of agreement that might be lawful, Judge Taft instanced covenants not to compete with the buyer of one's business or with a partner or former partner. Permitting sales of goodwill may be pro-competitive. It encourages the proprietor of the business to build up goodwill to sell later, and enables him to move on or retire and a younger man to take over. No one would pay for goodwill if next day the former proprietor could legally canvass his former customers. The reasonableness of the restraint can be judged by the amount of protection needed to enable the goodwill sold to keep its value. Under US law, as under the English common law, the restraint would have to be limited in time and space to the products and area for which the business had achieved a reputation.

A very similar analysis of covenants on the sale of a business has been adopted by the Commission in *Nutricia*[2] and confirmed by the Community Court in *Remia and Nutricia* v. *Commission*.[3] The Court said that the Commission was right to assert that such covenants do not, in themselves, infringe article 85(1). The situation with the restriction should be compared with that which would have prevailed without it: no one would have bought the business without some protection. Perceived *ex ante*, no competition that was possible was restrained: only perceived *ex post* was competition reduced. The protection must, however, be limited in time and space to what is necessary to make the transaction viable. Moreover, the Commission decided in *Quantel*[4] that the vendor may not protect itself territorially from the buyer of one of its subsidiaries, with whom it had previously not been competing. This decision may deter management from selling off parts of a business that could be better managed by third parties and so may reduce efficiency and competition rather than increase it.

Article 85(3), unlike US antitrust law, provides a possibility for exemption, and in many situations where US courts might now hold that competition is not restricted, the Commission has held to the contrary but granted an exemption under article 85(3). In this way it has centralised control in its own hands as only the Commission has power to grant exemptions. The drawback has been that it has insufficient resources to grant many exemptions and national courts asked to enforce a contract have no power to exempt. The problem was considered in Chapters 5 and 6 above and we will return to it when dealing with specific kinds of ancillary restraints, for instance, at 8.5.1 below when

2 [1984] 2 C.M.L.R. 165.
3 (42/84) [1985] E.C.R. 2545.
4 [1993] 5 C.M.L.R. 497.

considering the Court's judgment in *Pronuptia*, which adopted the ancillary restraints doctrine.

7.1.3 *Horizontal and vertical relationships*

A slightly different distinction from that between naked and ancillary restraints has been developed by some economists between horizontal agreements made by firms that would otherwise compete with each other at the same level of trade or industry — between manufacturers, between retailers or between licensees of competing products — and vertical restraints between firms at different levels of trade or industry, such as a supplier and his customer or a licensor of technology and his licensee.

Horizontal restraints are highly suspect, although some joint ventures between potential competitors may be necessary if economies of scale are to be realised or other pro-competitive developments are to take place. Competitors are likely to want to raise prices collectively and, if not exposed to substantial competition, may be able to do so. The Court stressed the distinction in *FEDETAB*,[5] without articulating the reasons for it and, in *SSI*,[6] it confirmed that high fines were appropriate for a horizontal, naked cartel to maintain dealers' margins.

A supplier or technology holder normally has no interest in protecting his dealers or licensees from competition between each other. The lower the price they charge the more will be sold and, other things being equal, the greater the profit of the firm upstream. It is in his interest to protect dealers or licensees from each other only to the extent necessary to induce investment that would not otherwise occur.

A dealer might not be prepared to advertise goods, enable the public to inspect them or provide technical advice that might increase the popularity of the brand, if a discount house, not having borne similar costs, could take a free ride on the investment and undercut the dealer investing in the service. For this sort of reason, the US Supreme Court held in *Continental TV* v. *GTE Sylvania*[7] that location clauses, whereby each retailer agreed to sell only from a specified address in order to protect dealers in a different city, were not necessarily illegal. Such a clause may make competition between brands possible, by restricting competition between dealers in the same brand.

Sylvania's market share increased after adopting the practice; it was not encouraging dealers to sell less on higher margins, but encouraging them to perform pre-sales services. Similarly, a patentee may have to protect a licensee if the latter is to develop a market and tool up to

5   (209–215 & 218/78) [1980] E.C.R. 3125, and 7.3 below.
6   (240–242, 261, 262, 268 & 269/82) [1985] E.C.R. 3831.
7   433 U.S. 36 (1977), 53 L.Ed.2d 568.

operate a system that may not even have been tried on an industrial scale. The first licensee might not undertake the investment at all if he feared that when he got the system to work smoothly and began to trade profitably, another licensee with lower costs, because the market is developed and improvements to the technology have been passed on to it, could reap where he has sown.

Possibly for this kind of reason, the Community Court ruled in *La Technique Minière* v. *Maschinenbau Ulm*[8] that to grant a dealer an exclusive territory does not infringe article 85(1) if exclusivity is necessary to penetrate a new market. An agreement should be appraised in its legal and economic context. Similarly, in *Nungesser*[9] it held that, in view of the investment by both the patentee and licensee, an open exclusive licence does not, in itself, infringe article 85(1). In *Pronuptia*,[10] many restrictions of conduct necessary to make distribution franchising viable were ruled not in themselves to restrict competition. Nevertheless, the Community Court has not embraced the American doctrine wholeheartedly. It has rarely accepted what it calls 'absolute territorial protection' and, apart from *Remia*,[11] its judgments seem to have been confined to exclusive agreements. The Commission has followed the Court to some extent, especially in some of the block exemptions, which permit exclusivity and some territorial protection under article 85(3),[12] but has rarely cleared agreements as outside the prohibition of article 85(1) on this ground.

It is regretted that the Commission and Court do not stress more clearly the distinctions between naked and ancillary, or between horizontal and vertical, restraints. Article 85(1) does not refer in so many words to horizontal or vertical agreements. The distinction is relevant only indirectly because the effects of each on competition differ according to the relationship of the parties before the transaction. Similarly, article 85(1) does not distinguish in words between naked and ancillary restraints. In *FEDETAB*[13] the Court clearly distinguished vertical from collective exclusive dealing in holding that provisions it had cleared in a vertical context were forbidden when adopted by competitors, but later, in *Salonia* v. *Poidomani*,[14] it advised a national court to apply the rule it had developed for vertical agreements to a horizontal agreement.

Professor, now Judge, Posner in the US has gone much further and

8   (56/65) [1966] E.C.R. 235.
9   (258/78) [1982] E.C.R. 2015, and 10.3 below.
10   (161/84) [1986] E.C.R. 353, and 8.5.1 below.
11   Cited at 7.1.2. above.
12   See Chaps. 8 and 10 below.
13   Cited at n. 5 above.
14   (126/80) [1981] E.C.R. 1563, and 7.3 below.

suggested that owing to the interest of the supplier or licensor in not raising the prices of the goods to the public, vertical restraints should be *per se* legal. This remains controversial even in the US. Not all kinds of goods need much pre-sales investment on which others could take a free ride. For some products, many buyers do not need pre-sales advice from the retailer. If a few marginal customers do, however, it may pay the brand owner to encourage the dealer to provide it, by promising him an exclusive territory or maintaining resale prices.

It is not always easy to detect a horizontal agreement between dealers to which effect is given vertically in supply contracts. Moreover, in Europe, efficiency is not the only aim of the competition rules; the well-being of small and medium sized firms is mentioned in the preamble to the treaty. This concern is not limited to those that produce efficiently what consumers want to buy. The preamble also refers to 'fair competition,' which some perceive as including the right of those that have not made the investment to share in its benefits. See 1.3.2.3 and 2.4 above.

Neither the distinction between naked and ancillary restraints nor that between horizontal and vertical agreements solves all the problems, although each helps. The ancillary restraint doctrine may apply both to vertical and to horizontal agreements.

In *Topco* v. *US*[15] some small supermarket chains had collaborated through a trade association to develop the Topco mark, and only one shop in any locality was allowed to join the association and use the mark. The Supreme Court rightly treated it as a horizontal agreement between the supermarkets rather than as a vertical licence. Was the development and licensing of the mark to be thought of as ancillary to a market sharing agreement or *vice versa*? Probably it increased competition by helping small supermarkets to compete with larger but, unfortunately, it was condemned as being an unreasonable restraint of trade.

In *Rothery Storage & Van Co.* v. *Atlas Van Lines,*[16] Judge Bork suggested that to the extent that *Topco* stands for the proposition that all horizontal restraints are automatically illegal even if ancillary to a pro-competitive transaction, it must be regarded as effectively overruled by various recent decisions of the American Supreme Court.

An agreement, rather similar to that in *Topco*, made through an association of small grocers was cleared by the Commission in *SPAR*,[17] but only because its effects were not appreciable, not because it enabled small grocers to compete with supermarket chains by combining their purchases.

---

15   405 U.S. 596 (1972).
16   792 F.2d 210 (D.C. Cir., 1986).
17   [1975] 2 C.M.L.R. D14.

7.2 Naked horizontal cartels affecting price and allocating markets

There is little point in notifying naked, horizontal cartels. They have been condemned clearly by the Commission in decisions, statements to the press and in its annual *Reports on Competition Policy*. Fines will not run for the period between notification and a decision by the Commission, but the latter may make a simplified decision under regulation 17, article 15(6), which would expose the parties again to the risk of fines if they continue the practice.

If one discovers that one's client or firm has entered into a horizontal cartel it is safer to ensure that it is terminated forthwith. After five years the Commission would no longer be able to impose fines.[18] Notification is but slight mitigation of fines for the period before notification, whereas voluntary termination coupled with the introduction of a compliance system fully backed by top management before any sign of enforcement interest would be a strong mitigating factor if the Commission discovers the cartel before the five years are up.[19]

To be forbidden, collusion must be capable of affecting trade between member states and have the object or effect of restricting competition within the common market. The list of practices set out in article 85(1), although not exhaustive, exemplifies agreements likely to restrict competition. The most immediate and effective competition between suppliers of goods or services satisfying similar needs is in price, and article 85(1)(a) expressly lists agreements which 'directly or indirectly fix purchase or selling prices or other trading conditions' as falling within the prohibition.

The *Quinine Cartel* decision[20] was the first to condemn a naked cartel to raise prices by restricting production. Undertakings in the Netherlands, France and Germany agreed not only on the prices they would charge, but also to keep out of each other's national markets. These restrictions are listed in article 85(1)(b) and (c). Quotas were also allocated for countries with no national producer. The decision that these restrictions contributed to the division of national markets and denied consumers the benefit of competition was upheld by the Court in *ACF Chemiefarma NV* v. *Commission*.[21] The *Dyestuffs* case[22] is an example of a simpler concerted practice affecting the levels of prices in different member states.

Recently, the Commission has devoted considerable resources to

18   Reg. 2988/74, and 5.11 above.
19   *National Panasonic* [1983] 1 C.M.L.R. 497.
20   [1969] C.M.L.R. D41.
21   (41/69) [1970] E.C.R. 661.
22   (48, 49, 51–57/69) [1972] E.C.R. 619, considered at 2.2.4.2 above.

detecting such agreements. In *Polypropylene*[23] and *Italian Flat Glass*,[24] the Court of First Instance quashed fines amounting to 10 million ECUs and more on individual firms only where it considered that the facts had not been proved. In 1994, a fine of over 100 million ECUs was imposed on the parties to a cartel in steel beams, some 32 million on British Steel.[25] An agreement may be condemned as having the prohibited effects even if the parties do not always abide by it,[26] although in some decisions by the Commission this has been found to reduce the gravity of the infringement and lead to lower fines.

7.2.1   Indirect influences on pricing policies

Restrictions inhibiting price competition indirectly are also prohibited. In *Re IFTRA Rules for Producers of Virgin Aluminium*,[27] the Commission treated the rules of a producers' association as an agreement between the members who signed them. They were found to restrict competition although they had not been enforced. Indeed, the excess supply which led to their introduction had been reduced by an increase in demand so soon that the rules had never come into play but they had been retained as a safety net.

The Commission considered that their existence, supported by an arbitration clause, was likely to discourage any action contrary to their letter and spirit. It added that their object would be to restrict competition if that were a reasonably foreseeable consequence of the application of the rules. Labelling the rules as being 'against unfair competition' did not prevent the application of article 85. The members agreed not to make 'destructive sales below cost.' Not only did this go beyond the law of unfair competition in some member states, it was so vague and difficult to apply that it was likely to discourage some commercial initiatives.

The parties agreed not to sell below their published prices and to exchange information about the prices charged. The Commission found that the restrictions had the object and effect of restricting competition. It confirmed that firms that do not enjoy a dominant position within the meaning of article 86 must be allowed to give secret discounts and that these might be necessary to obtain a foothold in a new market.

Other provisions for the exchange of information about costs were

23   *Hercules* v. *Commission* (T–7/89) [1991] E.C.R. II–1711 and others.
24   (T–68, 77 & 78/89) [1992] E.C.R. II–1403.
25   *European Producers of Beams*, O.J. 1994, L116/1. Appeals have been brought against the decision which was adopted under the ECSC.
26   *Belasco* (246/86) [1989] ECR 2117.
27   [1975] 2 C.M.L.R. D20.

also condemned as they enabled each firm to predict the others' pricing policy with greater certainty.

7.2.2 *Information agreements*

From the 1960s, Commission officials have considered that agreements to exchange information about prices that have been charged or paid might infringe article 85. According to the notice it issued in 1968 on Co-operation Agreements,[28] however, collaboration in producing joint statistics is permitted. The exchange of information about competitors is most likely to restrict competition when there are few of them; it takes place very rapidly, perhaps by telephone or facsimile through a trade association, and when it gives sufficient detail to identify specific contracts it enables competitors to react. In the *IFTRA Rules on Glass Containers*,[29] the Commission stated that:

> 'It is contrary to the provisions of article 85(1)... for a producer to communicate to his competitors the essential elements of his price policy, such as price lists, the discounts and terms of trade he applies; the rates and dates of change to them and the special exceptions he grants to specific customers.'

Where information about a discount that has been made to obtain an important order by one of only a few suppliers must be disseminated immediately to competitors, there is little incentive to make the price cut. Competitors are likely to make a similar cut when the next big order comes along, even if they do not actively retaliate against a firm that has rocked the boat. Consequently the initial discounter is unlikely to obtain additional turnover in the long run.

In *COBELPA*,[30] the Commission stated that there is no objection to national trade associations exchanging statistical information indicating the industry's output and sales, provided that individual firms cannot be identified. Under that agreement, however, the output of and prices charged by individual companies were disseminated, and the Commission proceeded to condemn the agreement although the parties amended it to comply with the Commission's suggestions. The parties:

> 'replaced the normal risks of competition by practical co-operation resulting in conditions of competition differing from those obtained in a normal market situation.'

The Commission objected even to the agreement to exchange

28   O.J. 1968, C84/14.
29   [1974] 2 C.M.L.R. D50.
30   [1977] 2 C.M.L.R. D28.

published price lists, on the ground that it was easier to get them directly from competitors, and they were an indication that the firms were not competing normally.

In its decision on *Vegetable Parchment*,[31] the Commission added that sending invoices, etc. on an individual basis would be evidence of a concerted practice, since individual information is not necessary for the preparation of trade statistics.

In the special circumstances of the Italian market for insuring engineering risks, however, the Commission exempted an arrangement whereby on the basis of information given to it about members' risk experience, *Nuovo Cegam*,[32] their association, prepared a common tariff of standard premiums for each kind of risk. The Commission did require that members should individually set their final premium to include a margin for costs and profit.

Since it is difficult to ensure that cheating does not break down an old fashioned cartel, it is unlikely that an agreement to exchange information about prices will for long keep prices much above the level they would reach in its absence. Nevertheless, the exchange of information may help to stabilise consciously parallel conduct, since a member realises that if it is caught cheating even once it will be treated as untrustworthy.

In *UK Agricultural Tractor Registration Exchange*,[33] there was no opportunity to cheat, since the UK ministry of transport provided detailed figures of deliveries within each of a large number of small areas with exact figures of sales by each member of each model. The Commission stressed that there were high entry barriers and that the market was concentrated. It is hardly surprising that it condemned the agreement, but the decision is useful in setting out the kinds of information that may safely be exchanged. The agreement was implemented for 12 years before it was notified, so it was somewhat surprising that the Commission did not consider the possibility of fines. It is currently investigating agreements to exchange far less detailed information.

7.2.3 *Joint sales organisations*

In the days when cartels were lawful, one of the most effective forms was a joint sales organisation. Members gave up their own marketing resources and could sell only through the joint organisation. This prevented cheating. Chiselling has always been a problem to those organising cartels. If the price is maintained above cost, including the normal

31   [1978] 1 C.M.L.R. 534.
32   [1984] 2 C.M.L.R. 484.
33   [1993] 4 C.M.L.R. 358.

return on capital, it pays each member to sell below the price agreed, if it can thereby increase its turnover. Such price cutting, however, leads to sales at lower prices, and conflicts with the interests of other members.

In *Dutch Nitrogenous Fertilisers*,[34] a joint sales organisation, confined to a single member state and sales outside the common market and where quotas were allocated to the parties, was condemned on the ground that the two members' co-operation within their joint venture affected their whole production and sales policy and so affected trade between member states. The Commission added that parallel imports might also be discouraged by the joint operations of firms supplying three-quarters of the Dutch market. There were various other circumstances deterring the parents from competing in other member states, such as joint ventures with foreign firms in which each participated.

In *Floral*,[35] the parties shared the profits of the joint sales organisation through their equity holding, and this was condemned. A firm that benefits from a substantial part of the profits earned by another member has less incentive to compete aggressively.

Nevertheless, in *Finnpap*[36] the Commission issued a notice stating that it did not intend to take action against a joint sales organisation of producers of newsprint outside the common market that was smaller than several of its competitors on the ground that it had no appreciable effect on trade between member states. It stated that there was no second hand market in newsprint as it is cut to the size used by a particular client. It did require the parties to alter their agreement, however, so as to permit buyers to meet unsolicited orders. It is at least possible that the decision was affected politically by the hope that Finland would join the EEA and, eventually, the EC.

In *UIP*[37] the Commission granted an exemption to a joint sales organisation that achieved substantial cost savings, where there were no quotas and profits could not be shared since each parent agreed to pay for the individual costs attributable to its products, and share only overhead costs. The joint sales organisation was established in such a way as not to make any profit.

It is thought that the favourable conclusions in both these later cases are sensible. Finnpap lacked market power, so could not increase prices by restricting output, but this was not the reason given, and there was no way that the parents in UIP could restrict production profitably to raise price. I am unhappy about the reasoning and would have been happier had *UIP* been cleared rather than exempted. The UIP exemption expires

34   *CSV* [1979] 1 C.M.L.R. 11.
35   [1980] 2 C.M.L.R. 285.
36   [1989] 4 C.M.L.R. 413.
37   [1990] 4 C.M.L.R. 749.

at a time when there is some hostility towards American films, so it will be interesting to see whether it is renewed and, if so, on what terms.

Where there are substantial savings in costs to be made through a joint sales organisation, one should be organised with these two cases in mind — avoid both quotas and the possibility of the sales organisation earning profits to be shared between the members.

Nevertheless, it would probably be dangerous not to notify the agreement, as Commission officials have often said in public that joint sales organisations should be treated as 'classic cartels.' The costs of notification are, however, substantial. The clearance in *Finnpap* took eight years and the exemption in *UIP* seven. Both organisations had to submit to changes in their agreements. Finnpap had to permit members to accept unsolicited orders, but as these still count against quota this is not likely to have had much effect on competition. UIP agreed to set up an arbitration system for unsatisfied dealers under pressure from the Commission, although it is difficult to see how this restored any competition that was restricted.

As I argued at 6.4.2.4 above, the Commission's practice of intervening in agreements long after they are made is most worrying, although bargaining power is less likely to have shifted when the relationship is horizontal than when it is vertical.

7.2.4 *Agreements about standard conditions of sale*

Agreements between competing suppliers not to sell a product in bulk, or to sell only on prescribed conditions of sale have been condemned, but in its Notice on Co-operation Agreements,[38] the Commission has stated that the issue of standard printed forms is unobjectionable, provided that firms are free not to use them and there is no tacit agreement or understanding on prices, discounts or conditions of sale.

7.2.5 *Market sharing*

Agreements between competitors to fix prices are often supported by quotas, so that each party can maintain its share of the demand, which is likely to be reduced if they are successful in raising prices. *Quinine*[39] concerned an agreement whereby quotas as well as prices were fixed.

Indirect market sharing is also prohibited. In *White Lead*[40] an agreement fixing quotas in an attempt to prevent prices falling still further was replaced in 1971 by an agreement under which quotas were fixed only for

38   Cited at 7.2.2. above.
39   Confirmed in *ACF Chemiefarma* discussed at 7.2 above.
40   [1979] 1 C.M.L.R. 464.

countries outside the EC, but members were required to notify all export deliveries, broken down by country, to a central office for distribution. The common market was excluded from this at the end of 1972, but the parties continued to notify the central office of their deliveries in each member state, and the Commission concluded that the quota system was intended to apply to the common market. It condemned the exchange of information as a concerted practice: it was not normal statistical information, since sellers were identified. The Commission also condemned a quota scheme, although it was not being adhered to very well, as having the object of restricting competition.

7.2.6 *Maximum buying prices*

Agreements to combine buying power are equally prohibited. After the Commission's intervention, the users of *Belgian Industrial Timber*[41] agreed to abandon an agreement about maximum buying prices.

7.3 Collective discrimination — boycotts and reciprocal exclusive dealing

In the Benelux it has been traditional for traders to collaborate through a trade association. There may well be half a dozen classes of members: manufacturers, importers, wholesalers, retailers, repairers, itinerant traders, restaurants and so forth. Rules or recommendations will determine with which classes of members each class may deal on trade terms. Importer and manufacturer members are entitled to sell only to wholesalers and wholesalers to buy only from them, and so on down the chain.

A non-member at any level of trade will be unable to deal on trade terms with members at any level. Except when there is a substantial part of the trade outside the association, an outsider will be unable to operate unless it can make the products or import them and sell at the retail level itself; frequently, multiple retailers are excluded from membership or are not permitted to undercut other retailers.

In *FEDETAB*[42] the Commission condemned many such restrictions, although some of them had ceased to operate after 1975. The restrictions included:

(1) the approval and classification of wholesalers and retailers into categories, with different profit margins provided for each category;

(2) the collective maintenance of resale prices during periods when

---

41 Press release [1976] 1 C.M.L.R. D11.
42 [1978] 3 C.M.L.R. 524.

price competition was compatible with the restrictive Belgian tax system;
(3) the criteria for approving traders and the collective boycott of those not approved;
(4) the standard terms of payment; and
(5) the requirement that some retailers should stock a minimum number of brands.

The decision was confirmed by the Court in 1980.[43] Even though the Court accepted that government measures made it impractical for manufacturers and importers to compete in ways that would affect retail sale prices, it condemned the collective fixing of margins which prevented price competition at intermediate stages. The Court clearly distinguished its case law on selective distribution, whereby an individual brand owner may restrict dealers from selling to traders who lack appropriate premises and staff (8.3.3 below) from collective agreements, whereby all manufacturers collectively set and apply the criteria, although later cases such as *Salonia* v. *Poidomani*[44] have ignored this important distinction. In confirming the decision of the Commission not to grant an exemption, the Court denied that increasing the number of outlets necessarily improved distribution:

'The quality of a distribution sector may be judged above all by its commercial flexibility and capacity to react to stimuli from both manufacturers and consumers.'

The Court stressed the importance of adaptation to new purchasing habits. Sales by supermarkets had increased, although they no longer stocked, as previously they were required to do, such a wide range of brands as did the specialist trade. This must have reduced their costs and enabled them to compete in price and freshness with more traditional outlets.

This clear judgment condemning such trade association practices should facilitate the Commission's task in restraining them.

In *APB*[45] the Commission intervened in a collective boycott organised by a trade association of pharmacists in Belgium. Pharmacists there are legally responsible for the products they sell and the association organised a testing facility to ensure that products corresponded to the claims made for them by their manufacturers. They seem to have carried on the testing without charge, and the manufacturers were then entitled to use the association's stamp on the product and required not to sell the product save to pharmacists. This seems to have been a serious

43   Cited at 7.1.3. above.
44   Cited at 7.1.3. above.
45   [1990] 4 C.M.L.R. 176.

restriction of competition, aggravated by the government licensing system, which limited the number of pharmacists permitted to operate.

The association altered its scheme so that manufacturers were entitled to sell tested products to other retailers in the same packaging, but without the stamp. The Commission decided that the restriction of competition was no longer appreciable. The association was providing a service, on which it could not let other retailers take a free ride, but I can see no reason why it could not have charged the manufacturers for the testing, and then permitted them to sell, with the stamp, wherever they wanted.

The Commission did not discuss the free rider problem in its decision, so it did not consider other ways of solving it. Nor did it say why a collective reciprocal arrangement like this did not have appreciable effects. It admitted that pharmacists charge more than other retailers. It is regretted that the reasons for the decisions were suppressed. (See 14.2.1 below.)

7.4 Collective aggregated discounts

In *Re German Ceramic Tiles*,[46] an aggregated discount scheme was condemned. Most German manufacturers of ceramic tiles agreed through their trade association to grant to buyers quantity discounts based on the total quantities bought by each during the year from all German producers. This deterred buyers from buying a small quantity of such tiles from Italy. Where that additional quantity would enable the firm to obtain a higher discount, an outside competitor would have to match that discount not only on the quantities it sold, but also on all the quantities bought from those whose sales were counted when calculating the amount of discount.

This effect was magnified by the uncertainty: most customers would not know during the year whether at the end they would have bought just under the amount needed to obtain a better rate of discount if they were to buy a particular lot of tiles from outsiders. The scheme had effects similar to a collective loyalty rebate. The Commission added that collectively agreed discount rates also inhibited almost the only form of price competition possible in an oligopolistic market.

The foreclosing effect is similar to progressive discounts offered by a dominant firm, as in *Michelin*,[47] but a dominant firm cannot be expected to compete with itself in price, so the second reason does not apply to unilateral conduct. Aggregated discounts are unlikely to generate any cost savings, but they help small suppliers to compete with larger ones.

---

46   [1971] C.M.L.R. D6.
47   (322/81) [1983] E.C.R. 3461, and 4.3.2.2 above.

7.5 Agreements to tie the sale of one item to another

In *FEDETAB*,[48] the Commission objected to the minimum range of brands that supermarkets were required to stock by the manufacturers' association. The general tenor of the Court's judgment,[49] and its observation that the requirement might increase costs, demonstrate its support for that view, although it did not find it necessary to deal with the question specifically.

The Commission has condemned individual tying agreements too as contrary to article 85. In *Vaessen/Moris*,[50] it objected to a patent licensee being required to buy from the patentee all the casings into which he packed *saucissons de Boulogne* with the aid of the patented device, on the ground that this extended his market power over the device to the market for casings. Lucio Zanon has suggested,[51] however, that the more significant effect was that the patentee was able to obtain more from those processors who used the device more intensively and to whom it was worth more. Had the patentee required payment of a royalty it might have been difficult to control cheating.

In *Tetra Pak II*,[52] the Commission imposed the highest fine ever, 75 million ECUs, on a Swiss firm that was very dominant over the supply of machinery for making and filling cartons with milk, fruit juice and the like in such aseptic conditions that the liquid would last for six months without refrigeration. Amongst other practices, Tetra Pak required those to whom it supplied machines to buy their cartons from it. The Commission considered that the tie would extend its dominance to the supply of the cartons. It did not address the question how Tetra Pak would be able to exploit its market power over the machines more effectively. To the extent that licensees disliked buying the licensor's cartons, they would pay less for the patented machines. Tetra Pak does not appear to have suggested that it was trying to extract more revenue from those who most used the machinery. So, one cannot criticise the Commission for not taking the point. The decision is subject to appeal before the Court of First Instance.[53]

7.6 Export bans

The Commission habitually imposes heavy fines on firms that have engaged in classic cartels, often supported by provisions that none shall

48   Cited at 7.3 above.
49   Cited at 7.1.3. above.
50   [1979] 1 C.M.L.R. 511.
51   See *op. cit.*, bibliography, 7.8 below.
52   [1992] 4 C.M.L.R. 551.
53   Case T–83/91.

sell in the home territory of the others. These are horizontal agreements between competitors and not ancillary to any pro-competitive transaction. So they are clearly anti-competitive.

The Commission has, however, taken a further more questionable step in habitually condemning export bans and deterrents accepted in vertical agreements between a single brand owner and its dealers. In the absence of a cartel at the level either of dealers or of manufacturers, a brand owner usually has an interest in letting its dealers compete with each other, as the lower the margin on which they operate the more they are likely to sell. Chicago economists argue that if a supplier does protect its dealers from each other, it is likely to be because the dealers have to invest in pre-sales services, for which it is difficult to charge, and which promote the brand generally.

If poaching were permitted, one dealer could take a free ride on the services of another. Buyers could make their selection in an expensive shop providing the services, but buy in a discount shop that does not. This would deter any shop from providing services that might be worth while for the brand as a whole.

The contrary argument is that cartels at both dealer and producer level are more likely in Europe than the United States, and that the Commission lacks the resources to discover them all, so is more hostile to agreements even if they appear to be vertical.[54] It is also possible that only a few marginal customers require the services, in which case it may be undesirable that those who do not should have to pay to encourage it.

It was the absolute territorial protection given to Consten and the sole distributors in other member states that prevented the Commission from exempting the exclusive dealing agreement in *Grundig*.[55] We will see in Chapter 8 that the exclusivity would probably have been exempted otherwise. If competition policy is seen as a buttress to the principle of the free movement of goods, services and so forth, and businessmen's strategic reactions to public control are ignored, then any artificial restriction on imports or encouragement to exports interferes with the functioning of the common market, and is very unlikely to be tolerated.

Subject to the *de minimis* rule accepted by the Court in *Völk* v. *Vervaecke*,[56] export restrictions have always been treated as prohibited by article 85 and not capable of exemption. The very large fine imposed on *Tetra Pak* under article 86 was due in part to its attempt to maintain different prices in different member states.

In *Miller Schallplatten*,[57] the Court condemned a no-poaching clause

54   See M. Waelbroeck, *op. cit.*, bibliography, 7.8 below.
55   [1964] C.M.L.R. 489, and 2.3.1 and 2.4 above.
56   (5/69) [1969] E.C.R. 295, and 2.4.1 above.
57   (19/77) [1978] E.C.R. 131.

without making any market analysis beyond stating that Miller supplied some 5 per cent. of the German market for records and without enquiring whether dealers would have been reluctant to incur sunk costs in the absence of protection.

Yet, provided that export bans do not lead to absolute territorial protection, the Court held in two cases on licences of intellectual property rights in 1982[58] that export bans do not in themselves infringe article 85(1).

7.6.1 Export deterrents

The Commission looks not only to the form of the agreement, but also to the substance. In *Distillers*[59] it condemned the export deterrent created by Distillers' dual pricing system as well as the absolute export ban which it replaced. The Commission refused to exempt The Distillers Company's conditions of sale, under which British dealers were required to forego discounts amounting to about £5 per case on any whisky that was to be exported. The market in the UK was extremely price sensitive, so Distillers could not afford to spend on advertising there. On most of the Continent, there were discriminatory taxes imposed on whisky to protect the locally made liquor. It was illegal even to advertise whisky in France. These rules had been condemned by the Community Court but had not then been abrogated by the French state and were enforced.

The Commission did not accept the argument that this was needed to protect Distillers' exclusive distributors on the Continent who spent considerable sums on promotion from which parallel importers would benefit.

On appeal,[60] however, Advocate General Warner strongly rejected the Commission's view. He accepted that the markets in the United Kingdom and on the Continent were very different, and that more promotion was needed on the Continent if whisky was to be sold there. He added that Distillers could not afford to raise its prices in the United Kingdom to cover the overseas promotional costs in view of the evidence given of the extreme elasticity of price there. The dual pricing system had not eliminated parallel exports as did the *Grundig* agreements (see 2.3.1 and 2.4 above) and 340,000 cases had been sold at the higher price for export to the Continent. He would, therefore, have recommended that the decision should be quashed had Distillers notified its agreement.

The Court did not deal with the points of substance, but merely confirmed that an exemption could not be granted as the agreement had

58   *Nungesser* and *Coditel (2)*, described at 10.3 below.
59   [1978] 1 C.M.L.R. 400, and 1.3.2.5 above.
60   (30/78) [1980] E.C.R. 2229.

not been properly notified. Mr. Warner's opinion was extremely cogent. Distillers reacted to the decision by raising the price of some brands in the United Kingdom, and those almost ceased to sell there. It also ceased to sell Johnny Walker Red Label Whisky in the UK. The other brands ceased to be promoted on the Continent.

The result was that the Distillers' brands sold in the United Kingdom differed from those sold on the Continent. This splitting of the brands and the Commission's decision that led to it must have retarded the integration of the common market once the discriminatory taxes and other disadvantages imposed on the sale of whisky on the Continent were abrogated.

The year after it split its brands, Distillers' turnover on the Continent for those brands the price of which in England had not been raised, and which ceased to be worth promoting, increased less than its turnover for those that suffered no parallel imports and whose price was higher. In 1983, the Commission announced that it was considering an exemption for a dual pricing scheme for Red Label, provided that the additional price charged in the UK to dealers for the quantities exported was used for promotion.[61] No such decision was ever adopted.

The Court confirmed the condemnation of export bans and the imposition of fines even where there was governmental price control leading to artificially low prices in the country of export in *BMW Belgium* v. *Commission*,[62] and the Commission continues to condemn such bans, without considering whether the effects of governmental price controls in one country should be spread in this way throughout the common market, or whether it would pay a firm to refuse to supply a country subject to such control.[63]

Even mild deterrents that may be important to people who move around the common market, such as military personnel and diplomats, have been prohibited. In *Zanussi*,[64] the Commission objected to a system of after-sales guarantees that did not apply to washing machines used in a different member state from that where they had been bought. This view was accepted by the Court in *Hasselblad* v. *Commission*.[65] In the first *Transocean* case,[66] however, members were allowed to agree to pass over part of the profit on exports to other member states, on the ground that the product was new and required promotion in many ports if it were to compete with marine paints from larger competitors. The

61 [1983] 3 C.M.L.R. 173.
62 (32 & 36–82/78) [1979] E.C.R. 2435.
63 *Johnson & Johnson* [1981] 2 C.M.L.R. 287.
64 [1979] 1 C.M.L.R. 81.
65 (86/82) [1984] E.C.R. 883.
66 [1967] C.M.L.R. D9.

agreement has been exempted again three times, but without the previous profit passover clause.

The Commission adopts simply argued decisions imposing fines for vertically imposed export bans, for instance in *Polistil/Arbois*,[67] although it has recognised the free rider argument and permitted limited territorial protection in its group exemptions. See Chapters 8 and 10–12 below.

7.6.2 *Export boosters*

These are just as incompatible with the concept of a common market as import deterrents. In *Cimbel*,[68] the Commission condemned the arrangements whereby Belgian cement producers collectively subsidised exports by equalising receipts between domestic sales and exports. It held that:

> 'the object and effect of the agreement regarding the equalisation of receipts is to reinforce artificially the competitive position of the various Belgian manufacturers in export markets ... the manufacturers in other member states are not in fact in competition with another manufacturer but with all the members of Cimbel.'

It added that the subsidisation of exports by domestic sales injures consumers within the home country. Since the Commission said that the arrangement helped to absorb surplus capacity, I would have enquired whether average export prices exceeded variable costs before concluding that there was a cross-subsidy. Similar examples are *Milchförderungsfonds*[69] and the *EATE levy*.[70]

7.7 Conclusion

Subject to a *de minimis* rule the Commission has habitually condemned agreements directly or indirectly, fixing buying or selling prices, or sharing markets. Collective boycotts and provisions that isolate part of the market, such as export boosters, import deterrents or aggregated discounts, have also habitually been forbidden.

There is little point in notifying such agreements to the Commission — usually only a few months' freedom from fines will be bought, and the firm will become involved in difficult negotiations under regulation 17/62, which may well be extended to other products or practices. It is better to avoid making such agreements or, if they already exist, to

67   [1984] 2 C.M.L.R. 594.
68   [1973] C.M.L.R. D167.
69   [1985] 3 C.M.L.R. 101.
70   [1988] 4 C.M.L.R. 677.

terminate them, both formally and in practice. The introduction of an effective compliance system caused the Commission to fine *National Panasonic*[71] very much more lightly than it had fined *Pioneer*.[72]

The following chapters will describe the kinds of agreement that may well enjoy exemption.

7.8 Bibliography

Charles Baden Fuller, 'Price Variations — the Distillers Case and Article 85 EEC' [1979] I.C.L.Q. 128.

——, 'Economic Issues Relating to Property Rights in Trademarks: Export Bans, Differential Pricing, Restrictions on Resale and Repackaging' (1981) 6 E.L.R. 162,

Ivo Van Bael, 'Heretical Reflections on the Basic Dogma of EEC Antitrust: Single Market Integration' [1980] 10 R.S.D.I.C. 39.

Frank H. Easterbrook, 'The Limits of Antitrust' (1984) 63 Texas L. Rev. 1.

——, 'Vertical Arrangements and the Rule of Reason' (1984) 53 Antitrust L.J. 135.

Valentine Korah, 'Goodbye Red Label: Condemnation of Dual Pricing by Distillers' [1978] 3 E.L.R. 62.

——, 'The Rise and Fall of Provisional Validity — the Need for a Rule of Reason in EEC Antitrust' [1981] 3 N.W.J. Int'l. L. & Bus. 320.

——, 'The Paucity of Economic Analysis in the EEC Decisions on Competition — *Tetra Pak II*' (1993) 46 Current Legal Problems 148,

Richard Posner, 'The Next Step in the Antitrust Enforcement treatment of Restricted Distribution: *per se* legality' (1981) 48 U. Chi. L. Rev. 6.

Michael Reynolds, 'Trade Associations and the EEC Competition Rules' (1985) 23 R.S.D.I.C. 49.

Scherer and *Ross*, *Industrial Market Structure and Economic Performance*, 3rd ed., 1990, pp.542–548.

Michel Waelbroeck, 'Vertical Agreements: Is the Commission right not to follow the current U.S. policy' (1985) 25 R.S.D.C.I. 45.

Lucio Zanon, 'Ties in Patent Licensing Agreements' (1980) 5 E.L.R. 391.

---

71   [1983] 1 C.M.L.R. 497.
72   [1980] 1 C.M.L.R. 457.

8 Distribution Agreements

8.1 Exemption of individual agreements

In its first decisions from the beginning of 1964, the Commission granted individual exemptions under regulation 17 to several exclusive distribution agreements. It decided that agreements whereby a manufacturer agrees to sell to a sole distributor for a large area, often the whole of a member state, have the object of restricting competition in that they restrain the manufacturer from supplying any other distributor directly, thus restricting competition between its distributors.

This reasoning was criticised at 2.4 above. If Grundig would not have been as successful in France without the help of Consten and if Consten would not have invested as much without protection from free riders, the exclusive territory might have increased competition by enabling Grundig to penetrate a new member state. The Advocate General recommended that the decision be quashed for lack of reasoning on this point. To use the language explained at 7.1.2 above, the exclusive provisions were ancillary to the pro-competitive transaction and may have been necessary to enable Grundig to penetrate the French market.

The Commission takes the view that agreements by the distributor not to handle competing goods make the entry of competing manufacturers into the industry or the expansion of existing suppliers more difficult, although this would be so only if it were difficult for a new dealer to enter the market, and if so many of the existing ones of all kinds were tied for so long that those remaining free could not absorb the output of a plant large enough to produce economically.[1]

Exclusive distribution agreements provide by far the easiest way for a manufacturer to start exporting to another member state and increase competition by increasing the number of brands available. So the Commission granted, first, individual exemptions and, later, a group exemption. In the sixth recital to regulation 1983/83 by which the Commission granted a group exemption,[2] the Commission stated:

'... exclusive distribution agreements facilitate the promotion of sales of a product and lead to intensive marketing and to continuity of supplies while at the same time rationalizing distribution; ... they stimulate competition between the products of different manufacturers; ... the appointment of an exclusive distributor who will take over sales promotion, customer services and carrying of stocks is often the most effective way, and sometimes indeed

1 See *Stergios Delimitis* v. *Henninger Bräu* (C–234/189) [1991] E.C.R. I–935, and 2.4 above and 8.4 below.
2 Analysed at 8.3 below.

the only way, for the manufacturer to enter a market and compete with other manufacturers already present; ... this is particularly so in the case of small and medium-sized undertakings;'

The Commission's reference to exclusive distribution as sometimes being the *only* way for small or medium-sized undertakings to compete in the market may be very helpful when justifying agreements that do not qualify under the group exemption. It may be difficult to find a non-exclusive dealer prepared to make the investment necessary to promote a new or foreign product. The costs of promotion, maintaining stocks and advertising, etc. may result in a loss during an initial period of months or even a few years and, unless protected for several years more from free riders distributing the same brand who would benefit from its advertising, a dealer might not be prepared to make the investment. Indeed, some protection from other dealers in the same brand may be needed to induce dealers to continue to promote well-known products. Moreover, it is often only a dealer confined to a single manufacturer's product who has sufficient incentive to pass on complaints and suggest that modifications be made to the product.

8.2 Clearance of exclusive dealing agreements

The Court is less likely to hold that exclusivity requires exemption than the Commission has been. In *La Technique Minière* v. *Maschinenbau Ulm*,[3] it ruled that an exclusive distribution agreement would not have the effect of restricting competition, if there was no other way of penetrating a new territory. Agreements should be appraised in their legal and economic context.

The Commission cleared a few agreements, mostly those whereby a common market manufacturer has appointed an exclusive distributor for a territory outside the common market. In *Grosfillex*[4] the Commission found that an agreement did not come within the prohibition of article 85(1), despite an export prohibition, on the ground that re-exports from the Swiss distributor to the common market were unlikely in any event, owing to the double customs barrier at that time. The Commission also mentioned the numbers of competing suppliers and competition at the distribution level. The restrictions were, therefore, not significant. If that be so, one wonders why the parties should insert them, unless they are needed to protect markets outside the common market. Their abrogation may avoid considerable risk and bother. *Grosfillex* must, however, now be applied with caution. For most products and countries that belong to the EC or EEA or with whom the

3   (56/65) [1966] E.C.R. 235, and 2.4 above.
4   [1964] C.M.L.R. 237.

Community has a Free Trade or association agreement the argument no longer applies as customs duties have been reduced or eliminated.

8.3 Group exemption for exclusive distribution agreements— regulation 1983/83

The Commission received about 30,000 notifications of exclusive distribution agreements soon after regulation 17 was passed. In an attempt to escape from such a load of paper and concentrate its resources on more serious restrictions of competition, it obtained from the Council of Ministers, under regulation 19/65, power to exempt by category exclusive distribution and purchasing agreements and agreements licensing intellectual property rights. It first exercised this power by adopting regulation 67/67 which exempted exclusive distribution and purchasing agreements. This has expired and been replaced by regulations 1983/83 and 1984/83, but the case law under regulation 67/67 remains relevant.

Regulation 1983/83 exempts exclusive distribution agreements whereby a supplier of goods for resale grants a dealer an exclusive territory, whether or not the dealer agrees to buy only from him. Regulation 1984 exempts exclusive purchasing agreements, whereby a dealer who is not granted an exclusive territory agrees to buy goods for resale only from the supplier. Articles 1 and 2 of each regulation set out the permissible, or 'white,' clauses and article 3 the 'black' list of conditions which prevent the application of the exemption. In regulation 1984/83, there are special provisions for beer and petrol to which regulation 1983/83 does not apply. They will not be dealt with in this book.

The Commission has published a notice[5] giving its interpretation of some aspects of the regulation. This does not bind anyone other than the Commission, but may be helpful in resolving ambiguities.

There are considerable advantages to be derived from bringing a contract within the terms of one of the new regulations. Such a contract enjoys exemption from article 85(1), although not from article 86,[6] unless and until the Commission makes a decision terminating the exemption for the future.[7] Consequently, the agreement can be enforced in national courts without the need for a market analysis, or the difficulty due to national courts having no power to grant an exemption. Where it is not possible to bring a contract within the terms of a group exemption, there is much to be said for getting as close as possible, as the Commission has occasionally granted an individual exemption by

---

5 As corrected, O.J. 1984, C101/2.
6 *Tetra Pak I* (T–51/89) [1990] E.C.R. II–309, and 8.3.6 below.
7 *Tetrapak II* (T–83/91), not yet reported.

analogy with the group exemption. The group exemptions reflect the policy of the Commission to various classes of transaction.

8.3.1 Article 1 — exclusive supply

Article 1(1) exempts from the prohibition of article 85(1):

'... agreements to which only two undertakings are party and whereby one party agrees with the other to supply certain goods for resale within the whole or a defined area of the common market only to that other.'

Unfortunately, although article 85 applies to services as much as to goods, the regulation applies only if goods be sold for resale, so it cannot apply to agreements for the distribution of services. Often this is done through agents, but contracts with agents frequently infringe article 85(1).[8] It is not easy for the Commission to overcome this *lacuna*, because regulation 19/65 empowers it to grant exemptions only for agreements for the supply of goods for resale. If it wanted to extend the group exemption to services, it would have to propose an extension to regulation 19/65 by the Council, and also amend the regulation appended to the EEA treaty.

It is not always clear whether goods are supplied 'for resale' if the final stage of manufacture is carried out by the dealer. This is known colloquially as the 'bottling' problem. If a fizzy drink producer should supply its distributor with a syrup which the distributor bottles before adding water and gas, is the syrup sold 'for resale? Almost certainly not.[9] The problem has also arisen in relation to pharmaceutical products, sold in bulk and later formulated and packaged into a form suitable for administration to patients. Retailers normally add distilled water to a car battery and charge it. It is still not clear how much processing can be left to the dealer, without losing the benefit of the group exemption.

The Commission's notice suggests that goods are 'resold' if they retain their identity. Where the reseller improves the goods, the answer will depend also on the proportion (unstated) of the value added. Trade usage is also relevant. Components incorporated as original equipment into a final product probably lose their identity and are not resold. If the reseller does more than repackage the goods, one might consider notifying the agreements with a request for individual exemption, although no provisional validity would be gained thereby.

In *Junghans*[10] the Commission decided that the regulation does not apply unless there be an exclusive territory. In that case, there were three dealers for one area, but Junghans promised each of them that it would

---

8   See 8.7 below.
9   *Campari* [1978] 2 C.M.L.R. 397.
10   [1977] 1 C.M.L.R. D82.

supply no others. The Commission exempted the agreement by analogy to the group exemption. In such a case, however, it would be necessary to notify the agreement to obtain an individual exemption and there would be no provisional validity meanwhile.

It is hoped that this will be altered when the regulation comes up for renewal at the end of the millennium. The Commission started to exempt restrictions of the same kind but more limited scope only in its group exemption for patent licences, adopted the year after regulation 1983/83. Nevertheless, some people argue that an exclusive territory provides benefits that merit favourable treatment which should not be given to a partially exclusive dealer. In my view, the Commission should be concerned, rather, with whether there is a free rider problem to be overcome. It is anomalous that a dealer may not be protected by an exclusive territory if there is more than one dealer, even if each is protected from the others for one field of use.

8.3.2   Article 2 — permitted clauses or 'white list'

If an exclusive territory is granted to the reseller in accordance with article 1, the restrictions of competition specified in article 2 may also be accepted. Article 2(1) provides that:

> 'Apart from the obligation referred to in Article 1 no restriction on competition shall be imposed on the supplier other than the obligation not to supply the contract goods to users in the contract territory.'

It is clear from recital 6 that this is an optional provision. Often the supplier wants to be able to supply at least large users directly. Provided it does not restrict its dealer from supplying them, it may continue to do this, but the exemption will still apply if it agrees not to supply for resale or use anyone in the territory. This provision, which was not included in the earlier version of the exemption in regulation 67/67, prevents the regulation applying when the supplier accepts other obligations which restrict competition.

Article 2(2) provides that:

> 'No restriction on competition shall be imposed on the exclusive distributor other than:
> (a) the obligation not to manufacture or distribute goods which compete with the contract goods;
> (b) the obligation to obtain the contract goods for resale only from the other party;
> (c) the obligation to refrain, outside the contract territory and in relation to the contract goods, from seeking customers, from establishing any branch and from maintaining any distribution depot.'

Unlike the corresponding provision in regulation 67/67, the first provision no longer applies for a year after the agreement is terminated.[11] Perceived from when the agreement is terminated it might, in limited circumstances,[12] be more competitive to enable the former dealer to compete. On the other hand, an unknown dealer could take a free ride on the reputation of an established brand owner by becoming its dealer in a specialised shop and receiving training, but then handling competing goods when its contract expires. Perceived *ex ante*, it may be better to permit an exclusive purchasing obligation to persist for a reasonable period[13] than to encourage the brand owner to do its own retailing or give up training its dealers. Where this argument does not apply, the supplier is unlikely to stipulate continued exclusive purchasing.

In contrast to the position under regulation 67/67, the exclusive purchasing obligation on the reseller is now exempt only if the dealer is granted an exclusive territory. If not, regulation 1984/83 may apply.

Paragraph (c) permits a limited export ban. If, however, the reseller agrees not to accept unsolicited orders from outside its territory, the group exemption does not apply. In the Commission's jargon, an active sales policy outside the dealer's territory may be restricted, but not a passive one.

Any other restriction of competition accepted by either party will prevent the group exemption from applying. Resale price maintenance or location clauses confining sales to particular premises may protect the dealer from free riders less than does article 2(2)(c), but if they do restrict competition — and the Commission believes that usually they do — they prevent the exemption from applying even to the clauses specifically exempt by articles 1 and 2. It is not stated even that the supplier may promise to impose on other dealers a limited export ban of the kind described by article 2(2)(c) in order to protect the contracting dealer. In the light of recital 6, quoted at 8.1 above, however, it is thought that such a provision cannot exclude the exemption.

The Commission has taken a strict and formalistic view against most post-sales restrictions.[14] Article 2(3), however, permits the supplier to require the reseller to take certain measures to promote sales: (a) to handle a full range or buy minimum quantities, (b) to sell the contract goods under trade marks or packed and presented as specified by the supplier, and (c) to promote the contract goods by advertising, maintaining a sales network or holding stocks, to provide pre- or post-sales

11 Recital 8.
12 Spelled out by the Court in *Delimitis*, discussed at 2.4 above and 14.2.2 below.
13 As cleared by the Court in *Pronuptia*, discussed at 8.5.1 below.
14 8.3.3 and 8.3.4 below.

services and to employ staff with specialised or technical training. Other obligations are allowed only if they do not restrict competition.

Although the Commission sometimes assumes that any restriction relating to goods bought by a dealer restricts competition and prevents the application of the exemption, it may well be argued that the protection of one dealer's investment from other dealers taking a free ride on it may not restrict any competition that was possible: without the protection no one might have made the investment necessary to exploit the territory. It may be more costly to develop a market in less populous areas, and local dealers may not be prepared to do so if dealers in other territories are able to exploit the towns. In a national or the Community Courts such an argument might well be accepted. It is clear that an obligation to keep products in ways reasonably necessary for their preservation, such as specific temperature ranges, freedom from light, humidity and so forth, does not restrict competition and would not prevent the regulation from applying.

8.3.3   Obligations not permitted by article 2 — selective distribution

The limitation by article 2 of the restrictions of competition that a dealer may accept may make it difficult for a brand owner to control its retail outlets. The term 'selective distribution' in EC practice is normally limited to multi-tier systems. If a supplier does not enjoy a dominant position within the ambit of article 86, he may unilaterally choose with whom he deals however arbitrary his choice, but may not impose unjustifiable obligations on his distributors or wholesalers as to who may buy from them. In *AEG Telefunken* v. *Commission*,[15] the Community Court stated that:

'... it has always been recognised in the case law of the Court that there are legitimate requirements, such as the maintenance of a specialist trade capable of providing specific services as regards high-quality and high technology products, which may justify a reduction of price competition in favour of competition relating to factors other than price. Systems of selective distribution, in so far as they aim at the attainment of a legitimate goal capable of improving competition in relation to factors other than price, therefore constitute an element of competition which is in conformity with Article 85(1)...

The Court specified in ... [*Metro* v. *Commission*[16]] that such systems are permissible, provided that resellers are chosen on the basis of objective criteria of a qualitative nature relating to the technical qualifications of the reseller and his staff and the suitability of his trading premises and that such conditions are laid down uniformly for all potential resellers and are not applied in a discriminatory fashion.'

15   (107/82) [1983] E.C.R. 3151, from para. 33 onwards.
16   (26/76) [1977] E.C.R. 1875.

In the second paragraph quoted, the Court distinguishes what are called 'quantitative criteria.' As soon as the supplier attempts to protect the investment of approved dealers in qualifying, the Court and Commission consider that article 85(1) is infringed, although such restrictions have occasionally been exempted.

The test given by the Court in *AEG* and other cases was interpreted narrowly by the Commission in *Ideal-Standard's distribution system*,[17] where it doubted whether plumbing fittings can be considered as technically advanced products justifying selective distribution. It also doubted whether limiting wholesalers rather than retailers to those technically qualified escapes the prohibition of article 85(1). In *Binon*,[18] however, the Court went the other way and considered that selective distribution of newspapers did not infringe article 85(1) provided there is no quantitative criterion. The judgment was not very cogent as the justification for limiting retail outlets was the need to deliver quickly in the morning, and for that, a quantitative restriction would be appropriate.

In *Grundig (2)*,[19] the Commission held that requiring retailers to make a substantial sales effort is caught by article 85(1) and it exempted but did not clear the obligation of such retailers to stock and display as full a range as reasonable and a requirement that the goods be demonstrated in suitable premises and attractively displayed.

The Commission seems to be stricter in ensuring that all dealers who meet the criteria are approved for vehicles and hi-fi than for perfumes. Grundig was persuaded to provide that dealers might suggest other dealers who might apply for admission, and if their applications were not dealt with within four weeks they would automatically be admitted.[20] In 1992, it had required perfume manufacturers to set up a system whereby those wanting approval would be inspected within a maximum of six months and an average of four months, and permitted to receive products from other dealers within the year.[21] One might have thought that the inspections were more complex for consumer electronics than for perfume and no reason has been given for the distinction. Different teams of officials deal with the two sectors.

Nevertheless, the Commission submitted to the Community Court in *Demo-Studio Schmidt*[22] that there is no duty to supply all approved

17 [1988] 4 C.M.L.R. 627.
18 (243/83) [1985] E.C.R. 2015.
19 O.J. 1985, L233/1.
20 *Grundig III*, O.J. 1994, L20/15.
21 *Yves Saint Laurent Parfums* [1993] 4 C.M.L.R. 120.
22 (210/81) [1983] E.C.R. 3045, at 3056.

dealers. The Court accepted this in *Metro (2)*.[23] The infringement of article 85(1) consists in prohibiting dealers admitted to the distribution network from supplying other resellers who are qualified but not admitted. Nevertheless, a unilateral refusal to supply a dealer on grounds other than those specified by the Court may lead to a finding that the supplier was tacitly colluding with the dealers he was protecting by not supplying retailers likely to operate on very slim margins, contrary to article 85.[24]

Even where the criteria for choosing retailers lower down the chain are justifiable, it is seldom possible to come within the Court's definition. Normally it is expensive to comply with the criteria. Consequently, a manufacturer or trade mark owner may also have to adopt quantitative criteria, promising not to select any other retailers within 50 kilometres, or in an area with a population of half a million, or some such limitation. The Commission and Court have treated such criteria as restricting competition contrary to article 85(1), although individual exemptions have occasionally been granted. Such selective distribution systems cannot benefit from the group exemption under regulation 1983/83. When granting individual exemptions, the Commission habitually requires that one approved dealer be allowed to sell to any other. This makes it difficult for the brand owner to maintain significantly different prices in different areas.

In *FEDETAB*,[25] the Court stated that its ruling that selective distribution based on qualitative criteria does not infringe article 85(1) applies only to the conduct of an individual brand owner and not to collective agreements. This was forgotten in *Salonia* v. *Poidomani*,[26] where the Court ruled on a collective system for distributing newspapers in Italy. It is thought that not only is *FEDETAB* more sensible, it is a better precedent since the judgment was on an appeal from the Commission rather than on a preliminary ruling, where the Court may be less familiar with the facts.

The Court's view that some restrictions of conduct imposed on dealers do not restrict competition is welcome, but the narrowness of the tests is regretted. The rules are nonsense commercially and economically speaking. It is very difficult for the holder of a prestige brand to become master of its retail outlets. The rules encourage a firm that is concerned about the services offered by retailers to integrate forward, and sell as far down the distribution chain as it can manage. This policy does not increase

---

23   (75/84) [1986] E.C.R. 3021, at para. 64.
24   *AEG*, n. 15 above.
25   (209–215 & 218/78) [1980] E.C.R. 3125, discussed at 7.3 above.
26   (126/80) [1981] E.C.R. 1563.

competition and may well reduce efficiency. Moreover, it cannot be adopted by small firms.

In *Villeroy & Boch*,[27] however, the Commission relented. A selective distribution scheme was operated for ceramic tableware in a very competitive market by a firm with several thousand retailers. Villeroy & Boch insisted on its approved retailers also selling other brands, so that customers could choose effectively. The Commission cleared a restriction on selling to non-approved retailers, and an obligation to promote the goods, in view of the competitive nature of the market and the large number of retailers, which made a dealers' cartel impossible. This represented a change of view by the Commission. As Professor Demaret suggests,[28] it is difficult to reconcile the decision with *Grundig (2)*. Unfortunately, different people are now in charge, and the Commission has returned to ignoring market conditions, and applying the rules formalistically.[29] Consequently, it is almost impossible for brand owners to control the retail outlets where their products are sold to consumers and to compete on pre-sales services rather than on price.

Firms that want to control the services provided by retailers may prefer to use the franchising route, analysed at 8.5 below. There is a separate group exemption granted by regulation 123/85 and explained in guidelines published by the Commission for the selective distribution of motor vehicles to be driven on public roads. Its validity has been questioned and, since its application is limited to a single range of products, it will not be considered in this book. It is due to expire at the end of 1995.

8.3.4 *Obligations not permitted by article 2 — resale price maintenance (r.p.m.)*

Originally, in the absence of export bans, the Commission used to clear r.p.m. on the ground that it was unlikely to have a perceptible effect on trade between member states. Since, however, it is a restriction on the reseller not permitted by article 2(2) of regulation 1983, its presence prevents the application of the group exemption.

In the context of individual decisions on exclusive distribution, too, the Commission seems adverse to r.p.m.[30] and in *Hennessy/Henkell*[31] it condemned the maintenance of the prices of its German exclusive dealer

27   [1988] 4 C.M.L.R. 461.
28   *Op. cit.*, bibliography, 8.9 below.
29   *Yves Saint Laurent Parfums*, n. 21 above, and *Parfums Givenchy* [1993] 5 C.M.L.R. 579; and the Court of First Instance in *Vichy* (T–19/91) [1991] E.C.R. II–265.
30   *Brooke Bond Liebig* [1978] 2 C.M.L.R. 116.
31   [1981] 1 C.M.L.R. 601.

by a French producer of cognac, although the prices of other brands were not maintained, and there might have been inter-brand competition in the Federal Republic of Germany. The Commission did not allege that prices in the Federal Republic were being kept up to guarantee the margins of Hennessy's dealers in other member states, nor did it allege that prices were maintained elsewhere in order to protect Henkell's margins, so the reasoning about the effect on inter-state trade is not as strong as it might have been.

Again, the Commission seems to be thinking of codes. One may protect one dealer from another by giving it an exclusive territory supported by restrictions on active sales imposed on other dealers, but one may not protect a retailer who provides services from free riders who do not by resale price maintenance, nor may one restrict dealers' customers.

This is supported by the Court's judgment in *Louis Erauw-Jacquéry* v. *La Hesbignonne*,[32] where it assumed that resale price maintenance has the object of restricting competition without considering the possibility of free riders, and questioned only whether it has a perceptible effect on trade between member states.[33]

8.3.5   *Article 3 — conditions precluding group exemption or 'black list'*

Article 3 provides that the regulation shall not apply in four specified situations, and is colloquially referred to as the 'black list.'

'Article 1 shall not apply where
(a) manufacturers of identical goods or of goods which are considered by users as equivalent in view of their characteristics, price and intended use enter into reciprocal exclusive distribution agreements between themselves in respect of such goods;
(b) manufacturers of identical goods or of goods which are considered by users as equivalent in view of their characteristics, price and intended use enter into a non-reciprocal exclusive distribution agreement between themselves in respect of such goods unless at least one of them has a total annual turnover of no more than 100 million ECU;'

The Commission has always feared that where there are few manufacturers of a product, A might appoint B its exclusive dealer in one part of the common market, and B appoint A in another. Neither would buy much from the other and, in effect, each would be kept out of the other's territory. Article 3(a) ensures that such an agreement is not exempted by the regulation. In *Siemens/Fanuc*,[34] the Commission imposed fines of

32   (27/87) [1988] E.C.R. 1919.
33   See also *Pronuptia*, discussed at 8.5.1 below.
34   [1988] 4 C.M.L.R. 945.

1 million ECUs each on firms entering into such reciprocal dealing agreements.

There may, however, be good reasons even for reciprocal exclusive dealing and then the Commission is prepared to send a comfort letter. In *Fluke/Philips*,[35] Philips had tried in vain to penetrate the market in North America and Fluke that in Europe. Both made measuring and testing devices but, apart from multimeters, their ranges were complementary. Together they supplied some 20 per cent. of the common market requirements of three kinds of multimeters, so the overlap was not *de minimis*.

The Commission pointed out that since neither firm had managed to sell much in the other's territory, it was unlikely that they had entered into the agreement to keep each other out. It was much more likely that each was trying to find a good distributor. Moreover, Philips could not afford to anger Fluke by not selling its products effectively in the common market. In these circumstances the reasons for blacklisting reciprocal exclusive dealing did not apply, and the Commission proposed to grant an exemption or send a comfort letter.

This precedent is important not merely in the field of distribution. There was a time when individual exemptions were refused with virtually no reasoning if there was a blacklisted clause. This no longer seems to be the case when the reason for blacklisting does not apply.

Two distinct problems arise from article 3(b). A large firm — according to articles 4 and 5 it is the turnover of the total group of companies, worldwide and in all products, that counts — may include a small manufacturing business. It may not be large enough to warrant a separate distribution network in all parts of the common market. The obvious kind of person to take on the distribution is a competing firm, whose salesmen will visit the appropriate kind of retailer. The manufacturer will now have to find a small firm to carry on its distribution or notify the agreement and hope for an exemption or comfort letter.

The other problem relates to what happens if an existing dealer who did not manufacture competing goods is taken over by a company that makes similar products somewhere in the world. Suddenly condition (b) prevails, and the Commission assumes that the block exemption ceases to apply to the dealer's restrictions on distributing competing goods, unless it would not be commercially sensible for the dealer's sister company to sell in the common market because of the cost of transport from a distance. The supplier may not even know. Yet, although the restrictive terms, including the exclusive territory and exclusive

---

35   O.J. 1990, C188/2. A formal decision was never adopted. See Commission's *19th Annual Report*, p.63.

purchasing obligations, may become void, it is possible that the duty to supply remains valid. That would prevent the appointment of a new exclusive distributor, unless provision were made in the original contract for the termination of the whole agreement should the group exemption cease to apply. When drafting exclusive distribution agreements, thought should be given to this problem.

The next two items in the black list are concerned with trade from other member states. The regulation does not apply where

'(c) users can obtain the contract goods in the contract territory only from the exclusive distributor and have no alternative source of supply outside the contract territory;'

The source of supply may be outside the common market, and would probably have to be if the territory covered the whole common market and there were only one tier of distribution. Users must be able actually to get the goods, so manufacturers may be advised to require their dealers to make passive sales outside their territory when requested.

Paragraph (d) prevents the application of the exemption if either party makes it difficult for users or dealers to obtain the goods through parallel imports. The trade mark may be vested in the dealer, provided it does not exercise its right to keep out goods lawfully sold elsewhere.[36]

8.3.6   Other provisions of regulation 1983/83

The regulation includes transitional provisions that have expired. The Commission may terminate the exemption by an individual decision if it considers that the agreement does not come within the terms of article 85(3). Such termination dates only from the date of the decision. In *Tetra Pak I*,[37] the Commission considered that the conditions of article 85(3) did not apply to a licence falling within the group exemption for patent licensing. It stated that it would have withdrawn the benefit of that regulation under provisions similar to those in regulation 1983/83 had the licensee not agreed with the licensor that it might appoint competing licensees (see 14.2.5 below). No group exemption has formally been withdrawn: the Commission's threat to withdraw it is enough to force the parties to amend or abrogate their agreement.

8.4   Exclusive purchasing agreements

Exclusive purchasing agreements by dealers do not fall within regulation 1983/83 unless they are given an exclusive territory (8.3.1 above). In *Brasserie de Haecht* v. *Wilkin*,[38] Advocate General Roemer made it

36   *Hydrotherm* v. *Andreoli* (170/83) [1984] E.C.R. 2999.
37   (T–51/89), cited at 8.3 above.
38   (23/67) [1967] E.C.R. 407.

clear that an exclusive purchasing agreement by a retailer would infringe article 85(1) only where there are barriers to entry at the dealer's level, and so many outlets of all kinds are tied for so long by exclusive purchasing agreements that it would be difficult for a new manufacturer to enter the market. He considered that the national court that had asked for the preliminary ruling should also take into account the possibility of a new entrant buying up retailers or chains of them. The Court did not dissent when it ruled that a national court should consider the agreement in its legal and economic context and see whether other cafés were tied before deciding that an agreement between a small brewery and a single café infringed article 85(1).

The Advocate General's view was accepted by the Court in *Stergios Delimitis v. Henninger Bräu*.[39] It pointed to the benefits an exclusive purchasing agreement brought to each party and concluded that such an agreement did not have the object of restricting competition. It then went on to advise a national court asked to enforce the agreement to consider the market as a whole before considering that an exclusive purchasing agreement had the effect of restricting competition.

The Commission, however, seems to ignore this part of the judgment in *Delimitis* and in the German ice cream cases, *Langnese* and *Schöller*,[40] talked of an exclusive purchasing obligation foreclosing competition from the particular outlet or freezer and therefore infringing article 85(1). Contrary to the ruling of the Court, it began to analyse the market only under article 85(3). It is the Court's judgment that should be followed by national courts rather than inconsistent analysis by the Commission. Nevertheless, it should be borne in mind that the Commission may take the less liberal view. On that view, a group exemption may be necessary for exclusive purchasing agreements.

8.4.1 *Group exemption in regulation 1984/83*

Regulation 1984/83 has much the same structure as regulation 1983/83. Article 1 exempts exclusive purchasing agreements by a dealer who is not given an exclusive territory. Article 2 is fairly similar to that in the companion regulation, save that there is no provision for a restriction on active sales, but article 3, after blacklisting reciprocal exclusive purchasing agreements — the converse of the reciprocal exclusive sales agreements blacklisted in regulation 1983/83 — continues differently.

39   (C–234/89) [1991] E.C.R. I–935.
40   *Langnese-Iglo* and *Schöller Lebensmittel* [1994] 4 C.M.L.R. 51, each subject to appeal on the grounds set out in the O.J. (T–24/92) O.J. 1992, C 121/16, and (T–28/92) O.J. 1992, C138/7.

The Commission is concerned to ensure that such agreements come to an end at least every five years and that they do not extend to more than one type of goods, where these are neither by their nature nor according to commercial usage connected to each other. According to the Commission's notice, this does not prevent several agreements being made between the same parties relating to different classes of goods as long as no agreement is dependent on the others being made.

There are specific provisions for the sale of beer to pubs and cafés and for the sale of petrol to petrol stations in view of the long term obligations undertaken in return for the suppliers' investment in the premises. These will not be considered in this book.

8.5 Franchising

Franchising was hardly known in Europe in the 1960s but has spread rapidly from the US and is now a common way to distribute goods when considerable control over retailers is desired. Unlike the agreements exempted by regulations 1983/83 and 1984/83, the block exemption for franchising extends also to the provision of services. The word, franchising, is a chameleon, and when it is referred to it is usually worth asking what is meant. Franchisors do not, necessarily, supply the franchisee with the products they sell, in which case it is hardly a method of distribution.

8.5.1   *The Court's judgment in Pronuptia*

In *Pronuptia*,[41] the Community Court was asked to make a preliminary ruling. Pronuptia de Paris and its subsidiaries franchised various retailers to sell wedding gowns according to its instructions in shops that looked as if they were owned by Pronuptia, but which in fact belonged to the franchisee. Pronuptia promised that it would franchise only Frau Shillgalis in three cities in Germany, the franchised territories, and she agreed only to sell from the contract premises. When sued for non-payment of royalties, she argued that the franchise agreements were anti-competitive and that, by virtue of article 85(2), the duty to pay royalties was void.

The Court confined its remarks to what it called 'distribution franchising,' — in the USA usually called 'retail format franchising.' It observed at paragraph 15 that franchising has desirable characteristics. It is not so much a method of distribution as a method for a firm that has found a

41   (161/84) [1986] E.C.R. 353.

good way to sell things to exploit its formula without using much of its own capital. It also permits firms without the necessary experience, but some capital, to enter the market with the aid of the instructions, assistance and established reputation of the franchisor. The Court did not conclude that the transaction increases competition, merely that it does not, in itself, restrict it, contrary to article 85(1). It then observed that, for such a transaction to be viable, the franchisor must be able to ensure that the assistance it gives to its franchisees does not benefit competitors even indirectly; and it must preserve the identity and reputation of the network.

On the first ground, it cleared a restriction on a franchisee opening a competing shop or selling its shop without the franchisor's approval. On the second ground, it cleared many methods of control. The franchisee may be required to sell only from premises laid out and decorated according to instructions; not to change its address without consent; to follow the franchisor's business methods; where it is not possible to specify the goods to be sold or there are too many franchisees to monitor, to buy goods only from designated sources, provided they may also be bought from other franchisees; and to obtain the franchisor's consent for the nature of any advertising, although the franchisor may not control the prices at which goods are advertised.

So far, the Court adopted the doctrine, described at 7.1.2 above, that ancillary restraints needed to support a transaction that is not anti-competitive do not restrict competition. Nevertheless at paragraph 24 it added that the obligation to sell only from the contract premises restrained the franchisees from opening a second shop without consent and, coupled with an exclusive territory, that gave each franchisee absolute territorial protection which, in accordance with the Court's judgment in *Consten and Grundig* v. *Commission*,[42] would infringe article 85(1) once the network was widespread. Nevertheless:

> '24. ... It is of course possible that a prospective franchisee would not take the risk of becoming part of the chain, investing its own money, paying a relatively high entry fee and undertaking to pay a substantial annual royalty, unless he could hope, thanks to a degree of protection against competition on the part of the franchisor and other franchisees, that his business would be profitable. That consideration, however, is relevant only to an examination of the agreement in the light of the conditions laid down in article 85(3).'

It is true that in *Consten and Grundig* (2.4 and 8.1 above) the Court mentioned that the product was of a very well known brand, but that was not true in France when the distributorship was negotiated. It is clear in *Pronuptia* that the Court is looking *ex ante* to the time when the

42 Cited at 2.3.1 above.

franchisee agrees to undertake commitments, and not *ex post* when he hopes to benefit from his investment. The Court's statement goes further than *Consten and Grundig* in one further way: it suggests that the Commission should exempt even absolute territorial protection if that were necessary to induce the franchisee to make commitments.

The Court added, in its summary at paragraph 27, that the agreement must be judged in the light of the particular provisions in the contract and their economic context. It may be that, as Advocate General Verloren Van Themaat had suggested, even an exclusive territory does not infringe article 85(1) if there is a great deal of competition from other brands, whether franchised or not.

The Court went on to rule that franchising agreements could not be brought within the group exemption granted by regulation 67/67, the predecessor of regulation 1983/83 (analysed from 8.3 above). Basically, the Court treated franchising as being different from distribution. I regret that the Court should perceive as different arrangements that have much in common in many cases, if not all. Where a franchisor does supply goods to a franchisee on the terms expressly permitted by the regulation, it is sad that it should be held not to apply without the Court giving any reason either of policy or based on the wording of the treaty or the regulation. Civil lawyers tend to think in legal categories more than common lawyers.

This part of the judgment placed considerable pressure on the Commission, which did not wish to discourage franchising, to grant a group exemption. Few franchisees would make commitments without at least a small exclusive territory. To come within the *vires* of regulation 19/65, the Commission had to gain experience by making individual decisions on franchising. It decided to include service franchises as well as those relating to goods.

Between the judgment in February 1986, and the adoption of the regulation in November 1988, the Commission exempted five standard agreements. They were very diverse, but every market seems to have been extremely competitive. The Commission might have cleared every one of them, but it believed that it had to make decisions exempting and not merely clearing franchising agreements if its powers to adopt the regulation were not to be challenged. It is regretted that now it has adopted its regulation, this practice may continue. In *Pronuptia*, the Court referred in its summing up in paragraph 27.1 to the economic context of the provisions which, presumably, means the amount of competition from outside the network. A national court asked to enforce a contract should follow the Court's judgment rather than the Commission's decisions when these are at variance.

8.5.2 Group exemption for franchising — regulation 4087/88

After adopting decisions that exempted rather than cleared franchising agreements in competitive markets,[43] the Commission adopted a regulation granting a group exemption to bilateral franchising agreements that confer an exclusive territory etc., but the definition of a franchising agreement is narrow. It must include obligations relating to:

'— the use of a common name or shop sign and a uniform presentation of contract premises and/or means of transport,
— the communication by the franchisor to the franchisee of know-how,
— the continuing provision by the franchisor to the franchisee of commercial or technical assistance during the life of the agreement.'

These items are cumulative, and qualifying 'know-how' is required by the definition clause to be 'secret, substantial and identified.' There is concern that in many agreements there will not be much know-how that qualifies in the manual. It is hoped that national courts asked to enforce an obligation to pay royalties will not lightly exclude the application of the regulation on this ground.

Article 2 lists the restrictions, said to be of competition, that are exempted by article 1. The licensor may grant an exclusive territory and agree not to grant a franchise, nor itself to exploit the franchise there, or supply the franchisor's goods there to third parties. It may also require the franchisee to exploit the franchise only from the contract premises and not to seek customers outside its territory; to buy the franchisor's goods only from nominated sources and not to buy competing goods, save for spare parts and accessories. There is rather less control permitted over sources of supply in relation to goods that do not qualify as franchisor's goods and this protection is circumscribed by article 5(b).

There is a long white list in article 3, but some clauses are said to be clear only if it is established that they are necessary to protect the franchisor's industrial or intellectual property rights or to maintain the common identity and reputation of the franchised network, while in *Pronuptia*, the Court alleged that they were necessary for these purposes *per se*.

The black list is divided into conditions that must be satisfied under article 4 and clauses that must not be included under article 5. The conditions mostly ensure cross-frontier trade. Unlike exclusive distribution exempted by regulation 1983/83, where the dealer may be required to obtain supplies only from the supplier, franchisees must be free to obtain goods from other franchisees. Moreover any guarantee the franchisee is obliged to give must apply also to goods bought from other

---

43 Discussed in my monograph, listed in the bibliography at 8.9 below, 1.5.1.1.

franchisees or distributors. Indeed territorial protection from distributors, where the franchisor uses both, is very limited.

On the other hand, greater control than is permissible under regulation 1983/83 (8.3.3 above) can be obtained over retail outlets under the franchising regulation. In a short, introductory book like this, it is inappropriate to go further into the detail of the regulation, which I have analysed at length in the monograph listed in the bibliography at 8.9 below.

8.6 General comments on the regulations

There are such advantages in ease of enforcement to be derived from bringing an agreement within a group exemption that this should be done wherever possible without serious commercial loss. Difficulty is to be expected where it is necessary to impose export restrictions or quantitative restrictions on the number of dealers to whom an intermediate dealer may sell.

If an exclusive distribution agreement cannot be brought within the group exemption, for instance one relating to services, it may not be possible to enforce it in the courts, unless and until an individual exemption be granted by the Commission. For this, it will be necessary to notify the agreement, unless it is absolved from notification under article 4(2) of regulation 17. If it becomes necessary to enforce the contract before the Commission makes a decision, the proceedings will probably be adjourned, and the Commission asked to give the case priority. Where there are quantitative restrictions on the retailers whom exclusive dealers may supply, which are justifiable to make commercially possible the necessary investment in stocks and skilled personnel, a national court may grant interlocutory relief, but in England this would be only on terms (6.1 above).

Franchise agreements that do not qualify under the group exemption may well not infringe article 85(1). Resale price maintenance must be avoided, although prices may be recommended. An exclusive territory does not require exemption until the network is widespread, and even then may not infringe article 85(1) if it operates in a competitive environment. This view of the Court, however, is contradicted by all the Commission's recent decisions.

The group exemptions do not expressly apply to article 86. The Court of First Instance decided in *Tetra Pak*,[44] however, that conduct that is stated in the recitals to the group exemptions to be desirable can be treated as an abuse of a dominant position. In that case, the Commission

44 Cited at 8.3.6 above.

found that the acquisition of a competitor with an exclusive licence to another source of technology infringed article 86 and the Court of First Instance confirmed that this would be a reason for withdrawing the exemption.

8.7 Agency

In 1962, when there was no case law and the Commission feared more notifications under regulation 17 than it could handle, it stated that, in its view, exclusive distribution agreements between principal and agent, including a *del credere* guarantee, do not infringe article 85(1). Vertical integration may, therefore, take the form of appointing agents instead of dealers.

The ambit of this possibility is, however, very narrow. In several cases such as *Pittsburg Corning Europe*[45], *Sugar*,[46] and *Belgian Travel Agents*,[47] both the Commission and the Court have made it clear that for an agreement to come within this exception, the agent must be integrated into the undertaking of the principal. It need not be an employee, but it must take its instructions in detail from the principal and, according to the Commission, not be a firm capable of acting in its own name and on its own behalf, nor must it act much on behalf of other principals. The Court refers to the agent being integrated into the undertaking of the principal — a test that is very difficult to apply as many dealers are closely integrated into the supplier's business. It is not enough to ensure that title to the goods should remain with the principal until it passes to a third party, since an agent is defined by reference to its commercial functions and not merely by reference to its legal position. The Commission has been working on a notice giving its views as to when an agreement with an agent infringes article 85(1). A draft circulated in 1991, but a final version has not yet been adopted. According to the draft, limitations on the authority of the agent will be cleared as not prohibited by article 85(1). When the agent is closely integrated into the organisation of the principal, only a restraint on passive sales will be treated as infringing article 85(1). One problem is that it is not easy to distinguish an agent from an independent dealer on the basis of integration, but that is the criterion that has been adopted by the Court.

A further limitation on this exception to the competition rules is that the law of many member states makes it very expensive ever to dismiss an agent, once it has acted for a few years. Commercial agents enjoy considerable protection under German and French law. The Council

45 [1973] C.M.L.R. D2.
46 (40–48, 50, 54–56, 111, 113 & 114/73) [1975] E.C.R. 1663.
47 *Vlaamse Reisbureaus* (311/85) [1987] E.C.R. 3801.

also adopted Directive 86/653,[48] which harmonises some of the rights and duties of agents and their principals. Some of the provisions can be avoided voluntarily, so it is important to check its terms. The wish to have independent entrepreneurs promoting one's products may be a stronger reason for not taking the agency route.

8.8 Collective exclusive dealing

This chapter has been concerned only with bilateral agreements between one supplier and each of its dealers. Collective agreements do not fall within the group exemption, and we saw at 7.3 that they are unlikely to receive exemption.

8.9 Bibliography

Ivo Van Bael, 'Heretical Reflections on the Basic Dogma of EEC Antitrust: Single Market Integration' [1980] 10 R.S.D.I.C. 39.

J. S. Chard, 'The Economics of the Application of Article 85 to Selective Distribution Systems' (1982) 7 E.L.Rev. 83.

Jean-Eric de Cockborne, 'New EEC Block Exemption Regulation on Franchising,' in Barry Hawk (ed.), [1988] *Fordham Corporate Law Institute*, Chap. 13.

Roger Daout, 'Distribution under EEC Law — an Official View,' in Barry Hawk (ed.) [1982] *Fordham Corporate Law Institute* 441.

Paul Demaret, 'Concurrence et Distribution en Droit Communautaire' [1984] *Juris Classeurs* 1–37.

——, 'Selective Distribution and EEC Law after the *Ford, Pronuptia* and *Metro II* judgments,' in Barry Hawk (ed.) [1986] *Fordham Corporate Law Institute* 151.

John Ferry, 'Selective Distribution and Other Post-Sales Restrictions' [1981] 2 E.C.L.R. 209.

Ian Forrester, 'Distribution and Agency Agreements in EEC Competition Law: A Survey,' 3 R.S.D.I.C. 3.

Frances Hanks and *Philip Williams*, 'The Treatment of Vertical Restraints under the Australian Trade Practices Act' (1985) 15 *Australian Business Law Review* 147.

Valentine Korah and *Warwick A. Rothnie*, *Exclusive Distribution and the EEC Competition rules — Regulations 1983/83 and 1984/83*, 1992, Sweet & Maxwell.

Valentine Korah, *Franchising and the EEC Competition Rules, Regulation 4087/88*, 1989, ESC, Oxford.

——, 'Exclusive Purchasing Obligations: *Mars* v. *Langnese and Schöller*' [1994] 3 E.C.L.R. 171.

——, 'Selective distribution' [1994] 2 E.C.L.R. 101.

Paul Lasok, case note on *Hydrotherm* v. *Andreoli* (170/83) [1984] 5 E.C.L.R. 241.

48   O.J. 1986, L382/17 on the co-ordination of the laws of the Member States relating to self-employed commercial agents.

9 Industrial Property Rights and the Free Movement of Goods

9.1 Intellectual property rights and competition

In order to encourage and reward investment in innovation, the law of most countries enables inventors or their employers to apply for patents. If these are granted, the patentee or holder may, generally, sue anyone who uses the patented process, or who makes, sells or imports goods made by use of the invention without a licence for a period, usually of 20 years. The patentee is protected from competition by others using the invention.

Copyright lasts even longer, under UK law generally for the lifetime of the author and 50 years thereafter,[1] and enables authors, or their successors in title, to sue those copying their work.

Trade marks may last indefinitely, as long as goods or services continue to be supplied under the mark. They enable the holder to identify goods and, in some countries including the UK, services as deriving ultimately from the same controlling source. The holder may change the specification, but has an interest in preserving any goodwill adhering to a mark and, consequently, has some incentive not to reduce quality.

On an analysis *ex post* — as perceived after the investment in innovation has been incurred — these exclusive intellectual property rights are anti-competitive since they restrain other people from taking advantage of innovation or reputation without the consent of the holder. They constitute barriers to entry. For this reason, German economists and political scientists after the second world war were distrustful of intellectual property rights and restrictive clauses in licences. This attitude has influenced the thinking of Commission officials dealing with licensing and may well have influenced the Court.

On the other hand, when analysed *ex ante* — from the time when the decision to invest or create was made — such rights encourage some forms of innovation that otherwise might not be worthwhile and so lead to a more competitive economy. Some inventions, once available, can be easily copied and, without protection, it would not be worth investing in making them. This is particularly true of pharmaceutical products that are costly to develop and take through their clinical trials, but can easily be copied. Many artistic works can be copied and, without copyright, authors and artists might have little chance to earn a living.

Trade marks enable the holder to sue those who confuse buyers into

---

1 Under the harmonisation directive described at 9.5 below, the period will be life plus 70 years throughout the EC and EEA.

thinking that their products emanate from him. They make possible competition in qualities that are not immediately obvious to shoppers, such as the taste of packaged food. They do not prevent others from selling identical goods unbranded or under their own mark. In the long term, protection of such rights may increase efficiency as well as consumer choice and so make the economy more competitive.

9.2 Birth of the distinction between the existence of rights and their exercise

The national limitations of intellectual property rights, however, are difficult to reconcile with the concept of a common market. A French patent extends only throughout France and a British one only throughout the United Kingdom. Exploitation of the invention in Belgium would not infringe either. Until the mid-1960s, it was widely believed that, for goods protected by such rights, the common market could be divided along frontiers through the use of national intellectual property rights.

Consten and Grundig v. *Commission*[2] was the beginning of a development preventing this. The way Grundig enabled its exclusive distributors for all member states except Germany to register the trade mark Gint, which it placed on all the apparatus made at that period, was described at 2.3.1 and 2.4 above. This enabled Consten to sue the parallel importer UNEF under French law for trade mark infringement in addition to unfair competition. The Advocate General considered merely that this was an abuse of trade mark law, since the Grundig mark adequately indicated the origin of the goods, that is, who was responsible for their specification.

The Community Court went further and distinguished the existence or ownership of such rights under national law, which may be protected under article 222 of the treaty, from their exercise, which is subject to the treaty provisions. In legal theory, it is impossible to draw the line between existence and exercise, except at the extremes. Analytically, the existence of a right consists of all the ways it may be exercised. In ruling that an important difference rests on a distinction which cannot be drawn by logical analysis, the Court created a very flexible instrument for it to develop the law and reduce the value of intellectual property rights.

2   (56 & 58/64) [1966] E.C.R. 299.

9.3 Free movement of goods

The principle stated in article 3(a) of the EC treaty[3] is crystallised in articles 30–36. Article 30 provides:

'Quantitative restrictions on imports and all measures having equivalent effect shall, without prejudice to the following provisions, be prohibited between member states.'

The Court has interpreted this provision, implementing one of the most fundamental principles of the common market, very widely. 'Quantitative restrictions' is a term referring to customs quotas — only so many widgets shall be imported from state A each year. An extreme quantitative restriction is a nil quota — no widgets shall be imported thence. The right of a patent or trade mark holder to restrain imports has been perceived as a measure of equivalent effect to a nil quota — no protected articles shall be imported without its consent. Article 34 makes similar provision for quantitative restrictions on exports.

Exceptions are provided in article 36 for measures justified on various grounds, including the protection of 'industrial or commercial property', but its provisions derogate from a fundamental principle of the treaty and have been narrowly construed. Moreover there is a sting in the tail:

'Such prohibitions or restrictions shall not, however, constitute a means of arbitrary discrimination or a disguised restriction on trade between member states.'

Article 36 confirms that the authors of the treaty thought that industrial and commercial property rights could be of equivalent effect to quantitative restrictions.

9.4 The exhaustion of intellectual property rights when a product has been sold by or with the consent of the holder in another member state

9.4.1 *Early cases on exhaustion*

The Court has developed the concept of the 'specific subject matter' of the particular kind of industrial or commercial property, in the light of which protection may be justified. In *Centrafarm* v. *Sterling*,[4] the Court stated:

'9. As regards patents, the specific subject matter of the industrial property is the guarantee that the patentee, to reward the creative effort of the inventor, has the exclusive right to use an invention with a view to

3 Set out in App. I.
4 (15/74) [1974] E.C.R. 1147.

manufacturing industrial products and putting them into circulation for the first time, either directly or by the grant of licences to third parties, as well as the right to oppose infringements.'

'The specific subject matter' includes both the nature of the right — the right to restrain others from using the invention or selling goods made through its use — and the reason the law grants it — the reward to those investing in innovation. *Parke Davis*[5] could not obtain a reward for its research and development from the items of the drug sold in Italy where it did not have a patent. The drug had been marketed by Parke Davis in Italy without it being able to extract a monopoly price from its purchaser or a royalty from a licensee.

Sterling was in a different position. It owned patents in the UK, Germany, the Netherlands and elsewhere. Centrafarm had bought the drug in England and Germany where Sterling had obtained some recompense; but the UK price for the drug was half the Dutch price, partly because of fluctuating currencies and partly because of the buying power of the government, which pays for most drugs used in the UK and which could obtain a compulsory licence under the Crown use provisions of the Patents Act 1949.

The Court does not seem to have been concerned about the size of the reward, and was not prepared to allow the national patent laws to divide the common market in order to permit Sterling to have a second bite of the cherry when its drug entered the Netherlands, where it was more highly valued:

'11. Whereas an obstacle to the free movement of goods of this kind may be justified on the ground of protection of industrial property where such protection is invoked against a product coming from a member state where it is not patentable and has been manufactured by third parties without the consent of the patentee
and in cases where there exist patents, the original proprietors of which are legally and economically independent,
a derogation from the principle of the free movement of goods is not, however, justified where the product has been put onto the market in a lawful manner, by the patentee himself or with his consent, in the member state from which it has been imported, in particular in the case of a proprietor of parallel patents.' [I have divided the sentence into three for ease of reference.]

The Court made clear the position at the two extremes, but there is some intermediate ground which it leaves open, part of which has been clarified by later cases. Later judgments have tended to apply paragraph 11 literally and treat a patent as exhausted by any sale in another member state by or with the consent of the holder, whether or not a

5   (24/67) [1968] E.C.R. 55.

monopoly profit could be earned. For some years, little attention was given to the need for a monopoly profit— the reward for creative effort mentioned in paragraph 9 which creates the incentive to invest in innovation. This is unfortunate and surprising in view of the teleological approach the Court claims to adopt.

In *Merck* v. *Stephar*,[6] Merck had sold or consented to the sale in Italy by its subsidiary of a drug called 'Moduretic.' It held patents for this in other member states but, as in *Parke Davis*, at the time of the discovery it was not possible to obtain a patent for pharmaceutical products in Italy. Although the law preventing the grant of patent protection for drugs had since been held unconstitutional by the highest Italian court, no transitional provisions were enacted for drugs discovered during that period, which cannot now be patented because they are no longer novel.

Prices for the drug were very different in different member states. In the Netherlands, Germany and Belgium, the patent law was strong and the price was high; in the UK, where the main purchaser was entitled to a compulsory licence under the Crown use provisions, the price was about half. In Italy the price was still lower, but it was lowest of all in France, where there was patent protection but the government imposed maximum price controls, restricting the returns on the drug even more tightly than did the lack of patent protection in Italy.

Although neither Merck nor its subsidiary had had any chance of earning a monopoly profit in Italy, the Court ruled that Merck could not rely on its Dutch patent to keep out a drug that had been sold in a member state by it or with its consent. The Advocate General had pointed out that not all patentees make a monopoly profit — they merely have a chance of doing so. One might reply that there are always commercial constraints. Some patents have little value because there are cheaper substitutes on the market or a drug is found to produce disastrous side effects, but the Italian law ensured that no inventor of pharmaceutical products who sold them in Italy could prevent firms taking a free ride on its investment in innovation.   The Court's only apparent reason for preventing Merck from using its Dutch patent to protect one of the countries where it could make a monopoly profit was that Merck must take the consequences of its conduct in selling the product in Italy. That is not a reason, but a conclusion. To discourage the patentee from selling in countries where it can obtain no protection may in theory lead to the products being sold only where they are protected by patent, and this might divide the market even more seriously than does differential pricing. It may be that patents for pharmaceutical products are weak in too many countries for this to be worthwhile. The Court's judgment,

6   (187/80) [1981] E.C.R. 2063.

however, must have reduced the returns from r & d, and may have marginally reduced that activity.

The only policy reason which in my view might justify the Court's decision is that it encouraged private firms to persuade their governments not to control a patentee's profit margin too tightly. I am told that, after the judgment, French pharmaceutical firms persuaded the French government to raise the maximum prices at which they were permitted to sell in France on the ground that this would enable them to make higher profits on exports to other member states. This had the advantage of bringing the national laws closer together. It is, however, tough for a firm in the private sector to be squeezed between the desire of government in some countries to keep down the cost of medicine and the Community rules for free movement, which seem to extend to the whole common market the rules of the member state giving least protection to innovators. It is also hard on the countries which provide strong patents because of their desire to encourage innovation.

In several subsequent cases the Community Court has drawn back somewhat from the erosion of intellectual property rights. Under the Benelux uniform law on designs, the first person to apply for a design is granted an exclusive right to sell goods that conform to it against anyone save the author or his assigns. In *Keurkoop* v. *Nancy Kean Gifts*,[7] Nancy Kean Gifts registered the design for a handbag in 1979. Apparently, it was similar to an earlier design filed in the US, but this did not affect the validity of the Benelux rights unless the original innovator objected. Nancy Kean had the bag made in Taiwan and despatched directly to the Netherlands. The following year, Keurkoop was found to be offering a bag of the same design, also made in Taiwan. Some items came directly from Taiwan and some via Germany.

When Nancy Kean Gifts tried to exercise its design rights to restrain commercial imports into the Netherlands the Community Court stated that, at the present stage of Community law where national intellectual property rights have not been harmonised, it is for national law to define their scope and ruled that a design law protecting persons other than the inventor does come within the class of industrial and commercial property rights mentioned in article 36. Not only can the design right be invoked to restrain direct imports from Taiwan which are not subject to article 30 since they do not constitute trade between member states, but also against those items first sold in the Federal Republic of Germany without the consent of the Benelux holder, which enjoyed no exclusive right in Germany. It must follow that had Moduretic been sold in Italy

7   (144/81) [1982] E.C.R. 2853.

by a third party without Merck's consent, Merck could have prevented exports therefrom to other member states.

In *Pharmon* v. *Hoechst*,[8] the Court held that a patent in the Netherlands can be exercised to keep out goods exported there by a compulsory licensee in the United Kingdom. The Advocate General considered that no distinction should be made between goods sold in the UK and exported by the buyer to the Netherlands and goods sold directly in the Netherlands by the compulsory licensee under United Kingdom law. The Court did not advert to this problem, which remains controversial. It treated manufacture or putting on the market by a compulsory licensee as being carried out without the consent of the holder. On this basis, it did not matter whether direct sales by a licensee exhaust the right.

Nevertheless, there must be no discrimination against imported goods. In cases against the UK[9] and Italy, the Court held that national provisions for granting compulsory patents when the patent was worked in another member state rather than locally were contrary to the principle of free movement, so the problem of excessive costs due to working nationally to avoid the grant of compulsory licences is disappearing.

9.4.2 Copyright — the Court emphasises the need for rewards and incentives

A problem similar to that in *Merck* had arisen earlier in *Musik-Vertrieb Membran* v. *GEMA*,[10] a reference for a preliminary ruling to the Community Court made by the German courts. Under section 8 of the UK Copyright Act 1956, once records of a musical work have been made in or imported into the United Kingdom for the purpose of retail sale, by or with the consent of the holder, any other manufacturer may make records of the work for sale by retail on giving notice to the holder and paying a royalty of 6·25 per cent. of the retail price. Consequently producers normally consent to such manufacture at that rate of royalty.

Advocate General Warner said there could be no exhaustion of a right when there was no power to prevent exploitation by others, and that GEMA, the performing rights society in Germany acting on behalf of the copyright holder, should be allowed to charge the importer of records from England to Germany the difference between the statutory 6·25 per cent. and the royalty that would have been obtainable in England but for section 8 — a difficult test to apply!

The Court accepted that copyright is included in the term 'industrial

8   (19/84) [1985] E.C.R. 2281.
9   *Commission* v. *UK* (C–30/90), judgment of 18 February 1992 [1992] E.C.R. I–829.
10   (55 & 57/78) [1981] E.C.R. 147.

and commercial property' in article 36 of the treaty, although article 36 does not refer to artistic property rights. The Court referred, however, to part of the judgment in *Centrafarm* v. *Sterling*[11] which was not described at 9.4.1 above and, without discussing the amount of the reward, repeated that the existence of differences in national law that may distort competition between member states cannot justify the protection by a member state of the practices of a private organisation that are incompatible with the free movement of goods. Anticipating its later judgment in *Merck*,[12] it added that the holder can choose in which state to market its records. Where there is some protection in the country where the goods were first sold, the common market is not divided.

Copyright in rights like broadcasts and performing rights, however, has been treated far more favourably. In *Coditel* v. *Ciné Vog Films*,[13] a Belgian cable television company picked up the transmission of a film from Germany and relayed it to clients in some parts of Belgium. The exclusive licensee in Belgium objected and the French copyright holder sued the cable company to protect it. The Community Court distinguished broadcast diffusion rights from copyright in a physical disk or cassette. The former are governed by the rules for the free movement of services, rather than for goods. It implied something like article 36 into the rules relating to services, but went considerably further.

It stated that a copyright holder and its assigns have a legitimate interest in calculating royalties on the basis of the number of performances by the licensee and that exploitation of copyright involves various methods, including television. It ruled that the holder was entitled to rely on his copyright to restrain Coditel from relaying the film transmitted with consent in another member state. That is broadcast diffusion rights are not exhausted by a performance in another member state.[14]

The distinction between the mechanical rights in a record, which are subject to the rules for the free movement of goods and the right to transmit a film in public, which is subject to those for the provision of services, is commercially artificial, although they are governed by different parts of the treaty. A film producer is induced to invest because of a series of exploiting acts. There are royalties to be obtained from cinemas downtown charging high prices, then from general release and television — all these derive from services. Now, an increasing proportion of the

11 Cited at 9.4.1, at paras. 22–24.
12 Discussed at 9.4.1 above.
13 (62/79) [1980] E.C.R. 881.
14 Subsequently, the Court found for the same reasons that exclusive licences to different broadcasters in different member states do not infringe art. 85(1), although Reischl A.G. observed that such a conclusion would result in absolute territorial protection. See *Coditel II*, at 10.3 below.

revenue comes from the sale and, recently, the hire of video cassettes. This is subject to the free movement of goods, but in a later case the Court did not rely on the distinction.

Warner Bros. and Metronome v. *Christiansen*[15] was concerned with the hiring out of video cassettes. Christiansen bought some in England with the consent of the copyright holder and imported them into Denmark for the purposes of hiring them out from his shop. Under Danish law, sale and hire are separate infringing acts. Under UK law at that time, copyright holders were able to oppose the sale but not the hire of the cassettes.

Citing *Keurkoop*[16] for the proposition that it is still for national law to define the scope of industrial and commercial property rights and *Coditel (2)*, the Community Court stressed the need for the holder to make an adequate return on its investment. The Danish law was not discriminatory. Had the cassettes been bought in Denmark, hiring them would still have infringed the copyright. The Court refused to follow its Advocate General, and its ruling came as a great surprise to experts. I welcome the Court's emphasis on the need for adequate remuneration, although it is not possible to say how much remuneration is needed to induce the producer to invest. That should be determined by the market — by the amount that producers can extract from the licensees and buyers of the protected goods.

Thetford v. *Fiamma*[17] concerned a patent, rather than copyright, but has brought together the ideas of reward and incentives for investment. Under UK law, it was possible to obtain a patent if an inventive idea had not been anticipated by any patent specification in the preceding 50 years, although it was not novel in the absolute sense. Following Advocate General Mischo, the Court recognised at paragraph 19 that the doctrine of relative novelty was adopted in the UK:

> '*to foster creative activity* on the part of inventors in the interest of industry. To that end the "fifty year rule" aimed to make it possible to give a reward, in the form of the grant of a patent, even in cases in which an "old" invention was "rediscovered." In such cases the U.K. legislation was designed to prevent the existence of a former patent specification which had never been utilised or published from constituting a ground for revoking a patent which had been validly issued.
>
> 20. Consequently, a rule such as the "fifty year rule" cannot be regarded as constituting a restriction on trade between member states.' [my emphasis]

The Court perceived the matter *ex ante*, at the time the investment in research was made, and not *ex post*. It brought together the concept of

15 (158/86) [1988] E.C.R. 2605.
16 9.4.1 above.
17 (35/87) [1988] E.C.R. 3585.

reward for the inventor, introduced in *Centrafarm* v. *Sterling*, and stressed in the *Coditel* and *Warner* judgments, and that of incentives. The expectation of a reward is the incentive to investment: it 'foster[s] creative activity.' On this basis, the exercise of the right is not anti-competitive. But for the hope of reward, there might have been no product to import.

The Court confirmed in *Thetford* that, where the national law discriminates against imports from another member state, this will amount to 'a disguised restriction of trade between member states' within the second sentence of article 36, and its exercise would infringe article 30.[18]

Shortly afterwards in *Volvo* v. *Veng*,[19] the Court ruled that, even if it enjoys a dominant position within the meaning of article 86, the holder of design rights is not obliged to grant a licence to third parties in return for a reasonable royalty. The right to sue for infringement 'constitutes the very subject matter of its exclusive right.' Nevertheless it would amount to the abuse of a dominant position neither to license nor to sell the goods. It might also be abusive to overcharge. This is a difficult concept to understand. There is no point in enjoying an exclusive right if the holder may not charge a monopoly rent: the monopoly rent is the incentive that led to the original design rights.[20]

9.4.3 *Law of unfair competition*

The Court has treated the national laws of unfair competition very much like industrial and commercial property rights, although it may be directly interpreting article 30 rather than article 36 which does not mention unfair competition as a possible justification. In *Béguelin*,[21] the Court ruled that an exclusive distributor cannot rely on national laws of unfair competition to exclude imports from another member state when such parallel trade, in itself, is alleged to amount to unfair competition.

In *Dansk Supermarked* v. *Imerco*,[22] however, it distinguished the use of rules for unfair competition to control the circumstances and methods in or by which the imported goods are put on the market. Imerco, a Danish retailing co-operative, ordered from an English firm sets of a special dinner service decorated with pictures of Danish castles to

---

18   In *Warner*, the Court reached the same conclusion by stating that the exercise of copyright would not then be justified by the first sentence of art. 36.
19   (238/87) [1988] E.C.R. 6211.
20   In *Ford Body Panels*, Press release IP(90)4, 10 January 1990, the Commission extracted from Ford an undertaking that represents a stricter policy than that accepted by the Court in *Volvo*.
21   (22/71) [1971] E.C.R. 949.
22   (58/80) [1981] E.C.R. 181.

celebrate its fiftieth anniversary. It stipulated high quality standards but, to save cost, permitted the sale of seconds in parts of England not much visited by tourists. One of Imerco's competitors, Dansk Supermarked, bought some 300 of the 1,000 sets of seconds and started to sell them in Denmark without any indication that they were seconds.

As it happened, the Danish Supreme Court, applying the ruling of the Community Court, held that Imerco was saved from competition in its home market because the indication that the sets were seconds had been removed, although not by Dansk Supermarked. Had they not been, members of Imerco would have been faced with competition in their home market. The Community Court's ruling may be criticised as simplistic. The ruling could have been avoided with the aid of sophisticated advice. Imerco might have had the service made in Denmark and article 30 would not have applied to sales within a single member state. It could, therefore, have restrained the maker from selling in any city where Imerco had a store. That would, of course, have divided the common market more than the actual agreement did. It could have bought the seconds itself and sold them to retailers at a distance from Denmark and in small quantities, but if it was not organised for such an operation its costs would have increased substantially; or it could have sold them in Sweden before the EEA was established (9.4.5.1 below). In eradicating obvious restrictions on inter-state trade, the Community Court has ignored the probable strategic reactions of intelligent businessmen to its ruling and may have reduced efficiency and consumer choice and even helped to segregate the common market.

9.4.4 Rights in reputation — trade marks

Trade marks may similarly be treated as quantitative restrictions on imports, the use of which is prohibited by article 30, unless justified on grounds of trade mark law. In the much criticised case of *Van Zuylen* v. *Hag*,[23] Hag's Belgian subsidiary was seized as reparations after the war and the Belgian mark came, by public act, to be separately owned from the German mark. The Community Court decided that where the same trade marks are held by different firms in different member states but were once of common origin, neither holder can prevent goods bearing the mark from being sold in the countries where it owns the right by either the other holder itself or by purchasers from it if the goods were genuinely put on the market, bearing the mark, in the area where the other has the right. The case was greatly criticised as the common origin had been rendered asunder by a government decree.

The judgment was firmly reversed by the Community Court,

23   (192/73) [1974] E.C.R. 731.

following Advocate General Jacobs, in *Hag II*.[24] The Court withdrew the scathing remarks it had made about trade marks in early cases and, at paragraph 13, referred to rights in a mark as being:

> 'an essential element in the system of undistorted competition which the Treaty aims to establish and maintain. In such a system enterprises must be able to gain customers by the quality of their products or services, which can be done only by virtue of the existence of distinctive signs permitting identification of those products and services. For a trade mark to be able to play this part, it must constitute a guarantee that all the products bearing it have been manufactured under the supervision of a single enterprise to which responsibility for their quality may be attributed.'

The Court went on to hold that the holder in Germany was entitled to use the mark 'Hag' to restrain the sale of coffee made by the successor in title from the Belgian sequestrator.

Some controversy remained in that the judgment was based both on the lack of consent by the German holder and on the possible confusion of the public. Where a business in one country is sold as a going concern with the local trade marks, any products will arguably have been sold with consent within the meaning of the Community Court's rules, but if there is no continuing relationship between the vendor and purchaser there is no guarantee that the specification of the products in the two areas will be the same and consumers may be confused.

Whether the mark may be used in such circumstances remained controversial, but in *Ideal-Standard*,[25] the Court ruled that it may. In a judgment based on first principles, it repeated its earlier statement that:

> 'The object of trade mark law is to protect owners against contrivances of third parties who might seek, by creating a risk of confusion amongst consumers, to take advantage of the reputation accruing to the mark.'

It considered that consent to an assignment was not the kind of consent relevant to the doctrine of exhaustion.

It repeated the statement it had made in *Hag II*, that 'trade marks are an essential element in the system of undistorted competition which the Treaty seeks to establish.' In the earlier cases where exhaustion occurred, the essential function of marks was not interfered with—the same firm had an opportunity to control the specification of the products to which the mark was attached. After even a voluntary assignment that would not be the case in the absence of economic links betweeen the two holders.

The Court stated that the assignment might infringe article 85 and be

24   (C–10/89) [1990] E.C.R. I–3711.
25   *IHT Internationale Heiztechnic GmbH and Uwe Danziger* v. *Ideal-Standard GmbH and Wabco Standard GmbH*, case C–9/93, judgment of 22 June 1994, para. 45.

void if it were made in pursuance of an agreement to partition the market, but that that view could not apply mechanically to every assignment limited to part of the common market.

'Before a trade-mark assignment can be treated as giving effect to an agreement prohibited under article 85, it is necessary to analyse the context, the commitment underlying the assignment, the intention of the parties and the consideration for the assignment.'

Consequently, the Court ruled that for the original holder to use its trade mark to exclude products made by the assignee for another member state on the ground that consumers would be confused, would not infringe the rules for free movement.

9.4.4.1 *Repackaging and relabelling of trade-marked goods* — Another problem to come before the Community Court in *Hoffmann-La Roche* v. *Centrafarm*[26] resulted from the purchase in England by Centrafarm of valium for sale in the Federal Republic of Germany, after the pills had been repacked in different quantities, and both the original mark and Centrafarm's name had been placed on the packaging. The Court ruled that the exercise of German trade mark rights in such circumstances to oppose import and sale was justified within the meaning of the first sentence of article 36. The specific subject matter of trade mark rights is to protect the holder against competitors who would abuse the reputation protected by the mark. The essential function of a mark is to guarantee to buyers or final users the original identity of the marked product, so as to avoid confusion. This implies that the goods have not been tampered with without the holder's authorisation.

Nevertheless, the Court added that the sale of the pills in smaller packages in England than in Germany coupled with the exercise of the trade mark right might constitute 'a disguised restriction of trade between member states' within the proviso to article 36, if it had the effect of dividing the market. The repackager, Centrafarm, would have to establish, however, that the repacking was not of a nature to affect the original state of the product. This might be possible if it removed only an outer packing, leaving the inner packing untouched, or repacked subject to the control of a public authority. The Court added that the repackager, to rely on the proviso to article 36, would have to give the holder advance warning, and indicate clearly on the final package that the goods had been repacked by it.[27] It made it clear that its judgment extends beyond the pharmaceutical industry.

26   (102/77) [1978] E.C.R. 1139.
27   *Pfizer* v. *Eurimfarm* (1/81) [1981] E.C.R. 2913 is a successful example.

Shortly afterwards, the Court ruled on a similar problem in *Centrafarm* v. *American Home Products*.[28] American Home Products sold under the mark 'Serenid' in the United Kingdom and 'Seresta' in the Netherlands tranquilisers that were pharmaceutically identical, but chemically different and tasted different. The Court treated these as identical products. Advocate General Capotorti pointed out that it would be difficult for Centrafarm to sell 'Serenid' in the Netherlands in competition with 'Seresta' unless it could benefit from the sales promotion paid for by American Home Products, and the Court ruled that although the use of the Dutch mark to restrain the marketing in the Netherlands under the 'Seresta' mark of 'Serenid' sold in the United Kingdom was justified within the meaning of the first sentence of article 36, it might constitute a disguised restriction on trade between member states within the second sentence of that article, if it were established that the holder used different marks for the *purpose* of partitioning the markets artificially.

The Advocate General in *American Home Products* referred to justifications for the use of different marks, and this may be implied by the Court's reference to the 'artificial' partitioning of markets. One may, therefore, be able to restrain the marketing of articles sold in another state under a different mark where the mark registered in one country cannot be used in another, either because it would be confused with a local mark or because it would sound ugly, misleading or scurrilous in the language of the second. One may be able to use different marks and restrain parallel imports when the products are different in respects important to the user and the trade marks have been changed. It may be that the import of a cheap, low quality product sold in one member state under one mark can be restrained if the goods have been relabelled under the mark used in the country of import for a more expensive but higher quality product.

For example, the change of emphasis by the Court from the effect on inter-state trade in the *Roche* case to the purpose of the holder has enabled Roche to defeat Centrafarm's Euro-defence to the German proceedings. Packaging in different quantities may have had the effect of dividing the common market, but it was difficult to show that Roche adopted different packages for this purpose. Hospitals in Germany habitually order pills packed in larger quantities than do those in England and this may have explained Roche's method of packaging.

Nevertheless, the Commission has proved hostile to attempts to divide the common market in this way, and in *Bayo-n-ox*[29] warned that they might attract fines. The Commission easily finds a concerted practice by the holder to protect the dealer in the higher priced territory.

28   (3/78) [1978] E.C.R. 1823.
29   [1990] 4 C.M.L.R. 930.

9.4.5 Sales outside the EEA do not exhaust intellectual property rights

The rules relating to the free movement of goods, however, relate only to imports and exports between member states. So in *EMI* v. *CBS*,[30] the Court held that where the mark had lawfully been affixed to the goods in the USA by the holder there, the holder in various common market states could rely on national law to prevent their import, although the marks were of common origin.

Goods bearing a mark may be imported from outside the common market to a member state where no similar mark is held, but they can be kept out of any other member states where the mark might be confused with one held independently in that state.[31] It is no longer clear whether a United Kingdom registered trade mark can be used to block parallel imports of goods sold by a sister subsidiary from a country outside the Community such as the United States.[32] If the parallel imports were admitted to the United Kingdom, by or with the consent of the owner of the UK mark, they would be able to circulate freely thereafter in other member states where the owner of the UK mark or different subsidiaries hold the mark.

In *Hauptzollamt Mainz* v. *Kupferberg*,[33] the Court ruled that the provisions on the free movement of goods between member states of the common market and countries with which it has entered into Free Trade or Association Agreements do have direct effect. Nevertheless, it held earlier, in *Polydor* v. *Harlequin Records*,[34] that they should be construed far more narrowly than the EC rules since they are not intended to create a common market. Consequently, an exclusive licensee of the copyright holder in the UK was entitled to exercise its copyright to restrain the import of records sold with the consent of the holder in Portugal, before its accession to the common market. The Court's reasoning is based on general considerations that apply equally to marks, patents and other intellectual property rights.

This rule will continue to apply to the association agreements the EC has made with Eastern European countries. Holders of intellectual property rights will be able to sell cheaply in those countries and prevent the goods from undermining the price in the common market.

9.4.5.1 Exhaustion applies to goods sold anywhere in the EEA — Protocol 28 of the EEA Agreement provides for exhaustion throughout the

30   (51, 86 & 96/75) [1976] E.C.R. 811.
31   This follows from *Keurkoop*, 9.4.1 above, and from *EMI* v. *CBS*.
32   Contrast *Revlon* v. *Cripps & Lee* [1980] F.S.R. 85 (C.A.) with *Colgate* v. *Markwell* [1989] R.P.C. 49 (C.A.), affirming [1988] R.P.C. 283.
33   (104/81) [1982] E.C.R. 3641.
34   (270/80) [1982] E.C.R. 329.

area in accordance with the case law of the Community Court. Goods sold in Scandinavia cannot be kept out of the Common Market or vice versa. Nor can a right in Finland be used to keep out goods sold in Sweden by or with the consent of the holder.

9.5 Harmonisation of intellectual property rights

The existence of intellectual property rights in only some of the member states may divide the common market. Free riders can sell where there are no rights but not elsewhere.

The problem caused for goods protected by patent by differences in national patent law remains: although pharmaceutical products can now be protected by patent in Italy, their value is reduced by price control there and in France, while in other member states, such as Greece, patent protection is less strong, although Portuguese and Spanish law have recently been changed to increase protection.

Copyright protection still lasts for different periods in different member states and in *EMI* v. *Patricia*,[35] the Court held that, where copyright has expired in the country of origin, it may be invoked to prevent the export into countries where it subsists. This followed from *Keurkoop*, but divided the common market.

As part of the programme for the internal market in 1992, therefore, the Commission proposed directives to the Council[36] to harmonise intellectual property rights where the differences are capable of dividing the common market. In the field of copyright, this has been done largely by raising the level of protection to the highest. For instance, copyright will be extended throughout the Community from the life of the author plus 50 years in the UK to the German period of life plus 70 years[37] so as to avoid the division of the market exemplified in *EMI* v. *Patricia*.

Some member states protected software by copyright, and now all have been required to do so by the software directive[38] which determines the scope of the right. The rights of third parties to decompile programs sufficiently to get to the interface to permit one program to work with another are now recognised throughout the EC and the directive is appended to the EEA treaty, which will, therefore, confer the same

---

35   (341/87) [1989] E.C.R. 79, para 12. See Gerald Dworkin, 'Authorship of films and the European Commission Proposals for Harmonising the Term of Copyright' [1993] E.I.P.R. 151.

36Under art. 100A of the EC treaty, inserted by the Single European Act. *E.g.* Dir. 92/100 of 19 November 1992 on rental right and lending right and on certain rights related to copyright in the field of intellectual property.

37   Dir. 93/98 of 29 October 1993 harmonising the term of protection of copyright and certain related rights.

38   Dir. 91/250, O.J. 1991, L122/42.

rights. Nevertheless, legislation by directive suffers from the drawback that the member states tend to implement the directives differently, adding them to what was national law before, so the effects may not be entirely uniform.

9.5.1 *Trade marks*

The first trade mark directive[39] should already have been implemented.[40] The Community trade mark regulation was finally adopted in 1993[41] and a trade mark office will be established in Alicante in Spain. Nevertheless, national marks will continue and honest concurrent user of independent marks will still give rise to difficulties and divide the market.

9.5.2 *Patents*

The Community Patent Convention was signed in 1976 but has not yet been fully ratified. If, however, the member states continue to insist on translations into all nine languages, the expense will prevent its being used much save for important pharmaceutical products.

The European Patent Convention was not adopted by the Community as such, but all the member states and some others have joined. It has worked well. If patents in two or three states that have joined the Convention are desired, it is cheaper to have a single international search made thereunder. This will result in patents being granted under the laws of those member states for which they are requested, valid from the time that the applications and claims have been translated into those languages. Additional fees are required for each additional country for which a patent is requested, but the bigger deterrent to multiple applications is the cost of translations into languages spoken by only a few million people.

9.6 Conclusion

In its determination to prevent limited national intellectual property rights dividing the common market, the Court initially developed the doctrine of exhaustion and applied it even when the right holder had not been able to earn a monopoly profit. More recently, its judgments have demonstrated an awareness that rewards and incentives are important

---

39 Dir. 89/104 to approximate the laws of the Member States relating to trade marks, O.J. 1989, L40/1.
40 It is not entirely clear whether these require service marks to be granted.
41 Council Reg. 40/94 of 20 December 1993 on the Community trade mark, O.J. 1994, L11/1.

and I hope that *Merck*,[42] if heard now, would not now be decided in the same way.

Since intellectual property rights may impede inter-state trade where the right holder in the country of import had no rights in the country of export, the Council has been adopting directives to ensure that differences in the law should not divide the common market. The process is a gradual one. Problems remain where protection is greater in the country of import than in that of export, and if *Merck* continues to be good law, right holders will have to consider carefully before marketing the goods themselves where the protection is weak, for instance because of maximum price controls.

It seems that any restrictions on inter-state trade will have to be imposed by contract, and be subject to the application of articles 85 and 86. The Commission has been hostile towards export bans and deterrents, but some limited protection is permitted by the group exemptions for exclusive distribution and technology licensing.

9.7 Bibliography

W. R. Cornish, *op cit.*, main bibliography.

Paul Demaret, *op. cit.*, main bibliography.

Karen Dyekjaer-Hansen, critical comment on *Imerco* v. *Dansk Supermarked* and the subsequent proceedings in Denmark [1982] 3 E.I.P.R. 85.

Georges Friden, 'Recent Developments in EEC Intellectual Property Law: The Distinction between Existence and Exercise Revisited' (1989) 26 C.M.L.Rev. 193.

Laurence Gormley, 'Prohibiting Restrictions of Trade within the EEC: the Theory and Applications of Articles 30-36 of the EEC Treaty', Kluwer, 1985.

——, Part 12, in David Vaughan (ed.), *Law of the European Communities*, vol. 2, being vol. 52 of *Halsbury's Laws of England* (1986).

Hugh Hansen (ed.), IV *Fordham Intellectual Property, Media & Entertainment Law Journal*, Summer 1993, Special Issue containing the papers of the First Fordham Conference on International Intellectual Property Law and Policy. The papers for the second conference will be published by Transnational Law, hopefully by the end of 1994.

René Joliet, 'Patented Articles and the Free Movement of Goods within the EEC' [1975] *Current Legal Problems* 15.

——, 'Trademark Licensing Agreements under the EEC law of Competition' (1983) 5 N.W. J. Int'l. L. & Bus. 755.

——, 'Territorial and Exclusive Trademark Licensing under the EEC Law of Competition' [1984] IIC 21.

Valentine Korah, *Know-how Licensing and the EEC Competition Rules, Regulation 556/89*, ESC, 1989, Oxford, section 1.5.1.

——, 'The Limitation of Copyright and Patents by the Rules for the Free

---

42   See 9.4.1 above.

Movement of Goods in the European Common Market' (1982) C.W.R. Int'l. L.J. 7.

Warwick A Rothnie, Parallel Imports, Sweet & Maxwell, 1993.

——, '*Hag II*: Putting the Common Origin Doctrine to Sleep' [1991] 1 E.I.P.R. 24.

Dr. H. Ullrich in Gijlstra and Murphy (eds.), *Competition Law of Western Europe and the USA*, Cmn. C–491.

Denis F. Waelbroeck, 'Les Conventions de Délimitation des Marques Face au Droit Communautaire' [1985], *Cahiers de Droit Européen* 402.

Michel Waelbroeck, 'The Effect of the Rome Treaty on the Exercise of National Industrial Property Rights' (1976) 21 *The Antitrust Bull.* 99.

10 Licences of Industrial and Commercial Property Rights

10.1 Introduction: rationale for the grant of patent protection

As explained at the beginning of Chapter 9, a patent is the exclusive right conferred by the law of a country to prevent others from exploiting an invention within its territory. Often innovating firms obtain patents, sometimes called 'parallel patents,' in many countries.

A patent may or may not confer a monopoly. The protected product may meet acute competition from substitutes or be capable of being produced by a process that does not infringe, in which cases the patent may provide little or no protection. The holder of an improvement patent may not be entitled to exploit it at all unless the holder of the basic patent grants it a licence, although the improvement patent may help the holder to negotiate such a licence in return for one under the improvement patent.

Although *ex post*, when the investment in innovation has been successful, valuable patents may raise barriers to entry by enabling the holder to restrain infringements. They are based on a competitive philosophy: they may encourage investment in research into kinds of innovation that are easily copied and which might otherwise not be worthwhile for any individual firm. So, perceived *ex ante*, from the time when the future holder decides whether to innovate, the hope of obtaining a patent may be necessary to induce its investment.

The holder of a patent is called the patentee. It may decide not to exploit the invention itself, but to license someone else to do so. An individual inventor can rarely raise the capital to finance the development of his ideas and set up production. In *Velcro/Aplix*,[1] the inventor's company did not start to manufacture itself until the basic patents had expired, presumably because it needed to build up licence fees to pay off its debts and finance a factory.

A licence merely permits the licensee to do something that would otherwise be unlawful, so clearly does not infringe article 85(1) unless it is coupled with other obligations that have the object or effect of restricting competition in some way. In the absence of an agreement or concerted practice, it is not contrary to article 85 to refuse to grant a

---

1 [1985] 4 C.M.L.R. 157.

licence.[2] Nevertheless, in *AEG*,[3] the Court stated that *tacit* collusion with authorised dealers to protect them from dealers operating on low margins might infringe article 85(1). In that case, there seems to have been sufficient evidence of actual collusion mentioned in the Commission's decision, but the reference to tacit collusion is worrying. The judgment in *AEG* suggests, *inter alia*, that the holder of an intellectual property right which refuses to grant a licence because it has already licensed others, might be in contravention of article 85.

Most systems of antitrust law have had difficulty in distinguishing permissible clauses from those that confer undue protection. In 1981, the Department of Justice in the USA took the view that a patentee is entitled to a property right granted by Congress and that any monopoly power conferred by the exclusive right provides the incentive for the innovative effort required to create the property.[4] Agreements between competitors to pool their patents are, however, suspect unless a problem with blocking patents can be shown.

It is arguable, moreover, that no control is needed over vertical agreements since the patentee has an interest in its licensees being subject to competition and earning the minimum margin. It is likely to protect each from the others only in so far as it thinks necessary to induce them to accept the risks of investing in plant, development and establishing a market. It is more likely to get the balance right than is an official enforcing the law since it is in the business and the decision will affect its profits. This argument, however, has not been accepted in the Community. Where marginal consumers require more service or higher quality than the majority, the argument may lead to a proliferation of services worth less than they cost. Moreover, it is not always easy to tell whether the licensee would have been likely to enter the market independently. Agreements restricting competition between potential competitors may require control.

10.2 The Commission's view

By 1972, the Commission had taken the view that any significant licence other than a non-exclusive one for the whole common market is caught by the prohibition of article 85(1).[5] This had not always been so.

---

2 In what circumstances a refusal by a dominant firm to grant a licence infringes art. 86 is an interesting question, considered at 4.3.3.4 above and 10.10 below.

3 (107/82) [1983] E.C.R. 3151, and 2.2.2.1 above.

4 Abbott B. Lipsky, Remarks before the ABA Antitrust Section, Washington D.C., 5 November 1981. The current administration is reconsidering its position on vertical restraints.

5 See *GEMA*, text to note 14 below.

In 1962, the Commission published a notice on patent licences,[6] since withdrawn, in which it accepted that where a licence for part of a member state was given, it was the patent that restrained sales in the other parts, so there was no need for export bans if the licensee was limited to exploiting the invention in part of a member state.

Many people read the notice carelessly and assumed that a licence limited to a whole member state did not restrict competition, and that one could rely on another national patent to keep the product out of the second member state. It has, however, been clear at least since *Centrafarm* v. *Sterling*[7] that a sale by a holder or his licensee in the UK exhausts the patent throughout the common market by virtue of the rules for the free movement of goods, so the customer of a patentee throughout the common market cannot be restrained from trading across frontiers. *Warner* v. *Christiansen*[8] has not altered the position where the infringing act in the country of import is the same as that originally approved in the country of export, although it is difficult to reconcile with the cases where the Court found exhaustion despite the lack of right in the country of export.[9]

The Commission also alleges that direct sales by the licensee into another member state are lawful because the intellectual property rights are exhausted by the licence. This is controversial, but supported by the Advocate General in *Pharmon* v. *Hoechst*,[10] although the Court did not address the point. The Court ruled in *Van Zuylen* v. *Hag*[11] and the Commission found in *Velcrol Aplix*[12] that direct sales by the holder of a trade mark in one member state cannot be opposed by the owner of the same mark in another member state, if the marks are of common origin. In *Hag II*,[13] however, the Court followed the advice of its Advocate General and overruled its earlier judgment on another ground. It is not clear how far the rest of the judgment in *Hag I* should be relied on.

The Commission has gone further and considers that a licence limited territorially is an unrestricted licence subject to a contractual ban on exploiting outside the territory, which is unlikely to merit exemption. In its press release about the settlement of proceedings against *GEMA*,[14] it stated that a copyright licence to make in one member state amounts to a licence to make, as well as to sell, anywhere in the common market. The

---

6   J.O. 1962, C139/2922.
7   (15/74) [1974] E.C.R. 1147, and 9.4.1 above.
8   (158/86) [1988] E.C.R. 2605, and 9.4.2 above.
9   *E.g.*, *Merck*, discussed at 9.4.1 above.
10   (19/84) [1985] E.C.R. 2281.
11   (192/73) [1974] E.C.R. 731.
12   Cited at 10.1 above.
13   *CNL-Sucal* v. *Hag* (C–10/89) [1990] E.C.R. I–3711. See 9.4.4 above.
14   *15th Annual Report*, p.81, [1985] 2 C.M.L.R. 1.

Commission does not set out its analysis and its proposition goes beyond the current case law. It may be based on a wide version of the doctrine of exhaustion.

Where the holder has patents for only some member states it cannot grant a licence for the others and failure to do so does not deter activities in the places where it holds no patents. So it is thought that a licence to exploit a patent in the areas where one has patent protection should not be treated as an export ban, unless there is a contractual ban on doing the licensed acts outside the territory. In *Delta Chemie*,[15] where an exclusive licence of pure know-how was in question, the Commission stated at point 25 that:

> 'the exclusive manufacturing right granted to the licensee [in the UK] implies by its very nature, that it is prohibited from manufacturing these products outside the licensed territory. This limitation affects [the licensee's] competitive position regarding the sale of the products in the member states not reserved for it.'

The clause infringed article 85(1) but was exempted. In *BBC/Brown Boveri*,[16] the exclusive licence from BBC to NGK for the Far East included substantial know-how (paragraph 8), as well as technology protected by patents in some member states and was treated as restraining production in those parts of the EC where there was no patent protection. No reasoning is expressed, but presumably the conclusion is based on the ground that the know-how licence limited to the Far East restrained sales in Europe. Since the licensee lacked the technology to make in Europe, it is difficult to see how the licence restrained any sales that would have been possible without it. It is an example of the Commission perceiving the transaction *ex post*.

As a result of its experience with exclusive dealing agreements, the Commission now considers that granting an exclusive territory infringes article 85(1) and requires exemption, even if an exclusive territory be necessary to persuade the licensee to take a licence and commit himself to tooling up and developing a market for the product.

In *Davidson Rubber*,[17] three licensees were each allocated an exclusive manufacturing and sales territory, one in France, one in Germany and one in Italy (multiple parallel licensing). The Commission found that this infringed article 85(1), since it restrained Davidson from licensing, say, another manufacturer in France who might have exported to Belgium. Once the restrictions on sales to other member states were abrogated by the parties and the exclusivity restricted to manufacture,

15   [1989] 4 C.M.L.R. 535.
16   [1989] 4 C.M.L.R. 610, criticised at 13.3 below.
17   [1972] C.M.L.R. D52.

however, the Commission exempted the agreement on the ground that, without the protection of exclusive manufacture, the Davidson process would not have been available in Europe.

Perceived *ex post*, after the technology had been introduced and a market created, the European market would be more competitive if further licensees were permitted in the territory. Perceived *ex ante*, however, this was not the case: when considering article 85(3) the Commission accepted that without the exclusive territories the Davidson process would not have been available in Europe, presumably because no licensee would have invested in tooling up and making a market without protection from free riders.

It is difficult to reconcile the Commission's view that a restriction without which the process would not have been introduced in Europe infringed article 85(1) with the Court's ruling in *La Technique Minière*[18] and later cases that article 85 is infringed only where competition that could have taken place is restricted.[19] Nevertheless, in its recent decisions on know-how licences granted shortly before adoption of the group exemption in 1988, the Commission seems to have accepted that exclusive licences, even if 'open,'[20] always infringe article 85(1), unless they are *de minimis*.

The Commission condemned and refused to exempt manufacturing exclusivity for the first time in *AOIP* v. *Beyrard*.[21] In *Bronbemaling* v. *Heidemaatschappij*,[22] it made a decision under regulation 17, article 15(6), terminating the freedom from fines obtained by notification (5.10 above), when opposition proceedings in the patent office were compromised by the grant of licences with an element of exclusivity. These licences, however, were granted to competitors. So, the relationship was horizontal.

The Commission has exempted exclusive territories in several individual decisions, although it is arguable in a national court that such an agreement is not caught by article 85(1) and the court should enforce the provisions without waiting for the Commission to grant an exemption.

10.3 The Court's view

In contrast to the Commission's practice, the Community Court held in the *Maize Seed* case, *Nungesser* v. *Commission*,[23] that an 'open exclusive licence' is not in itself contrary to article 85(1). INRA, a

18   (56/65) [1966] E.C.R. 235.
19   2.4 and 7.1.2 above and 10.3 below.
20   Contrast *Nungesser*, at 10.3 below.
21   [1976] 1 C.M.L.R. D14.
22   [1975] 2 C.M.L.R. D67.
23   (258/78) [1982] E.C.R. 2015.

research institute financed by the French Minister of Agriculture, developed an F1 hybrid maize seed that could be grown in the colder climate of Northern Europe. For a few years the variety was a great success, but it was finally superseded by other varieties. INRA was not permitted by French law to exploit its discoveries commercially, so it licensed various farmers in France to grow certified seed to be placed on the market.

To exploit the German market, INRA made contracts in 1960 and 1965 with Eisele and later his firm, Nungesser, enabling Eisele to acquire the plant breeders' rights in the Federal Republic of Germany. It promised him that it would try to prevent the seed grown in France from being exported to Germany, save to Nungesser, and there were various other restrictions condemned by the Commission, such as minimum prices to be charged by Nungesser on the German market and an obligation to take two-thirds of its requirements from the French growers.

Nungesser arranged for the seeds to be grown and tested in Germany, and approved by a public authority for general sale. By 1972, the variety was already being superseded in France, and two dealers in Germany tried to buy surplus quantities of certified seed from dealers in France. Long before *Centrafarm* v. *Sterling*[24] was decided, Eisele persuaded a German court to restrain one of them from doing so, although it would now appear that any intellectual property rights must have been exhausted by the French grower's sale of the certified seed to a dealer. With the advantage of hindsight, it might have been better had Eisele sued for unfair competition, on the ground that the imported seed was over two years old. That would reduce its germinating capacity considerably and harm the reputation of the INRA mark under which Nungesser was selling the newer seed.[25]

The Commission condemned the agreement without analysing the transaction to ascertain whether INRA could have arranged for the sale of its seed in Germany without granting what the Commission and Court treated as an exclusive licence. The Court, however, distinguished an open exclusive licence from one where absolute territorial protection is conferred. An 'open exclusive licence' is a novel term coined by the Court. It means an agreement:

'53. ... whereby the owner merely undertakes not to grant other licences in respect of the same territory and not to compete himself with the licensee in that territory.'

24 Cited at 10.2 above.
25 High germinating capacity is vital since, if there are bare patches in the field, the wind may get in and blow down the whole crop. Each year some seeds die, so it is vital that new seed be used each year. It is not clear whether the second dealer was importing old seed.

The Court therefore quashed the decision in so far as it condemned:

'an obligation upon INRA or those deriving rights through INRA to refrain from having the relevant seeds produced or sold by other licensees in Germany, and an obligation upon INRA or those deriving rights through INRA to refrain from producing or selling the relevant seeds in Germany themselves.' [operative part of the judgment]

It is not clear whether a licence remains open if the licensee in one territory is restrained from selling in another — different parts of the judgment are inconsistent on that point. The Commission, however, subsequently held in *Boussois/Interpane*[26] that it does not. Nor is it clear whether intellectual property rights are exhausted only when the licensee sells the protected goods within the terms of the licence, or by the grant of the licence itself (10.2 above).

To a significant extent the Court did expressly accept the free rider argument in relation to both parties when considering article 85(1). First, at paragraph 56, it referred to INRA's years of research and experimentation to justify the exclusivity. Presumably, a firm in the private sector would invest more in innovation if it expected to be able to earn the higher royalties to be obtained from an exclusive licence. The Court added:

'57. In fact, in the case of a licence of breeders' rights over hybrid maize seeds newly developed in one member state, an undertaking established in another member state which was not certain that it would not encounter competition from other licensees for the territory granted to it, or from the owner of the right himself, might be deterred from accepting the risk of cultivating and marketing that product; such a result would be damaging to the dissemination of a new technology and would prejudice competition in the Community between the new product and similar existing products.

58. Having regard to the specific nature of the products in question, the Court concludes that, in a case such as the present, the grant of an open exclusive licence, that is to say, a licence which does not affect the position of third parties such as parallel importers and licensees for other territories, is not in itself incompatible with article 85(1) of the Treaty.'

Despite the Court's concern in relation to article 85(1) that the Commission should investigate the effects of exclusivity and consider whether INRA's varieties could have been sold in the Federal Republic without protection from the French licensees, it was much more rigid when discussing the possibility of exemption. INRA had not granted open exclusivity, it had tried to prevent the French licensees from exporting, and Eisele had succeeded in restraining parallel imports by two dealers. The Court stated:

26   [1988] 4 C.M.L.R. 124.

'77. As it is a question of seeds intended to be used by a large number of farmers for the production of maize, which is an important product for human and animal foodstuffs, absolute territorial protection manifestly goes beyond what is indispensable for the improvement of production or distribution or the promotion of technical progress ...'

It is odd that the Community Court adopted a *per se* rule for an important licence under article 85(3), while not doing so in relation to article 85(1). In *Consten and Grundig* v. *Commission*,[27] the Community Court had stressed the complex economic appraisal needed in deciding whether to grant an exemption, which necessitates a wide discretionary power being exercised by the Commission. In both cases, however, the Court adopted a *per se* rule against absolute territorial protection. It did not articulate its reasons. The rule is arbitrary: open exclusivity gives considerable protection from parallel imports of goods of low value in relation to the cost of freight, but virtually no protection for more valuable products.

In its decisions made before adopting a block exemption for know-how, the Commission distinguished the judgment and its acceptance of 'open exclusivity' as not, in itself, restricting competition on the ground that the product was not new, although it was better than anything else on the market.[28] Nevertheless, a national court should follow the Court's precedents rather than those of the Commission.

The Court went much further in relation to a licence of performing rights in *Coditel (2)*.[29] It ruled that even absolute territorial protection may not infringe article 85(1) in the light of the commercial practice in the particular industry and the need for a film producer to obtain an adequate return.

The Court went further still in *Louis Erauw-Jacquéry* v. *La Hesbignonne*.[30] It referred to *Nungesser* and the investment needed to develop basic seed. It should be remembered that plant breeders' rights remain valid only so long as the variety is distinct, uniform, stable and useful. The Court ruled that the holder of the plant breeders' rights that result:

'must be able to obtain protection against improper handling of those seed varieties. For this purpose the breeder must have the right to reserve propagation for the propagating establishments chosen by him as licensees. To that extent the clause prohibiting the licensee from selling and exporting basic

27 (56 & 58/64) [1966] E.C.R. 299. Discussed at 2.3.1 and 2.4 above.
28 The Court rejected the Commission's view that INRA maize seed was not new, because the variety was better than what preceded it. See my monograph on know-how licensing, cited at 10.11 below, at 1.5.3–1.5.3.6.
29 (262/81) [1982] E.C.R. 3361, and 9.4.2 above.
30 (27/87) [1988] E.C.R. 1919.

seeds does not come within the prohibition laid down by article 85(1) of the Treaty.'

In *Erauw-Jacquéry*, the Court distinguished the basic seed supplied to propagators from the certified seed sold to farmers. Even absolute territorial protection for the basic seed sent to propagating establishments for multiplication before sale to farmers was cleared, whereas in *Nungesser* such a clause in relation to certified seed was held to go too far even for an exemption.

The Court's remarks in *Erauw-Jacquéry* were confined to basic seed, but the reference to investment is of wide application, so the judgment might be extended to other protected products that need careful handling, such as software. The Commission, however, is construing the precedent more narrowly to relate only to basic and certified seed.

10.4 The group exemption for patent licences — regulation 2349/84

A group exemption for exclusive and other patent licences was eventually adopted by the Commission in 1984. It is due to expire at the end of 1994 and will not be analysed in detail here. It is very similar in structure to that for know-how licences but, where there is both patent protection and secret, substantial know-how, the latter almost always permits more useful clauses than the patent regulation. The patent regulation has come to be used almost exclusively only when there is no qualifying know-how included in the licence — usually where a patent dispute between competitors is resolved by the grant of a licence.[31]

10.5 The group exemption for know-how licences — regulation 556/89

This regulation is not due to expire until the end of the millennium, but will probably be repealed at the end of 1994 and replaced by a new regulation. Transitional provisions are likely to exempt agreements that came within its terms until it was due to expire.

The basic scheme of the regulation is that article 1 exempts exclusive and some other know-how licences, whether or not some of the technology is protected by patent. Article 2 provides the white list of clauses that normally do not infringe article 85(1) but are exempted just in case. Article 3 contains the black list, which specifies conditions that prevent the application of the exemption and Article 4 provides for exemption under the opposition procedure[32] for agreements containing restrictions of competition that do not come within any of the lists.

31   My monographs on the regulations are listed at 10.11 below. The patent regulation will be of interest only when litigating or negotiating a settlement over facts that happened before its expiry.
32   Described at 3.3 above.

10.5.1 *The exemption (article 1)*

The know-how licensing agreements exempted by the regulation are defined in article 1(7). In addition to licences of pure know-how, the exemption applies to mixed licences of patents and know-how. The licence must include some technology that is secret, substantial and recorded, but these terms are defined widely and any know-how for which a licensee is prepared to pay is likely to suffice.

The exemption may apply where the licensed territory includes countries outside the common market (recital 4). The licence may relate to one or more means of exploitation, manufacture, use or putting on the market (article 1(7)(7)).

Article 1(1) provides:

> 'Pursuant to article 85(3) of the treaty and subject to the provisions of this regulation, it is hereby declared that article 85(1) of the treaty shall not apply to pure know-how licensing agreements and to mixed know-how and patent licensing agreements not exempted by [the patent regulation], including those agreements containing ancillary provisions relating to trade marks or other intellectual property rights, to which only two undertakings are party and which include one or more of the following obligations:'

The agreement must be made between not more than two undertakings. The regulation does not apply to technology pools; licences between competitors who hold interests in a joint venture, or by one of them to their joint venture if the licence relates to the activities of the joint venture and reciprocal agreements between competitors under which there are territorial restrictions (article 5).

The most important exclusion is for licences that include intellectual property rights other than patents, such as trade marks, copyright, design rights or software, unless the rights or software are ancillary to the know-how licence and no restrictions of competition are attached to them other than those also attached to the know-how and exempted by the regulation.

The question arises whether a trade mark is to be treated as ancillary when it is complementary. We will see at 10.7 below that in *Moosehead/Whitbread*,[33] where there was sufficient secret and substantial know-how passing to qualify under the regulation, an industrial franchise was not exempt because the Commission said that the licence of the trade mark was crucial, although it was previously unknown in Europe.

Article 1 specifies the obligations all, any combination or one of which may be accepted and which are exempted from article 85(1) of the treaty if the agreement includes no other provisions that infringe article 85(1).

The licensor may agree not to license anyone else in the licensee's

33   [1991] 4 C.M.L.R. 391.

territory and not to exploit the technology there himself (article 1(1)(1) and (2)). Such restrictions amount to open exclusivity according to the Court's judgment in *Nungesser* (10.3 above). The Commission accepts in recital 6 that the judgment applies to know-how and patents as well as plant breeders' rights, but only to products that are new. Nevertheless, the regulation is not so limited. The licensee may also agree not to exploit the licensed invention in the territory reserved for the licensor. Officials refer to 'absolute territorial protection as between licensor and licensee.' It must be remembered, however, that under the rules for the free movement of goods discussed in chapter 9, those to whom either party sells the protected product cannot be restrained through the exercise of national intellectual property rights from selling it throughout the common market and EEA, so the protection is limited. A reciprocal restriction to protect the licensor was not needed to protect INRA, since it was not allowed by French law to exploit its inventions commercially. Moreover, prices were higher in Germany than in France, so there was no incentive to sell in France. Such a restriction would be exempted by article 1(1)(3).

As to competition between licensees, each may agree with the licensor not to manufacture etc. in the territory of the others (article 1(1)(4)). Each may agree not actively to market the products in the others' territories (the provision is slightly narrower than article 2(2)(c) of regulation 1983/83) and not to sell even passively in their territories for a period of five years from the date of the first licence within the common market by the licensor or one of his licensees.

All these restrictions, other than the restriction on passive sales, may last as long as there is a patent that existed at the time of the licence within the territory to be protected (article 1(4)), or for periods of ten years from the first licence in the territory for restrictions between patentee and licensee, and from the first licence in the common market for those between licensees. The duration of the territorial protection cannot be extended even if new know-how is licensed. If substantial new, secret know-how is developed, however, a new licence can be granted with further periods of territorial protection. This may not be as important as it sounds, because once a market has been found for products made by the technology, the licensor may have less need to induce the licensee to invest in tooling up and making a market.

I infer from the recitals which state that exclusive licences are desirable that the licensor may promise to protect his first licensees by imposing such restrictions in subsequent licences, but this is not expressed in any of the provisions of the regulation. The longer territorial protection allowed between licensor and licensee than between licensees is difficult to defend on policy grounds. Each needs protection from everyone if it is to be induced to invest. The licensor enjoys some protection through the payment of royalties, and each manufacturer may enjoy some protection if transport costs are significant.

If the investment required to develop the innovation, set up production and develop a market exceeds the value of the natural protection from royalties and freight, further protection may be needed from every direction. If a roof leaks in five places, there is little point in mending four leaks as the rain may soak in through the fifth. The regulation was a compromise between the Commission's perception *ex post* and the views *ex ante* being urged by business.

The licensee may also be required to use only the licensor's mark or get up, although he must be allowed to identify himself as the manufacturer (article 1(1)(7)).

Article 1(5) provides that the sales restrictions exempted in paragraphs (2), (3), (5) and (6) do not apply to pure sales licences. They apply only where the licensee manufactures the licensed product itself or proposes to do so. Pure sales licences amount to distribution agreements, which may be exempt under regulation 1983 or 1984/83, but not under the know-how regulation.

Article 1(6) is a useful innovation that has become standard in group exemptions, although not included in that for franchising agreements. The exemption may apply when obligations of the same kind but of more limited scope are accepted, for instance where the licensor agrees not to grant a licence to more than one other person in the licensee's territory.

10.5.2 *The white list (article 2)*

Article 2(1) lists the provisions which in the Commission's view rarely infringe article 85(1) (recital 10), but are exempted just in case. Many of them are limited by items in the black list of article 3. Article 2(2) exempts the white listed clauses and this exemption also applies to restrictions of the same kind but more limited scope (article 2(3)).

10.5.3 *The black list (article 3)*

The black list of provisions that prevent the application of the exemption should be considered with care. The conditions blacklisted prevent article 1 and the opposition procedure, described at 10.5.4 below, from applying. This may well be the case even if the blacklisted clause does not itself infringe article 85(1): it probably prevents the exemption from applying to other clauses that qualify.

The Commission has long objected to clauses restricting the right of a licensee to challenge the validity of a licensed patent. Article 3(4) goes less far than the patent regulation[34] and blacklists restrictions on challenging the validity of any patents within the common market or the secrecy of the know-how belonging to the licensor's group of companies without prejudice to the licensor's right to terminate the agreement in the event of challenge. In practice, a licensee may acknowledge that the know-how is secret and substantial, and then it would have to show that the know-how has come into the public domain if it wished to avoid restrictions on selling outside its territory.

In *Bayer* v. *Süllhöfer*,[35] the Court held that no-challenge clauses may infringe article 85(1) even if they be contained in the settlement of opposition proceedings in the patent office or in a national court, but that they are not necessarily caught if not unfair. They should be assessed in their economic context. The judgment is confused, and the Commission fears that it may receive notifications of most resolutions of disputes. It is unlikely to clear restrictions on challenging the disputed rights, although it may be prepared to exempt them. Such agreements will seldom come within the know-how group exemption, as know how is unlikely to be included in a licence granted to compromise litigation.

Neither party must be restricted from competing in respect of r & d, manufacture, use or sales, save as allowed by article 1, without prejudice to requiring the licensee to use its best endeavours to exploit the licensed invention (article 3(9)). This condition is very wide and seems to cover many of the restrictions whitelisted in article 2. A minimum royalty clause whitelisted by article 2(9), for instance, may well deter a licensee from paying for rival technology to exploit. Commission officials, speaking in their personal capacity, have stated, however, that article 2 prevails over article 3. Careful draughtsmen change restrictions on competing to an obligation for the licensee to use its best endeavours to exploit the licensed technology and provide that once the licensee starts to use rival technology, he will inform the licensor, cease to be entitled to improvements and will have to prove that the products are no longer made by use of the licensor's technology.

There are further provisions about maximum quantities, which are perceived to restrict exports (article 3(7) and recital 19); prices must be set independently (article 3(8) and recital 19); markets must not be divided by class of customer (article 3(6) and recitals 16 and 18), although some field of use restrictions are allowed under article 2(1)(8) and recital 16. A new item is exempted by article 1(1) of the know-how regulation, however. One may grant a licence to a firm to manufacture

---

34   The patent regulation also blacklisted restrictions on challenging ancillary trade marks within the common market.

35   (65/86) [1988] E.C.R. 5249.

the licensed product as much as it wants for its own use only. The blacklisted provision for maximum quantities is also overridden by article 4(2). This provides that if a customer wants a second source of the licensed product, one may license such a second source to make limited quantities. For this to apply, the agreement must be notified, but an exemption under the regulation can be allowed without the Commission having to make all the translations necessary for a formal individual exemption.

Provisions requiring the licensee exclusively to feed back information about improvements or to assign intellectual property rights to them are included in the black list (article 3(2)), although non-exclusive and reciprocal feed and grant back clauses are whitelisted in article 2(1)(4) and recital 14. Tying one patent to another or to goods or services is also blacklisted (article 3(3)), as the Commission thinks this may extend market power from one product or patent to others, but package licensing is permitted when each item in the package is wanted by the licensee, or by virtue of article 2(1)(5) when technically justified. Both these elements are expressly excepted from article 3(5). Article 3(11) and (12) excludes territorial restrictions that exceed those permitted by article 1.

The main reason for the lengthy black list is that the Commission believes that, even if the licensee could not have entered the market without a licence, the agreement is horizontal once both licensee and licensor start to produce and sell. This is another example of the Commission looking at the matter *ex post* and not *ex ante*. It accounts for the generally negative approach towards technology licences that many consider vertical and pro-competitive.

10.5.4 *The opposition procedure (article 4)*

Provisions that restrict competition and are not listed in article 1 or 2 were thought to prevent the automatic application of the exemption to the obligations permitted by article 1 even if these are not blacklisted. To provide for this situation, the Commission has introduced the opposition procedure.

Article 4 provides that where a know how licence includes obligations restrictive of competition that do not come within any of the first three articles, the parties may notify the licensing agreement to the Commission, drawing attention to article 4. If the Commission does not oppose the exemption within six months or withdraws its opposition at any time, the agreement will be exempt under the regulation. Consequently, there will be no need for the Commission to write letters stating that an agreement merits exemption where the opposition procedure applies.

Since some Commission officials consider that many clauses restrict competition even though pro-competitive licensing could not take place without them, they may see this procedure as more important than do some legal advisers. The procedure is a technical minefield and has not often been successfully invoked, although a handful of technology licences have been exempted this way.

The Commission has only six months within which to oppose. Even after opposing, if it decides that an exemption is merited, it may merely withdraw its opposition and let the group exemption apply without having to go through the procedures for granting an individual exemption or comfort letter. The Commission's powers are discretionary.

It is clear that a national court asked to enforce the terms of a technology licence has jurisdiction to decide whether the agreement comes within the prohibition of article 85(1) of the treaty and whether it comes within the automatic provisions of the regulation[36] or qualifies for exemption under article 4. It almost certainly has no jurisdiction to decide whether the Commission has properly raised the opposition or failed to do so.

10.5.5 *Miscellaneous provisions (articles 6–13)*

Article 7 provides that the Commission may withdraw the benefit of the group exemption where it finds that a particular licensing agreement does not merit exemption. Articles 8–10 contain transitional provisions for know-how licences made before 1989. The provisions for confidentiality in article 11 go further than the treaty in that they prohibit authorities and officials of member states from disclosing confidential matters and the use of the information given under the opposition procedure for other matters, such as the enforcement of national competition laws.

10.5.6 *Conclusion*

After adopting the regulation for exclusive patent licences, the Commission sent standard letters to those who had notified know-how licences between 1963 and 1984, asking them to state whether the agreement remained in force and if so, whether it came within the new group exemption. It reduced its backlog of notifications without using

---

36 See *Hydrotherm* v. *Andreoli* (170/83) [1984] E.C.R. 2999, where the Court was prepared to answer questions about another group exemption, so must have considered that the answers were necessary to the judgment of the national court.

many of its resources. To my surprise, many technology licences negotiated before the group exemptions were published were found to come
within their terms.

10.6 The future of technology licences

The know-how regulation does not include pure patent licences that
are not supported by substantial, secret and recorded know-how. My
impression is that pure patent licences are rarely granted save as a
method of solving a dispute as to the validity of the patent. They are
often made between competitors. The Commission is preparing a single
new regulation to exempt all three categories of technology licence, pure
patent, pure know-how and mixed to come into force when the patent
regulation expires at the end of 1994.[37]

The most important change from the know-how regulation envisaged
when this is being written is that there is to be a limit of market share,
above which territorial restraints will not be exempted. Firms with
market power are expected to seek individual exemptions.

By virtue of article 1(5), the licensor may agree to grant no further
licences for the territory provided that the licensee is not already an
important producer of the products capable of being improved or
replaced by the licensed technology which are considered by users to be
equivalent. In other words, that ceiling will apply only if the licensee was
already an existing competitor of the licensed technology and either
produced 40 per cent. of the products so defined in the common market
or a substantial part of it or was one of the three firms with the largest
market shares and its market share was at least 10 per cent.

By virtue of article 1(6), the parties to be protected by the other
territorial restraints must not hold a market share of over 20 per cent.

The most important change from the earlier version circulating for
comment is that the ceilings are to be applied once and for all at the date
the licence is granted. There is no longer concern that it will be very
difficult to find a firm willing to commit itself to very risky investment if it
loses the territorial protection when the commercial venture is highly
successful.

The periods of territorial protection will differ as between the three
kinds of licences and the limits have still not been determined firmly. The
white list of provisions that rarely restrict competition is being retained

37   O.J. 1994, C 178/3, with corrigendum at O.J. 1994, C 187/16. See V. Korah,
Comment [1994] E.B.L.R. (July).
    I intend to write a monograph on the reg. when it has been adopted to replace my
monographs on the existing regs.

and lengthened. The black list has been significantly shortened, in view of the cap of market share. The opposition procedure has gone. The exclusion from the regulation of licences that include other intellectual property rights unless they are ancillary remains, but there is some hope of this being restricted as a result of pressure from industry.

10.7 Licences of other kinds of commercial and industrial property rights

The new group exemption will apply only to patent and know-how licences, not to licences of software, copyright or trade marks, unless these are ancillary to the licensed technology and no restrictions are attached to their use that are not attached to the know-how. Franchising agreements for the supply of goods or services which include a trade mark licence were considered at 8.5–8.5.2 above. As described there, many terms do not restrict competition, and even an exclusive territory coupled with a restriction on selling outside specified premises can often be brought within the group exemption.

Industrial franchises, however, do not fall within a group exemption. In *Moosehead/Whitbread*,[38] a Canadian firm decided to exploit the English market by providing Whitbread with the recipe and yeast needed to make its special brand of beer. Although the mark was formerly unknown in Europe, the Commission found that licensing it was crucial to the transaction rather than ancillary and that, by virtue of article 5(1)(4), the know-how regulation did not apply. Nevertheless, it granted an individual exemption to the exclusive licence.

The limitation of the exemption in article 5(1)(4) both of the know-how and the new draft exemption to marks and other intellectual property rights that are ancillary is very unsatisfactory. Usually they are complementary, and the distinction gives the Commission, or a court asked to apply the regulation, vast discretion, which reduces juridical certainty. It is hoped that the requirement that licences of other rights be ancillary will be relaxed. That may not entirely solve the problem as industrial franchises often include other restrictions on conduct to ensure the quality of the product when it is sold under the franchisor's mark. The Commission may prepare a specific regulation to exempt industrial franchises.

The Commission is considering granting a group exemption for software licences, but its study has not yet proceeded far. Article 4(c) of the software directive[39] confers on the holder the exclusive right to distribute

38 Cited at 10.5.1 above.
39 Council Dir. 91/250 of 14 May 1991, O.J. 1991, L122/42.

original computer programs or copies thereof. It is arguable that this enables him to supply copies for resale within the meaning of regulation 1983/83 and that exclusive distribution may fall within that group exemption.

Maurits Dolmans has suggested[40] that software licences to end users will not infringe article 85(1) when the end user operates in a different market from the holder. Where the licensee is to make modifications, however, it may well be a software company and at least a potential competitor and there may be problems. These he analyses.

It is not clear how far the know-how regulation is a good guide to the Commission's thinking about other kinds of intellectual property rights. Nevertheless, the Commission frequently states how concerned it is to encourage r & d, and it must take care not to discourage it through unduly strict control over the transfer of technology.

There were a few informal decisions on copyright reported some years ago in the *Annual Reports* but the law and policy have not yet been worked out. Some firms decide not to notify licences of rights not covered by a group exemption. They argue that, provided only the minimum of restrictive provisions necessary to ensure that the transaction is viable has been accepted, a national court or the Community Court might decide that the licence promotes rather than restricts competition, at least in the absence of significant market power. Others may notify the agreement in the hope of obtaining an individual exemption, but are more likely to receive a letter stating that the Commission thinks the agreement merits exemption, but is closing the file. This is more helpful now than it used to be.[41]

10.8 Agreements to avoid confusion between trade marks

Various problems relating to the exercise of trade marks have arisen. As branded goods are increasingly being sold throughout the common market, firms are finding that their marks may be confused with a mark already known in another member state. The firms may be prepared to collaborate to distinguish the marks, and in 1977 the Commission gave an informal clearance under article 85(1) to an understanding between the owners of the *Persil* mark[42] in different member states, whereby they were to take various measures, including the use of different colours and lettering, to distinguish the marks. This allowed the products marketed by either in an area where it held the mark to circulate freely throughout the Community.

40   *Op. cit.*, bibliography, 10.11 below.
41   See 6.3.4 above.
42   [1978] 1 C.M.L.R. 395, press release.

The Commission issued a press release[43] about the settlement of the *Hershey–Herschi* litigation. The confusing marks were of independent origin and the holder of the Herschi mark assigned it to the other for valuable consideration, retaining limited rights to use it on products for which it had already been used for five years. The Commission considered that this solved the dispute without restricting competition, in particular because it involved no territorial division of the common market.

The Commission will, however, challenge as contrary to article 85 agreements, such as that between *Sirdar and Phildar*,[44] whereby each party agrees not to use the mark in the other's territory. Those marks may not have been confusing, but the decision was based on the possibility that they might have been. The decision has been criticised as ensuring the free movement of marks rather than of goods, but the Commission has taken the view that it may well be difficult to tackle a new export market without the benefit of the reputation inherent in one's established trade mark. Others consider that it is permitting one firm to take a ride on the established reputation of others and so reducing the incentive to maintain quality and improve one's reputation. Marks are merely a way of identifying products, especially those that cannot be examined before purchase, or that are bought too seldom for many buyers to have had experience of the product. As recognised by the Court in *Ideal-Standard* (9.4.4 above), trade marks make important aspects of competition possible.

10.9 Article 86 — obligation to grant licences

The judgment in *Parke, Davis* v. *Probel*,[45] like that in *Consten and Grundig*,[46] was based on the competition rules. Parke Davis held the patent for the drug chloramphenicol in all the member states save Italy where, at that time, drugs were not capable of patent protection. The defendants imported the drug from Italy into the Netherlands, and Parke Davis sued them for infringement of its Dutch patent. As Advocate General Roemer observed, not to have permitted an infringement action would have emptied the rights of the patentee of all substance and reduced the incentives to innovation.

The Court did not advert to such policy issues but ruled that merely to enforce a patent right in the absence of a restrictive agreement does not

43   *20th Annual Report*, 1990, p.87.
44   [1975] 1 C.M.L.R. D93.
45   (24/67) [1968] E.C.R. 55.
46   See 10.3 above.

infringe article 85. It ignored the fact that Parke Davis was suing in order
to protect a licensee to whom it had granted an exclusive licence. The
Court added that a suit for patent infringement is not contrary to article
86, unless the patentee in fact enjoys a dominant position — in other
words, unless there are no close substitutes — and abuses it, possibly by
charging very high prices. The fact, however, that prices are higher than
in another member state where there is no patent does not necessarily
constitute an abuse (4.3.3.1 above). If, however, the patentee does enjoy
a dominant position, then discriminatory enforcement might infringe
article 86.

In several more recent cases decided under article 86, the Court has
confirmed that a firm that enjoys a dominant position may be required to
supply former trade customers even after any contractual obligations
have been performed (4.3.3.4 above). It is unclear whether this obligation extends to those not formerly supplied by the dominant firm. It
was, therefore, feared that, where intellectual property rights confer a
dominant position on the holder, the latter might be under an obligation
to grant a licence to anyone prepared to pay a reasonable royalty. Any
such obligation would reduce the value of the intellectual property right.
Usually, higher profits are to be made by exploiting intellectual property
rights oneself, so patent, copyright and design licences are usually
granted only where, for some reason, the holder is unable to exploit the
rights itself.

The judgment in *Volvo*,[47] therefore, came as a considerable relief to
those investing in innovation and their advisers. Independent repairers
wanted to make spare body parts for Volvo cars, but Volvo held a
registered design and was not prepared to grant a licence for a royalty.
Advocate General Mischo concluded that the holder of intellectual
property rights is dominant over the products they protect only if it is in
a position to prevent the maintenance of effective competition over a
considerable part of the relevant market. He added, however, that since
there were no substitute parts, Volvo did enjoy a dominant position over
the body parts once it began to exercise its design rights, a view slightly
narrower than that in *Hugin*.[48]

The Court did not decide whether Volvo enjoyed a dominant position
but, assuming that it did, followed Advocate General Mischo in holding
that the right to restrain third parties from exploiting the design 'constitutes the very subject-matter of his exclusive right.' Consequently, to
order the holder to grant a licence would deprive it of the substance of its
exclusive right and a refusal to license did not constitute an abuse of the

47   (238/87) [1988] E.C.R. 6211.
48   [1978] 1 C.M.L.R. D19, and 4.2.4 above.

right. Nevertheless, it added that the exercise of a holder's exclusive right might be prohibited by article 86 if it involves:

'certain abusive conduct such as the arbitrary refusal to supply spare parts to independent repairers, the fixing of prices for spare parts at an unfair level or a decision no longer to produce spare parts for a particular model even though many cars of that model are still in circulation, provided that such conduct is liable to affect trade between member states' (paragraph 9).

It seems then that the proprietor of an exclusive right, who is held to enjoy a dominant position, may be required either to license third parties, or to supply them with the protected product on terms that are not 'unfair,' whatever that may mean (see 4.3.3.1 above).

In proceedings for interim measures that ended without a formal decision, in *Ford Body Panels*, Ford undertook not to use its design rights more than three years after it had sold a certain number of vehicles of which they formed part.[49] It is difficult to understand the legal basis for requiring such an undertaking.

In *Magill*,[50] the Commission condemned under article 86 the refusal by three broadcasting organisations in Ireland to permit the reproduction weekly, in advance, of their programme listings. They had exercised their copyright to restrain publication by Magill, which wanted to publish a combined listing of the programmes of all three organisations which could be received in Ireland. The Court of First Instance upheld the decision[51] on grounds that would be very disturbing if applied generally to copyright. On the facts of the case, the copyright itself might be thought unjustified as the holder had invested neither effort nor originality, but the Court of First Instance stated that that remained a matter for national law. The matter is before the Community Court.[52] Advocate General Gulmann has recommended that the judgment of the Court of First Instance be quashed and the Court is likely to give judgment before three of the judges retire in early October.

10.10 The subcontracting notice

The Commission has issued a notice on subcontracting[53] stating that, in its view, certain restrictions on the conduct of those to whom work is given out, required to ensure the continued value of the technology and equipment, do not come within the prohibition of article 85(1). This is an interesting and early example of the Commission adopting a flexible

49   *20th Annual Report*, 1990, p. 87.
50   [1989] 4 C.M.L.R. 757.
51   (T–69, 70, 76–77, 91/89) [1991] E.C.R. II–485, at 535 and 575.
52   (C–241 & 242/91P), opinion of 1 June 1994.
53   O.J. 1979, C1/2.

approach under article 85(1). If the person requiring the work could not protect its technology, it would probably do it itself, and the result might be less competitive. The person undertaking the manufacture of the product is, therefore, not to be treated as an independent undertaking.

In so far as the technology or equipment is necessary to carry out the work under reasonable conditions, and the person undertaking it could not reasonably obtain access to it otherwise, it may promise not to use it except for the purpose of carrying out the agreement, not to make it available to others, nor to supply the goods resulting from its use to anyone else. Either party may also agree not to disclose secret know-how, and the person doing the work may agree not to use secret manufacturing processes or know-how even after the agreement has expired, until it becomes public knowledge. It may also agree to a feed and grant back clause, which must usually be non-exclusive.

According to its *10th Report on Competition Policy*, page 89, however, the Commission decided informally in *Bramley/Gilbert* that the:

> 'exclusive supply obligation may restrict competition where the licensee has made a sufficient contribution to the development of the invention covered by the patent for him to be regarded as a joint inventor with enforceable rights in this respect against the licensee.'

There have, however, been no formal decisions following this statement and it is hoped that the Commission has now changed its mind.

This notice has proved to be very useful. The official drafting it listened carefully to comments from industry and it is not too tightly circumscribed to be of use.

10.11 Bibliography

J. A. Bleeke and *James A. Rahl*, 'The Value of Territorial and Field-of-Use Restrictions in International Licensing of Unpatented Know-how: an Empirical Study,' (1979) 1/2 N.W. J. of Int'l. L. & Bus. 450.

Maurits Dolmans, 'Software Licensing in Europe — do we need a group exemption?' in Hugh Hansen (ed.), *Proceedings of the second annual Fordham Conference on International Intellectual Property Law and Policy*, to be published late in 1994 by Transnational Law.

Eleanor Fox, 'Maize Seed: A Comparative Comment,' Chap. 6 of Ed. Barry Hawk [1982] *Fordham Corporate Law Institute* 151.

Hugh Hansen (ed.), IV *Fordham Intellectual Property, Media & Entertainment Law Journal*, Summer 1993, special issue containing the papers of the *First Fordham Conference on International Intellectual Property Law and Policy*. The proceedings of the second annual conference will be published in hardback by Transnational Law late in 1994.

René Joliet, 'Territorial and Exclusive Trade Mark Licensing under EEC Law of Competition' [1984] IIC 21.

——, 'Trade mark Licensing Agreements Under the EEC Law of Competition' (1983–1984) 5 N.W. J. Int'l. L. & Bus. 757.

Valentine Korah, Patent Licensing and EEC Competition Rules: Regulation 2349/84, ESC, 1985.

——, *Know-how Licensing and EEC Competition Rules: Regulation 556/89*, ESC, 1989.

I plan to write a new monograph in 1995 on the new group exemption for technology licensing to replace these two.

——, 'Exclusive Licences of Patent and Plant Breeders' Rights under EEC Law after Maize Seed' (1983) XXVIII *Antitrust Bull.* 699.

Mario Siragusa, 'Technology Transfers under EEC Law: A Private View,' Chap. 5 of Barry Hawk (ed.) [1982] *Fordham Corporate Law Institute* 95.

James S. Venit, 'EEC Patent Licensing Revisited: The Commission's Patent Licensing Regulation' (1985) XXX *Antitrust Bull.* 457.

——, 'The Commission's Opposition Procedure — between the Scylla of *ultra vires* and the Charybdis of Perfume: Legal Consequences and Tactical Considerations' (1985) 22 C.M.L.Rev. 167.

——, 'In the Wake of *Windsurfing*: Patent Licensing in the Common Market,' in Barry Hawk (ed.) [1986] *Fordham Corporate Law Institute*, Chap. 22, from p.522.

Eric L. White, 'Research and Development Joint Ventures Under EEC Competition Law' [1985] IIC 663.

11 Specialisation Agreements

11.1 Introduction

Small and medium-sized firms in many industries may be too small to be able to utilise fully an automatic production line, or achieve other economies of scale or scope in either production or distribution. The Commission has encouraged specialisation agreements between such firms, especially where they operated in different member states. Specialisation agreements allocate the production of one range of products to one party and of another range to another and each appoints the other or others as its exclusive distributor in the other's home market. In this way, exports become easier because there is no need to set up a new sales network, the output of each party may increase rapidly and, if this warrants the installation and full use of an automatic production line, costs may be dramatically reduced.

One of the reasons for establishing the common market was to facilitate specialisation, so it is not surprising that the Commission has favoured such agreements. Frequently, the only competition restricted is the possibility of each firm extending production into the other's range. Both firms sell the full range, and the Commission considers this to be more competitive than a joint venture if the latter results in a single seller.

11.2 Effects of specialisation agreements on competition

Where there is a large number of firms making the full range of products that are subject to the specialisation agreement, any reduction of competition between the parties is likely to be insignificant and cost savings are likely to increase the effectiveness of each to such an extent that competition will be increased, not restricted. In accordance with its practice in other fields, however, and arguably inconsistently with the judgments of the Community Court,[1] where total market shares exceed 5 per cent., the Commission has considered only the reduction in the number of competitors under article 85(1), the effectiveness of their competition being taken into account under article 85(3).

From 1970, the Commission has been granting individual exemptions, not clearances, to such agreements[2] and, in 1972, it granted a group exemption, which was extended to rather larger firms in 1985.[3]

1 7.1.2, 8.5.1 and 10.3 above.
2 11.3 below.
3 11.4 below.

11.3 Individual decisions

An early individual decision was *Clima Chappée/Buderus*.[4] Each of two participants was allocated a list of air-conditioning products, which the other agreed not to make unless the turnover of the party to whom the products were allocated exceeded a level to be agreed. For those products not allocated to either party, each was to give preference to the other when buying, provided that price and quality were equal. Clima Chappée was a French firm, already established in supplying air-conditioning apparatus, while Buderus was a German firm new to this field. There were no restrictions on sale, save in the Federal Republic of Germany, where Clima Chappée agreed to sell only to Buderus, and in France, where Buderus agreed to sell only to Clima Chappée. The Commission stated that there were a large number of undertakings which made and sold air-conditioning equipment comparable to that made by the parties.

Despite the last statement, the Commission found that the agreement had the object of restricting potential competition, in that the parties each gave up their freedom of action in various respects. Each agreed not to make the products allocated to the other, not to sell in the other's country save through the other and to give preference to the other when buying the products that were not allocated to either. Neither gave up the manufacture of any products it was already making, but the specialisation arrangement did restrict potential competition in that each had the financial backing and other attributes necessary to extend its range.

The agreement was exempted on the ground that the elimination of duplication and the economies derived from passing to series production and so forth improved both production and distribution and increased consumer choice. If, as seems unlikely, the agreement did restrict potential competition, the key policy question should have been whether these benefits could have been obtained by any means that would have left possible any potential competition between the two firms. This issue was not addressed. The exemption expired in 1979.

There have been several similar decisions, in some of which the Commission seems merely to have certified the matters on which it must be satisfied if it is to apply article 85(3). An extreme example was *Fine Papers*,[5] where the specialisation between the French makers of cigarette and other very thin papers seems to have eliminated most of the competition that remained in that industry, without ensuring that any benefits were passed on to consumers.

In some decisions, the Commission makes no market analysis under

4   [1970] C.M.L.R. D7.
5   [1972] C.M.L.R. D94.

article 85(1). In *Rank/Sopelem*,[6] it held that an agreement infringed article 85(1) because it restrained the parties' freedom of action, and exempted it on the ground that the restrictions were indispensable as without them the parties could not have supplied such a comprehensive range of products.

By exempting rather than clearing the agreement, the Commission was able to put pressure on the parties to ensure that each would remain capable of selling in both countries when the agreement came to an end. It pointed out that the Sopelem lenses were to be sold under Rank trade marks, which would make it very difficult for Sopelem to distribute them independently when the exemption came to an end and seems to have persuaded the parties to modify the agreement, so that Sopelem would be entitled to buy the mark at the end of the period. There is much to be said for arranging that both the manufacturer's and the distributor's marks be used, so that when the agreement comes to an end each will have a reputation in all areas where its goods have been marketed, or where it has marketed the other's goods. On the other hand, the change in contractual terms enabled Rank to renegotiate the deal after Sopelem had invested in building up its reputation: the very evil the Commission was trying to avoid.

11.4 Group exemption — regulation 417/85

In regulation 2779/72, made under Council regulation 2821/71, the Commission granted a group exemption for specialisation agreements which expired at the end of 1977. Since then its scope has been extended and the current exemption is granted by regulation 417/85.[7] Unlike the regulations considered earlier in this book, the specialisation group exemption applies even if the agreement is made between more than two undertakings. Article 1 exempts:

'agreements on specialisation whereby, for the duration of the agreement, undertakings accept reciprocal obligations:
(a) not to manufacture certain products or to have them manufactured, but to leave it to other parties to manufacture the products or have them manufactured; or
(b) to manufacture certain products or have them manufactured only jointly.'

The final paragraph enables the economies of scale to be achieved even when there is but a single range of products, and the agreement could not be reciprocal.

Article 2(1) defines the only other restrictions of competition that may

6   [1975] 1 C.M.L.R. D72.
7   O.J. 1985, L53/1, extended to joint sales by reg. 151/93, O.J. 1993, L21/8.

be accepted. The first three items relate to exclusivity. The parties may agree:

(1) not to enter into specialisation agreements with others for goods that compete with those subject to the specialisation;
(2) to procure the goods subject to the agreement only from the others, or their joint venture, subject to a right to buy elsewhere on more favourable terms which the parties will not match, the so-called 'English clause'; and
(3) provided that dealers and users can obtain the products elsewhere, to grant the others exclusive distribution rights.

Regulation 151/93 has also permitted the parties to agree to joint sales until they achieve a market share of 10 per cent.

To revert to the facts of *Clima Chappée*,[8] had the regulation been in force at the time, Clima Chappée could have agreed not to make the items allocated to Buderus, to supply only Buderus in the Federal Republic of Germany and not to make similar agreements about air-conditioners with anyone else, and *vice versa*.

This gives considerable protection to each party from competition from the other parties. Clima Chappée could probably be restrained from distributing the products allocated to it in Germany directly to large users as well as to dealers. Nevertheless, buyers in France from Clima Chappée could not be deterred from selling in Germany. If there had been a third party from England, it could have been given exclusive distribution rights there by both the other parties, but would probably have had to be free to sell goods made by the other parties also in France and Germany.

Now, by virtue of regulation 151/93, joint sales may also be arranged by any of the parties, a joint venture or a third party who is not a competitor, until the market share of the parties exceeds 10 per cent.

Consequently, in the absence of effective barriers to cross-frontier trade, such as freight for cheap, bulky products or safety regulations that do not infringe article 30, there will remain indirect competition between the parties which, in theory, makes it harder to maintain large price differences between different parts of the common market. Moreover, there will be competing products made by those not party to the agreement.

Article 2(3) permits the acceptance of an obligation

— to supply the products to the other;
— to observe minimum standards of quality;

8   11.3 above.

— to maintain minimum stocks of the products subject to the
  specialisation and spare parts for them; and
— to provide customer and guarantee services.

Since the parties probably make complementary products, they may
well have been potential competitors and may actually have competed
before the conclusion of the agreement. It is therefore important that the
regulation should not apply if the parties collectively enjoy market
power. So article 3 imposes limitations of market share and size. The
exemption shall apply only if:

'(a) the products which are the subject of the specialisation together with
     the participating undertakings' other products which are considered
     by users to be equivalent in view of their characteristics, price and
     intended use do not represent more than 20% of the market for such
     products in the common market or a substantial part thereof;'

The market is defined only in terms of substitute products on the
demand side, not by reference to ease of entry or substitutes on the
supply side — firms that could stop making one product and easily turn
their productive capacity to the contract products.

The geographic market, on a literal interpretation, could be anything.
It is hoped that in the light of recital 6, which refers to the elimination of
competition, the Court will adopt a teleological approach and rule that
where the common market is integrated because freight is not a significant cost and there are no problems with safety regulations under the
national laws, it is the whole common market that is relevant, but that
where the goods cannot sensibly be moved far, a smaller area is appropriate. This, however, is not a literal construction of the regulation,
although the geographic market is so defined in the notice on minor
agreements.[9] In relation to article 86, Advocate General Warner interpreted a substantial part of the common market to be a *de minimis* rule
that did not exclude BP's customers for petrol in the Netherlands,
although they bought less than 0·5 per cent. of the supply in the common
market.[10] Such a small market would, it is hoped, be relevant only if
customers were insulated from other suppliers. Where the geographic
market is small, which bits should be added to comprise a substantial
part of the common market is arbitrary, so the test is inappropriate to a
group exemption.

The other limitation, that the aggregate annual turnover of all the

9 See 2.4.1 above, para. 14.
10 *BP* v. *Commission* (77/77) [1978] E.C.R. 1513, at 1537. See 4.3.1 above and also the
Commission's notice on agreements of minor importance, where it states that normally
the whole of the common market is relevant, unless the goods cannot travel far. It has
been applying this statement in other contexts.

participants (including their corporate groups and for all products) does
not exceed 500 million ECUs, may be exceeded if the agreement be
notified to the Commission under article 4, provided that the Commission does not oppose the exemption within six months. This is similar
to the opposition procedure described at 3.3 above but, unlike the other
group exemptions, relates to turnover and not to unlisted provisions.

12 Mergers

12.1 Control under articles 85 and 86

In *Continental Can*,[1] the Community Court held that article 86 prohibits the acquisition by a dominant firm of most of the shares in a potential competitor, where this would substantially reduce competition. The Commission intervened informally in a few large mergers after 1973 and either prevented or modified their accomplishment,[2] but it took no formal decisions. It believed that it lacked sufficient power to control anti-competitive mergers. It had no power to require firms to notify their mergers in advance. It was widely thought that it could not forbid mergers that create a dominant position, unless at least one of the firms was already dominant and the merger strengthened its position. Nor was it clear whether article 86 applied to small accretions of market power. The Commission even doubted whether it had power to grant interim relief to restrain a merger while it was considering the matter, and there were some doubts as to whether it had power to order divestiture after the event.[3]

In *Philip Morris*,[4] the Court stated that the acquisition of minority share holding in a competitor which led to control might infringe article 85 if the acquisition restricted competition. This caused great concern as it was not clear how much of the transaction might be void, nor whether minimal restrictions of competition would be forbidden.

12.2 The merger regulation

On 21 December 1989, under pressure from industry, the Council eventually adopted a regulation[5] requiring the pre-notification to the Commission of concentrations within its scope — those above the thresholds — and providing for possible prohibition by the Commission.

The parties to the concentration, or the bidder, are required to notify the concentration to the Commission before implementing it.[6] The

---

1 (6/72) [1973] E.C.R. 215, and 4.3.2–4.3.2.1 above.
2 These are summarised in the Commission's *Annual Reports on Competition Policy* and by James Venit, *op. cit.*, bibliography, 12.4 below.
3 See Karen Banks, *op. cit.*, bibliography, 12.4 below.
4 The Commission's decision to close the file is described in its *16th Annual Report*, point 98. The Court's judgment confirming that decision in *BAT and Reynolds* v. *Commission* (142 & 156/84) [1987] E.C.R. 4487.
5 Reg. 4064/89, originally published in O.J. 1989, L395/1, [1990] 4 C.M.L.R. 286, but republished as corrected in O.J. 1990, L257/14.
6 12.2.2 below.

Commission is required to decide within one month of receiving a complete notification whether the concentration gives rise to serious concern (stage I, see 12.2.6 below) and, if it does, the Commission has a further four months in which to decide whether to forbid it as incompatible with the common market on the ground that it creates or strengthens a dominant position as a result of which competition is significantly impeded (stage II, 12.2.7 below).

Mergers are dealt with by the merger task force. This includes some officials from other parts of DGIV but also a significant number of officials from member states who are used to working with economists and from other parts of the Commission. It also includes some economists, and economic advice is often obtained from DGII, another department of the Commission. Market analyses in the merger cases appear to be more sophisticated than in those under article 86. Nevertheless, the published decisions are short, because of the short time limits available. The Commission gives the reasons for selecting particular product and geographic markets, but it is difficult for an outsider to assess whether the selection is sensible unless he is familiar with the industry.

There has been only one outright prohibition, but several concentrations have been permitted only subject to conditions or after the parties changed the deal in response to the Commission's concerns. The definition of a concentration, in terms of common control, is broad enough to include joint ventures, and half the transactions notified have related to joint ventures between large firms.

There are at least five major advantages in devising joint ventures so as to qualify for investigation under the regulation. First, the substantive test is far more favourable than that under article 85(1). Secondly, the proceedings inevitably lead to a formal decision and, thirdly, the decision is not subject to time limits: so the problems of enforcement created by comfort letters are avoided. Fourthly, most transactions are cleared within a month and the ones raising serious doubts within a further four months. Fifthly, national authorities cannot apply national competition rules.

12.2.1 *Thresholds*

A concentration is treated as having a Community dimension and being subject to the regulation when it exceeds the thresholds provided by article 1:

'2. For the purposes of this regulation, a concentration has a Community dimension where;
   (a) the aggregate worldwide turnover of all the undertakings concerned is more than ECU 5000 million, and

(b) the aggregate Community-wide turnover of each of at least two of the
undertakings concerned is more than ECU 250 million,

unless each of the undertakings concerned achieves more than two-thirds of
its aggregate Community-wide turnover within one and the same member
state.'

The high thresholds gave both industry and the Commission time to
organise and recruit appropriate staff. They were to be reviewed by the
Council by the end of 1993 (article 1(3)), but it seemed unlikely that it
would agree to their being lowered and the review has been postponed
until 1996.

The method of calculating turnover is prescribed in article 5. Discounts and turnover taxes, transactions between parties and within
groups are to be disregarded. Where only some of the activities of the
target company are acquired, whether or not they be carried on by a
separate legal person, turnover relating only to the parts of the undertaking that are the subject of the transaction should be taken into account.
In the case of a joint venture, however, the total turnover of all the
parents is included. So far some half of the concentrations dealt with
have been joint ventures. The Commission has been dealing with some
50 notifications a year.

12.2.2 *Notification*

Concentrations with a Community dimension are required by article 4
to be notified not more than one week after the agreement, announcement of public bid or the acquisition of a controlling interest. The parties
may not put the concentration into effect before, or for three weeks after,
notification (article 7).[7] Nevertheless, with the Commission's permission, a public bid may be implemented if it was notified before its
announcement, and the acquirer does not exercise the voting rights
otherwise than in order to maintain the full value of those investments.

Article 7(5) provides that:

'the validity of any transaction carried out in contravention of the duty to
notify shall be dependent on a decision'

by the Commission as to whether the concentration be compatible with
the common market. It seems that if the Commission eventually ap-
proves of the concentration there will be no nullity, but that if it does not,
then something will be void: it is not clear what. It is feared that the
transfer itself may be void and become a 'wreck upon the sea of

7 The Commission may prolong the suspension further if it has serious doubts
whether the merger is compatible with the common market and decides to initiate the
stage II procedure.

commerce.' Innocent purchasers from the acquiring undertaking may not acquire title to the assets of the target undertaking unless the transaction is treated as voidable rather than void.

The regulation that governs notification, Commission regulation 2367/90[8] requires a great deal of information — it was modelled on the second request under the Hart/Scott/Rodino Act of the US. If, however, the parties consult the Commission in advance informally and it is clear that the merger is unlikely substantially to restrict competition, the Commission can waive the requirement of much of the information. In this it has been very helpful and realistic. Where the bid is friendly, or a party enters into many joint ventures, the parties often begin to put the information on to a computer in advance, but there may be problems in meeting the deadline for notification if hostile take-over bids become frequent again, as it may be difficult to obtain the information about the target company.

12.2.3 Criteria for appraisal by the Commission

Article 2 requires the Commission to appraise concentrations above the thresholds to see whether they are compatible with the common market.

Article 2(2) and (3) prescribes the criterion: whether:

> 'a concentration ... creates or strengthens a dominant position as a result of which effective competition would be significantly impeded in the common market or in a substantial part of it.'

If the concentration does create or strengthen a dominant position, the Commission should declare that it is incompatible with the common market and it may not proceed. More often, however, the parties either hive off some overlapping activities or undertake to do so, in which case the Commission may declare subject to conditions that the concentration is compatible with the common market. The conditions bind the parties only if imposed after an investigation that has progressed into stage II (article 8(2)), but are sometimes taken under stage I. In other cases, the deal that is allowed to proceed is altered before a formal decision is taken.

In assessing whether a dominant position is created or strengthened, Article 2(1) requires the Commission to take into account:

> '(a) the need to preserve and develop effective competition within the common market in view of, among other things, the structure of all the markets concerned and the actual or potential competition from undertakings located either within or without the Community;

8   O.J. 1990, L219/5.

(b) the market position of the undertakings concerned and their economic and financial power, the opportunities available to suppliers and users, their access to supplies or markets, any legal or other barriers to entry, supply and demand trends for the relevant goods and services, the interests of the intermediate and ultimate consumers, and the development of technical and economic progress provided that it is to consumers' advantage and does not form an obstacle to competition.'

The justification on non-competition grounds was removed from the earlier draft of this article, but article 21, which provides that only the Commission may implement the regulation and that member states may not normally apply their competition laws to concentrations with a Community dimension, adds that, nevertheless, member states may take appropriate measures to protect three specified legitimate interests: public security, plurality of the media and prudential rules, and other unspecified public interests that are recognised by the Commission after notification by the member state. They may also apply national rules that do not relate to competition, such as those that protect buyers of shares or minority interests.

The limitation to competitive criteria was controversial. Some of the matters to be taken into account could be interpreted to include non-competitive criteria. 'Economic and financial power' is not the same as power over price etc. in a market.

As suggested at 4.2.3.1 above, under the merger regulation the Commission has frequently taken rather wider markets as its starting point than it has done under article 86. Since it does not act on a complaint, it does not focus on particular conduct but on the structure of the market. Usually it has to focus on several overlapping activities of the parties. It has frequently defined the relevant market by reference to substitutes on the demand side but, when appraising whether the concentration is likely to create market power, it takes into account the possibility of specific firms entering the market and eroding it.   In *Alcatel/Telettra*,[9] for instance, there was concern about the Spanish market where Telefonica, the telephone monopoly, bought some 83 per cent. of some products from the parties. A market share of 50 per cent. raises a presumption of dominance within the meaning of article 86 according to *AKZO*.[10] Yet, the Commission looked to specific firms outside the common market which made similar equipment, and other makers of telephone equipment that were already operating in Spain.

Although the public procurement directive was not due to apply in Spain for several years, Telefonica stated that it favoured having two sources for each item of equipment and would be willing to buy abroad.

9   M 18, [1991] 4 C.M.L.R. 778.
10 See 4.2.5.1 above.

The Commission decided, therefore, that the market was contestable and that the concentration would not 'create . . . a dominant position as a result of which effective competition would be significantly impeded in the common market or in a substantial part of it.' Had the Commission adopted a definition of the geographic market that included all the firms that could potentially supply the equipment in Spain, however, the market shares cleared would have been far more modest.

There may be a gap in the regulation which does not expressly cover concentrations that reduce the number of suppliers to two or three. Concentrations may be forbidden only if they create or strengthen a dominant position as a result of which competition would be significantly impeded. In many countries, any merger which may substantially lessen competition may be forbidden.

The Commission has tried to fill the gap by stating that when, as a result of the merger, two firms will have large market shares, the concentration leads to a dualistic or oligopolistic dominant position. This it did for the first time in *Nestlé/Perrier*,[11] although it decided that the concentration was compatible with the common market in view of an undertaking from the parties that would create a third large player in the market.

Whether this view will ultimately be upheld by the Court is unclear. The judgment of the Court of First Instance in *Italian Flat Glass*[12] did not completely rule out a concept of joint dominance in relation to article 86, but did not encourage a wide application of the idea.

12.2.4 *Concentration defined*

The term 'concentration' is defined in article 3 in terms of a merger or of independent undertakings coming under common control. The definition includes concentrative joint ventures. Experts devote considerable time to making joint ventures concentrative so as to come within the more favourable regime of the regulation. Co-operative joint ventures are subject to article 85 and in Chapter 13 we will see that hardly any have been cleared or formally exempted.

Article 3(2) excludes 'collaborative' joint ventures from the regulation, but includes 'concentrative' joint ventures:

'2. An operation, including the creation of a joint venture, which has as its object or effect the coordination of the competitive behaviour of undertakings which remain independent shall not constitute a concentration within the meaning of paragraph 1(b).

The creation of a joint venture performing on a lasting basis all the functions of an autonomous economic entity, which does not give rise to

11   O.J. 1992, L356/1.
12   (T–68, 77, 78/89) [1992] E.C.R. II–1403. See 4.2.6 above.

coordination of the competitive behaviour of the parties amongst themselves
or between them and the joint venture, shall constitute a concentration within
the meaning paragraph 1(b).'

The Commission has a wide discretion to decide whether a joint
venture is concentrative or not. It has long, although not entirely consis-
tently, considered that concentrative joint ventures are not subject to
article 85.[13] It issued a *memorandum on concentrations* in 1966, after
receiving the reports of two groups of professors. It thought that mergers
often resulted in efficiencies and should be subject to a more lenient test
than that under article 85(1). It has tried to explain what is meant by the
term in a notice,[14] but in practice it has departed from the notice in its
actual decisions, largely in order to find that more joint ventures are
concentrative and come within the competence of the merger task force,
which can deal more rapidly and more favourably with joint ventures
than the rest of DGIV.

The distinction between concentrative and co-operative joint ventures
was never very satisfactory. Investment and the integration of resources
may justify both kinds of joint ventures. The idea seems to be that, when
a joint venture has access to all the resources it needs, it should be treated
as a firm independent of its parents, although for there to be a joint
venture, two or more parties must have at least *de facto* control in that
each must be able to veto important decisions of the joint venture.[15]
Consequently, any autonomy is a fiction.

The Commission is also concerned about parties co-ordinating their
market behaviour with each other and the joint venture, whether or not
the joint venture could have operated but for the transaction in question.
For the joint venture to be concentrative, therefore, the regulation
provides that the joint venture must 'perform on a lasting basis all the
functions of an autonomous legal entity and not have the object or effect
of coordinating the competitive behaviour of its parents.'

If the parties put all their assets relating to a wide geographic and
product market into the joint venture and agree not to compete with it,[16]
the joint venture will be autonomous and the parents will have left the
market on a long term basis. There will be no activities of the parents to
be co-ordinated. If they also ensure that neither parent remains in any
neighbouring market and arrange for the joint venture to include up-
and down-stream products, the concentration may come within the

13 See *SHV/Chevron* [1975] 1 C.M.L.R. D68, *Himont*, XVIIth Report on Competition Policy, point 69.
14 Commission's *Notice on concentrative and co-operative operations under Council
Regulation (EEC) No. 4064/89*, O.J. 1990, L203/10.
15 Paras. 11–14 of the notice.
16 *Mitsubishi/UCAR*, M7, [1992] 4 C.M.L.R. M50, para. 7.

more lenient test. It is difficult to explain to a client who wants the parent companies to compete up- and down-stream or in neighbouring product or geographic markets that, if all competition between the parents is removed, the joint venture will be subject to the more favourable test of the merger regulation. The need to avoid co-ordination to come within the more favourable test makes sense only *ex post*.

These rules are formalistic and absurd. It must be more anti-competitive for the parties to leave the market at the time of the joint venture than for there to be a chance for them to co-ordinate their activities through the joint venture. Yet if they leave the market on a lasting basis, the more lenient test of the merger regulation will apply. The danger is that, if the Commission finds that the transaction is co-operative, it is more likely to find it anti-competitive. The parties may have to renegotiate to satisfy the Commission.

The Commission is concerned about co-ordination not only between the parent companies, but also between one of them and the joint venture. This may be reasonable if the joint venture was an independent firm which the parents acquired, but should be irrelevant if it was an activity started by the parents. The Commission should perceive the transaction *ex ante*, not *ex post*, and compare the position with the joint venture with that which would have arisen without it. If the parties have created a new activity, they will not have restricted any competition that was possible without it.

Where one party does not leave the actual and neighbouring markets, the task force has tended to analyse the transaction as a full merger, on the basis that that party will become the industrial leader and take all the important decisions. The joint venture is then concentrative.[17] Sometimes when one of the parties remains active in a different geographic market, the joint venture has been treated as concentrative, since the parties are unlikely to co-ordinate their competitive behaviour.

When in doubt, it is common practice for a lawyer to approach the merger task force and ask its opinion. A transaction may be invalid under article 7(5) if not notified in the belief that a joint venture was co-operative, and the Commission eventually finds that it is concentrative and incompatible with the common market. Notification under the merger regulation can operate under regulation 17, but so much additional information is required under the merger regulation that a notification under regulation 17 is unlikely to be sufficiently complete to satisfy the requirements of the merger regulation. This may change as more information is required for the notification of structural joint

---

17   *E.g.*, *Thomson/Pilkington*, M51, [1991] 4 C.M.L.R. 897.

ventures[18] under regulation 17. Notification of the transaction as a concentration has the additional advantage that the task force may start its analysis and pass it on to the case handler who later deals with it as a co-operative joint venture under regulation 17.

12.2.5 *Earlier implementing regulations do not apply to concentrations*

Article 22 provides that regulation 17 and the implementing regulations relating to transport[19] no longer apply to concentrations above or below the thresholds. So these regulations will not apply to mergers or concentrative joint ventures.

If a concentration is above the thresholds, the Commission investigates under the merger regulation. This is true even under the EEA: the ESA is not competent to apply the merger regulation. If the turnover is below one of the thresholds, the regulation normally does not apply. Under article 22(3) a member state may ask the Commission to operate under the regulation in so far as the concentration creates or strengthens a dominant position within the territory of the member state concerned.

A Council regulation cannot deprive articles 85 and 86 of their direct effect. Nevertheless, unless the Court departs from earlier case law in the transport sector to which, also, regulation 17 ceased to apply, agreements for concentrative joint ventures below the thresholds and other mergers will enjoy provisional validity.[20] They may, however, be attacked in national courts under article 86[21] as well as under national law. It has not been argued, however, that article 22 is not valid. Article 235, under which many provisions of the regulation were adopted, provides for filling gaps in the treaty not for creating them.

Concentrations, including concentrative joint ventures below the thresholds, probably cannot be attacked under article 85. The dangers of nullity resulting from the *BAT* case,[22] therefore, have been largely avoided.

Nevertheless, it is unfortunate that business will be advised to negotiate acquisitions and concentrative joint ventures rather than co-operative joint ventures which remain subject to article 85. A permanent concentration which extends to joint distribution is likely to be more anti-competitive than a temporary joint venture, possibly limited to production and r & d, but the latter may be attacked under article 85 as

18 Those where substantial resources are invested in the joint venture.
19 Which was excluded from reg. 17 by reg. 141 in 1962.
20 *Ahmed Saeed* (66/86) [1989] E.C.R. 803, para. 29.
21 *Ahmed Saeed*, para. 33.
22 Cited at 12.1 above.

well as under national laws while the former enjoys the four benefits of falling within the merger regulation listed at 12.2 above.

Most member states now have legislation requiring the notification of concentrations and providing for their control. It can be very expensive to have to supply information, on different forms, to several national authorities all within differing, but short, time periods. The parties to concentrations above the thresholds, however, are absolved from having to notify national authorities under national law and sometimes an extra firm has been acquired solely to bring the concentration over the thresholds.

12.2.6 Powers of the Commission — stage I enquiry

Article 6 requires the Commission to examine notifications as soon as they are received and, if it concludes that the concentration does not fall within the scope of the regulation, it is required to adopt a formal decision to that effect. If it concludes that the concentration is clearly not incompatible with the common market, it is required to declare that it is compatible with it. If it has serious doubts about the merger's compatibility with the common market it is required to initiate proceedings to investigate the matter further. All these conclusions must be reached by formal decision, so are subject to appeal to the Court of First Instance. Reasons must be given but, in view of the time constraints, these are short.

Article 10(1) provides that such decisions shall be taken within one month of receipt of complete notification, which may be increased to six weeks if a member state makes a request under article 9 that the matter be referred to it.

Most notified mergers have been cleared within the first stage although, where the parties were competitors, sometimes only after the parties have agreed to hive off some asset or have done so.

12.2.7 Powers of the Commission — stage II enquiry

Within four months of initiating proceedings for stage II, the Commission should make a decision under article 8 or the concentration will be deemed to have been approved by virtue of article 10(6). The Commission may negotiate with the parties, and persuade them to agree to hive off some of the activities of one of the parties where they used to compete with each other, in which event it may declare the concentration compatible with the common market. Article 8(2) provides that it can attach obligations and conditions to such a decision made at stage II, and this less drastic remedy has enabled it to prohibit only one merger.[23]

If the concentration creates or strengthens a dominant position, by virtue of article 8(3) the Commission is required to adopt a decision that it is incompatible with the common market. If the merger has been legally implemented, for instance, more than three weeks after notification or under a derogation from the Commission, the Commission may order divestiture. This is far more satisfactory than invalidity under article 7(6), although the US experience of divestiture has not been very happy. The merger will not be very old by the time the Commission makes its decision and assets and activities will probably have been kept separate, so the EEC experience could be more successful.

The third great advantage of a concentration over an agreement subject to article 85 is that notification leads to a formal decision under stage I or II that binds the parties to whom it is addressed.

12.2.8 One stop control

Business supported the project of merger control by the Commission to achieve 'one stop control': on the basis that concentrations within the scope of the regulation would not have to be notified to the competent authorities in member states. Nevertheless, some of the smaller member states which do not control mergers under their national law wanted the power to control concentrations below the thresholds that were important in their national markets. Article 22(3) provides that a member state may request the Commission to investigate under the regulation a concentration below the thresholds. Moreover, article 9 provides that the Commission may, by decision, refer a notified concentration to a member state in limited circumstances. Within three weeks of receiving a copy of the notification, a member state may tell the Commission that a concentration threatens to create or strengthen a dominant position as a result of which effective competition would be significantly impeded on a market within the member state. If the market is distinct, whether or not it be a substantial part of the common market and the Commission agrees with the member state, it may deal with the matter itself under the regulation, or refer the case to the national competition authorities enabling them to deal with the matter under their national competition law. The Commission stated in the Council that it would rarely need to use the provision where the geographic market affected amounts to a substantial part of the common market.

Normally such a decision should be taken within the six week period envisaged by article 10(1), or within three months if the Commission has

---

23   *Aérospatiale-Alenia/De Haviland*, Case IV/M.053 [1992] 4 C.M.L.R. M2.

started a stage II proceeding, without taking preparatory steps, such as a statement of objection under article 8. If, despite a reminder from the member state concerned, the Commission fails to decide within the three months, it is deemed to have referred the matter to the member state.

Referral to national authorities has been made only twice, although the German authorities have more than one asked for a reference to be made to the Bundeskartellamt. The first referral[24] involved brick fields in England — a very local market, and the second was a case where the Commission had missed a deadline, so could not deal with the matter itself.[25] Usually more than one member state is involved and then the Commission will examine the concentration itself, often going to stage II.[26]

12.2.9 The Commission's power to obtain information

Article 11 is virtually identical with article 11 of regulation 17, allowing the Commission to request information, first without threat of sanctions and then by decision (5.7 above). Article 12 provides for the Commission to request national competent authorities to undertake investigations considered necessary by the Commission under the Commission's authorisation. There are unlikely to be many investigations under the regulation because of time pressure, but the power to carry out inspections may well be exercised by member states rather than by the Commission under article 13.

12.2.10 Fines

The Commission may impose fines not exceeding 10 per cent. of the aggregated turnover of the undertakings concerned for intentionally or negligently failing to comply with obligations to suspend or abrogate the concentration, or for implementing a concentration that has not been notified for three weeks. It may impose fines of between 1,000 and 50,000 ECUs for failing to notify, or notifying incorrectly or misleadingly, and so forth.

Article 15 provides for periodic penalties.[27]

12.2.11 Miscellaneous

The Court of First Instance has been given unlimited jurisdiction over the amount of a fine by article 16 and jurisdiction under article 173 of the

---

24   *Streetley/Tarmac.* The British then did not investigate the merger.
25   (M 330) *McCormick/CPC/Rabobank/Ostmann.*
26   *E.g., Varta/Bosch* M012, O.J. 1991, L320/26.
27   See 5.10 above.

EEC Treaty by article 21. Article 17 protects some kinds of confidential information from being used for other purposes or from being disclosed. Article 18 provides for undertakings with a legitimate interest to make their views known to the Commission. Article 19 provides for close and constant liaison with the competition authorities of member states. The Commission must publish decisions taken after the second stage of proceedings in the *Official Journal*. Decisions made after Stage I only are not published officially, but mimeographed versions in the language of the case only are made available after some delay and appear in some unofficial law reports. A majority of the decisions are in English.

12.3 Conclusion

Only some 50 concentrations a year, half of them joint ventures, have been notified under the regulation. However large an undertaking may be, it can acquire one firm with a turnover of under 250 million ECUs after another without the regulation applying. The regulation will catch a few conglomerate mergers and joint ventures, even tiny ones, between large firms, but concentrations below the thresholds, even if between competitors in concentrated markets, will be subject to little control at Community level.

12.4 Bibliography

Karen Banks, 'Mergers and Partial Mergers under EEC Law' in Barry Hawk (ed.) [1987] *Fordham Corporate Law Institute*, chap. 17 and reply by V. Korah, chap. 19, *ibid.*

Christopher Bellamy, 'Mergers outside the Scope of the New Merger Regulation — Implications of the *Philip Morris* judgment,' Barry Hawk (ed.), *ibid.*, chap. 22.

Bos, Stuyck and *Wytinck*, *Concentration Control in the European Community*, Graham & Trotman, 1992 (accurate, perceptive and doctrinal analysis of the merger regulation in the light of its history.)

John Cook and *Chris Kerse*, *EEC Merger Control*, Sweet & Maxwell, 1991 (Good comment by two lawyers, one influential when the regulation was being negotiated in the Council and the other frequently advising on mergers).

Frank L. Fine, *Mergers and Joint Ventures in Europe*, Graham & Trotman, 2nd ed., 1994.

Eleanor M. Fox, 'Federalism, Standards, and Common Market Merger Control' in Barry Hawk (ed.) [1988] *Fordham Corporate Law Institute*, chap. 23.

Barry Hawk and *Henry Husser*, 'A bright Line Shareholding test to end the Nightmare under the EEC Merger Regulation' (1993) 30 C.M.L.Rev. 115.

C. Jones and *Enrique Gonzalez-Diaz*, Colin Overbury (ed.), *The EEC Merger Regulation*, Sweet & Maxwell, 1992.

Jeremy Lever and *Paul Lasok*, in Weinberg and Blank, *Takeovers and Mergers*, chap. 3, section 2, on 'EEC Merger Law,' looseleaf, Sweet & Maxwell, 1990 and later releases.

Ernst-Joachim Mestmäcker, 'Merger control in the common market between competition policy and industrial policy' in Barry Hawk (ed.) [1988] *Fordham Corporate Law Institute*, chap. 20.

Damien Neven, *Robin Nuttall* and *Paul Seabright*, *Merger in Daylight — The Economics and Politics of European Merger Control*, CEPR, 1993.

Michael Reynolds, 'Merger control in the EEC' (1983) 17 J.W.T.L. 407.

F. M. Scherer, 'European Community Merger Policy; Why? Why not?' in Barry Hawk (ed.) [1988] *Fordham Corporate Law Institute*, chap. 24, and Panel Discussion, 'EEC Merger Policy,' *ibid.*, chap. 25.

Dieter Schwarz, 'New EEC Regulation on Mergers, Partial Mergers and Joint Ventures,' *ibid.*, chap. 21.

Robert Strivens (ed.), *Merger Control in the EEC*, Kluwer, 1988; second edition in preparation.

James S. Venit, 'The "Merger" Control Regulation: Europe Comes of Age. . . . or Caliban's Dinner' [1990] 1 C.M.L.Rev. 7.

13 Joint Ventures and Other Forms of Collaboration

13.1 Introduction

In markets where there are many suppliers or which lack barriers to entry, joint ventures are unlikely to restrict competition. Even if the venturers are unlikely to compete with their venture, other firms can. Indeed, a joint venture may be able to compete more effectively than each firm operating on its own.

13.2 The Commission's concerns about joint ventures

In concentrated markets where there are barriers to entry such as a minimum efficient scale that is large in relation to the expected demand, however, the Commission may rightly be concerned by a reduction in the number of competitors. Its published decisions have mostly related to concentrated markets, and many have been concerned with collaboration over sophisticated r & d. Where markets are not concentrated, the Commission has saved its resources by issuing informal comfort letters, many stating that article 85(1) is not infringed, but few of these have been published.

The Court has not yet been called upon to consider the merits of any of the decisions on joint ventures,[1] largely because few have been condemned, although some have been exempted subject to conditions and obligations.

The Commission is not concerned by the legal form of the joint venture unless it amounts to a concentrative joint venture as explained at 12.2.4 above: it may be a jointly owned subsidiary, a partnership or merely a joint committee to which each of the parties makes resources available. Joint ventures may also take the form of cross licences between the collaborators. The basic concerns are that each of the parties may be able to veto the expansion of the joint venture and might do so to protect its own activities, and neither is likely to compete aggressively with a joint venture in which it has a substantial equity interest.

1 The *Philip Morris* decision, considered at 12.1 above, was merely to reject the complaint, after the transaction had been altered, so the Court did not have to consider the Commission's causes for concern.

The Commission's decision to close the file is described in its *16th Annual Report*, point 98. The Court's judgment confirming that decision is *BAT and Reynolds* v. *Commission* (142 & 156/84) [1987] E.C.R. 4487.

13.2.1   Inherent effect: loss of potential competition

Whether or not the joint venturers agree not to compete with their joint venture, the Commission considers that those that have a substantial equity interest will be deterred from doing so. This concern has been felt whether the parties are both already in the market or are merely potential competitors.

The concern about potential competition, based on the US Supreme Court judgment in *US* v. *Penn/Olin*,[2] was often invoked until the early 1980s, but is seldom cogent. The Supreme Court held that even if not more than one of the parent companies would have entered the market without the joint venture, the joint venture would be anti-competitive if, in the absence of the joint venture, the other parent would have been in the wings waiting to enter if the first should overcharge. This possibility would constrain the performance of the entrant without actual entry by the other. Yet if one were to enter on a scale that would supply most of the expected increase in demand for some years, it would become less attractive to the other, especially if the minimum scale of operation is large in relation to the demand or its expected increase. The entrant will recognise this, so not be constrained. If the market is concentrated, there may well be a minimum scale of operation large in relation to the demand, so it is unlikely that a second would enter. The Supreme Court's theory also ignores the pro-competitive effect of the addition to supply from the joint venture, often faster than either parent could manage alone.

The practice of treating anyone sufficiently interested in a project to enter a joint venture as a potential competitor has enabled the Commission to attach conditions and obligations to an exemption. In *De Laval/Stork*,[3] for instance, De Laval was part of a large US group of companies just beginning to sell compressors and turbines in Europe. Stork was part of a Dutch group of companies operating under a technology licence from De Laval and with a more effective sales force in Europe. The firms were actual competitors, but had complementary strengths to contribute to their joint venture. The Commission exempted it for 15 years from its inception in 1971, but subject to conditions that would enable Stork to operate independently thereafter.

The market was one where each order had to be specifically designed by adapting basic designs and 85 per cent. of the work was based on designs contributed by De Laval. The same team of engineers had to negotiate a contract, co-operate technically with each customer to design a product, work out a production programme and carry out the

2   378 U.S. 158 (1964).
3   [1977] 2 C.M.L.R. D69.

after-sales service, which was an important element of competition. So, contrary to its preferred practice, the Commission exempted a transaction which included joint sales as well as development and manufacture.

The parties had agreed that on termination of the joint venture each would be entitled to use the technology licensed to the joint venture for a fixed rate of royalty for three years. The Commission, however, provided that on termination each party should be entitled to a licence for longer than the three years agreed by the parties and on a most favoured licensee basis. Each was to be entitled to sell products made thereby not only in the common market but also throughout the world.

The Commission's condition affected the commercial balance of the agreement since designs for 85 per cent. of the products came from De Laval. Worse still, since Stork provided some technology to the joint venture, it could refuse to grant any licence. This would ensure that the joint venture was not exempted, so it was in a position to renegotiate the entire agreement after receiving De Laval's technology.

Fear of such a condition being imposed has deterred some firms from notifying their joint ventures to the Commission, as will be considered at 14.2.5 and 14.2.6 below. Seen *ex post*, the changes required by the Commission may have made the market more competitive although, as it happened, it had to renew the exemption because the joint venture did not thrive during the recession.[4] The risk of having to renegotiate may deter some firms from entering into a joint venture that would, otherwise, have been viable.

13.2.2 *The group effect — spillover*

In several decisions, the Commission has been concerned that once the parties find that collaboration is convenient they may collude on other markets too. In *Wanol Schwarzpulver*,[5] for instance, where both parties had interests in explosives, explosives accessories and safety fuse, the Commission was concerned that their joint venture in black powder would give 'opportunities and strong inducements' for market sharing in safety fuse.

The parties may lessen this fear by arranging that only a limited number of employees will work on the joint venture and will not come into contact with the parents' other employees more than is necessary. Sometimes the parties agree that the joint venture will hire its own personnel and agree that they will not themselves employ anyone that has worked for the joint venture.

4 *De Laval (2)*, [1988] 4 C.M.L.R. 715.
5 [1979] 1 C.M.L.R. 403.

13.2.3 *Foreclosure*

The Commission should be concerned when firms with access to separate, rare resources combine to create a monopoly, in which case it may want to enable others to have access to it. This concern is exemplified by the Commission's informal action in *IGR Stereo Television*.[6] A trade association representing the German manufacturers of stereo TV sets acquired the patent rights for two rival technologies for making these. It then granted licences to its members, but refused one to the Finnish manufacturer, Salora, which was already operating on the German market. The Commission closed its file only when the association agreed to grant it licences too. Three years later, the Commission reported that the licence fees charged were too high and it intervened again to persuade the parties to reduce the royalties.

In *Tetra Pak*,[7] the Commission was concerned by an acquisition which brought into the same hands two competing technologies for treating milk to be placed in cartons aseptically. It ceased proceedings under article 86, when the technology licence acquired was made non-exclusive. This decision is criticised at 14.2.6 below.

It is hoped that the Commission would not be concerned when a joint venture produces a unique resource so valuable that it meets no competition. It is more competitive to have one source than none. Nevertheless, this is an example of circumstances in which the Commission may intervene to withdraw the benefit of the group exemptions for patent licensing or know-how. That power, however, is discretionary, and if the Commission seeks to exercise it, one may argue that it should think *ex ante*, and not remove the incentives to developing technology jointly by taking away the protection on which the commercial activity was based.

Another concern of the Commission is that too many firms from a particular industry may join in the joint venture, leaving no firms with which other undertakings might form a joint venture. It is for this reason that the group exemption, analysed at 13.5 below, applies only if the parties have a market share in the common market of under 30 per cent.[8]

13.2.4 *Ancillary restrictions*

Clearly, the Commission is right to check that cartel agreements are not attached to a valid joint venture. The ancillary restrictions should be only as wide as can be justified as necessary to make the basic transaction viable (7.1.2 above). Under the US case law, the ancillary restrictions

---

6 (1981 and 1984) *11th and 14th Annual Reports*, points 63 and 76 respectively.
7 [1990] 4 C.M.L.R. 47.
8 See also *Metal Box/Elopak/Odin* [1991] 4 C.M.L.R. 832, para. 27.

need only be reasonably necessary, and it is irrelevant that a slightly less restrictive provision can be devised with the advantage of hindsight. Despite the stricter language in the Community decisions, I am not sure that there is a difference of substance. The Commission does not always consider whether a less restrictive alternative exists. Nevertheless, unlike the Court, it seems to consider whether the ancillary restrictions are justified mainly under article 85(3) and rarely under article 85(1).[9]

13.2.4.1 *The need for each party to appropriate the benefits of its investment* — If investment in the joint venture is to be commercially viable, it is vital that the investor should be able to appropriate the fruits to itself. This is difficult enough for a single innovating firm, especially when patent protection is not possible or too expensive. It is even more difficult to ensure when the work is done jointly. It can be done only by contract, which must be enforceable.

When the parties need the results for different purposes, it may suffice merely to ensure that the other party keeps any results secret from the rest of the world, informs his partner of new technology and grants licences under any intellectual property rights he may acquire. Sometimes there may be field of use restrictions to restrain either from entering the other's market.

When the parties want the results for the same purpose each may have to ensure also that the other does not over-exploit the market at his expense. Often it is impossible to foretell at the time the agreement is being negotiated how much the work will cost or whether it will be successful, let alone how successful. Sometimes the only possible formula for joint r & d is that A will pay for a proportion of the cost and B for the rest and that they shall benefit from the results in the same proportions. In that event, the protection may take the form of agreed quotas or joint sales. Alternatively, the world market may be divided territorially. The protection may take various forms, but some protection against over-exploitation by the other may be necessary to induce investment.

Should these restrictions on conduct be seen as anti-competitive or as ancillary restraints necessary to make viable co-operation that may increase competition? For how long can they be shown to be indispensable? On the one hand, it may be argued that such an agreement results in a single seller and imposes quotas on both parties. No one should mind if A and B are unimportant in the market, but if there are only a few firms these restrictions on conduct may be important.

On the other hand, without these restrictions, neither party could be

9   The sub-contracting notice, 10.10 above, is a notable exception.

sure of recovering the benefit of the investment in joint research. It might be that neither would supply its best technology if the other could use it to compete immediately or soon afterwards, so such restrictions on conduct may be necessary for several years after the investment starts to bring in profits. On this argument, viewed *ex ante*, the restrictions are ancillary and pro-competitive as they enable each party to appropriate the expected benefit of its investment and so make the joint venture viable.

I have complained throughout this book of the Commission's practice of exempting rather than clearing agreements containing ancillary restrictions needed to make viable some agreement that may well increase competition.

13.2.4.2 *Joint sales organisations* — Joint sales organisations are seldom ancillary to a pro-competitive joint venture, and were considered at 7.2.3 above. The Commission cleared a joint sales organisation in *SAFCO*[10] whereby small makers of preserves were able to penetrate the German market where they met substantial competition. In *SPAR*,[11] it cleared a buying group that enabled small grocers to increase their buying power towards the level exercised by multiple retailers with whom they competed. Each was entitled to buy separately as much as it liked and many did so. In *Finnpap*,[12] where the Commission thought that trade between member states was unlikely to be appreciable, it granted an informal clearance after the agreement had been modified.

Only once has the Commission tolerated joint sales organisations that were not *de minimis*. In *UIP*,[13] it exempted a joint sales organisation for films when very substantial cost savings were expected. There were no quotas but the Commission perceived a slight possibility of the parties sharing profits through their dividends from the joint venture. This it prevented, so there was no way the parties could restrict production to raise price.

Even when a joint venture extends from production and development to marketing, the Commission will usually object to joint sales unless they can be justified, as they were in *De Laval/Stork* (13.2.1 above).

13.3 More realistic attitude to be taken to potential competition

In its *XIIIth Report on Competition Policy* for 1983 the Commission promised to look more realistically before finding an inherent anti-

10   [1972] C.M.L.R. D83.
11   [1975] 2 C.M.L.R. D14.
12   The Commission's decision under art. 19(3) to take a favourable view was published in [1989] 4 C.M.L.R. 413. This was followed by a press release IP(89)496.
13   [1990] 4 C.M.L.R. 749, and 7.2.3 above.

competitive effect in joint ventures.[14] It said that in deciding whether the parties were potential competitors the Commission would consider each party's ability to finance the operation independently, the productive capacity of each party, its familiarity with the process technology, the size of the demand and the distribution facilities of each party, as well as its ability to bear the risk.

It seemed that the Commission was prepared to analyse the situation *ex ante*, at the time the joint venture was entered into and neither party had access to the other's resources. We hoped for clearance, not exemption, of agreements between those with complementary resources, or where the risk was too great for a single firm and so forth.

In its next two decisions, the Commission did, indeed, not find that the parties were potential competitors, but in the first case, *BP/Kellogg*,[15] an arrangement for very limited exclusivity was found to infringe article 85(1) and exempted. The parties had complementary technology: BP had come across a catalyst it thought would be useful for making ammonia and Kellogg designs and builds process plants. They agreed to collaborate to design a plant in which to make ammonia using BP's catalyst. BP agreed to sell its catalyst only to Kellogg's customers and Kellogg not to invest in ways of producing ammonia without the use of the catalyst, without telling BP and giving it a chance to resile from the contract. The Commission found that ancillary restrictions which, when dealing with article 85(3), it described as 'reasonable and necessary' restricted competition and required exemption.

In *Optical Fibres*,[16] Corning Glass had developed optical fibres which revolutionised the technology used for telecommunications networks. It entered into two joint ventures to produce the fibres with BICC in the UK and Siemens in the Federal Republic. Corning could have made the fibres in Europe, but would have had difficulty in selling them to the PTTs, most of which tended to buy only from firms within the country. Neither Siemens nor BICC could have made the fibres without a technology licence from Corning. There were two other joint ventures, one between Corning and a French cable maker which was likely to be exempted once it had been renegotiated to conform to the Commission's ideas, and one was also being negotiated by Corning with a Spanish firm. Corning had also granted licences to firms in other member states. The Commission found that each individual joint venture did not restrict competition, since the parties contributed complementary technology.

---

14   At 50–52; confirmed by the Commission's notice on co-operative joint ventures, O.J. 1993, C43/2, para 15.
15   [1986] 2 C.M.L.R. 619.
16   O.J. 1986, L236/30.

Unaided, the cable makers could not have produced the fibres, nor Corning the cables.[17]

The Commission accepted that a licence to a joint venture is a good way to disseminate technology: it stated that each joint venture would not infringe article 85(1) because neither party could enter the other's market. This was the precedent for which we have waited since the Commission's *XIIIth Report*, stating that where not more than one of the parties could enter the market, a joint venture does not have an inherent anti-competitive effect.

The Commission added, however, that a network of joint ventures does infringe article 85(1) when a provider of technology has a substantial interest and control over each and the market is oligopolistic. Its theory is that Corning might use its control over one joint venture to prevent its expansion in order to protect one of the others. It granted an exemption only after Corning reduced its managerial control, the technology licence ceased to be exclusive, the territorial protection was reduced below that permitted by the patent licensing regulation, each party was entitled to expand the capacity of the joint venture either with the consent of the other or, if that was refused, by paying for the additional capacity and taking a larger share of the benefit. There were other provisions to ensure that information about each joint venture's prices and output was not passed on to the others.

In *BBC Brown Boveri/NGK*,[18] the Commission exempted a joint venture agreement which, in my view, should have been cleared rather than exempted. BBC was trying to develop a sodium sulphur battery for use in vehicles, but lacked technology in the ceramics required for insulation. NGK had developed the technology for ceramics, but had no access to technology relating to batteries. The Commission alleged that NGK became a potential competitor of BBC when it acquired the latter's technology through its share in the joint venture and that, consequently, its agreement not to export from the Far East infringed article 85(1) and required exemption. The joint venture, however, restricted no competition that would have been possible without it.

This is regretted. Impliedly, in *BP/Kellogg* and expressly in *Optical Fibres* the Commission looked *ex ante*: to the position that existed without the joint venture and licence in deciding whether the parties were potential competitors.

17   Para. 46.
18   [1989] 4 C.M.L.R. 610, and 10.2 above.

13.3.1 *ODIN*

At the end of July 1990, the Commission adopted a decision clearing the *ODIN* joint venture between Metal Box and Elopak to develop a carton with a replaceable metal lid to contain particulate foodstuffs.[19] The Commission decided, first, that the venturers were not even potential competitors: the technology and other resources provided by each were complementary. Secondly, the joint venture was unlikely to foreclose other parties, since each party to the joint venture had important competitors in its own field. Thirdly, the joint venture to make a completely new product was risky and would require substantial investment, so the ancillary restrictions were also cleared as necessary for the joint venture.

ODIN was given the exclusive right to exploit the know-how and any improvements made to it for the field of use specified which, according to the Commission, guaranteed that ODIN would concentrate its best efforts on the project. Each party would obtain access to the technology for the specified field of use, so would be able to compete in the field of the joint venture. The ancillary restrictions were very limited, but it was most encouraging that the agreement, including an exclusive right, was cleared and not exempted.

Unfortunately, with one exception,[20] all the formal decisions on joint ventures since *ODIN* have been exemptions and not clearances although it seems as if some of them foreclosed no competition that was possible without the joint venture.

13.4 Disadvantages to industry of the Commission's refusal to clear joint ventures

Only the Commission has power to exempt an individual agreement, and it has not got the resources to make many decisions each year: in the four years from 1990 to 1993 it granted 16 exemptions in all, for all industries save armaments, coal, steel and atomic energy in an area with a population of 320 million rising to 340 with the inclusion of East Germany. When negotiating a particular joint venture, therefore, the parties can be pretty sure that their agreement will not actually be exempted.

To obtain an exemption or even a comfort letter, it is necessary for the parties to notify their agreement in accordance with regulation 27,[21] as amended by regulation 2526/85.[22] This is a troublesome operation

19 [1991] 4 C.M.L.R. 832.
20 *Konsortium ECR 900* [1992] 4 C.M.L.R. 54.
21 J.O. 1962, 235.
22 O.J. 1985, L240/1.

requiring management time as well as highly skilled and expensive legal advice and is likely to become more onerous when the new form is required (6.3.4–6.4.2.4 above).

Unfortunately, there is no provisional validity for agreements that have been notified unless the Commission grants an exemption. If a national court follows the precedents of the Commission, it might well find that the agreement restricts competition contrary to article 85(1). It might then have to adjourn while the Commission decides whether to grant a formal exemption, since exemptions are in the Commission's exclusive remit and, following *Automec II*,[23] it seems clear that the Commission may be required to take a formal decision when an exemption is necessary.

Fortunately, the Commission has stated that it will send a comfort letter within two months of receiving a full notification of a structural joint venture unless it has serious doubts about whether it is compatible with the common market. A structural joint venture seems to be one involving substantial investment. Shortly before his retirement as Member of the Commission responsible for competition, Sir Leon Brittan said that it would not depart from the view taken in its comfort letters unless it had been told lies or circumstances had changed.[24]

It is feared, however, that the success of the joint venture, if it results in a large market share, may be treated as a change of circumstance, permitting the Commission not to abide by the views stated in a comfort letter. The ancillary restraints necessary to appropriate the benefit of investment may become invalid just when they are most valuable, leading the parties to invest only if sufficient fruits are likely before their market share becomes too high.

The conditions and changes in contracts imposed by the Commission in cases like *De Laval/Stork* (13.2.1 above) may have made the particular market more competitive after the event. Together the venturers were able to penetrate the common market more rapidly and, once it expires, each firm will be able to operate independently. The disadvantage of imposing a condition long after the contract has been negotiated, however, is the disincentive it creates for firms to attempt similar ventures in the future knowing that the Commission may intervene to force changes after the event. The parties must rely on their contract to appropriate the benefit of their investment but that protection may be undermined. Any changes required by the Commission may upset the commercial balance of the contract. Moreover, they enable any party whose consent is required to implement the condition or other changes to renegotiate the

23   (T–24/90) [1992] 5 C.M.L.R. 431, at para. 75. See 6.3.4 above.
24   See 6.3.4 above and the Commission's *22nd Annual Report*, p.81.

bargain as a whole after the parties' relative bargaining power may have shifted.

Now that the Commission has promised to deal rapidly with most structural joint ventures, the danger of bargaining power shifting before the Commission assesses an agreement has been considerably diminished.

13.5 The group exemption

Although the Commission is not prepared to exempt joint ventures generally by regulation, since the criteria are not easy to apply, in regulation 418/85,[25] it has exempted *en bloc* a limited class of joint ventures for r & d. It repeats in recital 2 the view it first expressed in a notice on co-operation agreements published in 1968, that joint ventures applying only to r & d and terminating short of industrial application rarely infringe article 85(1). This is the most important provision in the whole regulation. Where each party is entitled to use the results independently, therefore, the joint venture is unlikely to infringe article 85(1).

13.5.1 *The framework of the regulation*

The regulation exempts those agreements for which it is more difficult to establish that article 85(1) is not infringed. Article 1 exempts joint r & d as well as joint production or both. Both terms are widely defined, but the exemption is subject to conditions prescribed in articles 2 and 3. Article 4 exempts a list of ancillary restrictions, article 5 lists provisions that rarely infringe article 85(1) but which are exempted just in case and article 6 lists black provisions which prevent the application of the regulation. Article 7 provides for the opposition procedure, according to which a research and development agreement containing terms restrictive of competition that are not blacklisted may be notified. If the Commission does not oppose the exemption within six months, the agreement will be exempted by the regulation. Subsequent articles provide for withdrawing the exemption, confidentiality, agreements made before the regulation came into force and so forth.

13.5.2 *Conditions of its application (articles 2 and 3)*

The conditions of article 2 require that the joint venture's scope must be defined, results must be pooled although it *may* be possible to rely on the subcontracting notice if it is necessary to include someone who does not want to exploit the results. Joint exploitation is permitted only if the

25 O.J. 1985, L53/5.

joint venture achieves important innovations or if it obtains intellectual property rights (article 2(d)). This prevents the regulation applying to exploitation where all the important discoveries have already been made. If, however, there is a joint venture for r & d only, the parties may later agree to exploit the results jointly if they turn out to be sufficiently important.

The final condition imposed by articles 2 and 6(f) and the definition of 'exploitation' require that there should be no joint marketing and that each party shall be required to sell independently to outsiders. This was altered by regulation 151/93[26] and joint sales are now permitted until the joint venture achieves a market share of 10 per cent. It is strange that joint sales, which may restrain all competition between the parties, are permitted, but not quotas, which might not add up to 100 per cent. Sometimes, joint sales up to a market share of 10 per cent. may enable each party to appropriate the benefit of its investment, but where the r & d is very successful, the joint venture may well achieve far higher market shares, so this may not suffice.

Article 3 imposes conditions as to market shares. The Commission wishes to ensure that several centres of independent r & d remain in the common market. At the time of the agreement, the market share of the results will be nil, so one takes as the relevant market the products to be improved or replaced. If the venturers or any two of them compete in respect of such products, the initial ceiling is 20 per cent. of those products in the common market or a substantial part of it.

The second alternative, 'a substantial part,' is regretted. As in the exemption for specialisation (11.4 above), there is no recital to limit its application to products that cannot easily be moved. Moreover, r & d can travel even if the products are too heavy in relation to their value to do so. The earlier published draft of the regulation referred to three centres of research, presumably worldwide. If the parties' aggregate market shares in the products to be replaced exceed 20 per cent., the exemption does not apply at all. If none of the parties competes in the products to be replaced, or those who do compete do not together fulfil the 20 per cent. test the exemption applies. Whether or not production is joint, the market share is assessed again after the r & d programme is treated as complete,[27] five years after the products are first put on the market within the common market.

It is not clear when the five year period starts to run where the r & d continues: probably five years after putting the first results on the market. By then the parties will be competing in sales of the results and, if

---

26   O.J. 1993, L21/8.
27   Often the r & d will continue indefinitely.

together they sell over 20 per cent. of the products which compete with the results on the demand side of the market, the exemption ceases to apply, subject to some marginal relief.

13.5.3 *White and black lists*

The exempted provisions include restrictions on carrying out r & d independently or in another joint venture in the same field or in a closely connected field but not in an unconnected one. The parties may agree to acquire the contract products only from each other, the joint venture or persons charged with making them for the parties.

Quotas are blacklisted and the territorial protection permitted is very narrow. The parties may allocate manufacturing territories, and agree not actively to solicit sales for five years after the goods are first put on the market within the common market in each other's territories. Further protection is blacklisted even if the 10 per cent. market share permitted for joint sales is not attained. Less protection may be given than under the technology licensing regulations[28] because the relationship may well be horizontal.

Under the specialisation regulation if the ceiling for market shares is not exceeded, each may agree indefinitely to distribute the goods it makes only through the other(s) in particular territories. Many of the provisions in the black list of the regulation for r & d are also blacklisted in the patent and know-how licensing regulations, but the black list for licences will probably be shorter from next year. The r & d regulation, however, does permit a restriction on competing in a closely connected field, whereas only an obligation to use best endeavours to exploit is permitted for licensing.

Recital 14 provides that the parties may also take advantage of other group exemptions. The regulation presupposes some patent licences which may well come within regulation 2349/84 or the regulation that succeeds it (see 10.5 and 10.6 above), provided that there are only two undertakings. It seems that the Commission considers that the joint venture is a single undertaking, even if it is controlled by more than one undertaking, although this is not clear.

The parties may initially take advantage of the regulation for r & d to agree not to compete in innovation. When they start to produce the results they can enter into a specialisation agreement whereby each will make different products, or the joint venture will, but each will be allocated a sales territory where each of the others agrees to distribute the products it makes only through it. It is doubted whether they can

28 Active sales restrictions can last as long as the patents licensed, and passive sales restrictions for five years after first marketing.

make both such agreements from the start. To permit that would undermine the limitations to the territorial protection allowed under regulation 418/85, but to insist on separate agreements seems formalistic, increases the initial uncertainty and so may deter some marginal joint ventures.

Where there is an agreement for r & d within the meaning of the group exemption which includes no blacklisted clauses and if the conditions of articles 2 and 3 are not exceeded, the opposition procedure explained at 3.2 above will apply to any restrictions of competition that are not expressly permitted.

13.5.4 *Conclusion on the group exemption*

It is thought that few agreements will qualify under the regulation when the parties need the results for the same purpose: it does not apply when there are ancillary provisions enabling each joint venturer to ensure that the others do not over-exploit. Quotas are blacklisted, little territorial protection is permitted, although a field of use restriction may suffice when the parties need the results for different markets. Regulation 151/93 now permits joint sales until a market share of 10 per cent. is attained and may enable each to appropriate the benefit of its investment when the market is broad, but where the results will constitute a new market it will not protect each from over-exploitation by the others.

The importance of the regulation may lie in the recital that joint ventures for r & d that do not continue into exploitation usually do not need exemption as generally they are not caught by article 85(1). There is no need to tailor these to fit the regulation. Where the market shares permitted under article 3 are exceeded, it may well be possible to obtain an individual exemption or comfort letter, especially where there are competing centres of innovation outside the common market.

13.6 Concentrative joint ventures

If the parties are prepared to put into the joint venture on a lasting basis sufficient resources for it to constitute an autonomous legal entity, not dependent on its parents, the transaction may amount to a concentrative joint venture.[29] At the cost of having to fill in form CO, the parties will avoid problems under article 85, and if the joint venture is above the thresholds they will gain one stop control by the Commission under the favourable test of the merger regulation and the legal certainty resulting from a formal decision, usually within a month and, at the most, five.

It is difficult to persuade sensible clients that by putting everything

29   See 12.2.4 above.

into the joint venture from the beginning, and avoiding any possibility of co-ordination between the parties or one of them and the joint venture, they will obtain these advantages. The distinction between co-operative and concentrative joint ventures has best been criticised by Barry Hawk.[30] Only draughtsmen who think *ex post* could have invented it.

13.7 Conclusion

In the field of joint ventures there has been continuing tension between those who think *ex post* and those who think *ex ante*. Seen *ex ante*, substantial investment will not be made unless each joint venturer can ensure that it can supply an agreed proportion of the demand or obtain the agreed proportion of the results through dividends obtained from the joint venture, which makes the sale. Seen *ex post*, after the investments have been made, it would be more competitive for the venturers to compete with each other. For significant periods, able officials who think *ex ante* were in charge of joint ventures, and many comfort letters were written stating that the joint venture did not infringe article 85(1).

That has not been the experience over the last few years, but Sir Leon Brittan endeavoured to enable each joint venturer to appropriate the benefit of its investment. The Commission has stated that it will speed up its procedure for issuing a comfort letter about structural joint ventures and will abide by its comfort letters.[31] The Court of First Instance in *Automec II* has implied that the parties are entitled to a formal decision if they want an exemption. It is important that the Commission should abide by its comfort letters when joint r & d has been very successful and large market shares achieved.

Under article 85(3), it may well be that the Commission has been too generous in permitting joint ventures. Few have been forbidden, but the Commission has substantial discretion when applying article 85 and from the published decisions, it is impossible to be sure.

13.8 Bibliography

Joseph Brodley, 'Joint Ventures and Antitrust Policy' [1982] 95 Harv. L. Rev. 1521; the decision in *Optical Fibres* was largely based on Brodley's thinking.
Jonathan Faull, 'Joint Ventures Under the EEC Competition Rules' [1984] 5 E.C.L.R. 358.
Alexis Jacquemin and *Bernard Spinoit*, 'Economic and Legal Aspects of Cooperative Research: a European View,' in Barry Hawk (ed.) [1985] *Fordham Corporate Law Institute*, Chap. 24.

30   *Op. cit.*, bibliography, 13.8 below.
31   6.3.4 above.

Valentine Korah, *R & D Joint Ventures and the EEC Competition Rules: Regulation 418/85*, ESC, 1986.

——, 'Critical comments on the Commission's recent decisions exempting joint ventures to exploit research that needs further development' (1987) 12 E.L.R. 18.

——, 'Collaborative joint ventures for research and development where markets are concentrated: the competition rules of the common market and the invalidity of contracts' [1992] 2 Fordham I.L.J. 248.

Barry Hawk, 'Joint ventures under EEC law' [1992] 2 Fordham I.L.J. 303.

Barry Hawk and *Henry Husser*, 'A bright Line Shareholding test to end the Nightmare under the EEC Merger Regulation' (1993) 30 C.M.L.Rev. 115.

Angus Maciver, 'EEC Competition Policy in High Technology Industries' [1985] *Fordham Corporate Law Institute*, Chap. 25.

James S. Venit, 'The Research and Development Block Exemption Regulation' (1985) 10 E.L.Rev. 151.

Eric L. White, 'Research and Development Joint Ventures Under EEC Competition Law' (1985) IIC 663.

14 Conclusion — the Importance of Economic Analysis and of Contractual Validity

14.1 Introduction

The object of this chapter, written over 30 years after the adoption of regulation 17, is to assess some aspects of competition policy. It will express my personal convictions in the hope that the work may be used by those who are or will later become influential to persuade the Commission to draft more cogent decisions and to base the application and development of the law on principle, so as better to enable businessmen to ensure that each can appropriate the benefit of his investments. DGIV is more open to outsiders and their suggestions than any national bureaucracy I know.

14.2 The paucity of economic analysis in the Commission's public decisions

14.2.1 *Lack of reasoning to connect specific facts with the legal conclusions*

With a few notable exceptions, the Commission's practice in its formal decisions is to recite many primary facts, not all of them relevant to the decision, and then to give its legal appraisal. Unfortunately, the analysis in the legal appraisal relating to article 85(1) is seldom connected to specific facts. This gives the Commission a wide discretion in reaching its conclusions and makes them unpredictable. The uncertainty is increased by its practice of occasionally finding that the effect on trade between member states or on competition is not appreciable, as in *Finnpap*[1] and *APB*.[2]

The unpredictability is exacerbated by the reluctance of the Court to review under article 173 anything other than a 'manifest error of law' and its refusal to review the Commission's economic analysis.[3] The Court of first Instance has gone further into the facts, but its analysis of vertical agreements is often formalistic.[4] Even in the cases I welcomed at

---

1 [1989] 4 C.M.L.R. 413. See 7.2.3 and 13.2.4.2 above.
2 [1990] 4 C.M.L.R. 176, and 7.3 above.
3 *E.g., Consten and Grundig* v. *Commission* (56 & 58/64) [1966] E.C.R. 299; *Windsurfing* (193/83) [1986] E.C.R. 611; *Metro II* (75/84) [1986] E.C.R. 3021.
4 *E.g., Vichy* (T–19/91) [1991] E.C.R. II–265, which concerned a vertical restriction in a market admitted to be competitive, 8.3.3 above, and *Peugeot* (C–323/93P), judgment of 16 June 1994, where the need to protect dealers from free riding agents was not relevant, only the interpretation of the group exemption for vehicles.

10.3, such as *Nungesser*,[5] *Coditel (2)*,[6] and *Erauw-Jacquéry*,[7] there is little economic analysis — just assertions of principle. It is frequently not possible to advise businessmen what the attitude of the Court or Commission to their agreement is likely to be.

The recent decisions on joint ventures also lack much analysis. They seldom seem to analyse *ex ante* as promised in the Commission's *XIIIth Report on Competition Policy*, point 55 (14.2.5 below). In *Optical Fibres*,[8] a decision I welcome, the Commission spelled out its reasoning much more clearly. It stated at paragraphs 46 and 47 that, since Corning Glass was not in the cable market nor BICC or Siemens in that for optical fibre, the parties were not even potential competitors and each joint venture was not, in itself, caught by article 85(1). Moreover, when stating at paragraphs 48–53 that the network of joint ventures with a common partner which provided the technology did infringe article 85(1), the Commission explained its theory: that the common partner might restrict production in one joint venture in order to enable one of the others to increase its prices.

One of the great services performed by the reports of the Monopolies and Mergers Commission (MMC) in the UK is that they spell out why particular practices are pro- or anti-competitive or otherwise in or against the public interest and, in particular, whether they increase or decrease efficiency for the benefit of consumers. The MMC does not always write as tightly as would an economist, but it does usually provide reasons to connect particular facts to particular conclusions. It sets out the primary facts at great length, stressing those that are most relevant, but many people start with the chapter stating the MMC's conclusions and its reasons for them and read only the paragraphs in the statement of facts referred to in the conclusions chapter. One may disagree with the MMC. Indeed, cogent notes of dissent are often appended by one or more members. Nevertheless, there is enough argument to analyse. On this basis it is much easier to decide whether a precedent should be extended, for instance, to another practice that has some similar effects or different justifications.

By not spelling out the economic and legal arguments more precisely, the Commission loses a wonderful chance to educate not only business and its advisers, but also its own officials, national courts and the Community Courts. It should be an expert and experienced body and

---

5   (258/78) [1982] E.C.R. 2015.
6   (262/81) [1982] E.C.R. 3361.
7   (27/87) [1988] E.C.R. 1919.
8   O.J. 1986, L236/30, 13.3 above. See also *ODIN* [1991] 4 CMLR 832, 13.3.1 above, where the Commission spelled out all its causes for concern and explained why none of them applied to the joint venture.

develop its policy openly. It is being required to keep down the length of its annual reports on competition policy, so has nowhere but recitals to regulations, press releases, Commissioner's speeches and decisions where it can set forth its views. Well-analysed reasoning need not add to the length of the decision, as the Commission could limit the factual part of the decision to what is relevant for and against the conclusion.

14.2.2 The Commission's view that article 85(1) prohibits any restriction of conduct that is significant on the market

It is often difficult to reconcile the Commission's conclusions under article 85(1) with those under article 85(3) in the same case. Various ancillary restrictions necessary to make viable a transaction that may even increase competition are held to restrict competition contrary to article 85(1) because they limit the parties' freedom of action and have significant effects on the market. Yet, when granting the exemption the Commission describes them as 'necessary and reasonable' to make the transaction viable. These views are not consistent.

It is of the nature of contracts to restrict the parties' freedom of action. Every restriction cannot be anti-competitive. If the restriction is 'necessary and reasonable' to make the transaction viable — as the Commission often states in concluding that an exemption is merited, however *competition* rather than conduct cannot have been restricted when the parties were not already competitors.

For instance, the Commission exempted rather than cleared limited exclusivity in *De Laval/Stork*,[9] *BP/Kellogg*[10] and *Mitchell Cotts/Sofiltra*.[11] Indeed, until *ODIN*,[12] despite the Court's judgments cited at 2.4 above, the Commission has never cleared exclusivity in a formal decision save on *de minimis* grounds. It has, however, sometimes exempted exclusive territories, as in *Davidson*,[13] *Campari*[14] and *Delta Chemie*[15] on the ground that without an exclusive territory, the pro-competitive transaction would not have been viable and so would not have taken place without it. How then can the obligation have had the object or effect of restricting competition?

Expansion of firms into other member states was one of the driving ideas for the foundation of the Community. Cross-frontier trade would enable firms to take advantage of economies and spread new ideas

9   [1977] 2 C.M.L.R. D69.
10   [1986] 2 C.M.L.R. 619, and 13.3 above.
11   [1988] 4 C.M.L.R. 111.
12   [1991] 4 C.M.L.R. 832, discussed at 13.3.1 above.
13   [1972] C.M.L.R. D52, and 10.2 above.
14   [1978] 2 C.M.L.R. 397, and 8.3.1 above.
15   [1989] 4 C.M.L.R. 535, and 10.2 above.

quickly throughout the common market without making markets more concentrated. This was recognised by the Court as early as *La Technique Minière*,[16] where it stated that if an exclusive territory was necessary to enable the German firm to penetrate the French market, it would not have the effect of restricting competition contrary to article 85(1). The Court was even more explicit in *Pronuptia*,[17] where it stated that restrictions of conduct necessary to make distribution franchising viable did not, in themselves, restrict competition.

Moreover, in regulations, especially regulation 1983/83,[18] the Commission lists the ways in which exclusive distribution agreements help suppliers to penetrate another member state, yet grants an exemption rather than a negative clearance. In the group exemptions for technology licensing, the Commission recites that open exclusive licences do not usually infringe article 85(1). Yet in its individual decisions, it has always distinguished the Court's judgment in *Nungesser*[19] and granted an exemption.

When the Commission contemplates adopting a new group exemption, it is required by its empowering regulation to gain experience by deciding individual cases. If it were to clear the agreements with which it deals on the ground that the market is competitive or that the ancillary restrictions are necessary to make the transaction viable, the experience would hardly lead to the conclusion that a block exemption is required, so habitually it exempts several specific agreements.

When the franchising and know-how regulations were contemplated, the Commission granted individual exemptions to all the agreements it dealt with formally.[20] In my view, every one of them should have been cleared. The franchising markets were all very competitive and the territorial restrictions in the know-how agreements were exempted on the ground, in effect, that an exclusive territory encouraged the licensee to accept commitments to tool up and develop a market and so made the market more competitive.

It would be wonderful if now that the regulations have been adopted, the Commission were to decide that such agreements do not infringe article 85(1) and need no exemption. The co-ordination directorate of DGIV is now headed by an economist with a team of excellent officials

16   (56/65) [1966] E.C.R. 235, quoted at 2.4 above.
17   (161/84) [1986] E.C.R. 353, and 2.4 above.
18   The 6th recital.
19   See 10.3 above. It finds that the product is not 'new' even if it be better than anything else on the market. The cases are analysed in my monograph on know-how, cited in the main bibliography, at 1.5.3–1.5.3.4.
20   These have not been dealt with in this book, but are described in my monographs on the group exemptions listed in the main bibliography.

who are attempting to ensure that scrutiny is not confined to striking words like 'exclusive' out of agreements. Nevertheless, the co-ordination team does not write the decisions and will have to persuade case handlers to change their practice developed over 30 years of precedents relating to distribution, franchising, technology licensing and joint ventures. Change will be difficult to implement.

The Commission has seldom cleared a co-operative joint venture by formal decision,[21] although it has cleared some provisions, such as the obligation not to compete with the joint venture and an exclusive manufacturing territory in *Mitchell Cotts/Sofiltra*.[22]

Exclusive technology licences have been cleared by the Commission only when, *ex post*, the licensor and licensees obtained a small market share,[23] although, after the adoption of the patent regulation, the Commission limited its decision in *Velcro/Aplix*[24] to the period after the basic patents had expired.

Few exclusive dealing agreements that were significant have been cleared. Despite the Court's judgment in *Delimitis*,[25] ruling that exclusive purchasing agreements restrict competition only in very unusual circumstances, in *Langnese* and *Schöller*,[26]the Commission started to analyse the freezer and outlet exclusive purchasing agreements only under article 85(3) and in various cases concerning the most prestigious perfumes, a competitive market, no analysis of the market was attempted before finding that selective distribution agreements infringed article 85(1).[27]

In two decisions,[28] the Commission did not analyse the reasons there were no appreciable effects on trade between member states or on competition. *Finnpap* was an informal decision, but even a notice under article 19(3) followed by a press release operates as a precedent for later transactions. So it would be helpful to state which of the facts led to the particular conclusion. I am glad that on occasion the Commission finds

21   It did clear joint r & d in *ODIN*, consortia in several decisions, and a concentrative joint venture in *Metal Europe* [1991] 4 C.M.L.R. 222. In the last year or two, however, clearances of joint ventures have come only through the merger regulation.
22   [1988] 4 C.M.L.R. 111.
23   *E.g.*, *Burroughs* [1972] C.M.L.R. D67 and D72, decided before the adoption of the group exemption for patent licences.
24   [1985] 4 C.M.L.R. 157, and 10.2 above.
25   (C–234/89) [1991] E.C.R. I–935, described at 8.4 above.
26   *Langnese-Iglo* and *Schöller Lebensmittel* [1994] 4 C.M.L.R. 51, each subject to appeal on the grounds set out in the O.J., (T–24/92) O.J. 1992, C121/16, and (T–28/92) O.J. 1992, C138/7.
27   *Parfums Yves Saint Laurent* [1993] 4 C.M.L.R. 120 and *Parfums Givenchy* [1993] 5 C.M.L.R. 579 and the Court of First Instance in *Vichy* (T–19/91) [1991] E.C.R. II–265. See 8.3.3 above.
28   See *Finnpap* and *APB* cited at 14.2.1 above.

that the effects are not appreciable but, as argued at 7.2.3 above, it is difficult to see why it was necessary for the Commission to make the joint sales organisation abrogate the restriction on passive sales by members. At 7.3, the formal decision in *APB*[29] was criticised for failing to spell out the free rider problem that could have been overcome by less restrictive means — by letting the producers of the products pay for the test, and permitting them to sell the products with the stamp wherever they liked.

14.2.3 *Reasons why the Commission treated all important restrictions of conduct as restrictions of competition*

In the early days, the Commission proposed that it should have exclusive power to grant individual exemptions under article 9(1) of regulation 17 so that it could keep control over the key, difficult decisions. Otherwise the courts or authorities in the different member states might come to very different decisions (5.1 above).

By creating precedents that any restrictions on conduct of importance on the market restricted competition,[30] the Commission increased this control. The Commission's reasoning suffices to catch all contracts that have significant effects on the market, whether they increase, decrease or do not affect competition.[31] It can be argued that it has virtually unfettered discretion whether to grant an exemption. Since its legal conclusions are rarely related to specific facts, it can justify almost any decision in the difficult area where ancillary restraints are necessary to curb free riders and induce the investment required for some activity that may increase competition. It is easier for DGIV to draft a decision without articulating the appropriate economic analysis. Wide discretion makes work easy for those who enjoy the discretion, but impossible for those who advise firms whose business is affected by it.

14.2.4 *The notification and exemption process has broken down to the detriment of legal certainty*

The original concept that, if agreements were notified, the beneficial ones would receive an individual exemption has broken down. The Commission lacks the resources to make many formal decisions, and individual exemptions each require a formal decision. Few notifications will end in an exemption: in its best year, 1988, the Commission

29   Cited at 14.2.1 above.
30   See the examples given in the next few paras. See also Schröter, *op. cit.*, bibliography, 14.5 below, at pp.667 *et seq.*, where he cites some of the Court's judgments that support the Commission's views.
31   See 2.4 above.

managed ten for almost all sectors of industry and commerce in a common market of 320 million people. During the four years from 1990 to 1993 it managed 16 formal exemptions.

The unwillingness formally to clear agreements with ancillary restraints has begun to undermine the contract law of the common market countries. Competition law presupposes that there are markets and markets presuppose that there are rights to be traded and that contracts are enforceable. Otherwise products will not flow to their most strongly desired use.

There are signs that this is affecting the Commission's policy and that officials will be persuaded to clear exclusive agreements and others containing important restrictions on conduct where they are necessary to induce investment in sunk costs. I have always been an optimist and hope that this may succeed, but it may be difficult to change the working practices of some officials in view of the Commission's precedents.

National courts have no power to grant exemptions and it was widely thought that to enforce an agreement that requires exemption would amount to granting one and be illegal. All a national court can do is to adjourn and await the exempting decision of the Commission if the agreement has been notified before the period in issue in the proceedings.

Notification may lead to a comfort letter stating that, in the opinion of the Commission, the agreement does not infringe article 85(1) or that the agreement merits exemption. Previously any form of exclusivity might lead to a comfort letter stating that the agreement merits exemption. I am told that few are now being sent stating that the agreement does not restrict competition.

Comfort letters may be taken into account by national courts and one saying the agreement merits exemption implies that the agreement is caught by article 85(1) as, otherwise, it would not require any exemption (6.3.4 above).

As explained at the end of 6.3.4 above, two developments have reduced the problems of the recipients of such a letter. First, the Commission has taken steps to speed up its procedures in relation to structural joint ventures — those where investment is substantial. In other fields, too, the Commission is no longer taking so long to look seriously at notifications, so there is less risk of bargaining power having shifted by the time the Commission wants alterations to be made to the contract.

Secondly, in *Automec II*,[32] the Court of First Instance implied that where the Commission has exclusive competence, as it has over exemptions, the parties are entitled to insist on an actual exemption. This has

32   (T–28/90) [1992] 5 C.M.L.R. 431.

been accepted by the Commission, and the member formerly responsible for competition policy stated that it would not depart from the views expressed in its comfort letters unless conditions had changed or it had been misinformed.

If it be necessary to sue, the Commission may be asked to re-open its file and proceed to a decision under article 85(3). Two problems remain. First, litigation will be slowed down and made more expensive by the need to wait for an exemption. Secondly, the Commission may consider that when the investment has been successful commercially and market share has increased, conditions have changed and that it is no longer bound by its former comfort letter.

14.2.5 *The need to analyse ex ante: at the time the commitments are made*

It is vital that competition analysis should be made *ex ante*: at the time the undertaking is considering whether or not to make its investment. It is then that each party must be able to rely on its contract to appropriate the benefit of its investment. If it cannot rely on the contract, it may well not proceed with a risky investment that may be socially desirable.

In many situations, investment is unattractive unless the investor is protected from other undertakings taking a free ride on it. Parties to a joint venture usually promise not to derogate from their grant: to deal with the joint venture wherever practicable. Dealers who are required to invest in marketing resources may require an exclusive territory. So may technology licensees who have to create a market and tool up to serve it. This has been recognised by the Community Court: see 14.2.1 above. Once the investment is made, the market would be more competitive if free riders could compete. If, however, this happens too often, undertakings will learn, and will not make investments for free riders to share.

The analysis of joint ventures explained in the *XIIIth Report on Competition Policy* was *ex ante*. One should look at the ability of the parties at the date of the transaction. Unfortunately, the Commission has returned to its former practice of analysing *ex post* in many of its recent decisions on joint ventures (14.2.2 above).

14.2.6 *Agreements may have to be renegotiated after the bargaining power has shifted*

The lack of legal certainty has been increased by the Commission's habit of requiring the parties to make changes to their agreements years after they were concluded and when the relative bargaining power has altered. One decision where this was done, *De Laval/Stork*,[33] altered the commercial balance of the agreement in favour of Stork, which contributed only 15 per cent. of the basic designs, which the Commission required should be licensed by each parent to the other on most favoured licensee terms after the termination of the agreement.

More important still is the consideration that any change that a party can veto enables that party to renegotiate the whole deal after it has gained bargaining power through the contribution of the other. It is this consideration that has led to so few important joint ventures being notified. Some contracts provide that if some part of the agreement should become void, the parties will renegotiate in good faith to redress the commercial balance, but such an agreement to make a contract that is not defined could probably not be enforced by a court. It may also make it more difficult to argue that the clause was indispensable to the viability of the original transaction. Nevertheless, the parties may abide by it.

Let one recent case serve as an example of the balance of an agreement being altered. *ARD*[34] paid US$ 85 million to MGM and United Artists for exclusive broadcasting rights in various German-speaking areas in a large library of feature films. To simplify the facts, ARD was entitled to select 1,350 films out of some 3,000, and required to broadcast each at least once. The exclusive rights to transmit the films selected and new ones produced were to last for 16 years and were staggered so that the period for some of the films started only in 1998. The exclusive rights were subject to only short 'windows,' during which a quarter of the selection might be licensed by the film producers to third parties. ARD was one of two publicly owned national networks in Germany. There were also two privately owned national networks there and a third in the process of being developed.

Apparently, after ARD had been to the expense of scrutinising the whole library and selecting the most suitable films, the Commission intervened at the request of a complainant, and forced ARD to surrender its exclusive rights to the films it did not select. ARD also had to submit to the windows through which third parties might be licensed being substantially enlarged, and to supply print copies to its competitors and, where prints were not available, to meet half the cost of dubbing and preparing them.

According to its common, but not invariable, practice the Commission found that the agreement restricted the parties' freedom and thus competition. Too many films were withdrawn from the market for

33 [1977] 2 C.M.L.R. D69, and 13.2.1 above. See also *Davidson Rubber*, 10.2 above.
34 [1990] 4 C.M.L.R. 841, subject to appeal (T–168/89), grounds stated in O.J. 1990, C23/10. See W. A. Rothnie, *op. cit.*, 14.5 below.

too long, more films and for longer than was customary. The Commission attacked the innovative nature of the agreement, yet innovation may well be competitive. When a practice is customary in a sector it is more likely to foreclose. ARD's rights covered only 4·95 per cent. of the world's stock of films, although they included some of the more appealing ones, such as James Bond films. From the facts stated in the decision, it sounds as if the market was competitive.

Would ARD have paid so much and gone to the trouble of selecting the most suitable films had it not bargained for almost completely exclusive rights? Would the films have been made available for German television had someone like ARD not bought the exclusive rights? These vital questions were not considered in the published decision under article 85(1) or (3).

The Commission's intervention enabled the American film companies to earn extra licensing revenue and the complainant to obtain licences. Once ARD had taken the trouble to scrutinise the whole library and pick out the films that were worth televising, the bargaining power of the large producers and their joint sales organisation had increased at ARD's expense. Seen *ex post*, the Commission's intervention made the particular market more competitive, but enabled the film companies to act in an opportunistic manner by keeping the whole of the original payment while providing less exclusive rights.

Will such agreements, that must have made more feature films available for television, be made in future? Would another television company be prepared to scrutinise so large a library if it had to enable the copyright holder to license the more suitable films to its competitors?

At 14.2.1, I criticised the Commission for not articulating the reasons that had led it to persuade *Finnpap* and *APB* to modify their agreements in the way they did. Those were horizontal agreements made by trade associations, so bargaining power had probably not shifted and the changes must have been less damaging to the parties than they were in *ARD*. Nevertheless, better solutions might have been reached if the reasoning had been articulated in public.

The Economic and Social Committee[35] has strongly criticised the Commission for intervening in agreements after bargains have been struck. It objected to the decision in *Tetra Pak*[36]:

'By doing this [forcing Tetrapak to abrogate the exclusive nature of its

---

35 Opinion on the *18th Annual Report*, adopted at its 272nd plenary session, O.J. 1990, C62/14.

36 [1990] 4 C.M.L.R. 47. I do not agree with ECOSOC's criticism of the particular decision, which was upheld by the Court of First Instance. The acquisition by a very dominant firm of a competitor with access to rival potential technology may well exclude potential competitors otherwise than on the basis of competition on the merits.

technology licence, that had been exempted by a group exemption] the Commission interfered with a contractual relationship which was in existence before the merger and had no connection with that merger. This case leads the Committee (a) to stress the sometimes arbitrary attitude adopted by the Commission for a particular purpose, and (b) to oppose its attitude strongly in order to stop this becoming a trend.'

14.2.7 Steps taken by the Commission to remedy the lack of legal certainty

14.2.7.1 *Comfort letters and short form exemptions* — One of the Commission's responses to complaints about its inability to grant enough individual exemptions has been to write comfort letters (6.3.4 above) and grant short form exemptions. The first are not binding on national courts, and the latter are rare. Comfort letters stating that competition is not restricted owing to the parties' small market share may be of little use a few years later when their business has been successful. Short form exemptions may not include sufficient reasoning to amount to valid decisions.

Moreover, like traditional individual exemptions, both comfort letters and short form exemptions enable the Commission to intervene and persuade the parties to alter their agreements after investments have been made and relative bargaining power may have shifted.

14.2.7.2 *Group exemptions* — The other step taken by the Commission has been to adopt regulations granting a group exemption to the agreements that can be brought within its terms. There are two objections to the way the Commission has used this procedure.

First, instead of drawing its regulations in broad economic terms, such as vertical distribution agreements, vertical technology licensing or even vertical agreements, the Commission has drafted them in legalistic detail. It tends to define the kind of agreement being exempted by each regulation in terms of a typical agreement, rather than of the public policy being pursued. Some desirable agreements will fall between the exempted categories and so important clauses may be invalid.[37] On the other hand, the Commission's pigeon hole approach may lead to inconsistencies. Similar types of restriction may receive different treatment under different regulations or elements of case law.[38] Large business, which has readier access to expert legal advice, may structure

---

37 *E.g.*, *Pronuptia* O.J. 1989, L13/39, although the obligation to pay royalties may well have been enforceable.
38 *E.g.*, greater control over retailers can be obtained by using the franchise regulation than by relying on the Court's and Commission's case law on selective distribution.

agreements artificially to take advantage of the discrepancies. Smaller firms cannot afford that expense.

For example, a supplier wishing to distribute its goods through an independent firm would be well advised to look at the exemption for franchising if it is most interested in controlling its retail outlets, but will have great difficulty if arranging for an intermediary between it and the retailers as tripartite agreements are usually necessary to protect the holder's trade marks. If, on the other hand, it requires a distributor to set up a retail network and the retailers will not require an express trade mark licence, or it is interested in maintaining some price differences between different territories, a supplier might consider using the exclusive distribution regulation, as it can restrain one exclusive dealer, but not a franchisee, from buying from another. It might even think of using the exclusive purchasing regulation if the dealer is prepared to have only a principal sales area and not an exclusive territory. In that case it could rely on different trade marks in different member states if separate marks are justifiable, because the black list in regulation 1984/83 is not directed at restraining cross-frontier trade. Anomalously, the best way both to control one's dealers and segregate the common market is not to sell to independent firms but to sell through subsidiaries and employees, so no agreements are needed between independent undertakings.

The Commission argues that its formalism enhances legal certainty. Lawyers have only to read an agreement to see whether it is prohibited by article 85(1) and requires exemption and Commission officials can tell whether it falls within a group exemption. It is more difficult to decide whether the firms have market power or whether investment would have been forthcoming in the absence of the amount of protection granted. Jurists are not trained to recognise the height of entry barriers.

On the other hand, these formalistic categories have nothing to do with competition policy. Whether one is trying to protect the public from extortion or competitors from foreclosure, the legal nature of the contract is irrelevant. A brand owner supplying a reseller may have as great an interest as a franchisor in the final customer being able to buy its product only in outlets providing the appropriate range of services.

The appropriate questions relate to the structure of the market: are there many strong brands, or does the particular supplier supply a large part of the market? If it does, are there barriers to the entry of equally efficient firms? If the restriction on conduct is important on this basis, is it justified by the need to protect investors from free riders? It is absurd to encourage vertical integration rather than the supply to or licensing of independent firms, when they would be more efficient but for the problems created by a formalistic application of competition law.

The second drawback to the method of drafting narrow group

exemptions is that often it is virtually impossible to bring an agreement within them. I have doubts whether many r & d joint ventures can be brought within regulation 418/85.[39] It is absurd that regulation 1983/83 almost certainly does not apply to services which are not 'goods supplied for resale,' because of the limitations in the empowering regulation, no. 19/65, and that regulation 1983 does not apply when more than one undertaking is supplied in an area, with a restriction on more than the limited number being supplied.[40] Some officials claim that it is only exclusive distribution agreements that deserve exemption, but others that the idea of exempting similar restrictions of more limited scope was conceived only at the time the patent licensing block exemption was being drafted. To my mind, the restrictions should be allowed whenever a dealer or its supplier incurs sunk costs and needs protection from free riders, but this is not the kind of reasoning used in group exemptions.

The group exemption for patent licensing was held not to apply in *Boussois/Interpane*,[41] partly because of the narrow definition of 'patent licensing agreement' and partly because of its black list. Both grounds apply to most technology licences, so the group exemption lost most of its point and the Commission had to go through the complicated process of adopting another group exemption for the licensing of technology some of which was not protected by patents.

The Commission has tried to extend the ambit of group exemptions through the opposition procedure, but this does not broaden the definition of the kinds of agreements that qualify, nor may it be used if there is a blacklisted clause. In the draft of the new group exemption for technology licences, the opposition procedure has been abandoned. On the other hand, unlisted provisions that restrict competition will no longer prevent the application of the exemption to other provisions, although they may infringe article 85(1).

Moreover, some of the items in the black lists of the regulations for technology licensing are not clear in their application, for instance, the distinction between a promise by the licensee to use its best endeavours to exploit the licensed technology and a restriction on using rival technology within the meaning of article 3(9) of the know-how regulation.[42] This reduces the certainty normally attributable to applicable group exemptions.

Advisers sometimes persuade their clients to distort a transaction to come within the straitjacket of one of the group exemptions. This is worrying. One great virtue of contracts is that they are infinitely variable

39   13.5 above.
40   *Junghans* [1977] 1 C.M.L.R. D82, and 8.3.1 above.
41   [1988] 4 C.M.L.R. 124.
42   Now art. 3(2) of the draft new unifying regulation.

and can be drafted to fit any possible transaction. It would be so much more sensible for the Commission to develop broader rules, based on openly acknowledged economic considerations as to why particular provisions are or are not anti-competitive in specified circumstances.

There is widespread agreement that few vertical agreements restrict competition where markets are competitive. The Commission implicitly acknowledges this by granting *per se* exemption on its own terms to many of these agreements in its group exemptions. There is no need for separate rules for distribution, franchising, etc. Broader drafting of group exemptions would enable national courts to enforce agreements that are unlikely to restrict competition and may well increase it.

14.2.7.3 *Greater role for national courts?* — The Commission has managed to reduce its backlog of notifications and complaints considerably, but would like national courts to perform much of this task for it. There are, however, considerable problems in establishing an infringement before national courts and few such actions have been brought (6.1 above).

Evidence of an infringement is hard to obtain. In England, discovery would not be available to obtain evidence of an infringement for which penalties might be imposed. The evidence may be scattered in several member states, and the Commission's powers under regulation 17 would not be available to national courts, nor could the Commission make information it obtained under its powers available to a court, owing to the duties of confidentiality imposed by Community law. The plaintiff would be liable for the defendant's costs if it were not successful.

14.3 The Court's analysis is more helpful than that of the Commission

The judges of the Community Court and Court of First Instance give only a single judgment with no dissents or individual opinions, yet they are appointed *inter alia* because of their independence of mind. Consequently, they must have great difficulty agreeing to a common document. Key phrases have to be fudged and interesting paragraphs deleted in order to achieve a consensus. Some of the Advocates General, however, have taken advantage of their freedom to draft individual opinions to analyse the basic economic issues. Sometimes, but not always, the Court has been persuaded to follow them, although the reasons may be less fully articulated. Sometimes, as in *Delimitis* or *Pronuptia*, they are clearly articulated.

14.3.1 *Opinions and judgments have recognised the need for incentives to investment*

In *Consten and Grundig*,[43] Advocate General Roemer's opinion raised all the important points: the need to compare the situation after the agreement with that which would have prevailed in its absence; the need to examine incentives *ex ante*; the need to appraise vertical agreements in their economic context.

In *Brasserie de Haecht v. Wilkin (1)*,[44] however, he never reached the issue of incentives as he thought that exclusive purchasing obligations in return for a loan and equipment restrict competition only in very limited circumstances. De Haecht would need to ensure that its investment was not used for the benefit of its competitors. He stressed, however, that the obligation of a small café to take all its beer and soft drinks from a single brewer, even if considered in the context of many agreements under which other cafés bound themselves to other brewers, would restrict competition only if other brewers were foreclosed.

He pointed out how strict were the conditions for foreclosure. A foreign brewer would be able to enter the Belgian market and compete, unless so many outlets of all kinds (supermarkets as well as cafés) were tied for so many years to one or other of the existing breweries that a newcomer could not find enough free outlets to take the output of an efficient brewery. He even added that foreclosure would be serious only if it was not possible to open new retail outlets or buy up chains of them. His language was not as clear as this, but all these points are to be found in his opinion. The Court's judgment was very short, but its conclusions were congruent with Herr Roemer's opinion. Almost all his points were adopted by the Court in *Delimitis*.

Advocate General Verloren Van Themaat concluded in *Pronuptia*[45] that franchise agreements with the object or effect of restricting parallel imports would infringe article 85(1) only if:

> 'by way of its subsidiaries and franchisees in one or more of those other member states or in a significant part of their territory the franchisor has a substantial share of the market for the relevant product; and ...'

The Court said only that an exclusive territory coupled with an obligation to sell only from designated premises infringes article 85(1) once the reputation in the mark is widespread. In its summary of its conclusions, it added that the compatibility of a franchise agreement should be considered in the light of its economic context. The Court went further than the Advocate General in stating that certain ancillary

43   (56 & 58/64) [1966] E.C.R. 299. See 2.3.1 and 2.4 above.
44   (23/67) [1967] E.C.R. 407, and 8.4 above.
45   (161/84) [1986] E.C.R. 353, at 371. See 8.5.1 above.

restrictions were *per se* legal, since they were necessary to make franchise arrangements viable.

Herr Roemer also raised the proper issues in his opinions on intellectual property and the free movement of goods. In *Parke Davis*,[46] he pointed out that if the holder of a patent in the Netherlands could not keep out chloramphenicol imported from Italy where, at that time, one could not obtain a patent for drugs for treating human beings, the Dutch right 'would be hollowed of all substance' and incentives to r & d would be seriously reduced. In that case, too, the Court followed Herr Roemer, although it did not spell out the reasons.

More recently, in the cases on intellectual property rights, the Court has gone a long way in its judgments in expressly recognising the need for each party to appropriate the benefit of its investment. In *Nungesser*,[47] it held that open exclusivity did not infringe article 85(1), since it was required to encourage investment by both parties. In *Coditel (2)*,[48] it went further and ruled even that absolute territorial protection did not in itself infringe article 85, although excessive profits might do. In *Erauw-Jacquéry*,[49] it went even further in relation to plant breeders' rights.

Since the specific subject matter of intellectual property rights is equally relevant to the rules for the free movement of goods, these principles apply also in cases under articles 30 and 36. In *Thetford* v. *Fiamma*,[50] decided under article 36, it stated that the UK patents granted for inventions of relative novelty 'fostered creative activity.' In *Warner* v. *Christiansen*,[51] the Court also stressed the need for a film producer to obtain sufficient reward, not only from showing in the cinema, but also from the sale and hire of cassettes.

Most recently, in *Hag (2)*,[52] Advocate General Jacobs delivered a tightly reasoned, lucid and cogent opinion, saying why the full Court should expressly overrule its earlier judgment under articles 30 and 36 about trade marks of common origin. He considered the wording of the treaty, policy issues and the case law of the Court. The Court followed his advice and departed firmly from its earlier scathing remarks about the value of trade marks. It is hoped that this view will be extended to cases under the competition rules. The justification for using a mark in one member state to keep out goods bearing a confusing mark in another applies equally to article 36 and the competition rules.

46   (24/67) [1968] E.C.R. 55, and 9.4.1 above.
47   Cited at 14.2.1 above. See 10.3 above.
48   Cited at 14.2.1 above.
49   Cited at 14.2.1 above. See 10.3 above.
50   (35/87) [1988] E.C.R. 3585.
51   (158/86) [1988] E.C.R. 2605.
52   *CNL-Sucal* v. *Hag* (C–10/89) [1990] E.C.R. I–3711. See also *Ideal-Standard*, 9.4.4 above.

14.3.2 *The doctrine of ancillary restraints*

The Court's observation in the intellectual property cases that an exclusive territory may be necessary to induce investment by licensor and licensee may be an example of the ancillary restraint doctrine. In some other contexts, the Court has stated that ancillary restraints necessary to make viable a transaction not in itself anti-competitive do not restrict competition within the meaning of article 85(1).

As early as 1966, the Court ruled that an exclusive distribution agreement would not restrict competition if an exclusive territory were necessary for the manufacturer to have its earth moving equipment sold in France.[53] In *Remia and Nutricia* v. *Commission*,[54] it ruled that a covenant not to compete with a business sold as a going concern would not restrict competition if properly limited in space and time to what was reasonably necessary. In *Pronuptia*,[55] it ruled that distribution franchising does not, in itself, infringe article 85(1). It could not take place unless the franchisor was able, first, to control the outlets in its network symbolised by its name and, secondly, to ensure that the assistance it gave to its franchisees could not be used by those competing with the network. Restrictions necessary for those purposes were also outside article 85(1).

14.3.3 *Agreements are to be appraised in their legal and economic context*

Since the 1960s the Community Court has insisted, also, that agreements should be appraised in their legal and economic context. The strongest support for the proposition was in *Delimitis*. If this means that vertical restrictions in competitive markets are unlikely to infringe article 85(1), it would be far easier to enforce such contracts. Indeed, many firms, rather than distort their commercial agreements to come within one of the group exemptions, may already rely on this rule and not notify their agreements. They do, however, have to accept the risk of not being able to enforce vital terms of their contract when other parts may still be binding.

14.4 Conclusion

The Community Court has sometimes been prepared to rule that agreements do not restrict competition when either the market is

---

53   *La Technique Minière* v. *Maschinenbau Ulm* (56/65) [1966] E.C.R. 235. See also 2.4 above.
54   (42/84) [1985] E.C.R. 2545, and 7.1.2.
55   See 8.5.1 and 14.3.1 above.

competitive or the ancillary restraints are necessary to make viable some pro-competitive activity. The Community Court, however, rarely delved very deeply into the factual situation alleged by the Commission in its decisions. It does not have jurisdiction to rehear the cases, but only for judicial review. The Court of First Instance has the same jurisdiction as the Community Court, but has gone more deeply into the facts. My hope is that it will quash a few decisions of the Commission for defective reasoning where the legal appraisal has not been properly related to the facts in order to encourage more lucid analysis. In the long run, this should lead to a more effective competition policy. The Court of First Instance has received much praise for considering the evidence carefully to decide whether the Commission has sufficiently established that parties have participated in a cartel when they deny that they have done so.[56]

14.5 Bibliography

W. A. Rothnie, 'Commission Re-runs Same Old Bull (Film Purchases by German Television Stations)' [1990] 2 E.I.P.R. 72.

Helmuth Schröter, 'Antitrust Analysis under Article 85(1) and (3),' in Barry Hawk (ed.) [1987] *Fordham Corporate Law Institute*, chap. 27.

Michel Waelbroeck, 'Antitrust Analysis under article 85(1) and article 85(3),' *ibid.*, chap. 28, and the panel discussion in chap. 29.

See also some of the items listed in the bibliography to chapter 2 at 2.5 above: *Forrester & Norall, Luc Gyselen*, first item, *René Joliet*, second item, *Valentine Korah*, second and third items, *Mark Scheckter*.

---

56   See 2.2.2.2 above.

Main Bibliography

Ivo Van Bael and *Jean-François Bellis*, *Competition Law of the EEC*, CCH Editions Limited, 1987 (the named authors are very good and busy practitioners).

C. Bellamy and *G. Child*, *Common Market Law of Competition*, London, Sweet & Maxwell, 4th ed., 1993 (well organised, legal practitioners' work).

Berman, Goebel, Davey and *Fox*, *Cases and Materials of European Community Law*, West, American Case Book Series, 1993 (outstanding analysis, comments, questions and other materials in the chapter on competition — suitable for a short course on competition).

Bos, Stuyck and *Wytinck*, *Concentration Control in the European Community*, Graham & Trotman, 1992 (accurate, thorough, perceptive and doctrinal analysis of the merger regulation in the light of its history).

Dennis Carlton and *Jeffrey Perloff*, *Modern Industrial Organisation*, Harper Collins, 1990.

W. R. Cornish, *Intellectual Property: Patents, Copyright, Trade Marks & Allied Rights*, 2nd ed., 1989 (classic, basic, but amazingly full and critical analysis of whole area of UK intellectual property for so short a book. Accurate, lucid and perceptive. See, especially, Chaps. 3.4 'Justifying the Patent System' and 7.3 'Exhaustion in the Common Market').

P. Demaret, *Patents, Territorial Restrictions and EEC Law*, IIC Studies, Vol. 2, 1978 (describes economic analysis of the purpose of the patent system, nature of right and returns to be obtained by licensing. Effects on efficiency and on incentive to innovate of permitting territorial restrictions. Analysis of *Centrafarm* v. *Sterling* and Commission's decisions in light of the theory. Lucid, sharp and competent).

E. Fox and *R. Pitofski*, 'Introduction to Antitrust Economics' (1983) 52 Antitrust L.J. 513–837 (helpful collection from experts, not entirely persuaded by Chicago).

E. Gellhorn, *Antitrust Law and Economics*, West (UK distributor, Hammicks), 1986, Nutshell Series (basic and critical analysis of American law in the light of the latest as well as earlier economic theory. A readable and perceptive contrast to EEC thinking, 4th ed. with Kaplow expected soon).

D.J. Gijlstra (ed.), *Competition Law in Western Europe and the USA*, Kluwer, looseleaf multi-volume (contains the legislation relating to competition in the European Communities and under national laws. Substantial and critical commentaries thereon, as well as reprints of many of the decisions of Commission and Courts of the European Communities).

D. G. Goyder, *EC Competition Law*, Oxford University Press, European Community Law Series, 2nd ed., 1993 (accurate, elegant, largely historical description of the EEC competition rtules, with a critical appraisal in the last chapter. Rather few headings so difficult to find a point — easy to read through).

N. Green, *Commercial Agreements and Competition Law: Practice and Procedure in the U.K. and EEC*, Graham & Trotman, 1986 (substantial, accurate and full practitioners' text; new edition in preparation with Aidan Robertson).

Barry E. Hawk, *U.S., Common Market and International Antitrust: A Comparative Guide*, looseleaf, 2nd ed. (outstanding — full text. Accurate, lucid and critical; perceptive on comparisons and contrasts between US and EC practice: although the work is looseleaf, substantial updatings occur every two years or so. Mergers under national law were added in 1993).

R. Joliet, *Monopolization and Abuse of Dominant Position: A Comparative Study of American and European Approaches to the Control of Economic Power*, The Hague, Nijhoff, 1970 (classic, clear analysis of crucial issues in English, by Belgian law professor with deep understanding of economics, now a judge in the Community Court).

R. Joliet, *The Rule of Reason in Antitrust Law*, The Hague, Nijhoff, 1967 (ditto).

C. Jones, M. Van der Woude and **Z. Lewis**, *EEC Competition Law Handbook 1993 Edition*, Sweet & Maxwell, 1993 (a collection of the regulations and directives in the competition field, together with very useful references to relevant cases, etc., with very full citations. No commentary).

C. Jones and **Enrique González-Díaz**, ed. Colin Overbury, *The EEC Merger Regulation*, Sweet & Maxwell, 1992 (book by officials that addresses the critical issues — clear, readable and helpful as to the practice and thinking of the task force.)

C. S. Kerse and **John Cook**, *Merger Control — Regulation 4064/89*, Sweet & Maxwell, 1991 (good comment by two lawyers, one influential when the regulation was being negotiated in the Council and the other advising on mergers frequently. Little on the subject goes beyond September 1991.)

C. S. Kerse, *EEC Antitrust Procedure*, Sweet & Maxwell, 3rd. ed., 1994 (outstanding! accurate, lucid, tightly written and full analysis. A perceptive, most useful, thoroughly researched and practical guide).

V. Korah, *Competition Law in Britain and the Common Market*, Nijhoff, 3rd ed., 1982 (elementary — over 100pp. on the EEC law, tables of cases include citations of articles. In this edition more economic theory has been added).

V. Korah, *Exclusive Distribution Agreements and the EEC Competition Rules: Regulations 1983/83 and 1984/83* Sweet & Maxwell 1992, 2nd ed. (clause by clause critical commentary on regs. 1983 and 1984/83 in the context of the case law and economic analysis).

V. Korah, *Patent Licensing and the EEC Competition Rules — Regulation 2349/84*, ESC, 1985 (ditto).

V. Korah, *R & D and the EEC Competition Rules — Regulation 418/85*, ESC, 1986 (ditto).

V. Korah, *Franchising and the EEC Competition Rules — Regulation 4087/88*, ESC, 1989 (ditto).

V. Korah, *Know-how Licensing Agreements and the EEC Rules — Regulation 556/89*, ESC 1989 (ditto).

G. Lindrup, (ed.), *Butterworths Competition Law Handbook*, 1993 (carefully prepared collection of the primary and secondary legislation in the UK and EC. The corrigenda have been properly inserted in the EC regulations. Reliable and handy, although much bigger than the earlier edition.)

R. Merkin and *K. Williams*, Competition Law: Antitrust Policy in the U.K. and EEC, Sweet & Maxwell, 1984 (comparative student text. The economics are almost entirely Chicago.)

Damien Neven, Robin Nuttall and *Paul Seabright*, Merger in Daylight — the economics and politics of European Merger Control, CEPR, 1993 (analysis of the work of the merger task force in the light of the issues the authors argue are important).

L. Ritter, D. Braun and *Rawlinson*, EEC Competition Law — a Practitioners' Guide, Kluwer Law and Taxation, 1991 (accurate, well written work explaining, but not criticising, the Commission's current practice. Hard to find anything save through short table of contents. Good on the practice of the Commission.)

F. M. Scherer and *David Ross*, Industrial Market Structure and Economic Performance, 3rd ed., 1991 (lucid and thoughtful economic analyses of main problems arising from Antitrust. Not based on Chicago thinking, although familiar with it).

Thiesing–Schröter–Hochbaum, Les Ententes et les Positions Dominantes dans le Droit de la CEE, 1977 (particularly full on procedure of DGIV).

Piet Jan Slot and *Alison McDonnell* (eds.), Procedure and Enforcement in E.C. and U.S. Competition Law — Proceedings of the Leiden Europa Instituut Seminar on User-Friendly Competition Law, Sweet & Maxwell, 1993 (30 short and very perceptive contributions in under 300 pages, full of interesting ideas and information not widely known).

Dennis Swan, Economics of the Common Market, 7th ed., 1992 (a clear and helpful introduction, not specifically dealing with the competition provisions — excellent background reading.)

Jean Tirole, Theory of Industrial Organisation, 1988.

M. Waelbroeck, Le droit de la communauté économique européenne, Vol. 4, Concurrence, Brussels, Université libre de Bruxelles, 2nd ed., 1993 (most reliable, detailed, scholarly and practical commentary).

R. P. Whish, Competition Law, Butterworths, 3rd ed., 1993 (a lucid, interesting and up to date student text covering UK and EC law in the light of economic theory, both from Chicago and its critics).

R. P. Whish, P. Freeman and *M. Smith*, Butterworths Competition Law, looseleaf (well written, accurate analysis of EEC competition law).

Weinberg, Mergers and Acquisitions, ed. Lever and Lasok on the parts dealing with UK and EEC competition law respectively (looseleaf, full and careful analysis — perceptive — authors practise extensively in the field.)

Reports

Commission of European Communities, Reports on Competition Policy (sometimes referred to simply as the *Annual Reports*) — annual from 1971, published in May.

Commission of European Communities, Competition Law in the EEC and in the ECSC (collection of regulations and notices), 4th ed., 1991.

European Court Reports (E.C.R.), the official reports of the Community Court.

Official Journal — gazette of the Communities. The L volumes contain the decisions and regulations of the Commission, the C volumes short summaries of pending decisions, and issues before the Community Court, notices and draft regulations.

Common Market Law Reports (C.M.L.R.) (law reports, include cases in courts of member states, Commission decisions, authentic language of judgment until 1986. Vol. 4 of each year (and now vol. 5) is confined to the competition cases).

Common Market Reporter (C.M.R.), Commerce Clearing House (useful series of looseleaf volumes containing reports of the decisions of the Commission, judgments of the Court and press releases, Parliamentary questions etc., together with a comment on the treaty — not confined to competition. The recent cases are now reported as C.E.C.).

Some journals which publish commentaries on EC competition law

Cahiers de droit européen
Common Market Law Review
Europarecht
European Business Law Review
European Competition Law Review
European Intellectual Property Review
European Law Review
Fordham Corporate Law Institute, ed. Barry Hawk, Transnational Law (proceedings of annual conferences of extraordinarily high quality, thought provoking).
Fordham International Law Journal devotes one issue per year to EEC law, and usually has some outstanding articles on competition.
International and Comparative Law Quarterly
International Review of Industrial Property and Copyright
Journal of Business Law
Journal of World Trade Law
Legal Issues of European Integration
Northwestern Journal of International Law and Business
Revue du marché commun
Revue Suisse du Droit International de la Concurrence, more recently called *World Competition*
Revue trimestrielle de droit européen
World Competition, formerly called *Revue Suisse du Droit International de la Concurrence*

Glossary

Absolute territorial protection — protection given, usually to an exclusive dealer or licensee of intellectual property rights, from competition by sellers of goods of the same brand, or made by use of the protected innovation, not only by the supplier or licensor, but also dealers or licensees for other areas as well as from their customers. Since, however, the rules for the free movement of goods prevent either party from relying on intellectual property rights to restrain imports of goods sold in other member states with the consent of the holder, the protection is seldom absolute, although it may be for performing rights and basic seed (2.3.1 and Chapter 10).

Abuse of a dominant position — prohibited by article 86. Originally, it was thought to include only conduct that may harm those with whom a dominant firm deals, such as overcharging or paying too little. Such a prohibition is very difficult to apply and contrary to the liberal spirit of the treaty. The concept has been extended to include conduct that may harm those with whom a dominant firm deals indirectly by reducing such competition that remains in the market (Chap. 4).

Accession agreement — an agreement that came to infringe article 85 only on the accession of new member state, such as an agreement between a Spanish and Portuguese firm, prior to the accession of these states to the Communities, under which each promised to keep out of the other's market. A similar contract between a Spanish and French firm is almost certainly not an accession agreement as it probably restricted competition in France and may well have affected trade between France and some other member state. Accession agreements are treated as old agreements by article 25 of regulation 17, as added by the various acts of accession. If notified within six months of accession, accession agreements may be validated retrospectively if amended so as to escape the prohibition of article 85(1) or to merit exemption. They probably enjoy provisional validity (5.5. and 6.3.5).

Active sales policy, restriction on — a restriction on the active promotion of a product by an exclusive dealer or licensee of intellectual property rights outside his territory is permitted by some regulations, e.g., article 2(2)(c) of the group exemption for exclusive dealing; article 1(1)(f) of those for patent licensing and for know-how; or article 4(1)(f) of that for collaboration in research and development. Note that the exact scope of the permitted restriction differs.

Advocate General — member of the Community Court, of equal status to the judges. The opinion of the Advocate General is delivered before the judgment and may help the judges to focus on the crucial issues. Since he prepares his opinion on his own, it is more likely to be cogently reasoned than the judgment,

289

which has to accommodate the views of several judges. Opinions may point the way to subsequent developments. Frequently more of the issues are considered by the Advocate General than by the Court (1.4.3).

Agent — undertaking which sells on behalf of its principal, without owning the stocks it sells or being responsible for unsold stocks. If the agent is heavily dependent on its principal and integrated into its organisation, it may accept restrictions from the principal without infringing article 85. In any event the principal may limit the authority of the agent (8.7).

Aggregated discounts — discounts based on the total bought by each customer from all members of a trade association, or from all national manufacturers, and not just from the individual seller. They discourage buyers who hope to qualify for a larger discount from buying part of their requirements elsewhere, usually in another member state, and agreements to grant a particular scale of discounts discourage secret discounts (7.4). See also loyalty and other exclusionary rebates or discounts.

Case handler — term used colloquially to describe the official in directorate B, C or D of DGIV of the Commission (See DGIV, below) whose function is to prepare the Commission's case against possible infringements of article 85 or 86, or for the grant of an individual exemption, clearance or comfort letter. Most case handlers are lawyers, although few have practised. Their discretion is limited. Apart from the discipline inherent in a civil service hierarchy, including the co-ordination from directorate A, certain steps, such as the draft of the final decision, must be submitted to the legal service. The Advisory Committee of experts from member states must be consulted before the final draft of a decision condemning an infringement, granting an exemption or imposing a fine is submitted to the Members of the Commission themselves. Formal decisions must be made by the Members of the Commission acting collegiately, although they are prepared by the case handler (1.5.1 and Chapter 5).

Chiselling — selling at a price lower than that agreed with competitors in order to increase market share. The practice undermines cartels even when they are legal and few last for long without government protection (2.2.4.1).

Clearance, negative — decision by the Commission that an agreement or practice does not infringe article 85(1) or 86. Contrast an individual exemption, which implies that an agreement does infringe article 85(1), but merits exemption under article 85(3)(5.3).

Comfort letters — administrative letters of various kinds, usually signed by a senior official in DGIV. Some state that because of the small share of the market supplied by the parties, the Commission sees no reason to intervene under article 85(1) or 86. Some say that the agreement comes within the scope of one of the block exemptions. Others that the agreement is individually exemptable. Such letters probably used not to bind the Commission or a national court asked to enforce a contract, but may do so after the statement of Sir Leon Brittan just prior to his retirement as Commissioner in charge of competition matters (6.3.4).

Concerted practice — concept used to extend the prohibition of article 85(1) to forms of collaboration looser than a contract or agreement. It is thought that it does not extend to price leadership in the absence of some deliberate conduct reducing the risks of competition (2.2.4–2.2.4.3).

Community Court — my term for the Court of Justice of the European Communities (1.4.3 and 1.5.2.1).

Court of First Instance — attached to the Community Court, it hears appeals, *inter alia*, from the Commission, on competition matters. The Court of First Instance enjoys the same jurisdiction as the Community Court used to exercise, but it has tended to go more deeply into the facts. It does not hear cases brought by or against member states (1.4.3 and 1.5.1.1).

DGIV — abbreviation for Directorate General IV, the competition department of the Commission. It deals with state aids granted by national governments to industry as well as with articles 85 and 86. The senior civil servant is the Director General, now Dr. Ehlermann. He has fewer than 400 staff, including typists and secretaries but excluding translators (1.4.2).

Directorate A is responsible for advice on policy and the preparation of regulations and notices of general application. It is responsible also for co-ordinating individual cases. Directorates B, C and D deal with individual cases and are divided according to industry, so a case handler can start dealing with a file on the basis of familiarity with the market. Case handlers also act as inspectors in the cases they handle. The merger task force was established to deal with merger cases. Directorate E deals with state aids.

Directive — legislation adopted by the Council recently with the co-operation of the European Parliament requiring member states to bring their laws into conformity with the directive. Citizens may sue member states for damages if they fail to implement a directive properly.

Dominant position in the common market — This is a technical legal concept, not necessarily identical with the economists' idea of power over price. The Court habitually defines it as:

> 'a position of economic strength enjoyed by an undertaking which enables it to prevent effective competition being maintained on the relevant market by giving it power to behave to an appreciable extent independently of its competitors, customers and ultimately of its consumers.'

It includes the ability of a firm to foreclose its competitors (4.2–4.2.8).

ECU, European Currency Unit — based on a basket of currencies and quoted daily in the C series of the Official Journal. It is used for calculating fines under regulation 17 (1.8 and 5.10) and for measuring turnover when deciding whether an undertaking qualifies as small within various regulations and notices. It is also used to decide whether mergers have a Community scope (12.2.1). On 28 June 1994, it was worth £0·786749.

European Economic Area (EEA) — established by the EEA treaty from 1994. It creates a common market between Norway, Sweden, Finland, Austria, Iceland and the European Union (1.7).

EFTA Surveillance Authority — the administrative body of the EEA, which liaises closely with DGIV (1.7.).

Exclusionary rebates and discounts — see loyalty and other exclusionary discounts or rebates.

Exclusive dealer — independent trader who buys the stocks he later sells and is protected by the supplier's promise not to sell to any other dealer within his exclusive territory. Such agreements may come within a group exemption, provided *inter alia* that the dealer is not protected from goods coming indirectly from other dealers, in which case the dealer may agree also not to handle competing products. The territorial protection permitted is very slight (8.1–8.3.6).

Foreclosure — conduct of a dominant firm or combination of firms that prevents smaller firms from competing fairly. See also loyalty and other exclusionary rebates or discounts, below. Exclusive purchasing may also foreclose in limited circumstances.

Franchise — distribution franchise is a method of exploiting a formula for retailing without using much of the franchisor's capital. The franchisor supplies marketing advice to franchisees in return, usually for a royalty and down payment. The latter's shops look almost as if owned and managed by the franchisor, but are in fact owned and managed by the franchisees. Ancillary restrictions to ensure the control necessary to maintain a common reputation and to prevent the assistance coming into the hands of competitors do not infringe article 85(1), but an exclusive territory, coupled with a duty to sell only from specified premises within it, requires exemption once the network is widespread. For this there is a group exemption (8.5–8.5.2).

Production franchising consists of a trade mark licence, often coupled with technology. Since the technology is usually ancillary to the mark and not the other way round, such a franchise does not come within the group exemption for know-how. Nor does it come within the precedents on distribution franchising or the group exemption.

Free riders — those, such as parallel importers, who take advantage of the investment of others without paying enough towards it. The need for those incurring sunk costs to prevent free riding creates considerable difficulty when assessing the competitive impact of many practices and intellectual property rights.

Horizontal agreement — agreement between undertakings at the same level of trade or industry, for example, between two or more manufacturers, or two or more wholesalers of goods that compete with each other (7.1–7.4).

Information agreement — agreement to inform competitors of prices, production, capacity, etc. These are treated as restrictions on competition because they affect prices or market shares if the information is detailed and disseminated rapidly. They may also facilitate oligopolistic inter-dependence or collusion by reducing uncertainty (7.2.2).

Joint venture — collaboration between two or more firms in one or more areas of activity. This may take any legal form, joint subsidiary, joint committee, etc. It reduces the incentive for the venturers to compete with each other in those activities, and may deter competition between them in others. If more than one party could have operated alone, it may reduce the number of actual or potential competitors, etc. Joint ventures may, however, increase competition by enabling the parties to do what no one of them would have been prepared to undertake independently (Chapter 13).

Concentrative joint ventures are subject to the merger regulation.

Know-how — secret, technical information. Its communication is nowadays treated like a technology licence. Since national laws confer no exclusive right other than the obligation to keep it secret, it is more vulnerable than technology protected by patents. For this reason and others, the group exemption for the licence of substantial, secret know-how permits more ancillary restrictions than does that for patent licences (10.5). It may be replaced by a new regulation at the end of 1994 (10.6).

Loyalty and other exclusionary rebates or discounts — A discount is a deduction made when charging a customer, often proportional to the total bill, while the term 'rebate' is sometimes used when a repayment is made at the end of a period over which the amount is calculated. A firm may grant a rebate to those who in fact buy all or a large specified proportion of their requirements over a period from it, or a discount or rebate to those who promise to do so. Sometimes small buyers like to be assured of supplies whatever the amount they order and in return for such a promise will agree to buy exclusively from a single supplier.

The Commission and Court perceive loyalty rebates by a dominant firm as making it more difficult for smaller firms to compete. To compete for orders that would cause the buyer to forego the loyalty rebate, a firm would have to match the dominant firm's discounts not only on the amount bought from it, but also on the amount bought from the dominant firm. Since they cannot supply the total needs of large customers, small firms cannot compete by themselves giving such discounts unless they combine (4.3.2.2).

Similar practices may operate through a trade association where buyers agree to buy a large part of their requirements exclusively from members of the association or in fact do so (7.4).

Other kinds of discount given by a dominant firm or association may have similar effects in making it difficult for a single smaller firm to compete. The dominant firm or association may grant progressive quantity discounts or rebates so that, for instance, an extra 1 per cent. saving is made by the buyer on his total purchases for each extra thousand units taken. Where this reflects probable costs savings in planning production on a regular basis, or enabling shipments to be made in container or car lots etc., it encourages efficiency and should be treated as competition on the basis of performance. Where this cannot be shown, it may have an effect similar to a loyalty rebate or discount. A competitor wishing to supply the last thousand units would have to match the discount not only on what he sells but also the 1 per cent. the buyer will lose on all his other sales. The Commission and Court have not treated systematic discounts or rebates as competition on the basis of performance where they are not justified by cost savings (4.3.2.2).

Where a trade association arranges for discounts or rebates proportional to the amount bought from all its members by each firm, it may be easier for smaller firms in the association to compete in service for large buyers, but harder for outsiders. Such rebates are sometimes described as 'collective,' because arranged between competitors, and 'aggregated,' because the purchases from all members are relevant. They have the additional anti-competitive effect of preventing competition in discounts between the members (7.4).

New agreement — an agreement made after regulation 17 came into force. If such agreements fall under article 85(1), they can be exempted only from a date after their notification, and from a time when they qualified for exemption without further amendment. They do not enjoy provisional validity (5.5 and 6.3–6.3.5).

Notices of the Commission — statements made purporting to bind the Commission, but no one else, as to its view of the law or practice. The Court has stated that when the Commission promised to give greater access to its files than the Court had required, it was bound by the notice. The Commission is thinking, therefore, of withdrawing the notice. Notices stating that conduct is not forbidden do not bind a national court. Advocates General refer to them only to tell the Court to ignore them, which it has done, save as mitigation for a fine (2.4.1).

Official Journal (O.J.) — the gazette of the Communities. The L series includes formal decisions and legislation, the C series includes various notices.

Old agreement — an agreement made before regulation 17 came into force, or an accession agreement. Such agreements, if modified so as to escape the prohibition of article 85(1) or merit exemption, may be validated retrospectively under regulation 17, article 7. They enjoy provisional validity as long as there is a good chance of their being so validated (5.5 and 6.3–6.3.5).

Oligopoly — Greek term for few sellers, used by economists and the Commission for markets where there are few suppliers, each of which is likely to take into account the reactions of the others to its market conduct (2.2.4.1–2.2.4.3).

Open exclusive licence — a term coined by the Community Court in Nungesser (10.3). At paragraph 53 it defined a licence or assignment as open where:

> 'the exclusivity of the licence relates solely to the contractual relationship between the owner of the right and the licensee, whereby the owner merely undertakes not to grant other licences in respect of the same territory and not to compete himself with the licensee on that territory.'

It is contrasted with 'absolute territorial protection,' where the parties propose to eliminate competition from third parties such as parallel importers or licensees for other territories.

Parallel trade — mechanism on which the Commission relies to lead towards the equalisation of prices throughout the common market. If there are large price differentials between the member states, not accounted for by differences in cost, such as freight, taxes, etc., it may pay someone to buy in the low priced area and sell in the high (2.2 and Chapters 8–10).

Passive sales policy, restriction on — a restriction on accepting unsolicited offers within the territory of an exclusive dealer or licensee of an intellectual property right from those outside, as permitted by the group exemptions for exclusive distribution for an indefinite period and by the draft regulation for technology licensing for five years after the goods are first put on the market within the common market (8.3.2 and 10.5.1).

Patent — exclusive right conferred by national law to prevent others from using the invention covered by the patent, and also from selling, using or importing products made by use of the invention. A UK patent is infringed only by actions in the United Kingdom, and to use a UK patent to keep out goods made in France and protected by a corresponding French patent usually infringes the principle of the free movement of goods (Chapters 9 and 10).

Patent licence — permission to do what would otherwise infringe a patent. Usually, this is contained in a contract under which ancillary restrictions on competition may be accepted. The group exemption for patent licensing agreements is to be replaced by a new regulation at the end of 1994 and is being replaced (10.4 and 10.6).

Patents, parallel — situation where patents are obtained under the law of several member states in respect of virtually the same invention by the same person or company (9.4–9.4.1).

Preliminary ruling — ruling of the Community Court on the interpretation or validity of Community law, given at the request of a national court or tribunal (1.5.2.1).

Quantitative restrictions on imports and all measures having equivalent effect — These are prohibited by article 30 of the treaty. Quantitative restrictions are primarily import quotas — *e.g.* only 100 widgets shall be imported from state X in 1994. They were very common at the time the common market was established. They include a nil quota, *i.e.* a ban — no widgets shall be imported from state X this year. Laws granting industrial property rights, such as patents and trade marks, or, possibly, their exercise have been held to be measures of equivalent effect — no widgets shall be imported without the consent of the holder.

Consequently, national courts may not allow the exercise of such rights, save in so far as it is justified on the various grounds listed in article 36 and does not constitute a means of arbitrary discrimination or a disguised restriction on trade between member states. Where a quantitative restriction applies to domestic products but bears more heavily on imports from other member states, the Court has read into article 30 limitations for measures that protect consumers, the revenue etc. (Chapter 9).

Selective distribution — policy that may be adopted by a brand owner for ensuring that his output is sold only through competent dealers. Where glamour or pre-sales service is important, for example for jewellery, vehicles and television sets, he may restrain his wholesale dealers from selling to any retailer who does not meet objective criteria. To become approved the retailer may be required to keep specified premises, stocks of spare parts and have staff with specified skills available.

Provided that such requirements are objective, that is clearly specified, reasonably necessary to ensure adequate service to the consumer and applied without discrimination, the Court and Commission do not treat this as a restriction of competition. Where, however, to protect dealers who have invested in such staff and equipment, the brand owner also imposes quantitative restrictions — refuses to approve more retailers than he thinks the traffic will bear — article 85(1) may well apply. Consequently, the brand owner must now set up a system for approving those who want to deal in his goods, even though no one is under any duty to supply them.

Since the Commission considers that quantitative restrictions do restrict competition the group exemptions for exclusive distribution and purchasing do not apply. The Commission has sometimes exempted them on the ground that they are necessary to induce investment by dealers. In the absence of a dominant position, it has stated that there is no duty actually to supply all qualifying dealers; it is the restriction of the dealers' freedom that contravenes article 85(1) (8.3.3).

Sunk costs — investment that has no use save for a single purpose. If that purpose fails the investment is wasted, so such investments tend to be risky. They will be made only if higher profit than normal can be realised. The high profits suck in competitors. So before making such investments, one must ensure by contract that one can appropriate the benefit if the venture is a success. Seen after the investment is made, such terms appear anti-competitive, but without them the investment might never have been made.

Undertaking — includes any collection of resources to carry out economic activities: services, even professional services, as well as the supply of goods. Articles 85 and 86 are addressed to undertakings (2.2.1).

Unit of account — see ECU.

Vertical agreements — those between undertakings at different levels of trade or industry, for example those between supplier and customer or between licensor and licensee. Where the parties did or could have competed with each other without the agreement, it will also have horizontal elements (7.1 & 7.1.3).

Appendix I

Excerpts from the Treaty establishing the European Economic Community[1]

Part One
PRINCIPLES

Article 2

The Community shall have as its task, by establishing a common market and *an economic and monetary union and by implementing the common policies or activities referred to in articles 3 and 3a*, to promote throughout the Community a harmonious *and balanced* development of economic activities, *sustainable and non-inflationary growth respecting the environment, a high degree of convergence of economic performance, a high level of employment and of social protection, the* raising of the standard of living and *quality of life, and economic and social cohesion and solidarity among member states.*

Article 3

For the purposes set out in Article 2, the activities of the Community shall include, as provided in this Treaty and in accordance with the timetable set out therein:

(a) the elimination, as between Member States, of customs duties and of quantitative restrictions on the import and export of goods, and of all other measures having equivalent effect;

(b) *a common commercial policy;*

(c) *an internal market characterised by the abolition, as between member states, of obstacles to the free movement of goods, persons, services and capital;*

(d) *measures concerning the entry and movement of persons in the internal market as provided for in Article 100(c);*

(e) a common policy in the sphere of agriculture *and fisheries;*

(f) the adoption of a common policy in the sphere of transport;

(g) a system ensuring that competition in the *internal* market is not distorted;

(h) the approximation of the laws of Member States to the extent required for the proper functioning of the common market;

(i) *a policy in the social sphere comprising a European Social fund;*

(j) *the strengthening of the competitiveness of Community industry;*

(k) *a policy in the sphere of the environment;*

(l) *the strengthening of the competitiveness of Community industry;*

(m) *the promotion of research and technical development;*

(n) *encouragement for the establishment and development of trans-European networks;*

1 The additions made by the Maastricht treaty have been inserted in italics and the deletions made.

(o) a contribution to the attainment of a high level of health protection;
(p) a contribution to education and training of quality and to the flowering of
     the cultures of the Member-States;
(q) a policy in the sphere of development of co-operation.
(r) the association of the overseas countries and territories in order to increase
     trade and promote jointly economic and social development;
(s) a contribution to the strengthening of consumer protection;
(t) measures in the spheres of energy, civil protection and tourism.

Article 5

Member States shall take all appropriate measures, whether general or particular, to ensure fulfilment of the obligations arising out of this Treaty or
resulting from action taken by the institutions of the Community. They shall
facilitate the achievement of the Community's tasks.

They shall abstain from any measure which could jeopardise the attainment of
the objectives of this Treaty.

CHAPTER 2 — ELIMINATION OF QUANTITATIVE
RESTRICTIONS BETWEEN MEMBER STATES

Article 30

Quantitative restrictions on imports and all measures having equivalent effect
shall, without prejudice to the following provisions, be prohibited between
Member States.

Article 36

The provisions of Articles 30 to 34 shall not preclude prohibitions or restrictions on imports, exports or goods in transit justified on grounds of public
morality, public policy or public security; the protection of health and life of
humans, animals or plants; the protection of national treasures possessing
artistic, historic or archaeological value; or the protection of industrial and
commercial property. Such prohibitions or restrictions shall not, however,
constitute a means of arbitrary discrimination or a disguised restriction on trade
between Member States.

Part Three
POLICY OF THE COMMUNITY
TITLE I — COMMON RULES
CHAPTER 1 — RULES ON COMPETITION
SECTION 1
RULES APPLYING TO UNDERTAKINGS

Article 85

1. The following shall be prohibited as incompatible with the common
market: all agreements between undertakings, decisions by associations of
undertakings and concerted practices which may affect trade between Member
States and which have as their object or effect the prevention, restriction or

distortion of competition within the common market, and in particular those which:

(a) directly or indirectly fix purchase or selling prices or any other trading conditions;
(b) limit or control production, markets, technical development, or investment;
(c) share markets or sources of supply;
(d) apply dissimilar conditions to equivalent transactions with other trading parties, thereby placing them at a competitive disadvantage;
(e) make the conclusion of contracts subject to acceptance by the other parties of supplementary obligations which, by their nature or according to commercial usage, have no connection with the subject of such contracts.

2. Any agreements or decisions prohibited pursuant to this Article shall be automatically void.

3. The provisions of paragraph 1 may, however, be declared inapplicable in the case of:

— any agreement or category of agreements between undertakings;
— any decision or category of decisions by associations of undertakings;
— any concerted practice or category of concerted practices;

which contributes to improving the production or distribution of goods or to promoting technical or economic progress, while allowing consumers a fair share of the resulting benefit, and which does not:

(a) impose on the undertakings concerned restrictions which are not indispensable to the attainment of these objectives;
(b) afford such undertakings the possibility of eliminating competition in respect of a substantial part of the products in question.

Article 86

Any abuse by one or more undertakings of a dominant position within the common market or in a substantial part of it shall be prohibited as incompatible with the common market in so far as it may affect trade between Member States. Such abuse may, in particular, consist in:

(a) directly or indirectly imposing unfair purchase or selling prices or other unfair trading conditions;
(b) limiting production, markets or technical development to the prejudice of consumers;
(c) applying dissimilar conditions to equivalent transactions with other trading parties, thereby placing them at a competitive disadvantage;
(d) making the conclusion of contracts subject to acceptance by the other parties of supplementary obligations which, by their nature or according to commercial usage, have no connection with the subject of such contracts.

Article 90
1. In the case of public undertakings and undertakings to which Member States grant special or exclusive rights, Member States shall neither enact nor maintain in force any measure contrary to the rules contained in this Treaty, in particular to those rules provided for in Article 7 and Articles 85 to 94.
2. Undertakings entrusted with the operation of services of general economic interest or having the character of a revenue-producing monopoly shall be subject to the rules contained in this Treaty, in particular to the rules on competition, in so far as the application of such rules does not obstruct the performance, in law or in fact, of the particular tasks assigned to them. The development of trade must not be affected to such an extent as would be contrary to the interests of the Community.
3. The Commission shall ensure the application of the provisions of this Article and shall, where necessary, address appropriate directives or decisions to Member States.

Part Six
GENERAL AND FINAL PROVISIONS

Article 222
This Treaty shall in no way prejudice the rules of Member States governing the system of property ownership.

Excerpts from the Treaty establishing the European Economic Area

Article 53
1. The following shall be prohibited as incompatible with the functioning of this Agreement: all agreements between undertakings, decisions by associations of undertakings and concerted practices which may affect trade between Contracting Parties and which have as their object or effect the prevention, restriction or distortion of competition within the territory covered by this Agreement, and in particular those which:

(a) directly or indirectly fix purchase or selling prices or any other trading conditions;
(b) limit or control production, markets, technical development, or investment;
(c) share markets or sources of supply;
(d) apply dissimilar conditions to equivalent transactions with other trading parties, thereby placing them at a competitive disadvantage;
(e) make the conclusion of contracts subject to acceptance by the other parties of supplementary obligations which, by their nature or according to commercial usage, have no connection with the subject of such contracts.

2. Any agreements or decisions prohibited pursuant to this Article shall be automatically void.

3. The provisions of paragraph 1 may, however, be declared inapplicable in the case of:

— any agreement or category of agreements between undertakings;
— any decision or category of decisions by associations of undertakings;
— any concerted practice or category of concerted practices;

which contributes to improving the production or distribution of goods or to promoting technical or economic progress, while allowing consumers a fair share of the resulting benefit, and which does not:

(a) impose on the undertakings concerned restrictions which are not indispensable to the attainment of these objectives;
(b) afford such undertakings the possibility of eliminating competition in respect of a substantial part of the products in question.

Article 54
Any abuse by one or more undertakings of a dominant position within the territory covered by this Agreement or in a substantial part of it shall be prohibited as incompatible with the functioning of this Agreement in so far as it may affect trade between Contracting Parties. Such abuse may, in particular, consist in:

(a) directly or indirectly imposing unfair purchase or selling prices or other unfair trading conditions;
(b) limiting production, markets or technical development to the prejudice of consumers;
(c) applying dissimilar conditions to equivalent transactions with other trading parties, thereby placing them at a competitive disadvantage;
(d) making the conclusion of contracts subject to acceptance by the other parties of supplementary obligations which, by their nature or according to commercial usage, have no connection with the subject of such contracts.

Protocol 28 on Intellectual Property

Article 2 Exhaustion of rights
1. To the extent that exhaustion is dealt with in Community measures or jurisprudence, the Contracting Parties shall provide for such exhaustion of intellectual property rights as laid down in Community law. Without prejudice to future developments of case law, this provision shall be interpreted in accordance with the meaning established in the relevant rulings of the Court of Justice of the European Communities given prior to the signature of this agreement.

2. As regards patent rights, this provision shall take effect at the latest one year after the entry into force of this Agreement.

Appendix II

Text of Regulation 17

FIRST REGULATION IMPLEMENTING ARTICLES 85 AND 86 OF THE TREATY

Note: Council Regulation 17[1] enables the Commission to enforce articles 85 and 86. Article 3 provides for orders that firms should terminate an infringement and articles 6–9 provide for exemptions. Most agreements which the parties want exempted must be notified to the Commission under articles 4 and 5. Articles 11–14 enable the Commission to require information, while articles 15 and 16 provide for fines and penalties. Article 17 provides for appeals against decisions to the Court of Justice.

THE COUNCIL OF THE EUROPEAN ECONOMIC COMMUNITY,

Having regard to the Treaty establishing the European Economic Community, and in particular article 87 thereof;

Having regard to the proposal from the Commission;

Having regard to the Opinion of the Economic and Social Committee;

Having regard to the Opinion of the European Parliament;

1. Whereas, in order to establish a system ensuring that competition shall not be distorted in the common market, it is necessary to provide for balanced application of articles 85 and 86 in a uniform manner in the Member States;

2. Whereas in establishing the rules for applying article 85(3) account must be taken of the need to ensure effective supervision and to simplify administration to the greatest possible extent;

3. Whereas it is accordingly necessary to make it obligatory, as a general principle, for undertakings which seek application of article 85(3) to notify to the Commission their agreements, decisions and concerted practices;

4. Whereas, on the one hand, such agreements, decisions and concerted practices are probably very numerous and cannot therefore all be examined at the same time and, on the other hand, some of them have special features which may make them less prejudicial to the development of the common market;

5. Whereas there is consequently a need to make more flexible arrangements for the time being in respect of certain categories of agreement, decision and concerted practice without prejudging their validity under article 85;

6. Whereas it may be in the interest of undertakings to know whether any agreements, decisions or practices to which they are party, or propose to become party, may lead to action on the part of the Commission pursuant to article 8(1) or article 86;

7. Whereas, in order to secure uniform application of articles 85 and 86 in the common market, rules must be made under which the Commission, acting in

---

1 JO 1962, 204; OJ 1959–1962, 87; came into force on 13 March 1962.
   I have added numbers to the recitals for ease of reference.

close and constant liaison with the competent authorities of the Member States, may take the requisite measures for applying those articles;

8. Whereas for this purpose the Commission must have the co-operation of the competent authorities of the Member States and be empowered, throughout the common market, to require such information to be supplied and to undertake such investigations as are necessary to bring to light any agreement, decision or concerted practice prohibited by article 85(1) or any abuse of a dominant position prohibited by article 86;

9. Whereas, in order to carry out its duty of ensuring that the provisions of the Treaty are applied, the Commission must be empowered to address to undertakings or associations of undertakings recommendations and decisions for the purpose of bringing to an end infringements of articles 85 and 86;

10. Whereas compliance with articles 85 and 86 and the fulfilment of obligations imposed on undertakings and associations of undertakings under this Regulation must be enforceable by means of fines and periodic penalty payments;

11. Whereas undertakings concerned must be accorded the right to be heard by the Commission, third parties whose interests may be affected by a decision must be given the opportunity of submitting their comments beforehand, and it must be ensured that wide publicity is given to decisions taken;

12. Whereas all decisions taken by the Commission under this Regulation are subject to review by the Court of Justice under the conditions specified in the Treaty; whereas it is moreover desirable to confer upon the Court of Justice, pursuant to article 172, unlimited jurisdiction in respect of decisions under which the Commission imposes fines or periodic penalty payments;

13. Whereas this Regulation may enter into force without prejudice to any other provisions that may hereafter be adopted pursuant to article 87;

HAS ADOPTED THIS REGULATION:

Article 1
Basic provision
Without prejudice to articles 6, 7 and 23 of this Regulation, agreements, decisions and concerted practices of the kind described in article 85(1)of the Treaty and the abuse of a dominant position in the market, within the meaning of article 86 of the Treaty, shall be prohibited, no prior decision to that effect being required.

Article 2
Negative clearance
Upon application by the undertakings or associations of undertakings concerned, the Commission may certify that, on the basis of the facts in its possession, there are no grounds under article 85(1) or article 86 of the Treaty for action on its part in respect of an agreement, decision or practice.

Article 3
Termination of infringements
1. Where the Commission, upon application or upon its own initiative, finds

that there is infringement of article 85 or article 86 of the Treaty, it may by decision require the undertakings or associations of undertakings concerned to bring such infringement to an end.

2. Those entitled to make application are:

(a) Member States;

(b) natural or legal persons who claim a legitimate interest.

3. Without prejudice to the other provisions of this Regulation, the Commission may, before taking a decision under paragraph 1, address to the undertakings or associations of undertakings concerned recommendations for termination of the infringement.

Article 4
Notification of new agreements, decisions and practices

1. Agreements, decisions and concerted practices of the kind described in article 85(1) of the Treaty which come into existence after the entry into force of this Regulation and in respect of which the parties seek application of article 85(3) must be notified to the Commission. Until they have been notified, no decision in application of article 85(3) may be taken.

2. Paragraph 1 shall not apply to agreements, decisions or concerted practices where:

(1) the only parties thereto are undertakings from one Member State and the agreements, decisions or practices do not relate either to imports or to exports between Member States;

(2) not more that two undertakings are party thereto, and the agreements only:

　　(a) restrict the freedom of one party to the contract in determining the prices or conditions of business upon which the goods which he has obtained from the other party to the contract may be resold; or

　　(b) impose restrictions on the exercise of the rights of the assignee or user of industrial property rights — in particular patents, utility models, designs or trade marks — or of the person entitled under a contract to the assignment, or grant, of the right to use a method of manufacture or knowledge relating to the use and to the application of industrial processes;

(3) they have as their sole object:

　　(a) the development or uniform application of standards or types; or

　　(b) joint research and development;

　　(c) specialisation in the manufacture of products, including agreements necessary for achieving this,

　　　　— where the products which are the subject of specialisation do not, in a substantial part of the common market, represent more than 15 per cent of the volume of business done in identical products or those considered by the consumers to be similar by reason of their characteristics, price and use,

and
— where the total annual turnover of the participating undertakings does not exceed 200 million units of account.

These agreements, decisions and concerted practices may be notified to the Commission].[2]

Article 5
Notification of existing agreements, decisions and practices
1. Agreements, decisions and concerted practices of the kind described in article 85(1) of the Treaty which are in existence at the date of entry into force of this Regulation and in respect of which the parties seek application of article 85(3) shall be notified to the Commission [before 1 November 1962].[3] [However, notwithstanding the foregoing provisions, any agreements, decisions and concerted practices to which not more than two undertakings are party shall be notified before 1 February 1963].[4]
2. Paragraph 1 shall not apply to agreements, decisions or concerted practices falling within article 4(2); these may be notified to the Commission.

Article 6
Decisions pursuant to article 85(3)
1. Whenever the Commission takes a decision pursuant to article 85(3) of the Treaty, it shall specify therein the date from which the decision shall take effect. Such date shall not be earlier than the date of notification.
2. The second sentence of paragraph 1 shall not apply to agreements, decisions or concerted practices falling within article 4(2) and article 5(2), nor to those falling within article 5(1) which have been notified within the time limit specified in article 5(1).

Article 7
Special provisions for existing agreements, decisions and practices
1. Where agreements, decisions and concerted practices in existence at the date of entry into force of this Regulation and notified [within the time limits specified in article 5(1)][5] do not satisfy the requirements of article 85(3) of the Treaty and the undertakings or associations of undertakings concerned cease to give effect to them or modify them in such manner that they no longer fall within the prohibition contained in article 85(1) or that they satisfy the requirements of article 85(3), the prohibition contained in article 85(1) shall apply only for a period fixed by the Commission. A decision by the Commission pursuant to the foregoing sentence shall not apply as against undertakings and associations of undertakings which did not expressly consent to the notification.
2. Paragraph 1 shall apply to agreements, decisions and concerted practices

2   Amended by reg. 2822/71.
3   Substituted by reg. 59, art. 1(1). See also art. 25, below.
4   Added by reg. 59, art. 1(2).
5   Added by reg. 59, art. 1(3).

falling within article 4(2) which are in existence at the date of entry into force of this Regulation if they are notified [before 1 January 1967].[6]

Article 8
Duration and revocation of decisions under article 85(3)

1. A decision in application of article 85(3) of the Treaty shall be issued for a specified period and conditions and obligations may be attached thereto.

2. A decision may on application be renewed if the requirements of article 85(3) of the Treaty continue to be satisfied.

3. The Commission may revoke or amend its decision or prohibit specified acts by the parties:

(a) where there has been a change in any of the facts which were basic to the making of the decision;

(b) where the parties commit a breach of any obligation attached to the decision;

(c) where the decision is based on incorrect information or was induced by deceit;

(d) where the parties abuse the exemption from the provisions of article 85(1) of the Treaty granted to them by the decision.

In cases to which subparagraphs (b), (c) or (d) apply, the decision may be revoked with retroactive effect.

Article 9
Powers

1. Subject to review of its decision by the Court of Justice, the Commission shall have sole power to declare article 85(1) inapplicable pursuant to article 85(3) of the Treaty.

2. The Commission shall have power to apply article 85(1) and article 86 of the Treaty; this power may be exercised notwithstanding that the time limits specified in article 5(1) and in article 7(2) relating to notification have not expired.

3. As long as the Commission has not initiated any procedure under articles 2, 3 or 6, the authorities of the Member States shall remain competent to apply article 85(1) and article 86 in accordance with article 88 of the Treaty; they shall remain competent in this respect notwithstanding that the time limits specified in article 5(1) and in article 7(2) relating to notification have not expired.

Article 10
Liaison with the authorities of the Member States

1. The Commission shall forthwith transmit to the competent authorities of the Member States a copy of the applications and notifications together with copies of the most important documents lodged with the Commission for the purpose of establishing the existence of infringements of articles 85 or 86 of the Treaty or of obtaining negative clearance or a decision in application of article 85(3).

6 Substituted by reg. 118/63, art. 1. And see art. 25, *post.*

2. The Commission shall carry out the procedure set out in paragraph 1 in close and constant liaison with the competent authorities of the Member States; such authorities shall have the right to express their views upon that procedure.

3. An Advisory Committee on Restrictive Practices and Monopolies shall be consulted prior to the taking of any decision following upon a procedure under paragraph 1, and of any decision concerning the renewal, amendment or revocation of a decision pursuant to article 85(3) of the Treaty.

4. The Advisory Committee shall be composed of officials competent in the matter of restrictive practices and monopolies. Each Member State shall appoint an official to represent it who, if prevented from attending, may be replaced by another official.

5. The consultation shall take place at a joint meeting convened by the Commission; such meeting shall be held not earlier than fourteen days after dispatch of the notice convening it. The notice shall, in respect of each case to be examined, be accompanied by a summary of the case together with an indication of the most important documents, and a preliminary draft decision.

6. The Advisory Committee may deliver an opinion notwithstanding that some of its members or their alternates are not present. A report of the outcome of the consultative proceedings shal be annexed to the draft decision. It shall not be made public.

Article 11
Requests for information
1. In carrying out the duties assigned to it by article 89 and by provisions adopted under article 87 of the Treaty, the Commission may obtain all necessary information from the Governments and competent authorities of the Member States and from undertakings and associations of undertakings.

2. When sending a request for information to an undertaking or association of undertakings, the Commission shall at the same time forward a copy of the request to the competent authority of the Member State in whose territory the seat of the undertaking or association of undertakings is situated.

3. In its request the Commission shall state the legal basis and the purpose of the request and also the penalties provided for in article 15(1)(b) for supplying incorrect information.

4. The owners of the undertakings or their representatives and, in the case of legal persons, companies or firms, or of associations having no legal personality, the persons authorised to represent them by law or by their constitution shall supply the information requested.

5. Where an undertaking or association of undertakings does not supply the information requested within the time limit fixed by the Commission, or supplies incomplete information, the Commission shall by decision require the information to be supplied. The decision shall specify what information is required, fix an appropriate time limit within which it is to be supplied and indicate the penalties provided for in article 15(1)(b) and article 16(1)(c) and the right to have the decision reviewed by the Court of Justice.

6. The Commission shall at the same time forward a copy of its decision to the

competent authority of the Member State in whose territory the seat of the undertaking or association of undertakings is situated.

Article 12
Inquiry into sectors of the economy

1. If in any sector of the economy the trend of trade between Member States, price movements, inflexibility of prices or other circumstances suggest that in the economic sector concerned competition is being restricted or distorted within the common market, the Commission may decide to conduct a general inquiry into that economic sector and in the course thereof may request undertakings in the sector concerned to supply the information necessary for giving effect to the principles formulated in articles 85 and 86 of the Treaty and for carrying out the duties entrusted to the Commission.

2. The Commission may in particular request every undertaking or association of undertakings in the economic sector concerned to communicate to it all agreements, decisions and concerted practices which are exempt from notification by virtue of article 4(2) and article 5(2).

3. When making inquiries pursuant to paragraph 2, the Commission shall also request undertakings or groups of undertakings whose size suggests that they occupy a dominant position within the common market or a substantial part thereof to supply to the Commission such particulars of the structure of the undertakings and of their behaviour as are requisite to an appraisal of their position in the light of article 86 of the Treaty.

4. Article 10(3) to (6) and articles 11, 13 and 14 shall apply correspondingly.

Article 13
Investigations by the authorities of the Member States

1. At the request of the Commission, the competent authorities of the Member States shall undertake the investigations which the Commission considers to be necessary under article 14(1), or which it has ordered by decision pursuant to article 14(3). The officials of the competent authorities of the Member States responsible for conducting these investigations shall exercise their powers upon production of an authorisation in writing issued by the competent authority of the Member State in whose territory the investigation is to be made. Such authorisation shall specify the subject matter and purpose of the investigation.

2. If so requested by the Commission or by the competent authority of the Member State in whose territory the investigation is to be made, the officials of the Commission may assist the officials of such authorities in carrying out their duties.

Article 14
Investigating powers of the Commission

1. In carrying out the duties assigned to it by article 89 and by provisions adopted under article 87 of the Treaty, the Commission may undertake all necessary investigations into undertakings and associations of undertakings. To this end the officials authorised by the Commission are empowered:

(a) to examine the books and other business records;
(b) to take copies of or extracts from the books and business records;
(c) to ask for oral explanations on the spot;
(d) to enter any premises; land and means of transport of undertakings.

2. The officials of the Commission authorised for the purpose of these investigations shall exercise their powers upon production of an authorisation in writing specifying the subject matter and purpose of the investigation and the penalties provided for in article 15(1)(c) in cases where production of the required books or other business records is incomplete. In good time before the investigation, the Commission shall inform the competent authority of the Member State in whose territory the same is to be made of the investigation and of the identity of the authorised officials.

3. Undertakings and associations of undertakings shall submit to investigations ordered by decision of the Commission. The decision shall specify the subject matter and purpose of the investigation, appoint the date on which it is to begin and indicate the penalties provided for in article 15(1)(c) and article 16(1)(d) and the right to have the decision reviewed by the Court of Justice.

4. The Commission shall take decisions referred to in paragraph 3 after consultation with the competent authority of the Member State in whose territory the investigation is to be made.

5. Officials of the competent authority of the Member State in whose territory the investigation is to be made may, at the request of such authority or of the Commission, assist the officials of the Commission in carrying out their duties.

6. Where an undertaking opposes an investigation ordered pursuant to this article, the Member State concerned shall afford the necessary assistance to the officials authorised by the Commission to enable them to make their investigation. Member States shall, after consultation with the Commission, take the necessary measures to this end before 1 October 1962.[7]

Article 15
Fines

1. The Commission may by decision impose on undertakings or associations of undertakings fines of from 100 to 5000 units of account where, intentionally or negligently:

(a) they supply incorrect or misleading information in an application pursuant to article 2 or in a notification pursuant to articles 4 or 5; or
(b) they supply incorrect information in response to a request made pursuant to article 11(3) or (5) or to article 12, or do not supply information within the time limit fixed by a decision taken under article 11(5); or
(c) they produce the required books or other business records in incomplete form during investigations under article 13 or 14, or refuse to submit to an investigation ordered by decision isued in implementation of article 14(3).

2. The Commission may by decision impose on undertakings or associations of undertakings fines of from 1000 to 1 000 000 units of account, or a sum in excess thereof but not exceeding 10% of the turnover in the preceding business

7 See art. 25, *post*.

year of each of the undertakings participating in the infringement where, either intentionally or negligently:

(a) they infringe article 85(1) or article 86 of the Treaty;
or
(b) they commit a breach of any obligation imposed pursuant to article 8(1).

In fixing the amount of the fine, regard shall be had both to the gravity and to the duration of the infringement.

3. Article 10(3) to (6) shall apply.
4. Decisions taken pursuant to paragraphs 1 and 2 shall not be of a criminal law nature.
5. The fines provided for in paragraph 2(a) shall not be imposed in respect of acts taking place:

(a) after notification to the Commission and before its decision in application of article 85(3) of the Treaty, provided they fall within the limits of the activity described in the notification;
(b) before notification and in the course of agreements, decisions or concerted practices in existence at the date of entry into force of this Regulation, provided that notification was effected within the time limits specified in article 5(1) and article 7(2).

6. Paragraph 5 shall not have effect where the Commission has informed the undertakings concerned that after preliminary examination it is of opinion that article 85(1) of the Treaty applies and that application of article 85(3) is not justified.

Article 16
Periodic penalty payments

1. The Commission may by decision impose on undertakings or associations of undertakings periodic penalty payments of from 50 to 1000 units of account per day, calculated from the date appointed by the decision, in order to compel them:

(a) to put an end to an infringement of article 85 or 86 of the Treaty, in accordance with a decision taken pursuant to article 3 of this Regulation;
(b) to refrain from any act prohibited under article 8(3);
(c) to supply complete and correct information which it has requested by decision taken pursuant to article 11(5);
(d) to submit to an investigation which it has ordered by decision taken pursuant to article 14(3).

2. Where the undertakings or associations of undertakings have satisfied the obligation which it was the purpose of the periodic penalty payment to enforce, the Commission may fix the total amount of the periodic penalty payment at a lower figure than that which would arise under the original decision.

3. Article 10(3) to (6) shall apply.

Article 17
Review by the Court of Justice
The Court of Justice shall have unlimited jurisdiction within the meaning of article 172 of the Treaty to review decisions whereby the Commission has fixed a fine or periodic penalty payment; it may cancel, reduce or increase the fine or periodic penalty payment imposed.

Article 18
Unit of account
For the purposes of applying articles 15 to 17 the unit of account shall be that adopted in drawing up the budget of the Community in accordance with articles 207 and 209 of the Treaty.

Article 19
Hearing of the parties and of third persons
  1. Before taking decisions as provided for in articles 2, 3, 6, 7, 8, 15 and 16, the Commission shall give the undertakings or associations of undertakings concerned the opportunity of being heard on the matters to which the Commission has taken objection.
  2. If the Commission or the competent authorities of the Member States consider it necessary, they may also hear other natural or legal persons. Applications to be heard on the part of such persons shall, where they show a sufficient interest, be granted.
  3. Where the Commission intends to give negative clearance pursuant to article 2 or take a decision in application of article 85(3) of the Treaty, it shall publish a summary of the relevant application or notification and invite all interested third parties to submit their observations within a time limit which it shall fix being not less than one month. Publication shall have regard to the legitimate interest of undertakings in the protection of their business secrets.

Article 20
Professional secrecy
  1. Information acquired as a result of the application of articles 11, 12, 13 and 14 shall be used only for the purpose of the relevant request or investigation.
  2. Without prejudice to the provisions of articles 19 and 21, the Commission and the competent authorities of the Member States, their officials and other servants shall not disclose information acquired by them as a result of the application of this Regulation and of the kind covered by the obligation of professional secrecy.
  3. The provisions of paragraphs 1 and 2 shall not prevent publication of general information or surveys which do not contain information relating to particular undertakings or associations of undertakings.

Article 21
Publication of decisions
  1. The Commission shall publish the decisions which it takes pursuant to articles 2, 3, 6, 7 and 8.
  2. The publication shall state the names of the parties and the main content of

the decision; it shall have regard to the legitimate interest of undertakings in the protection of their business secrets.

Article 22
Special provisions
1. The Commission shall submit to the Council proposals for making certain categories of agreement, decision and concerted practice falling within article 4(2) or article 5(2) compulsorily notifiable under article 4 or 5.
2. Within one year from the date of entry into force of this Regulation, the Council shall examine, on a proposal from the Commission, what special provisions might be made for exempting from the provisions of this Regulation agreements, decisions and concerted practices falling within article 4(2) or article 5(2).

Article 23
Transitional provisions applicable to decisions of authorities of the Member States
1. Agreements, decisions and concerted practices of the kind described in article 85(1) of the Treaty to which, before the entry into force of this Regulation, the competent authority of a Member State has declared article 85(1) to be inapplicable pursuant to article 85(3) shall not be subject to compulsory notification under article 5. The decision of the competent authority of the Member State shall be deemed to be a decision within the meaning of article 6; it shall cease to be valid upon expiration of the period fixed by such authority but in any event not more than three years after the entry into force of this Regulation. Article 8(3) shall apply.
2. Applications for renewal of decisions of the kind described in paragraph 1 shall be decided upon by the Commission in accordance with article 8(2).

Article 24
Implementing provisions
The Commission shall have power to adopt implementing provisions concerning the form, content and other details of applications pursuant to articles 2 and 3 and of notifications pursuant to articles 4 and 5, and concerning hearings pursuant to article 19(1)and (2).

[Article 25
1. As regards agreements, decisions and concerted practices to which article 85 of the Treaty applies by virtue of accession, the date of accession shall be substituted for the date of entry into force of this Regulation in every place where reference is made in this Regulation to this latter date.
2. Agreements, decisions and concerted practices existing at the date of accession to which article 85 of the Treaty applies by virtue of accession shall be notified pursuant to article 5(1) or article 7(1) and (2) within six months from the date of accession.
3. Fines under article 15(2)(a) shall not be imposed in respect of any act prior

8   Added by the Act of Accession, Annex I.

to notification of the agreements, decisions and practices to which paragraph 2 applies and which have been notified within the period therein specified.

4. New Member States shall take the measures referred to in article 14(6) within six months from the date of accession after consulting the Commission.]⁸

This regulation shall be binding in its entirety and directly applicable in all Member States.

Done at Brussels, 6 February 1962.

Index